BLACK SEPTEMBER 1918

BLACK SEPTEMBER 1918

WWI'S DARKEST MONTH IN THE AIR

NORMAN FRANKS
RUSSELL GUEST
& FRANK BAILEY

GRUB STREET | LONDON

Published by
Grub Street
4 Rainham Close
London
SW11 6SS

An expanded and updated paperback edition, with new photography, of Part Two
of Bloody April, Black September (published by Grub Street in 1995).

Copyright © 2018 Grub Street, London
Text copyright © 2018 Norman L R Franks, Russell Guest and Frank Bailey

A CIP record for this title is available from the British Library

ISBN 978-1-911621-11-9

Cover and book design by Daniele Roa

Printed and bound by Finidr, Czech Republic

Our friend and co-author of Bloody April, Black September, Frank 'Bill' Bailey,
died in December 2010. He was a great WWI aviation researcher, especially
concerning the French air force. A WWII US Marine veteran (awarded two
Purple Hearts), in his post-war career in the USN he spent some years in Paris
where he was able to indulge his passion by spending long hours in the French
archives. We still miss him.

Contents

Acknowledgements

The authors wish to thank and acknowledge the help given by a number of friends and fellow historians, together with advice, support and photographs. Since the original work on *Black September* ended in 1995, a number of our pals have departed this life, but we remember them all. Neal O'Connor, George Williams, Ed Ferko, Richard Duiven, August Blume, Stewart Taylor, Stuart Leslie, Mike O'Connor, Greg Van Wyngarden, D MacGuinness, Russell Manning, Ola Sater, Dennis Connell, Paul Chamberlain, Dr Gustav Bock, Alex Imrie and Jörg Mückler.

Special acknowledgement must go to Trevor Henshaw not only for his massive work on WWI flying casualties with his book, *The Sky Their Battlefield II,* (Fetubi Books, 2014) but for his generous help over the years with this tremendous undertaking of recording the events of WWI in the air.

NB: Also to the keeper and staff at the Public Archives at Kew, Surrey, and the Bureau Central d'Incorporation et D'Archives, de l'Armée de l'Air, the Service Historique de l'Armée de l'Air (SHAA), France.

With Allied claims in these daily lists, we show the 'out of control' victories by the British, but as the French airmen had no comparable type of combat claim, there will be no figure for them under that heading.

Throughout the daily reporting we have tried to work chronologically but sometimes we do not know for certain the timing of a combat or a loss so these, while mentioned, will appear generally in the daily loss notes.

We have made little reference to losses due to non-combat sorties, or where an aircraft may have crashed returning from a sortie, but where the accident was not attributable to combat damage. Anyone reading through the daily aircraft loss reports will see just how many aircraft were lost, certainly by the British, through flying accidents and pilot error. To have included all those would have made the book unwieldy, so only crashes where combat damage was involved have been noted.

Where personnel casualties have been recorded, but the aircraft was not lost, even though damaged (which includes aircraft recovered from forced landings behind the front lines), a * will appear far right of the daily casualty entry to denote the aircraft was not a loss. Also, in the case of two-seater crews, the first named will always be the pilot; where only one crewman is recorded a (P) or (O) appears to denote pilot or observer.

In the narrative, during the periods where Allied and German times differed by one hour, reference to this will be emphasised by an (A) or (G) next to an Allied or German time, although generally the time attributable to an Allied or German action/report will, of course, be the time relevant to the side involved.

Introduction

In the new year of 1918, there was the familiar lull of winter, but with the release of German troops from the Russian front following the Russian Revolution and the ending of the war in the East, the Germans mounted a huge offensive with the First Battle of the Somme (20 March to 5 April), which so nearly achieved a complete breakthrough for the Central Powers. Other battles followed: the Lys (9 to 29 April), the Aisne (27 May to 6 June); while in the south, the Germans reached the Marne on 31 May.

The failure of the Germans' March offensives sent a chill through the German High Command, for it knew only too well that finally, after almost a year since declaring war on Germany, American might was beginning to arrive in France. Once men and munitions from across the Atlantic became a flood, Germany knew her ability to wage war would begin to crumble. The Allies just had too many men from the Empire and from the Americas to call upon.

Fully aware of the strength of American industrial might and men, the Germans had formulated their 'Amerika Program' over the winter of 1917-18 which led to an increase in the size of their air force. The number of Jastas was increased from 40 to 80, but it did not mean an immediate doubling of opposition for the Allied airmen. Many of the newly created units took time to become established, generally they had inferior aircraft types to begin with, and mostly the personnel were inexperienced, although led by an acknowledged veteran or ace.

The two-seater Schutzstaffeln were renamed Schlactstaffeln and used for infantry support and ground attack, first used with some effect at Cambrai in late 1917. With the ending of the war in Russia, a number of experienced flyers were released for duty on the Western Front in the spring of 1918.

The French began the Fourth Battle of Champagne (15 to 18 July) and as this ended came the Second Battle of the Marne which lasted until 7 August. The British fought the Battle of Amiens (8 to 11 August), which really began to cut deep into German territory, and began a series of battles which broke the German army apart. The British advance in Flanders (18 August), the Second Battle of the Somme (21 August) and the Second Battle of Arras (26 August), all hit home. These latter two came to an end on 3 September and now the stage was set for a mighty attack upon the German Hindenburg Line, while the French and Americans opened an assault at Saint-Mihiel (12 September) to be followed by the Champagne and Argonne Battles on the 26th.

In broad terms the air war had changed little since April 1917. The RFC had become the Royal Air Force, with the amalgamation of the RFC and Royal Naval Air Service on 1 April 1918, but was still fighting an offensive war, taking the fight to the Germans. For their part, the German Air Service were content to let the British and French come to them, and continued to let the Allied airmen dash themselves against their Jastas.

This German tactic had evolved since late 1916, due at that time to numbers. The British and French were always numerically superior in men and aircraft and so the German fighter pilots took up a defensive war. In many ways they were happy to be able, more or less, to choose the moment of combat, or decline it if odds and conditions proved unfavourable. They could wait on their fighter airfields until their enemies were reported to be crossing the lines and still have time to gain height and be ready to attack. They could also break off any time and land, whereas the British and French always had to remember that they had to fly back over the lines to reach safety. With drying fuel tanks, running short of ammunition and often against a prevailing west to east wind, the Allied airmen often had a bitter struggle to get back to the safety of their own lines. Knowing this, other German Jasta pilots would be waiting for them to do just that, but with full petrol tanks and gun-belts.

By the summer of 1918, the SE5a and Camel, plus the two-seater Bristol Fighter, were the main fighter equipment for the British, plus four squadrons of Sopwith Dolphins, a machine that was every bit as good as the Camel but could operate at greater altitudes too. The French fighters were now mostly all Spad XIIIs, while the Americans had come through their initial period with the Nieuport 28s and were also flying Spad XIIIs.

The Germans still flew Albatros Scouts, but had progressed from the DII and DIIIs of April 1917 to the DV and DVa, although neither was a real match for the Allied fighter opposition. Nor was another type, similar in general appearance to the Albatros, the Pfalz DIII, which swelled the Jasta ranks in the summer of 1917. In a few weeks in early autumn of that year, the Germans had brought out the Fokker DrI triplane, which produced a flurry of activity and success until a weakness in the upper wings – resulting in the death of several pilots – had caused the new type to be withdrawn and modified. In the spring of 1918 it reappeared, and for another brief period became a deadly opponent, notably in the hands of von Richthofen. But now, in the summer of 1918, the German Jasta pilots had perhaps their best ever fighter, the Fokker DVII biplane, a type with which both the novice and the expert fighter could meet any opposition on more than equal terms. And by this time, the Allied types were all beginning to look a bit long in the tooth, although far from being outdated.

Tactics and ideas had changed however. In mid-1917 the Germans had built on an earlier idea to group Jastas together, the first being Jastas 4, 6, 10 and 11. These became Jagdesgeschwader No.1 (JG1) under the command of the leading German ace, Manfred von Richthofen. The purpose of this permanent grouping was so that as a unit it could be moved to various parts of the battle front wherever it was needed, to oppose, for instance, an Allied offensive, which would naturally be supported in some strength by additional British or French squadrons.

With this mobility, and the increasingly colourful garb used by the German fighter pilots on their aircraft, these Jagdesgeschwader units soon became known as Flying Circuses. In total there were four Jagdesgeschwaderen, three Prussian – JG1, JG2 and JG3 – and one Bavarian, JG4.

The reader will notice we said 'permanent grouping'; there were, in addition, several non-permanent groupings of Jastas, and these became known as a Jagdgruppe, e.g. JGr1, JGr2 and so on. These were grouped together for specific duties and could be interchanged or even disbanded as was found necessary or expedient. Whether it was a JG or a JGr, a senior pilot would command such a unit, although not necessarily a leading ace. The German Air Service, like the Army and Navy, went on rank and ability, not just ability. Therefore one can find a number of Jasta or Jagdgruppes commanded by a pilot with few or even no air combat victories, leading other pilots with some quite sizeable scores. Even individual Jastas would not necessarily be commanded by a top-notch fighter pilot.

The Germans continued to employ a defensive stance, letting the Allied aircraft still come to them. In many ways this was still a good tactic, as it continued to give the German fighter pilots the choice of when to attack as well as the ability to break off combat and land if necessary, without being taken prisoner. The disadvantage, of course, was that German front-line troops would constantly see more Allied aircraft over them, often, by this later stage of the war, strafing and bombing them from low level, with very little interference from their own Fokker and Albatros pilots.

It also allowed the Allied airmen to become adept at forcing their way through packs of German fighters to raid a target, and even though several attacking bombers might be brought down, the target was often either destroyed or severely hit, causing not only casualties but the destruction of stores, ammunition, etc. and disruption to road and rail traffic bringing much needed troops and/or supplies to the front.

Numbers were still in the Allies' favour, which is why the Germans continued in the overall defensive air war, but this also hindered the German two-seater recce and artillery observation crews from doing their work. Any reconnaissance of the Allied rear areas was always flown unescorted, the crews using cloud cover and height for their main protection.

Both sides used front-line ground-attack aircraft. The Allied airmen were generally fighting pilots – mostly Camel flyers – who would take on this duty in addition to air fighting, whereas the SE5 pilots tended to keep to air combat, but not strictly so. Dolphins and Bristol Fighters could also be used in the ground-strafing role.

On the German side, they used two-seaters such as the Halberstadt CLII or III, and the Hannover CLIII, with extra armour, in units called Schutzstaffeleln. Some units also used the Junkers JI armoured monoplanes.

In fact, ground attack and ground strafing had really begun during April 1917, and by the summer of that year was used with increasing regularity by the British in particular, especially in the Cambrai battle. By the spring of 1918 and certainly by the summer, the RAF had this tactic down to a fine art. It often cost them men and aircraft, but the effect on the German ground soldiers was marked.

By 1918 the British and French were also using aircraft in groups, although they were not so rigidly organised as the German Jagdesgeschwader formations. The French formed Groupes de Combat (GC), the British using Wings, although this title should not be confused in any way with the Wings of WWII. When used, the British formation tended to be made up of specialist aircraft, e.g. Camels at a lower level, SE5s higher with Dolphins or Bristols above them. Bombing aircraft, such as the now well established DH4 and DH9s, or the Bréguet XIVs of the French, were now regularly escorted by fighters. It didn't always happen as planned, for this was still the era before air-to-air radio communications, so bombers and fighters making a rendezvous could lose each other/not find each other, and when the bombers 'pressed on' unescorted, they would find themselves under attack without any single-seater protection.

There was still no direct fighter protection for the Corps aircraft, their 'protection' still being in the form of fighter patrols in their area of activity. The poor old BEs had long gone, the main artillery machine being the RE8. This was still a 1917 machine but at least the crews were better trained now.

The French had begun to group their units together as early as 1916, although they tended to fight a less aggressive air war than their British counterparts. These Groupes de Combat totalled 16 by early 1918, and by February there were 21.

By 1918, larger groups of aircraft were needed by the French, to cover expanding ground operations, and under a central control. Therefore, they began reorganising a number of Groupes de Combat into Escadres de Combat, commanded by a Chef de Battaillon. Like the Germans, these units would be commanded by a senior officer, not necessarily a leading air ace. And just as JG1 had become known as the Richthofen Geschwader, so too did some of the Escadres de Combat become known by the name of their commander, e.g: Escadre de Combat No.1 was known as Groupement Ménard (being commanded by Victor Ménard).

In turn, units, groupes and escadres could be built into an even larger establishment of both fighter and bomber units. In May 1918 the French created the 1ère Division Aérienne, under the command of a general, which consisted of Groupement Ménard, plus three other Groupes de Combat plus Escadre de Bombardement No.12 (which was itself made up of three Groupes de Bombardement), together with Escadre No.2 (Groupement Fequant), three GCs and another full Escadre de Bombardement.

Each GC would generally have some 72 Spads, while each GB would muster 45 Bréguet bombers. In addition there were also some Escadrilles de Protection, equipped with large Caudron R11 aircraft, used in effect like gun ships to ward off attacking fighters. Both the British and the French had night-bombing units, and the RAF also had its Independent Air Force bombers, de Havilland 4s and 9s, and Handley Page 0/400 twin-engined three-seat bombers, used for attacking deep behind enemy lines, or even Germany itself.

For their part, by mid-1918, the American Air Service (USAS) were now operating in strength in support of their own and French ground troops. During August 1918 Colonel William (Billy) Mitchell was made commander of a recently organised (US) First Army Air Service and in co-operation with the ground commanders was preparing for an assault against the Saint-Mihiel front. Therefore, as the British to the north were pressing the Hindenburg Line, the French and Americans would attack at Saint-Mihiel, commencing 12 September.

For the drive on this front, Mitchell had convinced the French to fall in with his overall plan and had also managed to persuade them to put a large part of their air force at his disposal. As it turned out, by the time the attack began, Billy Mitchell had under his command, or co-operating with it, the largest number of units and aircraft to engage in a single offensive operation during WWI.

His own American forces consisted of 12 fighter (pursuit) squadrons, three day-bombing squadrons, ten observation (reconnaissance) squadrons and one night reconnaissance squadron. To this force the French assigned their 1ère Division Aérienne, which consisted of 42 fighter and day bombardment squadrons, two squadrons of French and three Italian night-bombing squadrons and 12 squadrons of French observation aircraft. He also had four French fighter squadrons attached to his 1st Pursuit Group (which itself consisted of four pursuit squadrons), which would move to this part of the front on the eve of the battle. To this force he could also call upon the eight bomber squadrons of Sir Hugh Trenchard's Independent Air Force, and while these were not under Mitchell's direct orders, they undertook missions in support of his overall battle plan.

As the Saint-Mihiel drive began, the number of aircraft Mitchell had under his orders was reputed to have been 701 fighters, 366 reconnaissance, 323 day bombers and 91 night bombers; a total of 1,481. Opposing this mighty force, the Germans had an estimated strength of some 213 aircraft – 72 fighters, 24 bombers, 105 reconnaissance, six battle (ground attack) and six long-distance photo machines. Some of the fighter units were in the midst of re-equipping from Albatros and Pfalz Scouts to the new Fokker DVII type.

The day after the drive began, the Germans reinforced their air units with the four Jastas of Jagdesgeschwader Nr.2, commanded by Oskar von Boenigk. Towards the end of the month, the 28th, JGI arrived, under Hermann Göring, but by this date the Saint-Mihiel offensive had ended, and the Meuse-Argonne battle had begun two days earlier.

Despite the numerical superiority of the combined American and French air forces, the German fighter pilots still managed to inflict tremendous losses on them. In fact, as will be seen, September was to be the worst month for Allied air casualties during the whole of WWI – and this all happened just six weeks prior to the Armistice. Thus, despite a gradual decimation of the top aces of the German Air Service, those who survived, supported by the successful up-and-coming air fighters, were able to wreak havoc upon the generally less aggressive French and the keen but more inexperienced Americans. JG2, in fact, claimed more than 80 victories for just five casualties. In the final analysis, however, it was weight of numbers, lack of adequate pilot replacements and scarcity of fuel which tended to defeat the Germans.

On the British fronts, gone were the days of 1917. Generally speaking the new pilots arriving to fill gaps in the single and two-seater squadrons had more flying hours in their logbooks than those of a year or eighteen months before. They also had the benefit of a more structured and aggressive training, especially in mock air combat, at such places as the School of Air Fighting at Ayr in Scotland. The instructors too were far more experienced, thanks to the School of Special Flying at Gosport, Hampshire, which helped not only to train new pilots but to train instructors how to instruct. The improved techniques were followed by other training establishments.

By September 1918 there were hardly any men still flying combat in the RAF who had been in action in April 1917. Those that had survived were by this time either instructors, squadron commanders (many non-flying), working at various headquarters or back in England. The British had the luxury of a constant stream of eager young airmen only too willing to take their place on the Western Front, not merely from Britain but from Canada, Australia, New Zealand, South Africa and other lands of the Empire.

The Germans, on the other hand, did have some of their spring 1917 flyers still in action. Many had fallen, among whom were some of the great aces such as Manfred von Richthofen, Werner Voss, Kurt Wolff, Karl Allmenröder, Emil Schäfer and so on. But Hermann Göring was a Jagdesgeschwader commander, and so too was Bruno Loerzer; Hermann Frommherz was an active Jasta commander while Julius Buckler was about to command Jasta 22, having been with Jasta 17 since 1916. Robert Greim, commanding Jagdgruppe 9 had been flying since 1915, and so had Josef Jacobs, who now commanded Jasta 7 as he had done since August 1917. Reinhold Jörke had scored his second kill in April 1917 and in September 1918 was commanding

Jasta 39. Emil Thuy also gained his second victory in April 1917, having then been Staffelführer of Jasta 28 since September of the same year. Ernst Udet, second only to von Richthofen in air victories, was still active, having downed his first adversary in March 1916, and now led Jasta 4. Josef Veltjens was another Bloody April veteran, and now commander of Jasta 15.

There were any number of others, either flying fighters in early 1917 or operating in two-seater units, who were still 'operational' in September 1918. Friedrich Altemeier had been scoring steadily with Jasta 24 since December 1916! Paul Baümer, Hermann Becker, Walter Blume, Franz Büchner, Carl Degelow, Alois Heldman, Rudolf Klimke, Otto Könnecke, Josef Mai, George Meyer, Karl Odebrett, Karl Ritscherle, Fritz Röth, Fritz Rumey, Emil Schäpe, Eduard von Schleich, Otto Schmidt and Paul Strähle, were just some of the aces of 1918 who had gained vast experience of air fighting and were still passing on their knowledge and skills to the latest recruits to their Jastas.

Among the French, there were some aces still flying over the front who had been active in the spring of 1917. René Fonck, the French ace of aces, was still scoring with Spa.103, having been with this unit for 16 months and recording victories since the summer of 1916. Bernard Barny de Romanet had been flying since 1915, and was now commanding Spa.167; François Battesti had gained his first victory in April 1917 with N.73 and was still operating with it. Maurice Boyau had been with N.77 in early 1917 and was still with it, his score now in the thirties. Jean Casale was another 1915 veteran, now flying Spads with Spa.38, while Gustave Daladier had gained his first kill in April 1917 flying Nieuports and was still with Spa.93. Paul d'Argueff had been fighting the Germans over the Russian front in early 1917, and was now with Spa.124. Armand de Turenne gained his second victory in April 1917, and was now commander of Spa.12. Claude Haegelen would score heavily in September 1918, having been with the Storks since early 1917, and Henri de Slade, commander of Spa.159, had been flying since 1916. Georges Madon had scored 40 victories by the end of August 1918, his 9th having been achieved during April 1917, all with Spa.38. Gilbert Sardier commanded Spa.48, and he too had been active since 1916.

So here too was experience after a long apprenticeship, with knowledge being passed to the embryo fighter pilots. Admittedly the French fought a less aggressive war than the RFC/RNAS/RAF, and often they generally faced less aggressive German units, but over many battles and especially during the heavy and prolonged fighting at Verdun, the French pilots had done well.

The scene was thus set for this mighty, final clash which took place in the September 1918 skies of France. The outcome was heavy material and personnel losses for the Allied air forces, but already the die was cast; Germany would be forced to sue for peace six weeks after Black September came to an end. For the German Jasta pilots, it was their last fling.*

* The authors will often refer to the events of April 1917 to September 1918, the former having been the worst month for aerial casualties prior to September. (see *Bloody April 1917* by Franks, Guest and Bailey, Grub Street, 2017.)

American Order of Battle

1st US ARMY AIR SERVICE HEADQUARTERS

Colonel William Mitchell (Ligny-en-Barrois)

AMERICAN AIR SERVICE UNITS WITH REINFORCEMENTS

1st Pursuit Group, USAS
Major Harold E Hartney (Rembercourt)

27th Pursuit Sqn	95th Pursuit Sqn	94th Pursuit Sqn	147th Pursuit Sqn	218th, 'C' Flt 648th Sqn
1/Lt Alfred A Grant	Capt David McK Peterson	Capt Kenneth Marr	1/Lt James A Meissner	

1st Pursuit Wing USAS
Major Bert M Atkinson (Toul)

2nd Pursuit Group
Major Davenport Johnson (Toul)

13th Pursuit Sqn	49th Pursuit Sqn	22nd Pursuit Sqn	139th Pursuit Sqn	'A' Flt 255th Sqn
Capt Charles J Biddle	1/Lt George F Fisher	Capt Ray C Bridgeman	1/Lt David E Putnam†	

3rd Pursuit Group
Major William Thaw (Vaucouleurs #1)

28th Pursuit Sqn	93rd Pursuit Sqn	103rd Pursuit Sqn	213th Pursuit Sqn	360th Sqn
1/Lt C Maury Jones	Major W F M Huffer	Capt Robert L Rockwell	1/Lt John A Hambleton	

Groupe de Combat 16
Capitaine Jules Menj (Vaucouleurs #2)

Escadrille Spa.78	Escadrille Spa.112	Escadrille Spa.150	Escadrille Spa.151
Capt Gustave Lagache	Capt Pierre Merat	Lt Albert Achard	Lt Henri de Sevin

1st Day Bombardment Group
Major J L Dunsworth (Amanty)

11th Bombardment Sqn (DH4)	20th Bombardment Sqn (DH4)	96th Bombardment Sqn (Bréguet 14.B2)	'A' Flight 648th Sqn
1/Lt Thornton D Hooper	1/Lt Cecil G Sellers	Capt James A Summersett, Jr	

Corps Observation Wing, USAS
Major Lewis H Brereton (Toul)

1st Corps Observation Group, USAS
Major Melvin A Hall (Saizerais)

1st Observation Sqn (Salmson 2A2)	12th Observation Sqn (Salmson 2A2)	50th Observation Sqn (DH4)
1/Lt Arthur J Coyle (Toul)	1/Lt Stephen H Noyes (Toul)	1/Lt Daniel P Morse, Jr (Toul)
'B' Flight 648th Sqn (Toul)	Escadrille Br.208	Escadrille Br.214
	Capt Proust (Bicqueley)	Lt Pierre de la Chapelle (Bicqueley)

---

† Acting CO in place of Major L C Angstrom who was ill, but who returned to duty on 13 September 1918.

Balloon Wing Company 'A'
1/Lt Allan P McFarland (Saizerais)

1st Balloon Company	2nd Balloon Company	5th Balloon Company	42nd Balloon Company
1/Lt Walter J Reed	1/Lt Ira R Koenig (Griscourt)	1/Lt M R Smith (Dieulouard)	1/Lt Ray W Thompson
(Domevre-en-Haye)			(Ville-au-Val)

4th Corps Observation Group, USAS
Major Harry B Anderson (Ourches)

8th Observation Sqn (DH 4)		90th Observation Sqn (Salmson 2A2)
1/Lt John G Winant		1/Lt William Gallop†
135th Observation Sqn (DH4)	'C' Flight 25th Sqn	Escadrille Br.218
1/Lt Bradley J Saunders, Jr		Capt Petit

Balloon Wing Company 'C'
Captain Paul Patterson (Toul)

9th Balloon Company	69th Balloon Company	3rd Balloon Company	43rd Balloon Company
1/Lt C M Felt (Roulecourt)	1/Lt James B Haight	Capt Birge M Clark	Capt O B Anderson (Ansauville)
	(Neuf-de-Mandres)	(Hamonville)	

5th Corps Air Service USAS
Lt Col Arthur R Christy (Souilly)

5th Corps Observation Group
Major Martin F Scanlon

88th Observation Sqn	99th Observation Sqn	104th Observation Sqn	Escadrille Spa.42
(Salmson 2A2)	(Salmson 2A2)	(Salmson 2A2)	Capt de Saint Seran
Capt Kenneth P Littauer	Capt James E Meredith	1/Lt Clearton H Reynolds	

Balloon Wing Company 'B'
Major John H Jouett (Benoite-Vaux)

6th Balloon Company	8th Balloon Company	7th Balloon Company	12th Balloon Company
1/Lt S W Ovitt	Capt M L Witherus	1/Lt Samuel T Moore	1/Lt Ashley C McKinley
(Villers-sur-Meuse)	(Dieue-sur-Meuse)	(Ft Génicourt)	(Sommedieue)

Army Observation Group, USAS
Major John N Reynolds (Gondreville)

24th Observation Sqn (Salmson 2A2)	91st Observation Sqn (Salmson 2A2)	'B' Flt 255th Sqn
1/Lt Maury Hill	1/Lt Everett R Cook	

Army Artillery Observation Group, USAS
Capitaine P A Block (Ligny-en-Barrois)

Escadrille Br.206	Escadrille Br.234	Escadrille Br.219	Escadrille Br.225
Capt Tastevin (Bicqueley)	Capt Emile Jansen (Lay-St-Remy)	Capt Touchard (Lay-St-Remy)	Capt Antoine Moraillon (Belrain)

(All with Bréguet 14.A2)

10th USAS Balloon Co	11th USAS Balloon Co	16th USAS Balloon Co
1/Lt Dale Mabry	1/Lt Charles E Barber	1/Lt Oscar Roman
39th French Balloon Co	41st French Balloon Co	93rd French Balloon Co
(Minorville-Domevre)	(Jouy-sous-les-Côtes)	(Génicourt-sur-Meuse)

---

† Acting CO in place of 1/Lt W G Schauffler, who was ill, and who returned to duty on 15 September 1918.

FRENCH NIGHT BOMBARDMENT GROUP

Commandant Emile Villome (Epiez)

Escadrille CAP 115 (Caproni)

Escadrille CAP 130 (Caproni)
Capt Léon Hebard

Italian Gruppo di Bombardement 18
(Capitano De Riso)

Italian Squadriglia 3, 14 & 15 (Caproni CA.3)
(Chermisy)

USAS 9th Night Recon Sqn (DH4)
1/Lt Thomas A Box (Amanty)

FRENCH 1st DIVISION AÉRIENNE

Colonel Albert Peting de Vaulgrenant (Tannois)

1st Brigade d'Aviation
Chef de Bataillon Louis de Goys de Mezeyrac (St Martin Sorcy)

Escadre de Combat No.1
Chef de Bataillon Victor Ménard (Ochey)

Groupe de Combat 15
Capitaine François Glaize (Ochey)

Spa.37	Spa.81	Spa.93	Spa.97
Lt Roger Poupon	Lt Jacques Leps	Capt Georges d'Geyer d'Orth	Lt Herve Conneau

Groupe de Combat 18
Capitaine Andre Laurent (Ochey)

Spa.48	Spa.94	Spa.153	Spa.155
Lt Gilbert Sardier	Lt Benjamin Bozon-Verdurez	Capt Jean Gigodot	Capt Edmond George

Groupe de Combat 19
Capitaine Albert Deullin (Ochey)

Spa.73	Spa.85	Spa.95	Spa.96
Lt Pierre Jaille	Lt Paul Dumas	Capt Marcel Hugues	Lt Pierre Fauquet-Lemaître

Escadre de Bombardement No.12
Chef d'Escadrons Joseph Vuillemin (Chaudeney)

Groupe de Bombardement 5
Capitaine Petit (Martigny)

Escadrille Br.117	Escadrille Br.120	Escadrille Br.127
S/Lt Charles Renard-Duverger	Lt Henri Lemaitre	Lt Blanchard

(All equipped with the Bréguet 14.B2)

Groupe de Bombardement 6
Capitaine Roux (Tantonville)

Escadrille Br.11	Escadrille Br.66	Escadrille Br.108
Lt Lucien Bozon-Verduraz	Lt Jean Ardisson de Perdiguier	Lt Jean Luciani

(All equipped with the Bréguet 14.B2)

Groupe de Bombardement 9
Capitaine Guy de Lavergne (Neufchâteau)

Escadrille Br.29	Escadrille Br.123	Escadrille Br.129
Lt Mongin	Lt Roger Delaitre	Lt Pierre Pascal

(All equipped with the Bréguet 14.B2)

Escadrilles de Protection

Escadrille C 239	Escadrille C 240
Lieutenant Jean de Verchere	Capitaine de Durat

(Both equipped with Caudron R11)

2ème Brigade d'Aviation
Chef d'Escadrons Philippe Fequant (Combles)

Escadre de Combat No.2
Chef d'Escadrons Edouard Duseigneur (Combles)

Groupe de Combat 13
Capitaine Jean D'Harcourt (Brabant-le-Roi)

Spa.15	Spa.65	Spa.84	Spa.88
Capt Fernand Chevillon	Capt Louis Sejourne	S/Lt Pierre Wertheim	Lt Arthur Coadou

Groupe de Combat 17
Capitaine Joseph de l'Hermitte (Rancourt)

Spa.77	Spa.89	Spa.91	Spa.100
Capt Henri Decoin	Capt Guy Tourangin	Capt Robert Lafon	Capt Louis Koenig Belliard de Vaubicourt

Groupe de Combat 20
Capitaine Raymond Bailly (Pargny)

Spa.69	Spa.99	Spa.159	Spa.162
Capt Paul Malavaille	Lt Rougevin-Baville	Lt Henri Hay de Slade	Capt Daniel Chambarière

Escadre de Bombardement No.13
Chef d'Escadrons Armand des Prez de la Morlais (Villers-en-Lieu)

Groupe de Bombardement 3
Capitaine Hubert de Geffrier (Combles)

Escadrille Br.107	Escadrille Br.126	Escadrille Br.128
Capt Hubert de Geffrier	Lt Louis Barjaud	Capt René le Forestier

(All equipped with the Bréguet 14.B2)

Groupe de Bombardement 4
Capitaine Pierre Etournaud (St Dizier)

Escadrille Br.131	Escadrille Br.132	Escadrille Br.134
Capt Albert Mezergues	Capt Jean Jennekeyn	Lt Pierre Rousselet

(All equipped with the Bréguet 14.B2)

Escadrille de Protection
Capitaine Marcel Bloch
C46 (Caudron R11) St Dizier

Chief of Air Service 2nd Colonial Corps (French)
Commandant Pennes (Rumont)

Sal.28	C47	Br.236	Sal.277
Rumont	Rumont	Belrain	Rumont

20th French Balloon Co	52nd French Balloon Co	53rd French Balloon Co	183rd Aero Squadron
(Thillombois)	(Boncourt)	(Vignot)	(Mobile Park No 1)

British Independent Air Force
Major General Hugh Trenchard (Azelot)

Day Bombardment

No.55 Sqn	No.99 Sqn	No.104 Sqn	No.110 Sqn
Maj A Gray	Maj L A Pattinson	Maj J C Quinnell	Maj H R Nicholl
DH9/DH9A	DH9A	DH9/DH10	DH9/DH9A

Night Bombardment

No.97 Sqn	No.100 Sqn	No.115 Sqn	No. 215 Sqn	No. 216 Sqn
Maj V A Albrecht	Maj C G Burge	Maj W E Gardner	Maj J F Jones	Maj W R Read
HP O/400	HP O/400	HP O/400	HP O/400	HP O/400

01 SEPTEMBER 1918
M T W T F S **S**

British Front

This late summer opened with fair visibility but a high wind. The British army was pushing forward along both sides of the Somme River, following up a series of attacks that had begun on 8 August 1918, with the Canadians and Australians breaking open the German front facing Amiens. On this day the Australians attacked the heavily defended Mont Saint-Quentin, just north of Péronne and Péronne town itself. Péronne lay on the Somme, and crossing the river here would roll up the Germans to the north, forcing a retreat behind their prepared positions on the Hindenburg Line.

Further to the north, August had seen General Sir Julian Byng's 3rd Army attack on the 21st. They were now facing the infamous Drocourt-Quéant switch-line of April 1917 fame. They would attack it on the morrow. Bapaume had fallen on the 29th and the northern flank of the 4th Army was also closing on the Hindenburg Line. The German army was on the defensive and showing increasing signs of disintegration.

In the air, things were different. The RAF had suffered heavily in August, and now faced well-equipped opposition in the shape of firmly established Jastas flying Fokker DVIIs. The RAF's day bombers needed escorting now as a matter of course, otherwise casualties were high. The four types of RAF fighters had seen long service, and indeed, only the Sopwith Dolphin was a 1918 aeroplane, and there were only four squadrons of them. The SE5a could hold its own with Fokker DVIIs but the main fighter, the Sopwith Camel, was rapidly becoming obsolete. This was evidenced in the last ten days of August, which witnessed the loss of five American-flown Camels in one fight on the 26th, while 43 Squadron lost another six the next day. The last main fighter-type was the Bristol F2b two-seat fighter, which had started life so ingloriously in April 1917, but which now had become a formidable foe. There were six squadrons of 'Brisfits' in France used also extensively for long-range reconnaissance sorties. The Germans were suffering their own difficulties, attrition was hard to replace, aviation fuel was in short supply, while their two-seater crews were now restricted in their operations by their lack of ability to avoid, out-fly or out-fight Allied fighters.

Aerial operations on the RAF's front as the month opened can be characterised in terms of the three main sectors of aerial activity: army co-operation, day bombing and fighter operations – including low bombing and strafing. (Night bombing was also becoming a regular feature, especially with the Independent Air Force's Handley Page bombers, under Hugh Trenchard.)

The prime initiation of aerial combat was when RAF patrols encountered patrols of German fighters that were prepared to engage. The German pilots still preferred to engage only when they had a distinct advantage, whereas the British and American pilots invariably attacked everything whatever the odds against them. As the Germans concentrated their resources on key sectors of the front, aerial activity was much more intense over the area of an offensive by the Army. In early September the active Jagdgeschwader on the British front was JGI and JGIII, both of which operated

Oberleutnant Robert Ritter von Greim had a long and varied flying war, serving with FFA3, Jasta 34b, leading Jagdgruppe 10 and 9, before returning to Jasta 34b. His victory tally reached twenty-eight by October 1918, four of which were scored in September. Holder of the Pour le Mérite, he remained in the German air force rising to Generaloberst in WWII. Captured by US troops in 1945 he committed suicide on 24 May that year.

near Cambrai. Also still near Cambrai was Jasta 5, which was by far the most successful non-'Circus' Staffel in September 1918. Consequently, most of the major encounters in September were over the Cambrai area, the Arras area, and later in the month in the north, around Ypres, following an Allied ground attack there.

Almost separately was something of a small private, but intense war between the mainly ex-RNAS squadrons (de Havilland bombers and Camel fighters) based around Dunkirk, and the German Marine Jastas, along the North Sea coast. The combatants also resorted to intensive night bombing, and the RAF also had a dedicated night fighter squadron in France to counter this threat – No.151, with Camels.

The morning of the 1st was fairly quiet, but Lieutenant W E G 'Pedro' Mann, in a Camel of 208 Squadron, claimed a German two-seater at 0750, in flames south of the Scarpe River for his 8th victory. Of its crew of Unteroffizier Gottfried Ebert and Vizefeldwebel Pilarz, of FA(A) 294, only the latter survived, wounded. 40 Squadron's SE5s claimed another, Captain George Dixon achieving his 6th victory at 0815, south-east of Henin-Liétard. The Germans only made one claim before midday: the commander of Bavarian Jasta 34b, Oberleutnant Robert Ritter von Greim claiming a Camel at 1000 near St Pierre Vaast Wood, just south of Sailly-Saillisel – probably a 73 Squadron machine. The four or five other victories of the morning were balloons by Allied pilots:

0740	Lt Len Taplin	(7th victory)	4 AFC Sqdn	at Fromelles
0745	Lt Roy King	(14th victory)	4 AFC Sqdn	at Le Grand Riez
0830	Lt Fred Luff	(3rd victory)	74 Sqdn	at Menin
1025	Capt Ernest Hoy	(6th victory)	29 Sqdn	nr Armentières

and a Fokker DVII by Lieutenant J W Wright of 4 AFC, south-east of Bailleul at 0925 – his first victory.

At 1100 hours, Captain Basil Catchpole MC DFC led out six Bristols of 'L' Flight – a long-range recce unit – to photograph the Sensée Canal, north of Cambrai. They lost one of their number, probably to Unteroffizier Schaack of Jasta 28 – his second victory. It seemed that the crew failed to spot the others turn for the lines and became separated – highly dangerous when enemy fighters were about. Later Catchpole returned alone to the area but with a large fighter escort and completed the photo sortie, producing a fine mosaic for 1st Army HQ. Further south over the Somme bridges at Brie, Lieutenant Russell McCrae of 46 Squadron claimed a Fokker out of control at 1125.

In the afternoon, at 1345, 57 Squadron lost a DH4 while bombing Cambrai and had another shot up by an estimated 20 attacking fighters. Their escort of 62 Squadron lost a Bristol and had another force-land. 57 Squadron crews claimed four Fokkers and 62, two more. Sergeant Mechanic J Grant, gunner to Lieutenant E M Coles of 57, saw a Fokker coming up beneath the 'Four' next to them, and shot it down.

The Fokkers were from Bruno Loerzer's JGIII, which consisted of Jastas 2, 26, 27 and 36. Loerzer claimed one Bristol for his 34th kill, Leutnant Ernst Bormann of Jasta 2 (Boelcke), another south of Lecluse for his 5th. The DH4 was brought down by Vizefeldwebel Skworz of Jasta 36 at Brunemont. Despite the RAF claims, there are no known German losses.

To the north, near Armentières, one of the many Americans serving with the RAF, Lieutenant Fred Gillet, in a Dolphin of 79 Squadron, shot down an LVG C at 1320, the 4th victory of the pilot who would be the most successful RAF pilot between the beginning of September and the end of the war. Another successful pilot, but on the German side, was Flieger Hans Nülle of Jasta 39. The Jasta intercepted Camels of 209 Squadron at 1650, Nülle gaining his first victory, Vizefeldwebel Gockel his third. More will be heard of Nülle during the month.

A Dolphin of 79 Squadron was lost to flak around Armentières at 1830 the pilot, Second Lieutenant D S Merton, chancing his luck. He had taken off at 1645 for a practice flight and strayed too close to the front lines. If he was looking for trouble he found it, ground fire bringing him down south of the town to become a prisoner. German flak fire had been very active during the day, three artillery observation aircraft having been hit, damaged, and forced to land.

More engagements between fighters occurred in the early evening, 29 Squadron having a scrap near Armentières at 1810, claiming two Fokkers, one to Captain Hoy for his second of the day, 7th overall. Another of the unit's aces, Lieutenant Arthur Eden Reed, a South African, claimed his 15th victory. Nos. 208 and 56 Squadrons each claimed a Fokker shortly before 1900. More fights went on near the Ypres Salient, Lieutenant Edwin Swale of 210 Squadron claimed a Fokker east of the city at 1830, then 88's Bristols got a Fokker in flames east of Becelaere at 1910. Despite these claims, no German aircraft were apparently lost, certainly no pilots.

On the German side, Leutnant Wilhelm Sommer of Jasta 39 achieved his third victory by burning the Tilloy balloon – SR59 of the 28th Balloon Company – at 2110. The observers, Lieutenants Kitcat and Freshney, both parachuted to safety. Flieger Abteilung (A) 208 lost Leutnants Hermann Aschoff and Friedrich Ohlf at Handecourt during the day, presumably to anti-aircraft fire, as no two-seaters were encountered anywhere near this area. Another two-seater crew, Vizefeldwebel Gunther and Leutnant Schwertfeger, of FA(A) 252, shot up a British tank which burst into flames, then directed artillery fire onto another which was also destroyed. This night, the RAF lost a night bomber, either to flak or to engine failure.

French Front

The French front line stretched from south of the Somme to the Swiss border. The Americans were arriving in force opposite the Saint-Mihiel salient, south of Verdun and held the line to the north and south of Verdun. Although we shall record the activities of both air forces separately, both French and American forces were defending what was the French Front. Due to the vagaries of the French climate, there was rather more low cloud and rain over the French lines than further north today, thus air activity was rather slow.

Vizefeldwebel Karl Schlegel, a recent and rapidly rising 'Kanone' (the German term for what the French called an ace) from Jasta 45, made an intrusion over the French lines and scored his 19th victory by flaming the balloon of the French 29th Company, in the X Armée sector. The observer, Adjutant Proust, took to his parachute and landed safely. Balloon observers were the only Allied participants in the air war to have parachutes as escape routes. Unlike the Germans, who had registered successful jumps from aeroplanes in combat from June 1918, Allied aircrew never had the opportunity. This was a bureaucratic if not autocratic (even murderous) decision that was to cost the lives of countless British, French and American airmen in the last year of the war. One line of thought was that with a way out, the airmen would be more inclined to bale out if in a fix, whereas most probably the pilot would have been more aggressive, knowing that he had a line of escape if all else failed. It has also been said that as the Allies had so many airmen there was less inclination from on high to save a few! The Germans, with dwindling numbers, obviously had the opposite view.

On the Aisne River front, the 29-year-old, devoutly religious Sous Lieutenant Léon Bourjade combined with Sous Lieutenant Ernest Maunoury to burn the German balloon at Pont Arcy at 1840. It was the 16th and 6th victories respectively of these two pilots of Spa.152. Over Flavy le Meldeux, Spa.150 claimed two aircraft, one credited to Sergent Charles Veil, an American serving with the French, the other shared between Lieutenant Henry Stickney, yet another American, and Sergent Bagarry, for their joint first victory. Vizefeldwebel Friedrich Poeschke of Jasta 53 claimed a Spad for his second victory, over Brétigny.

Thirty-seven aircraft of Escadre de Bombardement 14, comprising Groupes de Bombardement 8 and 10, carried out night raids against railway depots at Laon, Marie, Ham and other sites, dropping a total of 9,866 kilos of bombs and firing 700 rounds at barrack lights. One Voisin bomber was lost, probably to flak.

Top Sous Lieutenant L J-P. Bourjade of Spa.152. He ended the war with twenty-eight combat victories, all but one being German kite balloons. Four of these were achieved in September 1918. He became an officer of the Legion d'Honneur, became a missionary post-war and died in 1924.
Bottom Sous Lieutenant E J J Maunoury flew with Escadrille Spa.152 and most of his victories were balloons, four of which he burned in September. He received the Legion d'Honneur, but was killed in a flying accident in 1921.

	A/C	KB			DES	OOC	KB
British losses	14	1		British claims	13	11	5
French losses	1	1		French claims	2		1
American losses	–	–		American claims	–		–
IAF losses	–	–		IAF claims	–	–	–
German claims	12†	2		German losses	3		2

† Includes two to flak.

British Casualties

Aircraft type	No.	Squadron	Crew	
AWFK8	D5134	35 Sqdn	2/Lt H Phillips	Safe
			2/Lt H Griffiths	Safe
RE8	E67	15 Sqdn	Capt C C Snow	Safe
			2/Lt R C Capel-Cave	WIA
DH4	F6096	57 Sqdn	2/Lt J C Dugdale	POW
			2/Lt F B Robinson	POW
DH4	D8382	57 Sqdn	Sgt D E Edgeley	Safe *
			Sgt N Sandison	WIA
BF2b	E2521	L Flt	Lt G L Barritt	POW
			2/Lt R H G Boys	POW
BF2b	E2479	62 Sqdn	2/Lt L B Raymond	POW
			2/Lt D S Hamilton	KIA
BF2b	–	62 Sqdn	2/Lt J K Stewart	WIA
BF2b	E2494	62 Sqdn	Lt L W Hudson	Safe
			2/Lt J Hall	WIA
BF2b	C843	20 Sqdn	Lt F E Smith	Safe
			Pbr E S Harvey	Safe

Aircraft type	No.	Squadron	Crew	
SE5a	B7890	32 Sqdn	Lt E C Klingman (USAS)	POW
SE5a	E5939	32 Sqdn	2/Lt J O Donaldson (USAS)	POW
Dolphin	E4433	79 Sqdn	2/Lt D A Martin (USAS)	POW
Camel	E4388	209 Sqdn	2/Lt H V Peeling	POW
Camel	E4393	209 Sqdn	2/Lt R L Scharff	POW
Camel	D1922	73 Sqdn	Lt H V Fellows	POW
Camel	B7162	203 Sqdn	2/Lt T Nolan	Inj
FE2b (night)	C9790	101 Sqdn	2/Lt M E Challis 2/Lt R D Hughes	POW POW
AWFK8	F7394	8 Sqdn	2/Lt T Brandon 2/Lt R F Talbot	WIA * Safe
BF2b	–	L Flt	2/Lt M Wallace (O)	WIA *
BF2b	–	48 Sqdn	2/Lt J N Kier (O)	WIA *
RE8	–	53 Sqdn	2/Lt D C Burke (O)	WIA *
SE5a	–	74 Sqdn	Lt J Adamson	WIA *
DH4	F6168	57 Sqdn	Lt A L Platt Lt J Howard-Brown	Safe * WIA
SE5a	F6421	32 Sqdn	Lt A E Sandys-Winsch	WIA *
RE8	–	5 Sqdn	Lt E A Locke-Walters (P)	WIA *
RE8	C2244	53 Sqdn	Lt S W Cowper-Coles Lt G L Pargeter	WIA * Safe

		French Casualties		
Voisin		V106	Cpl Revolte Soldat Robin	MIA MIA

02 SEPTEMBER 1918
M T W T F S S

British Front

At 0500 the Canadian Corps of the British 1st Army and the XVIII Corps of the 3rd Army attacked the Drocourt-Quéant switch line, supported by tanks. V Corps attacked between Sailly-Saillisel and Le Transloy, IV Corps between Haplincourt and Beugny and VI Corps between Morchies and Lagnicourt. The Canadians broke right through and by mid-morning they had captured Cagnicourt. By the end of the day the British had reached a line along the Sensée River and the Canal du Nord. Along the Somme front, they were pressing up to the Hindenburg Line. On the British right, the French were also advancing, with the Germans losing all their gains from the March 1918 offensive.

Two American pilots who flew with 73 Squadron in 1918. Lts H V Fellows (POW 1 September 1918), and D B Sinclair, captured the following day.

In the air on this day, despite showery weather and an abundance of cloud, there were clear bright intervals with good visibility. Over the offensive, 5 and 52 Squadrons co-operated with the Canadians, 13 Squadron with XVII Corps and 8 Squadron with the Tank Corps. The Camels of 73 Squadron bombed and strafed enemy tank defences, while 40 and 22 Squadrons provided air cover directly over the advance.

The German policy of giving the elite Circus units the best equipment paid off, as the BMW-engined Fokker biplanes of JGIII had a significant impact on the air war. BMW Fokkers looked identical to the Mercedes-powered ones but they had 20-plus more horsepower, giving a significantly better performance. JGIII flew three main missions this day, claiming 26 victories out of the 35 or 37 claims made against the RAF. In all, the Germans claimed a massive 59 victories, details of 57 being presented here. It is assumed that the other two were by JGIII – as 24 are known – or by Jastas flying near JGIII and winning disputed claims. Certainly other Jastas claimed in the same area and time as JGIII. Another possibility is that two-seater crews made the claims.

The carnage began at 0630, as 201 Squadron attacked 12 Fokker DVIIs at 12,000 feet over Heudicourt. Captain Reg Brading, a 19-year-old Englishman, claimed his 9th victory by sending one down 'out of control' and 45 minutes later he got another. He attacked Fokkers operating under the cloud layer at 4,000 feet that were attacking Corps aircraft, shooting down his second victim over Lagnicourt. At the same time Lieutenant Ron Sykes, another 19-year-old, claimed a Fokker after his flight had been pounced on by 25 of these biplanes. This was confirmed at 1530 that afternoon, Brading seeing another wrecked Fokker near the crashed DVII he brought down, flying over to take a look at it. However, this could be deemed somewhat circumstantial.

The first major fight was at 0820, Jasta 36 clashing with the Camels of 3 Squadron, who lost Lieutenant Vic McElroy to Leutnant Quandt. However, the German then spoilt his performance somewhat by shooting up a Rumpler CIV of FA(A) 210 by mistake. Quandt would eventually lose a fight and be killed by a French fighter pilot, but not until June 1940 – in World War II!

From 0930 onwards, Jasta 27 of JGIII was in action, encountering two Bristols of 22 Squadron, one of which the Jasta commander promptly shot down. This was Hermann Frommherz's 17th victory. No. 22 claimed two Fokkers in return, one by the crew of Lieutenant Ian O Stead and Second Lieutenant W A Cowie, before they had to force-land – unharmed – in British lines, apparently not being claimed by the Germans. No. 22 also reported the presence of Camels and SE5s in this fight, and Pfalz DXIIs – which looked so similar to the more numerous DVIIs that few were actually reported that summer.

Then Jasta 26 claimed two SE5s at Villers at 1015/1020, one to Leutnant Otto Frühner, his 19th, the other to Leutnant Herman Lange, his 5th. They were fighting 40 Squadron who lost just one aircraft; the other claim may have been a Camel. Jasta 26 went on to engage Camels, the whole Geschwader encountering a formation of Camels and two-seaters between 1100 and 1130, east of Cambrai. They made the following seven claims, making ten in all for the sortie:

Ltn F Noltenius	Jasta 27	Camel	Étaing	1100	5th victory
Ltn O Löffler	Jasta 2	Camel	S Pelves	–	5th victory
Ltn E Bormann	Jasta 2	Camel	Drury	–	6th victory
"	"	Camel	Souchy	–	7th victory
Ltn F Heinz	Jasta 2	Camel	Boiry	–	2nd victory
Ltn O Frühner	Jasta 26	SE5a	Barelle	1110	20th victory
Ltn F Noltenius	Jasta 27	Camel	Rumaucourt	1120	6th victory

Whilst this was going on, another of the Bloody April veterans, Vizefeldwebel Jörke of Jasta 39, claimed an RE8 of 5 Squadron over Ballieul-Sir-Berthoult at 1125 – his 13th victory. For JGIII this was an example of accurate claiming, as 208 and 209 both lost two Camels, 73 and 201 one each. No. 56 Squadron lost an SE5a – probably to Frühner – and Noltenius's claim was probably a 35 Squadron AWFK8 – the Germans often confusing DH4s, AWFK8s and BF2bs.

Meanwhile, at 1005, Lieutenant M D Sinclair in a SE5a of 60 Squadron attacked an LVG C at the extremely low altitude of 30 feet, got underneath it (!) and opened fire from 100 yards, killing the observer moments before the C-type dove into the ground. Ten minutes later, Major F I Tanner, from 80 Squadron, claimed a DFW C, south of Cartigny, which spun in and burnt. At the same time, Lieutenant J Collier, also from 80 Squadron, claimed another just south of Mons-en-Chaussée – two rare victories for this Camel unit, dedicated to supporting British tanks.

Just after midday, JGIII and other Jastas were airborne again, this time making no fewer than 14 claims between 1220 and 1250 German time:

Vzfw C Mesch	Jasta 26	Camel	Haucourt	1240	7th victory
Oblt T H Dahlmann	JGIII	Camel	Haucourt	1240	4th victory
Vzfw C Mesch	Jasta 26	Camel	Haucourt	1242	8th victory
Ltn Ehlers	Jasta 26	Camel	NE Barelle	1245	1st victory
Ltn H Lange	Jasta 26	Camel	NE Barelle	1245	6th victory
Hpt B Loerzer	JGIII	Camel	Dury	1245	35th victory
Vzfw A Lux	Jasta 27	RE8	Hamel	–	5th victory
Ltn Stoltenhoff	Jasta 27	RE8	–	–	2nd victory
Vzfw A Lux	Jasta 27	BF2b	Vis-en-Artois	–	6th victory
Ltn O Löffler	Jasta 2	Camel	Beugnatre	–	6th victory
Ltn E Bormann	Jasta 2	Camel	W Havrincourt	–	8th victory

Fw W Kahle	Jasta 27	Camel	Beugnatre	–	1st victory
Ltn O Löffler	Jasta 2	Camel	S Palleul	–	7th victory
Ltn M Demisch	Jasta 58	RE8	Vis-en-Artois	1330	5th victory

Top Captain Field E Kindley began his war fighting with the RAF, in 65 Squadron. Moved to the 148th Aero Squadron, he claimed a total of 12 victories, seven in September. He too received US and British DFCs but was killed in a flying accident in Texas in 1920. **Bottom** Jesse Orinn Creech, flew with the 148th Aero Squadron under RAF control. By the end of the war he had achieved eight victories, four of them during September 1918.

Either Martin Demisch (sometimes spelt Dehmisch) was flying with JGIII, or more likely he won a disputed claim with a JGIII pilot, giving JGIII 24 confirmed kills rather than the initial 26 claimed for the day – for no loss. After both their engagements, JGIII remained over the battlefield and engaged in some extensive ground strafing. The root cause of their success – apart from superior aeroplanes – was the capacity of Bruno Loerzer to co-ordinate four Jastas into one large force, which simply swamped the flight-sized RAF patrols. Co-ordination between RAF units was hindered by their vertical separation which only seemed to work well when there were no clouds interfering with visual contact between each layer. The SE5a top cover often arrived too late, not having seen anything. Unfortunately, all too often no top cover was provided at all.

For example, the 148th Aero Squadron had been flying in two flights, with 'A' Flight, led by First Lieutenant Field Kindley in front, passing under a large bank of cloud which was at 3,000 feet south of Rumaucourt, while First Lieutenant Elliott Springs and 'B' Flight were in the open behind and below. When Jasta 26 dropped out of low cloud right into the middle of B Flight, Kindley turned his Flight back into the fight, just as the other Jastas arrived. He claimed a Fokker but had 36 bullet holes punched into his Camel, ten of which had hit his guns a foot in front of his face!

The Camels were fighting a continuously reinforced formation of Fokkers, as Springs' combat report noted four Fokkers at 1145, four miles south-east of Haucourt on the Arras-Cambrai road, reinforced by three more, followed by a further seven from the south-east, and finally more to bring the total to 25. Elliott Springs also left an account of this fight, quoted in his biography *War Bird,* by Burke Davis:

'The Huns meant business and so did we. As soon as I would get on the tail of one, another would get me and as soon as I would shake him off there would be another... My lower left wing buckled. I went into a spin. I thought my machine was falling to pieces and reflected with pleasure that I had forgotten my pocketbook. I thought of Mac [1/Lt John Grider USAS, KIA 18 June 1918, and a close friend of Springs] and how glad he would be to see me. But my plane held together... and I got out of the spin in time to hop a Hun. I don't know how many Huns we got out of it. I'm the only one of my Flight who returned.'

First Lieutenant Jesse Creech had earlier fallen out of the patrol due to a broken con-rod, getting down unhurt, but the rest had been severely mauled. Kindley claimed a Fokker at 1150 south of Rumaucourt, which he saw turn over onto its back and spin in. Lieutenant Charles McLean claimed another over Buissy after he had shot at it, the Fokker nose diving. Soon afterwards, McLean flew back past Buissy and saw a wreck burning on the ground where the Fokker would have crashed. This would, without doubt, have been a burning Camel and is another indication of how the optimism of a fighter pilot results in exaggerated claims. Lieutenant Walter Knox claimed another destroyed.

The RAF lost at least three RE8s to fighters. No. 52 Squadron sent nine machines to bomb Vitry and the last vic of three were shot up and force-landed in Allied lines – shades of 59 Squadron in April 1917. At least this time the Camels of 148 had been covering them, but they were decimated by JGIII. In the fight too were the SEs of 64 Squadron and the BF2bs of 22 Squadron, who between them claimed a further five Fokkers, the former being engaged in ground strafing. One of the SE pilots, Sergeant A S Cowlishaw, was obviously on a balloon hunt when he joined combat, for his guns were primed with the highly sensitive Buckingham ammunition, designed for igniting balloons, but he drove down a Fokker over Marquion, smoking!

For the two American Camel squadrons serving with the RAF, it was their second hiding in a week from JGIII. The other squadron, the 17th Aero, were the main sufferers on 26 August. The reason was the same; caught low down and having to fight their way out against high odds. JGIII double-claimed on the Camels in this fight, as can be seen by two claims at the same time and/or location for most of the victims, i.e. ten claims, four losses if we ignore Creech, who it is believed dropped out before the fight began. During this period the 'lesser' Jasta were also active and at 1220 Leutnant Wilhelm Sommer of Jasta 39 scored for the second day straight, shooting down an RE8 over Fampoux, in British lines, probably one of 52 Squadron's machines – and he wasn't finished for the day yet. Jasta 7's Leutnant Willi Nebgen claimed an AWFK8 at 1230 over Lomme, near Lille, for his 3rd victory while Vize-feldwebel Maack of Jasta 63 got his first, another Big Ack, at exactly the same time and place. However, 82 Squadron only lost one Ack-W!

During the day, Hauptmann Eduard von Schleich claimed an RE8 (his 31st kill) near Bapaume and in the late evening the Richthofen Circus (JG1) made its first claim in September. Oberleutnant Erich von Wedel, commander of Jasta 11, brought down another RE8 near Le Catelet at 1945 for his own 11th kill. Wilhelm Sommer got his second of the day by burning the 43 Company's balloon near Bapaume at 2100 hours.

This evening also saw a fight between Bristols of 48 Squadron and Jasta 20 over Gheluvelt at 2000. Leutnant Raven von Barnekow scored his 5th and Leutnant Bruno Hobein his 3rd, shooting down the two Brisfits which failed to return. No. 48's crews claimed four Fokkers, but Jasta 20 suffered no losses as far as is known. In fact the only known Fokker loss on the whole front was that flown by Vizefeldwebel Heinrich Gockel of Jasta 33. He baled out of his burning fighter, believed near Cambrai, while his young Staffelführer, Leutnant Karl von Schonebeck, scored his 7th victory.

During the day, the RAF organised a mass strafe of Linselles aerodrome. The SE5s of 29 and 74 Squadron bombed from 6,000 feet and then remained above while 41 Squadron and the Camels of 70 strafed from 100 to 50 feet. The aerodrome was reported as gutted, and none of the raiders were lost, a demonstration of air power that the RFC was incapable of 18 months earlier.

Another significant feature of the day was that, just like Bloody April, the German fighters broke through and got to a large number of artillery observation and close-support aircraft. However, unlike Bloody April, this was happening about once a month of late, and was not to happen significantly again during the war. The RAF fighters managed to keep the Jastas off the front most of the time, but more importantly, the far better trained RE8 and AWFK8 crews could now look after themselves, a great improvement on the previous spring.

French Front

The weather improved here and aerial combat picked up. In the V Armée sector, three Spad two-seaters of Spa.20 on a photo-recce mission were engaged in combat near Thil at 1030 by eight Fokkers. During the fight, Adjutant Dutrey and Sergent Latapie claimed a biplane at 1030 over La Neuvillette, 3 kilometres north-west of Reims, but were in turn attacked by Leutnant Gustav Dörr of Jasta 45. Latapie was wounded but Dutrey evaded the attack and they managed to return to base. Dörr then attacked the photo Spad and shot it down, the crew posted as missing. Dörr was credited with his 24th and 25th victories. Leutnant Meixner of Jasta 45 also claimed a Spad at this time for his first victory. The third Spad of the trio, Sous Lieutenant Clavel and Lieutenant Puisieux, claimed a Fokker in the fight.

Twenty minutes later, Jasta 45 commander, Leutnant Konrad Brendle, attacked a balloon near Reims, but did not return. He was killed in action behind the French lines but received credit for his 8th victory through his colleagues for downing a balloon.

In the X Armée sector, during the course of a combat with five Fokker DVIIs, Maréchal-des-Logis Verges and Lieutenant Barat, of Spa.34, succeeded in downing one near Courcy-la-Ville. However, during the scrap Verges was killed, although Barat managed to fly their two-seater, which had been riddled with bullets, down safely into French territory. Also in this sector, near Reims, Caporal Fournier and Lieutenant de Boeuxis of Br.289, were shot down by three Fokkers; this time the pilot was wounded and the observer killed. Two-seaters were claimed by Leutnant Werner Preuss of Jasta 66 – for his 13th victory – and Leutnant Herman Häbich of Jasta 49, his 2nd, the latter claiming near Châlons-Suippes at 1220, although the Jasta had Unteroffizier Hennies wounded.

Spad two-seaters were also claimed by Gefreiter Jakob of Jasta 17 at Savigny at 1000 hrs, and Leutnant Buddeberg of Jasta 50 over Braisne at the same time. Two more Bréguets were claimed in French lines near the Remser Wald, by Verdun by Jasta 68 – Leutnant Rudolf Otto, Staffelführer, and Vizefeldwebel Huar.

Over the V Armée sector, another Bréguet, from Br.260 on a two-plane photo mission, was engaged by six Fokkers. Lieutenant Fournier was wounded, his observer being killed. Fournier managed to force-land in French lines. A Spad two-seater from an unknown unit was shot up as well, Caporal Maurel being wounded, his observer, Lieutenant de Boeuric, unhurt.

During the day Adjutant Lucas of Spa.97 claimed a balloon for his first victory. Another Spad Escadrille that was climbing back from being heavily thrashed by the Germans during the early summer was Spa.159, under the expert guidance of their new CO, Lieutenant Henri Hay de Slade; they claimed two victories. De Slade got one between Terny and Sorny at 1045, Sergent Rozes the 2nd, over Sorny itself. Both villages are due north of Soissons. De Slade was 25 years old and had been operational since December 1916 with Spa.86, before taking over Spa.159 in late July 1918.

Another French ace, Lieutenant Ferdinand Bonneton, 28, now flying with Spa.69, had already served in Russia, Romania and Italy. He shot down a balloon at Pontavert for his 7th victory, followed by a probable Fokker DVII over Beaurieux.

There was no end of combats over the front on this day, the Germans claiming nine Spad fighters:

Uffz O Bieleit	Jasta 45	Baslieux	0820	1st victory
Ltn Fritz Höhn	Jasta 81	Coucy-le-Château	–	11th victory
Ltn A Brandenstein	Jasta 49	Suippes	1010	5th victory
Ltn Christians	Jasta 21	NW Fismes	1110	1st victory
"	"	E Fismes	1640	2nd victory
Ltn Hentzen	Jasta 9	W Terny Sorny	1733	2nd victory
Flgr F Wolff	Jasta 17	Savigny	1830	1st victory
Ltn H Brünig	Jasta 50	Fismes	1920	7th victory
Flgr Eyssler	Jasta 66	N Soissons	–	1st victory

The 22-year-old ace of Spa.88, Lieutenant Gabriel Thomas, had a fight with a German two-seater crew and was wounded for his pains. He would return in October and bring his wartime score to seven.

The French also attacked the German balloon lines during the day. At 0900 the 'drachen' of Ballonzug 22 was burnt by Lieutenant Henri Dencaussée of Spa.90 at Geline. Half an hour later Spa.90 struck again, Sous Lieutenant Marc Ambrogi, Adjutants Maurice Bizot and Jean Pezon shared the flaming of Ballonzug 36's gasbag at Juvelize, thereby gaining their 9th, 6th and 3rd victories respectively. During this team attack (normal for the French as it increased the chance of success while splitting the defensive fire) Bizot was hit by shrapnel from a defending gun but was able to fly home.

Spa.124 'Joan d'Arc' Escadrille, the French unit that replaced the earlier unit of the same number – the famed Lafayette Escadrille of American volunteers – claimed two balloons. The first went to Adjutant Bentejac and Sergent Grillot at Manre, the second to Lieutenant Berge and Sergent Caton at Bois de la Taille. Meantime, a patrol of Spa.163 burnt the German balloon at Bouconville.

In reply the Germans made determined efforts to go after French balloons. In the V Armée sector, the balloon of the 27th Company was destroyed at 1430 (A) by Leutnant Krayer of Jasta 45, Aspirant Simondi, the observer, parachuting to safety. The balloon of the 72nd Company was lost in the IV Armée sector, and again the observer – Sous Lieutenant Brutus – descended safely. The aircraft that flamed this balloon was shot down near Arcy St Restitute, and was probably Leutnant Gottfried Clausnitzer of the Saxon Jasta 72, who was shot down in flames after downing a balloon for his first victory. Two other balloons were attacked but not destroyed – probably those attacked by Brendle of Jasta 45 as mentioned above. The loss of Brendle – the experienced ace – and Clausnitzer makes it evident that the downing of a balloon was still no easy task, no matter how experienced the pilot.

A further two French balloons were lost in the II Armée sector by Jasta 67 pilots. Unteroffizier Baumgartner got the balloon of Sous Lieutenant Lamaud of the 81st Cié (Company), who made a safe jump, while Leutnant Quartier destroyed that of the 52nd Company, Sous Lieutenant Gravier parachuting down. Gravier was no doubt delighted to learn that his victor had been shot down by ground fire and captured, after having gained his second victory.

Three balloons were lost in the VII Armée sector in the late afternoon. Leutnant Josef Filbig of Jasta 80 got the 34th Company one at 1600, while the 89th Company lost theirs to Leutnant Gustav Burck of Jasta 54 at 1615. Earlier, the Americans had lost the balloon of their 3rd Balloon Company, which was flamed at 1400 hours by Jasta 80's commander, Oberleutnant Gottlieb Rassberger – his first victory.

American Sector

Also operating near Reims was a squadron of the USAS. The 88th Observation Squadron was in the IV Armée sector and three of their Salmson 2A2s, engaged on photo work, were attacked by eight German fighters. The Americans claimed the German leader shot down but lost Lieutenants R W Hitchcock and F M Moore behind the lines near Dhuizy. Hitchcock had only recently been awarded the DSC for an action which had occurred on 11 August, after his observer had been killed and his body had jammed the controls. Despite this impediment, Hitchcock managed to bring the plane home, but this time he was not so lucky. Captain Richard Page and Lieutenant Pitt F Carl came down in French lines south of Reims.

Unfortunately, no time is known for this action and it may relate to Jasta 45 and the loss of Brendle, but more likely to three Spad two-seaters claimed by this unit near Magneux at around 1600. Leutnant Hans Rolfes claimed two – his 12th and 13th victories – the other credited to Leutnant Koennemann for his second. Another casualty mentioned as being related to this fight is the two-seater crew of Unteroffizier Josef Kraemer and Leutnant Eugen Weber of FA2, who came down in French lines. However, they were lost further north-west, near Nesle, probably falling to a patrol of GC14 that downed a DFW which had had the audacity to attack the 68th Company balloon.

The Spads of the 22nd Aero Squadron shot down a Rumpler C at 0930, near Armaucourt, the victor being Lieutenant Arthur Ray Brooks, the 2nd of his six victories. Ray Brooks died on 17 July 1991, the last USAS – but not the last American ace – to die.

	A/C	KB		DES	OOC	KB
British losses	32	2	British claims	15	8	–
French losses	5	6	French claims	9		7
American losses	1	1	American claims	2		–
IAF losses	–	–	IAF claims	–	–	–
German claims	51	11	German losses	4		6

British Casualties

Aircraft type	No.	Squadron	Crew	
FE2b (night)	B1879	148 Sqdn	Lt E Alder	Safe
			Lt A V Collins	Inj
RE8	C2729	5 Sqdn	Lt L Coleman	KIA
			2/Lt C E Gardner	KIA
RE8	C2536	5 Sqdn	Lt C C Fraser	Safe
			2/Lt A J Bishop	WIA
RE8	C4590	5 Sqdn	Lt J Town	Safe
			Lt A C Pollard	Safe
RE8	E91	6 Sqdn	Lt Martin	Safe
			Lt G D Churchward	Safe

Aircraft type	No.	Squadron	Crew		
RE8	F5880	6 Sqdn	Lt Fenwick	Safe	*
			2/Lt J A Holmes	Safe	
RE8	C5072	6 Sqdn	Lt D Pettit	Safe	
			Lt Clark	Safe	
RE8	F5978	13 Sqdn	2/Lt J S Stringer	POW	
			Lt R A Pope MC	POW	
RE8	F6015	52 Sqdn	2/Lt J C Garlake	Safe	*
			2/Lt L Sharp	WIA	
RE8	C2467	52 Sqdn	2/Lt R G Walton	WIA	*
			2/Lt G Bradbury	WIA	
RE8	D4899	52 Sqdn	2/Lt J B Elton	Safe	*
			2/Lt W E China	Safe	
RE8	D4903	53 Sqdn	2/Lt A J Macqueen	Safe	
			2/Lt D A Lawson	Safe	
AWFK8	D5185	8 Sqdn	Capt G H Dykes	WIA	
			Lt F Birkett	Safe	
AWFK8	B4161	8 Sqdn	2/Lt W L Chapman	Safe	
			2/Lt F E L Elliott	Safe	
AWFK8	F4268	8 Sqdn	Lt W Spriggs	Safe	*
			Lt J A Cogan	WIA	
AWFK8	F7394	8 Sqdn	2/Lt C W Appleby	KIA	
			2/Lt R F Talbot	KIA	
AWFK8	D5121	8 Sqdn	Lt W Spriggs	Safe	
			2/Lt J A Cogan	WIA	
AWFK8	F4263	10 Sqdn	2/Lt R A Coulthurst	WIA	
			2/Lt A R Macpherson	Safe	
AWFK8	B4174	35 Sqdn	2/Lt H Nottrass	WIA	*
			Lt F A Lawson	WIA	
AWFK8	D5174	82 Sqdn	2/Lt D Rose	POW	
			2/Lt J B Cockin	POW	
DH9	D3226	206 Sqdn	2/Lt H A Scrivener	POW/WIA	
			Sgt C H Davidson	KIA	
BF2b	E2516	22 Sqdn	Lt I O Stead	Safe	*
			2/Lt W A Cowie	WIA	
BF2b	D7990	22 Sqdn	Capt B L Dowling	KIA	
			Lt V StB Collins	KIA	
BF2b	E2214	48 Sqdn	2/Lt O O'Connor	POW	
			2/Lt J J Ambler	POW	
BF2b	E2455	48 Sqdn	2/Lt I M B McCulloch	POW	
			2/Lt L P Penny	KIA	
SE5a	D8445	40 Sqdn	2/Lt H W Clarke	DOW	
SE5a	C8706	56 Sqdn	Lt W M Strathearn	POW	
SE5a	C6468	74 Sqdn	Capt S Carlin MC	Safe	
Camel	C8344	3 Sqdn	Lt V H McElroy	KIA	
Camel	F6190	3 Sqdn	Lt G F Young	KIA	
Camel	F5968	54 Sqdn	Capt E J Salter	WIA	*
Camel	F2145	54 Sqdn	2/Lt W J Densham	Safe	*
Camel	D8114	73 Sqdn	2/Lt D B Sinclair	POW	
Camel	E1471	148th US	2/Lt J E Frobisher	DOW	

Aircraft type	No.	Squadron	Crew		
Camel	E1414	148th US	2/Lt O Mandel	POW	
Camel	D6700	148th US	2/Lt D Kenyon	POW	
Camel	E1412	148th US	Lt L H Forster	KIA	
Camel	E4399	201 Sqdn	2/Lt W A Hall	POW	
Camel	E1545	208 Sqdn	2/Lt C H Living	POW	
Camel	D1873	208 Sqdn	Lt J W Marshall	POW/WIA	
Camel	F5970	209 Sqdn	Capt R C Grant	KIA	
Camel	E4381	209 Sqdn	Lt W M Wormold	KIA	
RE8	–	5 Sqdn	2/Lt G J Carr (O)	WIA	*
RE8	–	6 Sqdn	Lt E C Clegg (O)	WIA	*
RE8	–	7 Sqdn	2/Lt J McAslan (O)	WIA	*
RE8	–	13 Sqdn	Lt P J Travis (O)	WIA	*
AWFK8	F3487	8 Sqdn	Capt J T Quick Lt H A Mould	Safe WIA	*
DH4	A7887	18 Sqdn	2/Lt C W Snook Lt R S Aslin	Safe WIA	*
SE5a	E4018	41 Sqdn	1/Lt E H Barksdale (USAS)	WIA	*

French Casualties

Bréguet XIV		Br.207	Capt P de Ribes Soldat Peret	KIA Safe	
Bréguet XIV		Br.224	Capt H Lamasse 2/Lt G Jean-Marie	KIA KIA	
Bréguet XIV		Br.260	Lt V Fournier Soldat L Guimbertau	WIA KIA	*
Bréguet XIV		Br.289	Sgt Proiss Cpl Gamain	MIA MIA	
Bréguet XIV		Br.289	Cpl Fournier Lt de Boeuxis	WIA Safe	*
Bréguet XIV		Br.104	Lt Hoppelt (O)	DOW	*
Spad XI		Spa.34	MdL Verges Lt Barat	KIA Inj	*
Spad XI		Spa.20	Sgt Deglise-Favre Lt Brasseur	MIA MIA	
Spad XI		Spa.20	Adj F Dutrey Sgt J Latapie	Safe WIA	*
Spad XIII		Spa.99	MdL H Billiet	MIA	
Spad XIII		?	MdL Poitte	WIA	*
Spad XIII		Spa. 88	Lt G Thomas	WIA	*
Spad XIII		Spa.87	S/Lt C Bouisset	WIA	*
Spad XIII		Spa.38	Sgt L Juge	WIA	*

Aircraft type	No.	Squadron	Crew		
Spad XIII		Spa.87	Cpl R Perier	WIA	*
Spad XIII		Spa.159	S/Lt R d'Aux	WIA	
Spad XIII		Spa.90	Adj M Bizot	WIA	*
Spad XI	?		Cpl Maurel	WIA	*
			Lt du Boueric	Safe	

American Casualties

Aircraft type	Squadron	Crew		
Salmson 2A2	88 Sqdn	1/Lt R W Hitchcock DSC	KIA	
		2/Lt F M Moore	KIA	
Salmson 2A2	88 Sqdn	Capt R Page	Safe	*
		1/Lt P F Carl Jr	Safe	

03 SEPTEMBER 1918
M **T** W T F S S

British Front

At 0630, Captain W A Southey led a patrol of 84 Squadron to start the day, during which the weather improved to being fine but cloudy. The SE5s trapped a Rumpler C-type over the Manancourt to Nurlu Road and shot it down. Continuing their patrol, Southey burnt the balloon at Fins – his 12th victory – at 0645. The Germans lost another two-seater, this time a DFW, over Barelle at 0630, to a RE8 crew of 5 Squadron, Lieutenants S E Searson and T K Green, who spotted it flying along above the Canal du Nord.

On the ground this day, the two leading brigades of the 4th Canadian Division continued to advance, in order to secure the high ground overlooking the Canal du Nord, then pushing beyond it. Two-seater recce aircraft reported no sign of Germans west of the canal, while an 8 Squadron machine, on a tank contact patrol, was able to strafe German soldiers without seeing any enemy aircraft. With little opposition to their jobs, crews such as Canadian Lieutenants C F Galbraith and A T Sprangle of 5 Squadron were able to range artillery on guns and troops to good effect.

The Australians, as was their manner, were out hunting early and at 0705, Lieutenant Len Taplin of the Camel-equipped 4 AFC Squadron, burnt a balloon at La Plouich, thus achieving his 9th victory. Also out early were the Camels of 54 Squadron, who just five minutes earlier, but much further south, had claimed a Hannover CLIII at Moeuvres. No.54 had been out low bombing but Lieutenant M G Burger spotted the two-seater and sent it down to crash.

The first fighter versus fighter battle occurred at 0710, 56 Squadron meeting Fokker DVIIs at 13,500 feet near Étaing and claiming four for the loss of Second Lieutenant Alfred Vickers, a new boy from Northampton, who had only arrived on 19 August with under 52 hours in his logbook.

Top Australian L T E Taplin of 4 AFC Squadron claimed a dozen victories in WWI, the last six during September: five of these were balloons.
Bottom Another successful pilot with 79 Squadron was Lt F I Lord DFC, an American from Wisconsin. He achieved 12 victories, the last six during September 1918 to win the DFC.

The Germans claimed no fewer than nine SE5s on this day, two over Abancourt and Aubenscheul (time unknown), and seven more in the afternoon, Jasta 36's Vize-feldwebels Wilhelm Skworz and Alfred Hübner made the untimed claims. However, Skworz failed to return, and was found the next day having crashed next to his victim at Sancourt, south of Abancourt. This is near to where Captain W R Irwin of 56 shot a Fokker in flames off Vickers' tail, which seems to tie these combats together.

There were more combats, and then 12 Squadron lost an RE8 – most likely to ground fire, but possibly the one claimed by Leutnant Frommherz of Jasta 27 near Beugnatre between 1000-1100 for his 18th victory.

To the north of Ypres, the first serious fighting of the month occurred at 0910 as 70 Squadron ran into Fokkers south of Roulers and claimed four, three being out of control. At 0935, Lieutenant J A Glen flamed a balloon near Deulemont. At 0915, Leutnant W Schramm of Jasta 56 gained his 3rd kill by claiming a BF2b over Moor-seele. None were in fact lost and the only fight recorded in this area was 70 Squadron's. No. 84 were out again, flaming a balloon south of Poeuilly at 0930.

The next main action was mid-morning, Captain John Doyle of 60 Squadron claiming another Fokker over Inchy at 1010. Once again the fight was with Jasta 36 and once more Leutnant Quandt claimed, bringing down Lieutenant J F M Kerr, who force-landed at Cagnicourt at 1025.

The action swung back north of Ypres around 11 o'clock, 65 Squadron's Camels claiming four Fokkers over Engel. The pilot of a Fokker shot down at 1150 by Captain Fred Lord – his 6th – the young (supposedly 18-year-old) American ace of the notably 'Colonial' 79 Squadron, baled out of his burning fighter, but the parachute caught fire and the German fell to his death over Armentières.

Camels of 204 Squadron fought Fokkers at 1150, gaining three victories. The pilots had mixed experience: Ronald C Pattullo was a 22-year-old Canadian who'd been just three weeks with the squadron. Lieutenant Bliss Edward Barnum was another Canadian, aged 21 but a veteran of nine months. The last claimant was Lieutenant Robert M Gordon, a Scot who would turn 19 on the last day of September, by which time he would have a DFC for his three months of active service. Gordon would live to the 1990s, serving his community as a doctor, including WWII in which he would win the DSO as a medic with the 51st Highland Division.

After midday the action intensified. Another two-seat Hannover was claimed at 1315, in flames east of Moeuvres, having received 200 rounds from Lieutenant A S Compton of 54 Squadron whilst it was flying at 1,500 feet. Captain Gates of 201 claimed another two-seater he encountered at 3,500 feet. 500 rounds sent it diving into the ground.

The other American Dolphin pilot in 79 Squadron, Lieutenant Fred Gillet, reached his 5th victory at 1325, by burning the balloon at Armentières. One hour later another Fokker was claimed by 208's Captain 'Pedro' Mann at Marquion. This victory, his 9th, was made returning from patrol, spotting four Fokkers attacking the balloons along the Cambrai-Arras road. The 19-year-old Mann attacked one of them, firing from 100 to 50 yards, whereupon the Fokker spun away, engine on, out of control. This action matches Jasta 39's attack described in the next paragraph, and although this unit reported no loss, it is possible a Fokker got back over German lines without a pilot casualty. As will be seen, it certainly was not the victor over the two balloons lost by the RAF.

They were burnt at 1415 and 1417 by Gefreiter Hans Nülle. These, his 2nd and 3rd victories, were the 37-3-1 and 5-10-1 balloons positioned at Vis-en-Artois and Haucourt. The 10th Balloon Company balloon was numbered AR71, Lieutenant Henry and Corporal Banks both parachuting down after Nülle's attack. For the second day in a row, Nülle burnt the 5th Company balloon – AR74 – with Lieutenant Lockwood and Acting Corporal Knights baling out.

No.57 Squadron were escorted on a bomb raid to Roisel, by 56 Squadron. Eight Fokkers engaged the SEs at 1520, one attacking Lieutenant L G Bowen, a Canadian, head-on. Bowen ducked, then stalled his machine upwards under the Fokker, firing 100 rounds from close range, seeing it spin down out of control.

Just after this, at 1525, Jastas 2 and 23 intercepted the DH9s of 98 Squadron, shooting down two. One crew fell near Cambrai, a second, with its observer dead, managed to scrape back over the lines to force-land near Cappy. Unteroffizier Michael Hutterer of Jasta 23 had thus achieved his 4th kill at Arleux, Jasta 2's Leutnant Otto Löffler his 8th at Épehy. Also at this time, Captain Southey of 84 Squadron made it three for the day and his 13th overall, by downing a balloon north of Fins.

Hauptmann Bruno Loerzer got into a fight with 32 Squadron, shooting down an SE5 near Douai at 1640 for his 36th victory, five minutes after Leutnant Otto Frühner got his 21st – claimed as a Camel – at Sin-le-Noble. No.32's Lieutenant H R Carson reported a Fokker shot down over Douai at 1645. Flieger Hermann Wirth of Jasta 32b was killed on this day over Douai, possibly in this fight.

This shows how difficult it can be to tie up claims and losses when even some of the more experienced fighter pilots did not identify their opponents accurately. At around 1700, Frommherz got his 19th victory by downing an RE8 at Beugny, and soon afterwards, two BF2bs were claimed by Leutnant Alfred Lindenberger of Jasta 2 Boelcke – his 9th kill – at Combles on the Allied side of the line, with the other claimed by the prolific Theo Quandt, his 14th. The one loss was probably, in fact, a DH4 of 18 Squadron, whose crew were killed west of Bourlon Wood.

At 1740, another pilot, Leutnant Friedrich Vollbracht of Jasta 5, who like Lindenberger would live to see fighter combat in WWII, gained his second victory by downing another BF2b. The vastly experienced pilots of Jasta 5 were in amongst 20 Squadron south of Péronne. Leutnant Josef Mai claimed one, his 24th, Leutnant

Fritz Rumey shooting down his 30th. In fact only one Bristol was lost, although Captain H P Lale's machine was badly shot up and his observer killed, but he got back. 20 Squadron claimed three Fokkers and two Pfalz DXIIs.

Meantime, the undisputed 'ace' RE8 crew of the war, 12 Squadron's Lieutenants C R Pithey and H Rhodes (in F6097), who never hesitated to attack anything despite the type of machine they flew, shot down an LVG two-seater over Lagnicourt at 1715. Harvey Rhodes later became Lord Rhodes, although Croye Pithey was to die in 1919, but both men had won the DFC and bar for their unique achievements. Their ten victories included two balloons, three two-seaters and five fighters, and Rhodes made his own score 11 with another pilot. Not bad for the old 'Harry Tate'.

The Fokkers did not have it all their own way. No.27 Squadron's DH9s, escorted by 1 Squadron, were south-west of Valenciennes at 1815, meeting a Fokker which appeared to be returning to its lines with engine trouble. Lieutenants E J Jacques and N P Wood dived on it, Wood firing three bursts to send the biplane into a flat spin before diving straight into some houses on the outskirts of Valenciennes.

At 1820, the diminutive American, Lieutenant Howard Kullberg, of 1 Squadron, serving in the RAF because the USAS said he was too small, attacked a Fokker as the formation returned over Cambrai. Kullberg engaged the biplane as several went for the DHs they were protecting, sending it down to crash near Avesnes-le-Sec.

There were numerous combats during this evening period. No.210 Squadron fought several Fokkers after initially scrapping with a Fokker pilot they described as a 'star', although they eventually shot him down. Then 41 Squadron got mixed up with Jasta 29 at 1845, and although the Germans claimed three, only Second Lieutenant C E Turner crashed, wounded, at Arras. No.41 claimed one in return.

Just as this action ended, Jasta 23's Unteroffizier Hutterer got his second of the day by downing Lieutenant F W Ferguson of 87 Squadron, the British squadron also claiming two Fokkers. Later that evening, Lieutenant Leslie Hollinghurst, also of 87 Squadron, (a future air chief marshal) shot down a Hannover CLIII at Masnières.

Other British squadrons in action were DH4s of 18 Squadron at 1915, 29 Squadron at 1930 and 201 Squadron at the same time. Captain George Gates of the latter unit got an Albatros C-type east of Metz-en-Couture, watched by his patrol as it fell burning. Gates was the scourge of two-seaters in September, and his likely victims were Gefreiter Karl Noelpp and Leutnant Wilhelm Asmius of FA(A) 248.

Up in the far north, a 205 Squadron DH4 on a recce along the Channel coast was shot up and forced to land with a dead observer, which was probably the 'Bréguet' claimed by Leutnant Brockhoff of MFJ 3 at Furnes at 1950. And the incomparable balloon buster, Belgium's Lieutenant Willy Coppens, shot down the Tenbrielen balloon for his 29th victory – his 27th balloon in 1918. More was to come from Coppens; nobody would get near his total of destroyed 'drachens'.

Over the day the German losses had been relatively light. Most RAF claims have to be discounted, as there is simply no evidence of any losses in the records of the Jastas they are known to have been fighting. Only two Jasta pilots appear as casualties: Vizefeldwebel Willy Skworz of Jasta 36 over Abancourt and Flieger Hermann Wirth killed over Douai.

French Front

The air war was quieter on this southern part of the front, due to bad weather. Most of the French losses of two killed, one missing and five wounded were to ground fire. However, Jastas 9, 17, 60 and 81 did claim five Spads between them. In addition, the Germans claimed five French and American balloons, but only details of four are known.

The balloon of the 76 Cié was working in the 5th Armée sector when it was flamed at 0905, the observer making a safe descent. The balloon of 44 Cié was also burnt in this sector, Adjutant J Branche also jumping to safety. One other French balloon was lost in the Aisne sector, the observer too surviving a jump. The three victors were Vizefeldwebel Willi Stör of Jasta 68, near Remy Wald; Unteroffizier Friedrich Engler of Jasta 62, who was severely wounded in the arm for his pains; and Leutnant Gustav Wember of Jasta 61, timed at 1600.

In the German 19 Armee sector, Gefreiter Erich Mix of Jasta 54 claimed the balloon of the American 1st Balloon Company, at 0940, near Tremblecourt as his 2nd victory. His Fokker was hit at least 19 times by protective fire and was smoking badly on his return flight, forcing him to put down south-west of Preny. Mix would have to wait until WWII to add two more victories to his final WWI score in order to make 'ace' status. By 1941 his overall score was 11. On the French side, Adjutant Jean Pezon of Spa.90 burnt the Ballonzug 152 balloon at 1700, near Goin. Spa.98 claimed two enemy aircraft.

Further north, one of the great figures of French fighter aviation, Lieutenant Georges Madon, claimed another victory north of Fismes, his 41st and last confirmed kill. Because of the strict French confirmation system, he had upwards of 60 probable victories. Under the RAF method of scoring, Madon, like Capitaine René Fonck, would have over 100 victory claims by this time.

Pilots in Spa.91 and Spa.152 claimed aircraft this day, Spa.15 and Spa.152 adding two balloons at Concevreaux and north of Fismes, while Spa.77 also added two

Left Gefreiter Erich Mix claimed three victories with Jasta 54 in 1918, two of them in September. In WWII he was again in fighter conflict, flying with JG52 and then JG2, over France, Dunkirk, the Battle of Britain and once more over France in 1941, raising his score to 11. By 1944 he was an Oberst.

Right Leutnant Walter Blume, Jasta 9. Four kills in September were part of his overall score of 28, mostly against the French. Awarded the Pour le Mérite at the beginning of October, post-war he became an aircraft designer.

balloons to their tally. A Bréguet XIV crew of Br.203 also reported downing a two-seater as well. The Germans lost a two-seater crew at Anizy-le-Château, and a pilot at Reims. In turn, the Germans claimed a number of French aircraft: Unteroffizier Mack of Jasta 60, a Spad; Leutnant Fritz Höhn and Vizefeldwebel Dietrich Averes of Jasta 81, two Spads near Soissons – one probably being flown by Caporal Dumont of Spa.91 who failed to return; Leutnant Walter Blume, CO of Jasta 9, brought his score to 20 (he would be the post-war designer of Arado aircraft); and Leutnant Herbert Rolle, also Jasta 9, downing two Spads at 1030 near Fismes. Of the two casualties of Spa.15 in this last attack, one had probably just flamed the balloon kill – Lieutenant Schneider – who was wounded, while Caporal Chambert was killed. Rittmeister von Bredelow, the CO of Jagdgruppe II, also claimed a Spad near Soissons, as did Vizefeldwebel Hans Christian Donhauser of Jasta 17. Caporal Pradel of Spa.96 failed to return.

American Sector

During a bomb raid over Conflans, six Bréguets of the 96th Bombardment Squadron, which had departed at 1710(A) hours, were attacked by five Pfalz Scouts with green and brown fuselages and yellow tails. The fight ran from Hannonville to Lebeuville, the whole flight being credited with a share in one which was shot down.

	A/C	KB		DES	OOC	KB
British losses	12	2	British claims	29	28	7
French losses	2	3	French claims	4		4
American losses	–	1	American claims	1		–
IAF losses	–		IAF claims	–	–	–
German claims	33	6	German losses	5†		?

† At least; Schlasta 16 had a crew killed, supposedly in action, and the Germans had an airman killed at Valenciennes and another at Reims. There was also another pair (crew?) killed at Anizy-le-Château, but no unit shown.

	British Casualties				

Aircraft type	No.	Squadron	Crew		
RE8	F5885	5 Sqdn	Lt J Scholes	Safe	
			Lt R Boyle	Safe	
SE5a	E4064	56 Sqdn	2/Lt A Vickers	KIA	
RE8	B7888	12 Sqdn	Lt A W MacNamara DFC	KIA	
			Lt H Johnson MC	KIA	
RE8	F5874	59 Sqdn	Capt G J Scott	WIA	*
			2/Lt J N Schofield	WIA	
SE5a	E6000	60 Sqdn	Lt J F M Kerr	Safe	*
RE8	C2377	53 Sqdn	Lt D C Dunlop	Safe	*
			Lt B E Scott MC DFC	WIA	
DH9	D511	108 Sqdn	2/Lt A Preston	POW	
			Sgt H Stewart	POW	
DH4	F5839	18 Sqdn	Lt F M Macfarland	KIA	
			2/Lt A Peterson	KIA	
DH4	A7852	18 Sqdn	2/Lt H Cardwell	Safe	*
			2/Lt H O'Mort	Safe	
SE5a	D6935	32 Sqdn	2/Lt F C Pacey	KIA	

Aircraft type	No.	Squadron	Crew	
SE5a	C1124	32 Sqdn	Capt J H L W Flynn	KIA
DH9	D7202	98 Sqdn	2/Lt R T Ingram	KIA
			2/Lt K J W Dennitts	KIA
DH9	D2863	98 Sqdn	Lt C G Gowing	Safe *
			2/Lt J G W Halliday	KIA
DH4	D9235	25 Sqdn	Lt S Crossfield	Safe *
			2/Lt E F Boyce	KIA
SE5a	B8503	60 Sqdn	Lt C S Hall	Safe
BF2b	B1344	20 Sqdn	2/Lt W F Washington	KIA
			2/Lt K Penrose	KIA
BF2b	E2181	20 Sqdn	Capt H P Lale	Safe *
			2/Lt F J Ralph DFC	KIA
Dolphin	C4163	87 Sqdn	Lt F W Ferguson	KIA
SE5a	C9259	41 Sqdn	2/Lt C E Turner	WIA
DH9	–	49 Sqdn	2/Lt A Dewhurst (O)	WIA *
RE8	–	4 Sqdn	2/Lt P Ff Giles (P)	WIA *
AWFK8	D5057	10 Sqdn	Capt R Ivelaw-Chapman	Safe
			2/Lt W J Miles	DOW *
BF2b	–	48 Sqdn	2/Lt P A Clayson (O)	WIA *
RE8	C2699	12 Sqdn	Lt T S Bulman	WIA
			Lt Smith	WIA
French Casualties				
Salmson 2A2		Sal.?	Cpl van Troyen	WIA *
			Adj Langlois	WIA
Spad XIII		Spa.15	Brig Robert Hazemann	WIA *
Spad XIII		Spa.96	Cpl R Pradel	MIA
Spad XIII		Spa.91	Cpl A Dumont	KIA
Spad XIII		Spa.15	Cpl Chambert	WIA *
Spad XIII		Spa.15	Lt P Schneider	WIA *
Bréguet XIV		Br.210	S/Lt F Wachter (O)	WIA *
Bréguet XIV	B2	Br.66	1/Lt D Schaeffer (O) USAS	WIA *

04 SEPTEMBER 1918
M T **W** T F S S

British Front

The air action on this day began at 0555, with 4 Australian Flying Corps Squadron's Captain E J K McCloughry destroying a balloon at Erquinghem, near Armentières, for his 18th victory. Ten minutes later Lieutenant O B Ramsey got another over La Bassée – for his 1st. As it got lighter, the airmen could see that the day was bringing the best weather so far this September – fine but cloudy.

Further south, on the Cambrai front, the action started as eleven SE5a fighters from 60 Squadron, patrolling above the US 148th's Camels, attacked five Fokker biplanes, claiming three, between 0630 and 0635. Lieutenant M D Sinclair shot down one off the tail of Lieutenant McEntagart, the Fokker spinning in between Paillencourt and Bourlon. A second Fokker went down in flames to an American with 60, Lieutenant Oliver Johnson over Épinoy, following which five others got on his tail:

> '…shot me up and drove me to the ground. My engine had cut out and my prop was completely shot off. Ten Fokkers were between the lines and me and I had to dive steeply and land near Quéant at 0700.'

A third Fokker went to a 19-year-old Scot from Edinburgh, Lieutenant George Metcalfe Duncan at Cambrai for his 6th victory. Duncan reported the initial five Fokkers, then five more – then another five! This was typical of the way the multiple layered Jasta formations fed into a fight. Duncan claimed the leader of the last five.

Leutnant Theo Quandt of the blue-tailed Jasta 36 claimed again, this time an SE5a over Quéant for his 15th victory, but the unit lost Leutnant Kurt Waldheim over Abancourt and Unteroffizier Reinhold Neumann, the latter being shot through the stomach, although he got back and landed at base. He died in hospital later that day. The Americans of 148th Squadron located the fight over Marquion, west of Cambrai, claiming five Fokkers.

First Lieutenant Henry Clay, who claimed two, saw an SE5 being chased by ten DVIIs across the Canal du Nord, south of Sains-lès-Marquion, which, he said, sported blue tails and black noses. Clay's first victim was witnessed by McEntagart of 60, then he shot another from the tail of Lieutenant Starkey's Camel. Clay had then to be rescued from the attentions of three Fokkers by Lieutenant Clayton Bissell, who also claimed two kills. His first dove into a wood near the Canal du Nord, then as he went into a vertical dive and climbing turn, he got on to the tail of a second Fokker, firing 300 rounds before it went down out of control.

Vizefeldwebel Alfred Hübner of Jasta 36 claimed another SE5 over Mercatel which was flown by Lieutenant H T McKinnie of 64 Squadron. This unit was seen entering the fight by Duncan. McKinnie was initially reported missing at about 0700 but was later found wounded inside British lines. Earlier on 64's patrol, at 0645 above Hernu, Lieutenants A M Stahl and T C Sifton collided, with only Sifton surviving a crash-landing – injured – in Allied lines.

Something truly unusual occurred at 0700. The very experienced and aggressive DH9 two-seat bomber crew of Captain R N G Atkinson and Second

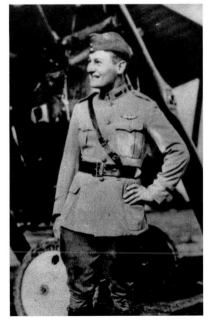

Henry Clay Jr, another member of the 148th Squadron, ended the war with eight victories, the last four in September 1918. Sadly he was to die in the post-war flu epidemic, in February 1919. He received both the American and British DFC medals.

Lieutenant W T Ganter burnt a balloon over Frelinghien having spotted gas bags up! Atkinson later reported:

> '...three dives were made on one of these and 200 rounds fired into it. While aiming through the Aldis sight, the HKB started smoking at 500 feet, and on turning around to avoid collision, same was not visible and a shroud of smoke only was seen rising from the ground.'

Both 10 Squadron and 15 Corps ground observers saw it burn. At 0745, Captain Sidney 'Timbertoes' Carlin of 74 Squadron, so named because of a wooden leg, shot down another balloon north-west of Armentières for his 9th victory. (Carlin would serve in WWII, flying as a gunner on bombers before being killed on 9 May 1941.) Twenty minutes later, Lieutenant Fred Gordon of the same unit claimed another balloon south of Roulers.

Leutnant Friedrich Noltenius was with Jasta 27 by the summer of 1918, and during September he gained eight victories, ending the war with 21 victories. He was killed in a flying accident in 1936.

To the south, meantime, the Australian Lieutenant Roy King brought down an LVG CV over Wattignies at 0710 for his 15th victory. Five minutes later, Captain A H 'Harry' Cobby scored his 29th and last victory, sending down a Fokker DVII out of control over the same locality.

Coming back from a bomb raid on Aubigny-au-Bac, 18 Squadron were intercepted by Fokkers, the bomber crews claiming two. One of the crews, Captain G W F Darvill and Lieutenant W Miller, both already with over five kills to their name, turned into the attack. Darvill then discovered his front gun had jammed, so he turned west with a Fokker following. Miller fired back at it, the DVII falling in flames at Cantin at 0750. Miller was then wounded, but continued to fire at another Fokker which they both saw crash at Aubigny-au-Bac. Their bomber (A7815) was shot about and they had to force-land inside the front line.

The initial interception was by Jasta 27, Leutnant Noltenius shooting up Darvill and getting as good in return, as will be seen. 18 Squadron lost A7853 to Leutnant Frommherz at Recourt – the German's 20th victory. Immediately after this, Jasta 27 and Jasta 26 became involved in a fight with 70 Squadron's Camels.

This occurred soon after 0800, a patrol, 12-strong, running into serious trouble in the form of JGIII. Of the 12 Camels – two entire flights – only four returned. Two Camel pilots claimed two victories over Escaillon (some 12 km due east of Douai) at 0815, one destroyed in flames, by the Canadian Lieutenant Ken Watson, and the other shared by Lieutenants D H S Gilbertson and J S Wilson. Gilbertson's victory was reported by Wilson on his return, as the former was among the missing. Both claims were for the ubiquitous Fokkers of JGIII, who in this combat inflicted the single biggest loss of fighters in one fight suffered by the Allies in WWI. Wilson described the fight as beginning when Gilbertson and he:

> '...dived on several EA. We engaged one machine and I fired about 120 rounds into it. The EA stalled and spun towards the ground well out of control. I also saw another Fokker diving vertically with clouds of smoke coming from the cockpit.'

This was confirmed by Captain Morgan, the only other returnee. Ken Watson reported:

'While on OP at 0815 over Escaillon, the patrol dived on 15 Fokker biplanes and a further 15 Fokkers dived on the patrol, coming out of clouds from 12,000 feet. I saw one EA on Lt Gower's tail. I engaged him at close range and shot him down in flames.'

JGIII claimed eleven Camels between the Sensée Canal and Douai, to the west of Escaillon, credited as follows:

0910	Ltn Ehlers	Jasta 26	Palleul	2nd victory
0910	Oblt T H Dahlmann	JGIII	Palleul	5th victory
0912	Vfw E Buder	Jasta 26	Cantin	9th victory
0912	Oblt T H Dahlmann	JGIII	Palleul	6th victory
0915	Ltn O Frühner	Jasta 26	Cantin West	22nd victory
0918	Vfw F Classen	Jasta 26	Cantin	6th victory
0920	Hpt B Loerzer	JGIII	Monchecourt	37th victory
0920	Ltn O Frühner	Jasta 26	S Douai	23rd victory
0925	Vfw E Buder	Jasta 26	Gouy	12th victory
0930	Ltn O Frühner	Jasta 26	S Douai	24th victory
–	Vfw A Lux	Jasta 27	Cantin	6th victory

Of the eight pilots lost, four were captured, including patrol leader Captain John Forman and Second Lieutenant Bill Rochford, younger brother of Captain L H 'Tich' Rochford, the star turn of 203 Squadron and one of its flight commanders. In Rochford's book (*I Chose the Sky*, Grub Street, 2015) he noted that 70 Squadron had been caught well over the lines by superior numbers. Certainly two of JGIII's three BMW-Fokker DVII Jastas were involved and, significantly, 70's Camels were described as Clerget-powered machines, with 20 less horsepower than the Bentley-motored machines 203 were flying. Bill Rochford and Forman escaped from their captors and were at large for a few days, but were eventually picked up again. Leutnant Noltenius may have been directly involved, as evidenced by this extract from his diary:

'After a while a lively aerial battle with a strong Sopwith squadron commenced. I tried hard to get higher up in order to catch one of them, if possible, when he attempted to fly back to his lines. I was successful in this: I caught one and spiralled downward with him to 300 metres. Then a section of my top wing broke off – the part aft of the second main spar – and I had to give up. [In a fight with "Bristols" – most likely 18 Squadron's DHs – he had been well shot up, including a grazing hit along his flying helmet.] The Sopwith afterwards landed in a normal manner. In the course of the fight another Sopwith came to the assistance of the first one. I evaded him and continued to pursue the first opponent. This plane was later shot down by Lux. Frühner also claimed this one. The decision had not yet been made, but it will no doubt be like this: Lux one, Frühner the other one.'

Noltenius was not happy with the way some of what he saw as his victims were awarded to other pilots. The Germans, unlike the Allies, did not 'share' victories. They were also, on this occasion, credited with three more Camels than were lost. Jasta 57, led by Leutnant Paul Strähle, was also involved in this fight, observing JGIII shoot down two DH4s. They were then attacked by 23 (!) Camels and survived until JGIII attacked. Leutnant Johannes Jensen and Vizefeldwebel Hechler were severely shot about, and Gefreiter Tegtmeyer badly wounded by a shot in the stomach.

Oberleutnant Fritz Röth, the leader of Bavarian Jasta 16, claimed a DH9 over Neuf-Berquin at 0830 for his 23rd victory. This was either a 4 Squadron RE8 that force-landed at 0815, or it may have been a Bristol from 88 Squadron, who were in a fight timed slightly later. This was at 0900, 88 becoming involved in a half-hour combat south-west of Lille with Fokker DVIIs and triplanes. Captain Edgar Johnston and his gunner, Lieutenant W I N Grant, claimed two of the former and one of the latter. Four more German machines were claimed, mostly out of control, although Johnston's veteran machine – C4867 – which he'd flown since March, was damaged. The four Bristol crews were all 'ace' teams.

Soon after this DH9s of 107 Squadron, out on a bombing raid to Valenciennes, were intercepted. The bombers, as was usual at this stage of the war, were escorted by Bristols – this time from 62 Squadron. The resulting fight lasted half an hour and drifted well to the south and east of Cambrai, where Jasta 58's aerodrome at Émerchicourt was situated. Leutnant Martin Demisch of this unit captured the Bristol of Lieutenant W K Swayze and his observer Second Lieutenant W E Hale at 1000. After the war, 'Pete' Swayze, who had achieved six victories, reported that he had suffered engine failure and was then forced down onto the German airfield. Swayze only survived the war by a couple of years, dying in 1920 in Toronto.

Meantime, Jasta 58 shot down two DH9s, one falling to Leutnant Spille at Helesmes, the other to Vizefeldwebel Jeep at d'Hivergies Ferme. One Fokker was seen in flames over La Sentinelle, being hit by Second Lieutenant F T Scott and Sergeant W J Palmer from 107 Squadron. Jasta 39 pilots saw the scrap and waded in, shooting down two more DHs; Unteroffizier Müller at Chelmes at 1010, and Unteroffizier Nülle at St Aubert five minutes later. No.107 lost three aircraft, while Jasta 58's Vizefeldwebel Dünnhaupt was wounded.

Pilots of 2 AFC, 32 and 48 Squadrons were in action shortly before 1000, and just after the hour, Camels of 3 Squadron, operating in the Bapaume to Cambrai area, encountered Fokkers. Lieutenant David Hughes was driven back to the lines by three of them when two broke off. The other continued to fight, but Hughes, a Welshman, in F1972, managed to shoot it down. Flieger Otto Wagner of Jasta 79b fell into British lines and was captured. Hughes also had to come down, his Camel having been hit in the fuel tank, and written off.

Wagner was the fourth of five victories for Hughes, who was still only 19 years old. He had only been in the services since August 1917. As an interesting aside, Hughes trained between then and November, then served as an instructor at 37 TDS. Taught to fly fighters in April 1918, he became an instructor again until June at which time he joined 3 Squadron with a total of 270 flying hours – far above the average. He obviously had talent which he used to good effect.

Other 3 Squadron pilots were engaged and three more Fokkers were claimed, but they lost a 20-year-old Londoner, Second Lieutenant Ralph Tedbury, who had been

Six pilots of 92 Squadron. Rear: E F Crabb (Canadian), E Shapard, Millar; Front: Hadden-Smith, O J Rose, and T S Horry. Oren Rose, an American, claimed four of his 16 victories during September 1918.

with the unit since 10 August. He died of his injuries later this day. Aside from Jasta 79b, this combat involved Jastas 1 and 6. Vizefeldwebel Georg Staudacher, aged 20, shot down a Camel at 1010 in the Sailly-Cambrai area, while Leutnant Richard Wenzl got one south of Paillencourt. Lieutenant William Hubbard, an experienced ace of 23, claimed one of the Fokkers which had a yellow tail with black and white stripes on elevators and top wing. Hubbard had first attacked a biplane which was shooting down a Camel but had to turn in pursuit of the colourful machine described. On the edge of this action, 57 Squadron's bombers were returning from a raid on Marcoing, claiming one Fokker crashed and another out of control.

Bristol Fighters of 11 Squadron had a fight east of Cambrai at 1045, and at the same time Captain Tom Falcon Hazell gained his 38th and 39th victories by downing two balloons at Bernes and Gouzeaucourt. One of his flight, Lieutenant Ernest P Crossen, strafed the parachute of one of the observers. This may sound a bit unsporting, but this often happened, the view being that a downed balloon was one thing, a dead observer who would no longer be able to bring fire and destruction to Allied troops, a bonus. More likely it was spite too, as balloonists had parachutes and Allied pilots did not.

Near Arras, Leutnant Ernst Bormann of Jasta 2 gained his 9th victory by downing the SE5a flown by Lieutenant V H Harley of 64 Squadron. Ten minutes later, an American who would run up the highest score in 92 Squadron, Lieutenant Oren J Rose, claimed a Halberstadt C-type just west of Douai.

Shortly after midday, 4 AFC burnt two balloons south-east of La Bassée and south of Armentières. Later in the afternoon, 84 Squadron flamed the Douvieux balloon, shared by Second Lieutenants Stephen Highwood and C R Thompson. Stephen Highwood was a 21-year-old from Morden, Surrey. An exceptionally aggressive pilot, his claim was the first of nine balloons and an aeroplane during September. 'Ruggles' Thompson, whose 5th victory this was, was a 23-year-old South African.

One of the former RNAS veterans from April 1917, Captain Art Whealy DSC DFC of 203 Squadron brought down, at 1615, a Fokker which had just set a balloon on fire near Trescault. The balloon, 11-9-13, had been shot down by Leutnant Erich Just of Jasta 11, his 6th victory, causing Lieutenants H Tallboy and J McGilchrist to parachute to safety. In fact Just survived the encounter and Whealy's victim was likely to have been Vizefeldwebel Hans Reimers of Jasta 6, who had achieved two victories, and who was shot down and mortally wounded by a Camel. He died the next day. This was the Canadian's 27th and last victory, and by the end of this momentous month, he was on his way back to Canada.

Another April 1917 veteran was in combat at 1815 near Auberchicourt south of Douai. Six Bristols out on a recce job were attacked by five Fokkers from cloud. Captain Alex Morrison, a 24-year-old from Middlesborough on his second tour with 11 Squadron, saw one coming and his observer, Sergeant R Allen, shot it down into a field near Hamel. The squadron claimed another out of control south of Douai. (As a matter of interest, the post-war idea that small formations of two or three Bristols cruised about over the lines looking for Germans was a total myth by this stage of the war. Where opposition was expected, the recce squadrons like 11, sent out large patrols of one or two flights.)

Another top German pilot gained a kill this day, Leutnant Arthur Laumann, Staffelführer of Jasta 10 being credited with his 28th and final kill of the war. No details are known, other than that the German daily communiqué specifically mentioned it. The most likely victim was Lieutenant E O Champagne, who force-landed mid-afternoon after being hit by a Fokker, following which his Camel burnt out.

During the day, the leading balloon buster of the war, Belgian Lieutenant Willy Coppens, burnt the Boverkerke balloon, to bring his score to 30.

South African Lieutenant C R Thompson of 84 Squadron in his SE5a. In September 1918 he destroyed three kite balloons, bringing his score to six, although he was wounded downing his last victory on the 15th. He received the DFC.

French Front

As with the British front, the weather was good in the morning before clouding over in the afternoon. The French suffered seven combat casualties as well as losing four balloons.

Three of the balloons were shot down by the Germans on the 7 Armee sector. The first by Unteroffizier Heinrich Haase of Jasta 21 west of Sarcy at 0915 was that of a V Armée balloon of the 27 Cié, from which Sergent Euribert baled out. Another balloon was lost in this sector, that of 26 Cié, which burnt at 1104, Adjutant Boitard jumping safely. This was the 21st victory of Vizefeldwebel Karl Schlegel, who had been with Jasta 45 since May 1918. Obviously the loss of the unit's Staffelführer a few days before had not deterred Schlegel from his path to becoming the third most successful balloon buster on the German side. Coincidentally, Jasta 45 was also the third highest claimer against balloons and the highest scoring Jasta of the 'Amerika Program' Jastas formed from late 1917.

Interestingly, the German communiqué noted that at the location of Haase's and Schlegel's claims, an unsuccessful attack was made on a balloon, resulting in a Fokker landing in French territory, with 30 hits from three Spads. The unknown pilot then repaired the engine and flew home before being captured! Adjutant Armand Berthelot, a 24-year-old from the Finistère area of France, shared an EA with Sergents Faucade and Barat at 1130, and these events are believed to be connected. It was Berthelot's 8th victory, the others' first.

Leutnant Berling, another Jasta 45 pilot, claimed a balloon at 1830 and whilst Sergent Godefroy was injured jumping from the basket, his balloon did not catch fire. The 25 Cié's balloon was lost to Unteroffizier Baumgarten of Jasta 67, with both observers, Caporals Aboucaya and Guilbert, making safe landings.

Not to be outdone, the French too attacked balloons. Spa.152's leading balloon buster, Sous Lieutenant Léon Bourjade, aided by Sous Lieutenant Ernest Maunoury and Caporal Etienne Manson, combined to burn the Pont Arcy balloon (west of Soissons) at 0645.

Capitaine Jean de Luppe, the CO of Spa.83, attacked the German balloon lines near Filain, in company with Sous Lieutenant Devilder. They flamed one but de Luppe was brought down and captured near Celles-sur-Aisne, probably falling to Leutnant Arthur Korff of Jasta 60. It is often very difficult to tie up victim and victor with certainty, and this applies to the loss of a Bréguet of Br.19 in the IV Armée sector. It was hit by AA fire and came down in the front lines, its pilot wounded. However, Leutnant Werner Preuss of Jasta 66 gained his 14th victory by downing a French two-seater near Crécy-en-Mont, which may relate to this event, pilots and flak units often contesting claims.

Two other German aircraft were claimed by pilots of GC13 and GC17, covering the sector across from the 18 Armee. Adjutant Jacquot of Spa.100 claimed a fighter near Breuil-sur-Vesles at 1145, while Sous Lieutenant Marcel Coadou, aged 21, of Spa.15 and Adjutant Delzenne of Spa.88 – both future aces – shared, with Adjutant Pinot of Spa.84, a scout in German lines. At midday, near Lavannes, Sous Lieutenant Robert Volmerange, who had joined Spa.38 on 1 June, claimed a C-type.

On the debit side, Jasta 17's Leutnant Seifert claimed a Spad near Souilly at 1130. Sergent René Touchard of Spa.68 was killed in action by either Offizierstellvertreter Gustav Dörr or Leutnant Hans Rolfes, both of the highly active Jasta 45. They

claimed Spads north of Fismes at 1300, their 26th and
16th victories respectively. Maréchal-des-Logis Camille
Chambrey of Spa.92 was shot down and captured,
probably by Leutnant Werner Peckmann of Jasta 9,
timed at 1715 near Soissons. At an unrecorded time,
Vizefeldwebel Fritz Jacobsen of Jasta 73 downed an AR2
for his 8th victory.

The British Independent Air Force sent 55, 99 and
104 Squadrons to bomb Buhl and Morhange aerodromes, without loss.

American Sector

Concentrating now on the Saint-Mihiel salient, the
Americans suffered six casualties, plus two balloons,
against claims for three aircraft with two more
probables.

First Lieutenants J Dickenson Este and Rob Roy S
Converse of the 13th Pursuit Squadron were on patrol
and engaged a Rumpler C above Nancy, which, they
reported, had a green fuselage and white tail. They
chased it from 1019 to 1027, seeing it going down in a
wide spiral over Pont-à-Mousson. This was not credited,
nor was another two-seater – an Albatros – chased by

the veteran commander of the 13th, Captain Charles Biddle, near Mamey at 1015.
Biddle, who was 28, and a cool leader, had previously served with the French Spa.73
and then the US 103rd Pursuit, before becoming the CO of the 13th Aero 'Grim
Reapers' in July 1918.

The 96th Bombardment Squadron sent out eight aircraft to bomb the rail facilities
at Dommary-Baroncourt at 1050. The formation was attacked by ten Pfalz Scouts,
some sporting red fuselages; one was seen to have black wings and another, a white
triangle pennant-shaped design on the fuselage, aft of the cockpit. One Pfalz, caught
in the cross-fire from the Bréguets, was seen to crash near Laubeville. First Lieutenants
Arthur Hadden Alexander and John Charles Earle McLannan were both wounded,
Alexander in the small of the back, McLannan four times in the legs, but the pilot
brought them back. For this action Alexander received the DSC. Two other observers
were wounded, First Lieutenants Donald D Warner being hit in the hip, while
Avrone N Hexter caught a bullet above the eyes. The bloodletting of the 'First Team'
– as the American day bombers have since been called – was beginning.

Four Salmson 2A2S of the 91st Observation Squadron were operating over Rembercourt, but were spotted by four Fokkers. One of the two-seaters, crewed by
25-year-old First Lieutenants Frederick Vernon Foster and Raymond R Sebring, had
taken off late and was trying to catch up the others. Leutnant Eugen Siempelkamp
of Jasta 64w dived on them at 1105, shooting them down over Thiaucourt for his
4th victory. Foster survived as a prisoner and lived well into his nineties. Meantime,
First Lieutenant Victor Strahm and Captain James A Wallis, shot down a Pfalz over
Rembercourt, with another EA unconfirmed. These were the first victories by the
91st Aero. Strahm, from Nashville, Tennessee, would become a two-seater ace.

One of the balloons lost on the American sector was that of the 10th Balloon Company, which was flamed at 1230, with observers Lieutenants E R Likens and D G Boyd making safe descents. The other loss was a French balloon of the 43rd Cié, burnt near Ansauville five minutes earlier. Unteroffizier Bader of Jasta 64 got the American balloon – his 2nd victory – but he was pounced on by Lieutenants Frank B Tyndall, Arthur Raymond Brooks and Clinton Jones of the 22nd Aero, who sent his Fokker down into German lines after wounding the man.

	A/C	KB			DES	OOC	KB
British losses	24	1		British claims	30	21	11
French losses	3	4		French claims	4		3
American losses	1	2		American claims	3		–
IAF losses	–			IAF claims	–	–	–
German claims	40†	6		German losses	5		9

† Four to flak.

British Casualties

Aircraft type	No.	Squadron	Crew		
RE8	E111	4 Sqdn	Lt E L Barrington MC	WIA	*
			2/Lt W G Greenaway MC	WIA	
DH4	A7853	18 Sqdn	Lt W B Hogg	KIA	
			2/Lt A E Stock	KIA	
DH9	D3106	107 Sqdn	2/Lt J C Boyle	POW	
			2/Lt F C B Eaton	KIA	
DH9	F6172	107 Sqdn	Lt E R L Sproule	POW	
			2/Lt G T Coles	POW	
DH9	C6169	107 Sqdn	Lt B E Gammell	KIA	
			2/Lt F Player	KIA	
BF2b	D7945	62 Sqdn	Lt W K Swayze	POW	
			2/Lt W E Hall	POW	
BF2b	C4867	88 Sqdn	Capt E C Johnston MC	Safe	*
			2/Lt W I N Grant	Safe	
Camel	F1972	3 Sqdn	Lt D J Hughes	Safe	
Camel	C8333	3 Sqdn	2/Lt R N Tedbury	DOW	
Camel	B5434	46 Sqdn	2/Lt C H P Killick	POW	
Camel	B9269	70 Sqdn	Lt J L Gower	POW	
Camel	D9416	70 Sqdn	Lt J A Spilhaus	KIA	
Camel	D9458	70 Sqdn	2/Lt K H Wallace	KIA	
Camel	E1472	70 Sqdn	Lt D H S Gilbertson	KIA	
Camel	D3406	70 Sqdn	2/Lt W M Herriott	POW	
Camel	D9418	70 Sqdn	2/Lt S W Rochford	POW	
Camel	C8239	70 Sqdn	Capt J H Forman DFC	POW	

Aircraft type	No.	Squadron	Crew		
Camel	D1930	70 Sqdn	Lt R McPhee	POW	
Camel	D9501	80 Sqdn	2/Lt E O Champagne	Safe	
SE5a	E5991	60 Sqdn	Lt O P Johnson	Safe	
SE5a	D6988	64 Sqdn	Lt T C Sifton	Inj	
BF2b	E2611	48 Sqdn	Lt G F Manning	Safe	
			2/Lt P A Clayson	WIA	
DH9	B9355	104 Sqdn	Lt J Wrighton	Safe	
			Sgt F H J Denney	WIA	
SE5a	E1273	64 Sqdn	2/Lt A M Stahl	KIA	
SE5a	E4002	64 Sqdn	2/Lt H T McKinnie	WIA	
SE5a	E5979	64 Sqdn	Lt V H Harley	POW	
AWFK8	D5164	10 Sqdn	Capt R D Blackman	Safe	*
			Lt A H E King	WIA	
DH4	A7815	18 Sqdn	Capt G W F Darvill	Safe	*
			Lt W N Miller (O)	WIA	
DH4	F6001	18 Sqdn	Sgt G A Cribbes	WIA	*
Dolphin	–	87 Sqdn	Lt V G Snyder	WIA	*
RE8	–	13 Sqdn	2/Lt H Dobing (O)	WIA	*

French Casualties

Aircraft type	No.	Squadron	Crew		
Bréguet XIV	3-309	Br.9	Sgt Gauthier	WIA	*
			Sgt Mulot	Safe	
Bréguet XIV		?	S/Lt Malot	WIA	*
			S/Lt Chevrel	DOW	
Spad XIII		Spa.68	Sgt R Trouchard	KIA	
Spad XIII		Spa.92	MdL C Chaimbaz	POW	
Spad XIII		Spa.83	Capt J de Luppe	POW	
Bréguet XIV		Br.104	Lt Hoppelt (O)	WIA	*
Bréguet XIV		Br.289	Sgt Tardieu (P)	WIA	*

American Casualties

Aircraft type	No.	Squadron	Crew		
Salmson 2A2	5225	91st	1/Lt F V Foster	POW	
			1/Lt R S Sebring	KIA	
Bréguet XIV B2	#18	96th	1/Lt A H Alexander DSC	WIA	*
			2/Lt J C E McLannan	WIA	
Bréguet XIV B2		96th	1/Lt E E Bates	Safe	*
			2/Lt A N Hexter	WIA	
Bréguet XIV B2		96th	1/Lt C P Young	Safe	*
			1/Lt D D Warner	WIA	

05 SEPTEMBER 1918
M T W **T** F S S

British Front

The weather this day was described as warm and hazy. Activity built up slowly but by late evening the RAF had made 67 claims. 4 AFC started the ball rolling with another of their early morning marauding raids, during which Lieutenant A H Lockley burnt the Pérenchies balloon at 0625. Half an hour later, east of Ploegsteert Wood, Lieutenant C L Childs of 70 Squadron flamed a Fokker DVII. On the German side, Leutnant Fritz Rumey of Jasta 5 shot down the SE5a of Second Lieutenant W A F Cowgill of 64 Squadron, north of Bouchain.

The next action was down at Cambrai at 0950. No.84 Squadron burnt two balloons south of Poeuilly, credited to the Highwood/Thompson team, a repeat performance of the previous day.

At 1015, a further patrol by 64 Squadron met Fokkers – again Jasta 5. Although the SE pilots claimed four either destroyed or out of control, the Jasta only recorded Leutnant Schenk wounded. Soon afterwards, 60 Squadron lost an SE5a to ground fire, north of Hayencourt. Between 1030 and 1100, 80 and 74 Squadrons had tussles with Fokkers, claims being made, for one 74 Squadron loss.

The first large-scale encounter of the day happened at 1100 hours. No. 92 Squadron's SE5s ran into JGIII, flying in company with Jastas 37 and 46. The British unit lost three with another pilot forced to land:

1100	Ltn G Meyer	Jasta 37	E Havrincourt	16th victory
1110	Hpt B Loerzer	JGIII	Inchy/Brebières	38th victory
1110	Ltn T Himmer	Jasta 37	NE Ribecourt	2nd victory

Both of the Jasta 37 claims were disputed by Leutnant auf der Haar of Jasta 46 who failed to have either awarded. No. 92, in turn, claimed three Fokkers shot down: one by the CO, Major Arthur Coningham MC (a future air marshal); one to Lieutenant Evander Shapard; the third to a 1917 Spad veteran, Captain W E Reed, on his second tour. Jasta 37 lost Unteroffizier Otto Rösler killed over Flesquières. Lieutenant H B Good, one of the pilots lost by 92, was an ace; another a flight commander, the Australian Captain George Wells, who was captured. The pilot who was lucky to get back was Shapard, being forced to spin almost to the ground, then flying back at a height of 20 feet. On landing it was found that the main spars of all four wings had been shot through as well as both longerons, while a bullet had also lodged in one of the magnetos.

The usual advantage of SE5a units can't be seen from this fight. This was the worst loss suffered by the most junior SE unit in France – only operational since late July; and generally they had the capacity to take someone with them. SE5s could, unlike Camels, run from the huge formations which, the RAF communiqués noted, were cruising around all day. Mostly, the SEs also operated at height, which gave them the capacity to dive away from trouble, again unlike the recent Camel slaughters, which had all taken place at very low level. Camel pilots generally had to fight their way out of tight spots.

The bombers of 57 Squadron were on a raid at this time, near Marcoing, and also claimed Fokkers. Captain Andrew MacGregor, with Sergeant J Grant, claimed one over the town at 1125, other crews claiming two more. One victim was possibly Leutnant Heinrich Hagar of Jasta 32, wounded at 1200 (G). If not, he was likely to have been a victim of 92 Squadron. MacGregor ended his air force career as an air vice-marshal with many decorations. The 20-year-old Scot had started as an infantry officer in the Argyll and Sutherland Highlanders in 1917 before flying training, joining 57 in March 1918. He would die the day before his 87th birthday. For Sergeant Grant, this victory was his 6th.

There were a number of isolated skirmishes from just before noon until the late afternoon, when an avalanche of fights occurred from 1700 hours onwards. One reason for this was that the RAF were slackening their rate of offensive operations, preserving strength for the major offensives. This was a vast change from the previous year. The pilots did not complain, glad of any respite, and this one was an actual request by RAF HQ in a memorandum dated 5 September, only to react if enemy activity increased. Fine words, but there was still a good deal of work to do supporting the ground battles.

One of the encounters involved an April 1917 veteran, Captain Edmund Zink, a former FE2b pilot and now flying an SE5 with 32 Squadron. He manoeuvred behind a two-seater and shot it down over Équancourt for his 5th victory. Another was a scrap between 48 Squadron's Bristols and Jasta 20, the second encounter this month. No.48 lost a crew to Leutnant Bruno Hobein over Espières at 1250 although the squadron did claim a Fokker in flames and another out of control. At 1315 the Germans reported that a single-seater landed near Ostricourt due to engine failure, which was a 73 Squadron Camel.

There was also action up on the North Sea coast. Camels of 65 Squadron claimed five Fokkers east of Ostende, the unit being led by another Bloody April pilot, Captain A G Jones-Williams MC. Their opposition was generally German Marine units, which had, on 2 September, been formed into the Marine Jagdgeschwader, comprising all five MFJ units under the command of Leutnant Gotthardt Sachsenburg.

Another unit who often tangled with the Marine pilots was 213 Squadron, formally the Dunkirk Seaplane Defence Flight of the RNAS. Their Camels claimed two Fokkers this afternoon just south of the German air base at Varsenare. Second Lieutenant C E Francis was lost to MFJ 3's Vizeflugmaatrose Mayer at Stalhille at 1425. Flugmaatrose Karl Engelfried of MFJ 5 made his second kill by downing a DH9 of 218 Squadron, west of Knocke, that had been bombing Bruges. Getting into trouble, Lieutenants J G Munro and T W Brodie staggered across into nearby neutral Holland. This was normal procedure for airmen that could not make it back down the coast. It was also usual for the Marine pilots to claim them. MFJ 5's records do not time this action, but 218 did claim a Pfalz DIII over Bruges at 1650.

In the early afternoon, down on the Bapaume front, the Germans launched an assault on British balloon lines, Vizefeldwebel Kautz of Jasta 46 burning one at Beugny at 1415. Ten minutes later Jasta 6 shot down two at Croisilles, 45-12-3 and 35-12-3, credited to Leutnants Richard Wenzl and Fritz Schliewen. The observers, Lieutenant C T L Smith from the 45th's and Second Lieutenant E F Caton and Sergeant Mechanic A W Woolgar from the other, all jumped safely.

Major Raymond Collishaw, CO of 203, attacked a Fokker that had been balloon strafing near Inchy-en-Artois at 1500 and shot it down into Allied lines where it burned. It was the Canadian's 56th victory – the highest of any pilot still operational in the RAF.

Between 1605 and 1610, 57 Squadron were once more intercepted on a bombing raid. In the area of Marcoing and Avesnes-le-Sec, Captain A MacGregor and Sergeant Grant claimed two destroyed in flames, from the second of which the pilot baled out but his parachute apparently failed. These claims brought Grant's score to eight. Another claim took one of the rare sergeant pilots to his 5th victory – Sergeant D E Edgley's observer, Sergeant J H Bowler, sending down a Fokker out of control.

Bristols of 22 Squadron and Camels of the 148th had fights during the afternoon, but on the Ypres front, near Roulers, 210 Squadron got into a scrap with Fokkers. One was claimed by an 18-year-old from Buckinghamshire, Lieutenant Ivan Sanderson for his 11th and final victory. Another was credited to Lieutenant Lowell Yerex, a 23-year-old American from Indiana – both timed at 1730. Upon their return, 210 posted Yerex and his flight commander, Captain Herbert Patey – a 6 Naval Squadron veteran of Bloody April, and an 11-victory ace – as missing. Patey would spend his 20th birthday (25 September) as a prisoner before dying during the influenza epidemic, in February 1919. Yerex was also captured, these pilots being shot down by Jasta 56's Leutnant Lutz Beckmann, the Staffelführer, for his 8th kill, at Winckel St Eloi, and Unteroffizier Ludwig Jeckert.

Captain Harry Cobby, the most successful Australian Flying Corps ace, had finished his tour on the previous day. On the 5th, his old flight went out without him, and only the leader, Lieutenant Norman Trescowthick, returned. No. 4 AFC were supposed to sweep the Douai area in conjunction with two other flights, one of Bristols of 88 Squadron, and one of 2 AFC's SE5s.

Rendezvous was made over Serny aerodrome but they became separated in cloud, so that south-west of Douai only the Camels met two sudden formations of Fokkers, that sandwiched the patrol of five. Four pilots were shot down, only Lieutenant Len Taplin, an ace, surviving as a prisoner. They had been caught at 1800, well south of Brebières by Jastas 26 and 27 of JGIII. The Camels had been flying in the usual 'V' formation and were attacked from above and from two directions at once. Trescowthick gave the signal to avoid action and dived away, but the others were unable to do so and went down to the Fokker pilots:

1800	Ltn H Frommherz	Jasta 27	Marquion	21st victory
1800	Vzfw C Mesch	Jasta 26	Cuincy	9th victory
1805	Vzfw A Lux	Jasta 27	Baralle	7th victory
1805	Vzfw F Classen	Jasta 26	Henin-Liétard	7th victory

Leutnant Noltenius briefly mentioned the fight in his diary:

'Almost no activity, when suddenly I saw a burst of flak on my port side over our territory. I did not notice the Englishmen until suddenly two Sopwiths passed by in front of me. I immediately pursued and hit one of them, for a mighty petrol vapour streamer began to issue from the machine, but I had to let him go as the other Sopwith prepared to attack me. Was unable to find my victim, however, and a confirmation was unobtainable.'

Mesch was credited with Taplin. Trescowthick saw Lockley shoot down a Fokker out of control as he was diving away. On return from prison camp, Taplin left this graphic account of his fate:

'The formation went over the line in V-formation, Trescowthick leading, Eddie and Carter above and behind him, and Lockley and myself above and behind them again. When a few miles over we turned north. We were flying at about 14,000 feet and our escort could not be seen; I did not like the situation and climbed another 1,000 feet above the patrol. Soon after this, when in the region of Douai, we were attacked. There were three formations in the attacking enemy, all Fokker biplanes. Two formations of about 12 to 15 machines attacked almost simultaneously, one from high up in the west and one from the north. Later a very much larger formation came in from the east, which I first thought was our escort coming to our rescue.

'Trescowthick dived away under the formation coming from the direction of our own lines, but the others were cut off. No German attempted to follow Trescowthick, so evidently he was unobserved. Meanwhile, I was gaining all the height I could and as the formation from the north closed in, I dived into the middle of them. The leader, a red and white tailed Fokker, pulled up and we went at it head-on. I got a good burst into his radiator and he went down on a glide – not out of control, just engine out of action. Next moment I was right in the middle of them and before I could do anything, a German below me pulled his nose up and put a burst right through the bottom of my machine. One bullet went through my right hand, smashing it up and breaking the wrist. My Camel immediately stalled and half rolled itself and to conform with poetic justice, came out of the stall right on the tail of my attacker, who was recovering from his own stall. I was now under control with my left hand and easily shot this German down. Just then I saw Lockley dropping past me completely out of control. I also saw during the fight two machines in flames, which I suppose were Eddie and Carter.

'I was getting shot about and firing at anything I saw, when a Fokker from somewhere (the sky seemed full of them) again got a burst into me. One bullet, an explosive, smashed the breech and crank-handle of one of my guns and sent a splinter through my nose. This dazed me and I fell out of control in an engine-spin. I spun down to about 1,000 feet and then recovered, to find two Fokkers had followed me down. I again had to fight, and luckily shot one down easily; the other then left me alone. After this fight I was down to about 100 feet and started off towards home. My engine was just about done, from being shot about and from running full throttle through everything. I had only one hand and could not properly control the engine to gain height, so just staggered along. After running the gauntlet of ground fire for several miles I was shot down from the ground when within a few hundred yards of the German front line, and taken prisoner. I found out from the Germans that Lockley was buried in Henin-Liétard cemetery but could get no news of the others.'

Jasta 39 continued balloon busting, Unteroffizier Ruppert burning the Dury balloon at 1810, the British losing a 5th Company gas bag – SR134 – from which Lieutenant Birchal and Corporal Kneller parachuted down.

Soon afterwards, to the north of Cambrai, 60 Squadron, out on patrol 11-strong escorting DH4s, ran into another large formation of 25 Fokkers near Avesnes-le-Sec and claimed six between them. Captain John Doyle claimed one in flames and one out of control before he was wounded, shot down and captured. A feature of the battle was that it was fought in a heavy rain storm! One Fokker pilot was seen to bale out. Jasta 4 were the main opponents, and they lost Leutnant Joachim von Winterfeld, in flames, and Unteroffizier Josef Doerflinger who survived. Doyle was claimed by the acting commander of the Staffel – and future Luftwaffe General – Leutnant Egon Koepsch, south of Paillencourt at 1815, his 8th victory. Ernst Udet, the Jasta CO, was on leave.

During the final skirmishes, 29 Squadron made claims for a two-seater south-east of Armentières and 88 Squadron's Bristols claimed five Fokkers between here and Douai. 80 Squadron lost a Camel to flak north of Méricourt, while Leutnant Paul Baümer of Jasta 2 Boelcke shot down a DH4 of the long-suffering 57 Squadron for his 23rd victory. Finally 79 Squadron's Dolphins claimed two Fokkers by the two Americans, Gillet and Lord, with 74 Squadron ending the fighting with two out of control Fokkers near Lille at 1910. During the day, Gefreiter Katzner from Jasta 43 was killed when separated from his patrol – time unknown.

An interesting item by another Jasta 43 pilot, Josef Raesch, who had just returned to the front after being shot down on 25 July, confirms the German Air Service's problems. Back on active duty in mid-August, he found there was no aeroplane for him until 3 September and that on the 5th, the Jasta's fuel allocation was cut to 2,000 litres per month. He noted: 'The British are superior to us, not only in numbers but in their tactics and organisation.' Fine words, considering the Germans were knocking down more Allied planes than the Allies were of them, but as can be seen, they were losing the war. Raesch put his finger on the main points as to why.

French Front

Action here was rather light, although the weather was good as it had been the day before. An American serving with the French, Lieutenant F C McCormick in Spa.164, was wounded and forced down at Mons. Two aircraft were claimed as probables by this unit and Spa.124 another.

Two Spads were claimed by the Germans, one to Leutnant Karl Ritscherle of Jasta 60, his 6th, north of Soissons and one to Vizefeldwebel Donhauser of Jasta 17 at 1210 – the latter probably Lieutenant Mantcewitch of Spa.76, forced down near Champfleury. Leutnant Werner Preuss of Jasta 66 claimed a Bréguet for his 15th victory, over Villeneuve inside French lines, supposedly Caporal Gaillard and Aspirant Marielle.

Sous Lieutenant Claude Haegelen, Brigadier Guérin and Sergent Peuch of Spa.100 shared a balloon at Boult-sur-Suippe for the French (Haegelen's 14th victory), while on the German side, Vizefeldwebel Karl Schlegel claimed a balloon at Fismes at 1720 for his 20th victory. Sous Lieutenant Fournier parachuted down without injury. There was no recorded action on the American sector.

	A/C	KB			DES	OOC	KB
British losses	18		British claims		32	32	3
French losses	–	1	French claims		–		1
American losses	–	–	American claims		–		–
IAF losses	–		IAF claims		–	–	–
German claims	25†	5	German losses		6		?

† Including at least one to flak and one FTL inside German lines.

British Casualties

Aircraft type	No.	Squadron	Crew		
DH9	C1294	218 Sqdn	Lt J G Munro	Interned	
			2/Lt T W Brodie	Interned	
BF2b	E2495	48 Sqdn	2/Lt R Beesley	POW	
			2/Lt A M Miller	POW	
Camel	B778	4 AFC	2/Lt M H Eddie	KIA	
Camel	E1407	4 AFC	Lt L E Taplin DFC	POW	
Camel	E7174	4 AFC	Lt D C Carter	KIA	
Camel	D8136	4 AFC	Lt A H Lockley	KIA	
Camel	F5945	73 Sqdn	Lt T K G Oliver	KIA	
SE5a	D6864	74 Sqdn	Maj K L Caldwell	Safe	
Camel	F2133	80 Sqdn	2/Lt A R Thatcher	POW	
Camel	F2143	80 Sqdn	Lt G B Wootton	Safe	*
Camel	B7280	210 Sqdn	Capt H A Patey DSC	POW	
Camel	E4390	210 Sqdn	2/Lt L Yerex	POW	
Camel	D1824	213 Sqdn	2/Lt C E Francis	POW	
SE5a	E1397	60 Sqdn	Capt J E Doyle DFC	POW/WIA	
SE5a	C1876	60 Sqdn	2/Lt S A Thomson	KIA	
SE5a	C1909	64 Sqdn	Lt W A F Cowgill	POW	
SE5a	B8428	92 Sqdn	Capt G A Wells MC	POW	
SE5a	D6889	92 Sqdn	Lt E V Holland	POW	
SE5a	D372	92 Sqdn	Lt H B Good	KIA	
DH4	F5828	57 Sqdn	Sgt D E Edgley	Safe	*
			Sgt J H Bowler (O)	WIA	
DH4	F6168	57 Sqdn	Lt A L Platt	Safe	
			Lt G A Riley	WIA	*
SE5a	E4070	60 Sqdn	Lt R C Blessley USAS	WIA	*

French Casualties

Bréguet XIV	?		Cpl Gaillard	Safe	*
			Asp Marielle	Safe	
Spad XIII		Spa.164	Lt F C McCormick	WIA	*
Spad XIII		Spa.76	Lt A Mantcewitch	Safe	*

British Front

Despite the weather being described as fair, there was not much activity this Friday. The ground offensive was winding down, although still continuing, with the front approaching Cambrai in the south.

Not deterred by their setback of the previous evening, 4 AFC were out early once again, with the 6' 3" tall Lieutenant Roy King claiming a DFW C as his 16th victory east of Wavrin (between Lens and Lille) at 0630. Also out early was Lieutenant Jesse Creech of the 148th Aero, claiming a Fokker DVII destroyed 1,000 yards north of Bourlon at 0705. He reported that the patrol was attacked by five enemy fighters. A climbing turn brought him back on the tail of the Fokker and he fired 150 rounds from 50 yards.

The first major fight of the day was between the Bristols of 20 Squadron and Fokkers near Saint-Quentin, with no less than seven being claimed by the 'Brisfits'. Despite two in flames and another two seen to crash, there is no corresponding information as to which Fokker unit this was.

At 0915, the Dolphins of 23 Squadron were escorting 205 Squadron on a raid which was intercepted by more Fokkers. Each unit claimed one, but 23 lost Captain N Howarth who was killed. Leutnant Wolfram von Richthofen of Jasta 11 (cousin of the famous Richthofen brothers) claimed a Dolphin east of Saint-Quentin at 0945 (G), whilst Oberleutnant Paul Blumenbach, the Staffelführer of Jasta 31, claimed one at 0950 (G) north of the town, but only the one was lost.

Another German victory was that claimed by Jasta 4's Leutnant Heinrich Maushacke, who shot down a Camel of 80 Squadron flown by Lieutenant J A McGill at 0953 over Le Catelet. Honours were even at 1025 and once again an RE8 crew proved they could survive in combat. Lieutenants G N Dennis and H D Hewett were taking photographs over Bourlon Wood but were suddenly attacked by seven Fokkers. Hewett grabbed his gun and sent one down in flames.

Five minutes later another large fight erupted over an area west of Cambrai. No. 11 Squadron on a 12-machine patrol were engaged by several formations of Fokkers. Four were claimed but two Bristols were lost in the process. Jasta 2 claimed two BF2bs, the 8th victory of Leutnant Otto Löffler north of Bourlon Wood, and the recently returned Paul Baümer, who had been injured in May, got his second kill in two days – his 23rd overall. He was on the way to 16 kills this September. Another German ace, Leutnant Martin Demisch of Jasta 58, shot down a 52 Squadron RE8 near Monchy on the Arras front 40 minutes later, to bring his own score to seven. Victory no. 8 for him came at 1245, downing the 8-1-1 balloon at Monchy-le-Preux. Just over an hour later the British lost another balloon, this time the 14th Company, to Vizefeldwebel Oskar Hennrich of Jasta 46, his 11th victory.

From midday to late afternoon there were few actions, although 103 Squadron fought Fokkers during a bomb raid near Lille and 32 and 29 Squadrons were in action; around Ostende 213 Squadron were in combat too.

At 1830, 208 Squadron claimed four Fokkers over the Canal du Nord on the Arras-Cambrai road but they lost Lieutenant A H Hiscoe. Two Camel claims were made, by Leutnants Alfred Lindberger and Ernst Bormann of Jasta 2 Boelcke. During this late period, 210, 88, 29, 201 and 2 AFC all had combats and made claims. At 1900 4 AFC and 22 Squadron had the last fights of the day, the latter with a Pfalz DXII over Cambrai.

French Front

Action was quite heavy, as the weather was mostly clear with good visibility. In the VIII Armée sector at 1215 hours, a patrol of Spa.90, consisting of Lieutenants Marc Ambrogi, Jean Lemarie and Sergent Gerard Florentin, engaged a two-seater over Azelot. Florentin forced the machine to land at Romain, east of Bayon for his first victory, but he was himself hit and mortally wounded, dying later. The occupants, Unteroffiziers Weiser and Scharg of Schlachstaffel 20, were on an orientation flight that in reality became a disorientation flight, and were taken prisoner.

In the X Armée sector, a flight of four aircraft from Sal.18 on a photo mission became engaged in two combats, the first against eight, the second against 20 enemy fighters. During these, Caporal Nal and Soldat Jeandemange were shot down in flames, although their comrades claimed one kill and one probable. The Salmson most probably fell to Hans Rolfes of Jasta 45 who claimed one at 1535 near Magneux. The Jasta, on their way to attack balloons, suffered no losses.

On this Aisne front, five balloons were attacked and two destroyed. Balloons of the 68 and 83 Ciés were flamed along the X Armée sector, with the observers, Lieutenant Charotte and Sergent Gaitz-Hocki making safe jumps. At 1645 (G), Jasta 45, continuing on after the Salmson fight, went for these balloons near Magneux, Rolfes, Leutnants Berling and Krayer claiming one each but only the two were lost.

Over the V Armée sector, a Bréguet XIV of Br.260, flown by Sergent Blovac and Lieutenant Millot, was attacked by two Fokkers, two kilometres inside the French lines above Puisieux (SE Reims) and shot down in flames. The victor was Leutnant Max Näther of Jasta 62, his 12th victory, recorded as shot down at 1742 (G) at Sillery, in the above area.

Other combats this day involved Spa.163 at 0830, and later at 1930; then at 1720, north of Soissons, Vizefeldwebel Knaak of Jasta 9 claimed a Spad fighter. Another went to Unteroffizier Dost of Jasta 21 east of Braisne at 1905. Two Spad pilots were wounded during the day, one each from Spa.75 and Spa.86. Leutnant Martin Haenichen, technical officer with Jasta 53, claimed two Spad two-seaters near Coucy-le-Château for his 2nd and 3rd kills. Another Spad two-seater went down to Leutnant Buddeberg of Jasta 50, south of Soissons, at 1120. One of these was crewed by Lieutenant Salvetat and Sous Lieutenant Descousis of Spa.269, who failed to return.

No activity of note was reported in the American sector.

	A/C	KB		DES	OOC	KB
British losses	6	2	British claims	21	23	–
French losses	5	2	French claims	5		–
American losses	–	–	American claims	–		–

	A/C	KB			DES	OOC	KB
IAF losses	–		IAF claims		–	–	–
German claims	17†	4	German losses		2‡		–

† Two to flak. ‡ Two two-seaters, with two other airmen killed, one belonging to FA(A) 219 falling near Bray.

British Casualties

Aircraft type	No.	Squadron	Crew		
RE8	C2479	52 Sqdn	Lt J Talbot	WIA	*
			Sgt H J Sampson	DOW	
DH9	D3249	206 Sqdn	2/Lt S M Desmond	KIA	
			3AM A Halliwell	DOI	
BF2b	D7906	11 Sqdn	2/Lt E N Underwood	KIA	
			2/Lt C M Coleman	KIA	
BF2b	C4745	11 Sqdn	2/Lt C B Seymour	KIA	
			2/Lt E G Bugg	KIA	
BF2b	F5820	22 Sqdn	Lt L C Rowney	Safe	
			Sgt J Goodman	WIA	
Dolphin	C8166	23 Sqdn	Capt N Howarth	KIA	
Camel	D9483	80 Sqdn	Lt J A McGill	KIA	
Camel	D9484	208 Sqdn	2/Lt A H Hiscox	DOW	*
DH4	A7815	18 Sqdn	Capt G W F Darvill DFC	Safe	
			Lt W N Miller	WIA	
HP O/400	–	207 Sqdn	Sgt C J E J Jones (O)	WIA	
HP O/400	–	207 Sqdn	Lt C Roberts (P)	WIA	
DH4	–	57 Sqdn	Lt G Anderson (P)	WIA	
Camel	D6434	201 Sqdn	2/Lt L G Teale	WIA	*
SE5a	B8392	2 AFC	Lt J S Ross	WIA	*

French Casualties

Spad XIII		Spa.75	S/Lt S Tourné	WIA	*
Spad XIII		Spa.83	MdL A Perrot	WIA	*
Bréguet XIV		Br.260	Sgt A Blovac	KIA	
			Lt P Millot	KIA	
Salmson 2A2		Sal.18	Cpl G Nal	KIA	
			Sol Jeandemange	KIA	
Salmson 2A2		Sal.17	MdL Baillodz	Safe	
			Lt Le Floch	KIA	
Bréguet XIV		Br.269	Lt Salvetat	MIA	
			S/Lt Descousis	MIA	
Spad XIII		Spa.90	Sgt G Florentin	DOW	

2

3

5

6

1 The RE8 aircraft was the backbone of artillery observation missions over the front throughout the last two years of the war. The crew shown from 5 Squadron are Captain C G Galbraith DFC (Canadian) and Lt A T Spangle. Galbraith died of wounds received on 15 September 1918, the next day.

2 The crews of the BF2b two-seat fighters were well to the fore in September 1918. Seen here is the successful crew of Lt S A W Knights MC, the observer to Captain G E Gibbons, of 62 Squadron. Gibbons achieved his last four victories on 3rd and 4th September, bringing his score to 17. He received the MC and DFC.

3 Two aces of 73 Squadron, South African G L Graham and E J Lussier DFC, French-Canadian. Emile Lusssier claimed his 10th victory on 15 September.

4 Two other BF2b pilots were Captains W McK Thomson and V E Groom of 20 Squadron. Thomson achieved 26 victories, while Groom scored eight. Groom became Sir Victor KCVO, KBE, CB, DFC.

5 Alfred Mills DFC, observer with Lt L M.Price of 20 Squadron, scored 15 victories with his various pilots. From Belfast, Mills claimed his six final victories during September 1918.

6 A French Bréguet XIV of the 96th Aero. Both the French and the USAS used this type for day bombing during the last years of the

British Front

A 19-year-old from Warrington, Lancashire, who would not survive the war, opened the aerial combat on this day of low clouds and afternoon rainstorms. At 0655, Lieutenant Guy Wareing of 29 Squadron destroyed a balloon at Gheluvelt for his 5th victory. A brave, but not entirely sensible German, rushed out of a nearby building and fired at Wareing with a rifle. He was promptly gunned down by Wareing, whose flight commander, Captain Camille 'Large-arse' Lagesse, strafed the defences during the attack. Five minutes later, 4 AFC shot down a two-seater at Henin-Liétard, the claimant being Lieutenant Thomas H Barkell.

At 0700, the whole of 203 Squadron took off from Izel-lès-Hameau aerodrome, led by Captain Leonard Henry Rochford – known universally as 'Tich' due to his small stature. At 0815 they attacked five Fokkers and Rochford shot down one north of Bourlon Wood for his 27th victory.

Major F I Tanner, serving with 80 Squadron following an extensive stay with 4 AFC, claimed a two-seater in flames south of Cartigny at 0930, while Captain George Gates of 201 Squadron gained his 10th victory with another two-seater at Noyelles. Gates noted that the observer baled out successfully, although actually, both crewmen had jumped from their FA(A) 263 machine, but only the pilot – Vizefeldwebel Hansen – survived. The observer's parachute failed, sending 24-year-old Leutnant Rudolf Brammer to his death. This two-seater was also claimed by Captain M E Ashton and Lieutenant T D Fitzsimon, in a 12 Squadron RE8.

Leutnant Fritz Rumey of Jasta 5 made the first German kill of the day, by downing a lone recce DH4 from 205 Squadron, for his 33rd victory. The pilot, Lieutenant Mellor, died but the observer, Lieutenant J C Walker, survived a prisoner. Jasta 5's CO, Oberleutnant Otto Schmidt, gained his 13th victory by claiming a balloon at Bertincourt.

DH9s of 211 Squadron were bombing a road northeast of Gravelines mid-morning, losing one machine possibly through a collision, which dived into the sea. Although the French rescued the men, the observer died.

At around 1130, 84 Squadron went on a balloon strafe and burnt four balloons between Saint-Quentin and Bellenglise. One was the 44th victory of the squadron's star turn, Captain A W Beauchamp-Proctor who would later be awarded the Victoria Cross. Another SE5a pilot, Second Lieutenant J B Bowen, an American serving with 32 Squadron, was not so lucky as he was caught and shot down by Leutnant Julius Schulte-Frohlinde of Jasta 11.

Oberleutnant Otto Schmidt in front of his Fokker DVII, commander of Jasta 5 in the summer of 1918. By the war's end he had achieved 20 victories, five of which he claimed during September 1918. He also led Jagdgruppe 2 on occasion.

Bad weather now curtailed flying until the late afternoon. No. 20 Squadron's Bristols and 98 Squadron's DH9s both had combats in the early evening, and then the Dolphins of 23 Squadron claimed a Fokker. Another Jasta 11 pilot, Wolfram von Richthofen, gained his 6th victory by downing an SE5a west of Le Catelet at 1840. This was probably Lieutenant R F Bush of 92 Squadron who failed to return but, due to imprecise records, may only have force-landed. Five minutes later von Richthofen and Jasta 11 ran into a patrol of 84 Squadron, he and Oberleutnant Erich von Wedel each shooting down one. Very unusually, the RAF made no claims at all in this fight.

The last RAF claim for the day was a two-seater at 1910, north-east of Marquion, to a patrol of 54 Squadron. During the day the Germans lost two more two-seater crews in British lines, presumed to ground fire. They were Gefreiter Rudolf Knust, who was killed, and Oberleutnant von Neufville, prisoner, of FA(A) 259 at St Leger. The other was an LVG crew, Vizefeldwebel Hermann and Leutnant Schneider of FA(A) 219, both taken prisoner.

French Front

The weather on the French front was described as cloudy and windy, but despite this the level of combats was high. Second Lieutenant David W Lewis, an American serving with Spa.79, was engaged by four enemy aircraft near La Fère. He reported shooting one down but the others pursued him, riddling his Spad and wounding him. He crash-landed in the front lines, evidently the victim of Leutnant Hofmann of Jasta 79, who was credited with a Spad at 0710 by Villequier-Aumont, about ten kilometres west-south-west from La Fère, for his 2nd victory.

It was a rough day for the French two-seater crews. On the Aisne front the Spad XI of Sergent Malot and Sous Lieutenant Monin was shot down in flames but they managed to survive – probably downed by Leutnant Bornträger of Jasta 49, near Auberive at 1030. On the IV Armée sector, Sergent Thomas and Sous Lieutenant Miles of Spa.140, on a photo mission, were attacked by two Fokkers and failed to return. They fell victim to Leutnant Hermann Häbich, also of Jasta 49, at St Hilaire at 1035.

Another was lost in the II Armée sector, Adjutant Videcoq and Lieutenant Broca of Spa.47 failing to get back from a sortie; they were seen going down near Pannes. They were probably the 'Salmson' shot down by Lieutenant Oliver Freiherr von Beaulieu-Marconnay at 1225, north-east of Montsec, where Pannes is located. 'Beauli' had been the Staffelführer of Jasta 19 for just five days, and this was his 14th victory; one week precisely before his 20th birthday and ten months after he had become operational. Jasta 19 was part of JGII – the BMW Fokker-equipped Circus which was just moving into the Saint-Mihiel salient area.

On the VII Armée sector, Maréchal-des-Logis Clerc and Sous Lieutenant Thirion of Sal.5 were shot down – probably to ground fire – and crashed north of Einville at 1645, the pilot killed and the observer wounded. Adjutant Chenard and Sous Lieutenant Plebert of Br.221 were killed in combat near Chavannes-les-Grandes, apparent victims of Leutnant Hermann Stutz, Staffelführer of Jasta 71, who claimed a Bréguet XIV west of St Ulrich for his 4th victory. This was the only claim and loss in the VII Armée sector, opposite the German Armee-Abteilung 'B' sector.

To offset these losses, a balloon was burnt by Sous Lieutenant Austin of Spa.92 north of Beaurieux in the X Armée sector, while another was claimed in the V Armée sector by Sous Lieutenants Michel Coiffard, Théophile Condemine and a newcomer of three weeks, Sergent Charles Peillard. Coiffard, who was 26 years old, and had now scored 25 victories, had been wounded six times in the infantry before becoming unfit for military service. He promptly joined the aviation service, eventually being assigned to Spa.154 on 28 June 1917. His medal citations, written with Gallic flair, for once, did not overstate their case. He was lauded as being a man of 'exceptional fighting qualities', 'rash bravery' and 'exceptional bravery'. Condemine was 23 and came from the infantry via a severe wound while with the cavalry. He was also a recent arrival, having joined the Escadrille on 22 August, but would gain nine victories by the Armistice. On the Champagne front, Sous Lieutenant Louis Douillet and Sergent Max Caton of Spa.124 claimed a Fokker west of Dontrien.

Another successful French ace was M J C M Coiffard of Spa.154. Sadly he did not survive the war, dying of wounds in October 1918 having achieved 34 victories. Seven of these were balloons, which he shot down in September. He received the Legion d'Honneur, Medaille Militaire and the British Military Cross.

American Sector

A Salmson of the 91st Observation Squadron, crewed by Lieutenants A W Lawson and H W Verwohlt, was attacked at 1130 hours over Conflans by six EA and was forced to land behind German lines. It was later learned that both men had been captured, with Verwohlt wounded. They had fallen to one of the units of JGII, the second organised Circus, which was beginning to operate against the US forces. They were to inflict massive losses on the Americans, for the same reason JGIII was doing it to the RAF: the best aircraft and pilots available, added to the general level of inexperience of the Americans. Vizefeldwebel Albert Haussmann of Jasta 13 shot them down – his 13th victory – at 1130, near Jeandelize. Haussmann had been operating since 1916, a fighter pilot since Bloody April, and knew his stuff.

First Lieutenant Warren T Kent, 49th Pursuit Squadron, departed on patrol at 1205 with three other pilots. The patrol was attacked by eight Fokkers over Thiaucourt, and Kent was last seen going down in this vicinity. Later in the month the American infantry found a grave marker being made in a house at Pannes, which is between Thiaucourt and Essey. The marker was for an American First Lieutenant who was killed this day. Vizefeldwebel Josef Hohly of Jasta 65 claimed his 5th victory, a Spad, at 1315, near Essey, about three kilometres south of Pannes.

At 1600, three men of the 213th Aero claimed a two-seater south of Essey, near Flirey, while the 22nd and 94th Squadrons each damaged a two-seater.

IAF

For the first time during this month, the IAF was intercepted in the process of dropping two and three-quarter tons of bombs on various targets. Six planes of 55 Squadron bombed the railway at Ehange, while 11 DH9s of 99 Squadron, led by Major Lawrence A Pattinson and Captain W G Stevenson, with ten more DHs from 104 Squadron, led by Captains R J Gammon and E J Garland, attacked Mannheim with two tons of bombs. Take-off was around 1100, with height and position assumed over base 40 minutes later. Soon after reaching German lines, the force was attacked by six-plus enemy fighters. 104 Squadron's gunners claimed three Germans destroyed, two by Gammon and gunner Second Lieutenant P E Appleby (one a flamer) timed at 1230 and 1400 – while at the latter time, Lieutenant J W Richards and Sergeant W E Reast destroyed another. Richards and Reast had a slightly defective engine and staggered to and from the target, 2,000 feet below the rest of the formation. For their courage, they were badly shot up and Reast mortally wounded. Observer gunners, protected only by a piece of fabric, often suffered high casualties, for there was no armour plate in WWI. Given the proximity of the pilot to the observer in a DH9 (they were farther apart in the DH4), the rear man tended, on occasion, to act as 'armour' for the pilot's back!

The fight lasted 70 miles to the target and another 70 back, lasting four hours in all. Three crews of 104 and one from 99 failed to return. Two were shot down by Leutnant Georg Weiner, the commander – since 1 September – of Jasta 3, falling at Burscheid and Dassberg. Weiner, who had turned 23 on 22 August, and who would end up a major general in the Luftwaffe, had served previously with Kest 3 since August 1917 after being wounded with Jasta 20. He died on 24 January 1957; these DHs brought his score to six. The other two fell to Kest 1a, led by a Jasta 5 veteran of Bloody April, Oberleutnant Rudolf Nebel, for his 2nd kill, and Unteroffizier Heinrich Forstmann for his 1st. One of Kest 1a's victims fell at Frankenthal, the other at Zabern (99 Squadron's machine) where it was contested by Kest 3. Nebel's combat report reads as follows:

> 'Just before 2 p.m. on 7 September 1918, as leader of the formation often aircraft of Kest 1a, I attacked a British bomber formation of 19 DH9s. I was immediately hit three times in the propeller, and once by an explosive bullet in the hand pump, which was shattered. One part struck me in the face causing me to momentarily lose my senses. In order to assess damage, I descended beneath the enemy formation and then immediately unsuccessfully attacked from there.
>
> 'Thereupon I dropped behind the enemy formation and despite most extreme enemy opposition, attacked the last DH9 about ten times. Because of the volume of fire which was met by each attack, I was forced to turn away. I could follow my fire well because I used 'Leucht-spur-Munition' (tracer bullets). Because of my accurate fire, the enemy aeroplane descended lower and lower below his formation. I last attacked in the region of Neidersbrund. During this attack, I received hits which damaged the engine mounting. This, and the damaged propeller, caused excessive vibration which made flying impossible. Whilst the fall of the Englishman was clearly a matter of time, I was denied the pleasure of seeing the crash of the machine I had hit. The enemy aircraft fell about 800 metres beyond the place of my last attack and shortly after my emergency landing. I enquired of its fate and was told that it had fallen at Buchsweiler. I fired 650 rounds at very close range during my attacks, received 29 hits in my propeller, engine, pressure pump and one glancing bullet which hit my shoe.'

Nebel's machine, Fokker DVII (Alb) 666/18, was equipped with wireless telegraphy which had enabled Kest 1a to be directed on to the DH9 formation south-west of Mannheim, where they attacked the bombers at 3,400 metres height. The IAF's bombing missed hitting any significant targets. Whilst Nebel was attacking, Feldwebel Schiller was hit in the lower jaw and spun down unconscious, recovering just in time to pull out of the spin and land. Unteroffizier Forstmann reported:

> 'On 7 September 1918 near 2.15 p.m., in my Albatros DVa, in the company of my Kettenführer, Leutnant Korner and Unteroffizier Sonnabend, I attacked

an enemy bombing formation SW of Mannheim. After I had fired about 100 rounds I saw the Englishman suddenly go down. In the meantime, I had come so close to the enemy formation that my radiator was shot up and I had to land immediately. I saw the Englishman, who was gliding down, chased first by a Fokker and then a Roland aeroplane. I could see no more because of hot water splashing in my face.'

Leutnant Kurt Seit of Jasta 80b, also claimed a DH9 as his third victory, which he saw stagger into Allied lines and force-land – Richards and Reast! Major Pattinson, Captain Gammon and Lieutenant Appleby all received the DFC five days later.

As this raid was ending, a lone recce DH4 of 55 Squadron, flown by one of the unit's Americans, Lieutenant Don J Waterous, with Second Lieutenant C L Rayment as observer, was intercepted and shot up by seven EA. The DH4 crew staggered back over the lines, claiming one German possibly out of control over Saarburg at about 1400.

The bloody battles which had been going on all summer between the Germans and the IAF were continuing into September. Most of the damage was inflicted by the German front-line Jastas over whose territory the IAF had to fly to reach their mainly German targets. In turn, the IAF, as can be seen, could and did take a lot of their opponents with them. The performance and armament differentials were so small between bomber and fighter that no one had a clear advantage, unless the Fokker DVII-equipped units broke up the IAF formations.

	A/C	KB		DES	OOC	KB
British losses	6		British claims	11	4	5
French losses	4		French claims	1		2
American losses	2	–	American claims	–		–
IAF losses	4		IAF claims	3	1	–
German claims	18†		German losses	4		4‡

† Three to flak. ‡ Plus one that broke loose.

British Casualties

Aircraft type	No.	Squadron	Crew		
DH4	D9271	25 Sqdn	2/Lt C H Saffery	Safe	•
			2/Lt J Harrington	WIA	
DH4	A7587	205 Sqdn	Lt D J Mellor	KIA	
			2/Lt J C Walker	POW	
DH9	D2918	211 Sqdn	Lt E S Morgan DFC	KIA	
			2/Lt R Simpson	KIA	
SE5a	C1123	32 Sqdn	2/Lt J B Bowen	KIA	
SE5a	C8895	84 Sqdn	2/Lt W B Aldred	DOW	
SE5a	D6917	84 Sqdn	Lt E C Bateman	KIA	
SE5a	C9064	92 Sqdn	Lt R F Bush	MIA	
Camel	D1887	65 Sqdn	Capt A W Jones-Williams MC	Safe	•
Dolphin	–	79 Sqdn	Capt H P Rushforth	WIA	•

Aircraft type	No.	Squadron	Crew	
DH9	D3268	104 Sqdn	Sgt E Mellor	KIA
			Sgt J Bryden	KIA
DH9	B7653	104 Sqdn	2/Lt J E Kemp	POW
			2/Lt E B Smailes	DOW
DH9	D7210	104 Sqdn	2/Lt W E L Courtney	POW
			2/Lt A R Sabey	DOW
DH9	D2916	99 Sqdn	Lt G Broadbent	POW
			Lt M A Dunn	POW
DH9	D7318	104 Sqdn	Lt J W Richards	Safe *
			Sgt W E Reast	DOW
DH4	A7942	55 Sqdn	2/Lt D J Waterous	Safe *
			2/Lt C L Rayment	Safe

French Casualties

Spad XIII		Spa.79	2/Lt D W Lewis US	WIA *
Spad XI		Spa.140	Sgt Thomas	MIA
			S/Lt Moles	MIA
Bréguet XIV		Br.221	Adj Chenard	KIA
			S/Lt Plebert	KIA
Salmson 2A2		Sal.5	MdL Clerc	KIA
			S/Lt Thirion	WIA
Spad XI		Spa.47	Adj Videcocq	MIA
			Lt Broca	MIA
Spad XI		Spa.?	Sgt Malot	Safe *
			S/Lt Morin	Safe

American Casualties

Spad XIII		49th Aero	1/Lt W T Kent	KIA
Salmson 2A2		91st Aero	1/Lt A W Lawson	POW
			1/Lt H W Verwohlt	POW

08 SEPTEMBER 1918
M T W T F S **S**

British Front

The weather was overcast with some rain. Combats were the fewest for the month so far. At 0635, Captain D H M Carberry and Lieutenant J B V Clements of 59 Squadron, in RE8 C2327, encountered and shot down a Halberstadt two-seater, sent another down out of control ten minutes later and then forced a third to land. The first constituted Carberry's 4th success in air fighting. One victim was from FA(A) 239, crewed by Leutnants von Scheve and von Rudno-Rudzinsky, who were wounded and crashed near Flesquières. Lieutenant Roy McConnel of 46 Squadron got another two-seater, this time a Rumpler, in flames south of Péronne at 0700.

The first fighter versus fighter clash came at 0815, 24 Squadron claiming three Fokkers between Le Catelet and Saint-Quentin. The known loss was Gefreiter Kurt Blumener of Jasta 6 who baled out over Beaurevoir but his parachute failed to open. Captain G B Gates of 201 Squadron burnt yet another two-seater over Cantaing at 0650. The Albatros's observer baled out too but the 'chute caught fire. This was probably Leutnant Albert Klingsporn, just eight days short of his 22nd birthday, observer with FA(A) 252.

The Germans made no claims against the RAF, who none the less lost two RE8s to ground fire – 3 AFC and 15 Squadron.

French Front

As on the British front, aerial activity was light, due to the weather turning to cloud and rain in the afternoon. One aircraft was shot down by ground fire on the X Armée front, coming down between the lines west of Prosnes. Both men scrambled to the safety of their front-line trenches despite intense rifle and machine-gun fire directed at them. Another airman was killed by ground fire in this area.

American Sector

Some action took place here, although most units were held back because of the preparations for the St Mihiel offensive. A five-strong Spad patrol from the 95th Aero departed at 0830 to patrol between Watronville and Saint-Mihiel, but lost Lieutenant Norman Archibald to flak about 0900, being forced to land near Étain to become a prisoner. He later wrote the book *Heaven High, Hell Deep* covering his experiences.

In the afternoon, First Lieutenant Jacques Swaab of the 22nd Aero became separated from his patrol and encountered Fokkers over Morhange. He claimed one in flames at 1235 at 150 metres, having come out of low cloud near a German airfield. He then had to fight his way back, claiming two more Fokkers at 1305 before becoming lost and landing well away from his base aerodrome.

Jacques M Swaab of the 22nd Aero gained his first four victories in September, three on the 8th. Ending the war with ten victories and the DSC he was later technical advisor to the 1938 film *Dawn Patrol*, starring Errol Flynn and David Niven.

	A/C	KB		DES	OOC	KB
British losses	–	–	British claims	5	2	–
French losses	1	–	French claims	–		–
American losses	1	–	American claims	3		–
IAF losses	–		IAF claims	–		–
German claims	1		German losses	3		–

British Casualties

Aircraft type	No.	Squadron	Crew		
RE8	D4814	3 AFC	Lt T J Pengilly	Safe	•
			Lt O G Whitcombe	Safe	
RE8	D4847	15 Sqdn	Capt A R Cross	Safe	•
			Lt H A Coysh	Safe	
DH9	–	206 Sqdn	2/Lt J D Russell (P)	WIA	•

French Casualties

Aircraft type	No.	Squadron	Crew	
Two-seater	–	7.CA	Lt Verdieret	Safe
			Lt Moulloud	Safe
Caudron R11	–	C.46	S/Lt P Artur (O)	KIA *

American Casualties

Aircraft type	No.	Squadron	Crew	
Spad XIII	4662	28th Aero	2/Lt L Moriarty	WIA *
Spad XIII		95th Aero	1/Lt N S Archibald	POW
Salmson 2A2		88th Aero	1/Lt E A Wagner (O)	WIA
Spad XIII		22nd Aero	1/Lt J M Swaab	WIA

09 SEPTEMBER 1918
M **T** W T F S S

Strong winds, low clouds and heavy rain storms set in on this day and would remain for the next few days. Very little aerial activity occurred, with almost all flying stopped. This gave the aviators a welcome respite, especially in view of the major offensives coming up.

The RAF made no claims and only reported one combat casualty, a 35 Squadron AWFK8, which force-landed near Épehy at 1600, and had to be struck off, having survived a near disastrous encounter with a shell.

The French and Americans had no combat losses either. The Germans made one claim, by Hauptmann Eduard von Schleich, the commander of Jagdgruppe 8, who claimed a Camel over Quéant.

British Casualties

Aircraft type	No.	Squadron	Crew	
AWFK8	B4179	35 Sqdn	Lt P E Mercer	WIA
			2/Lt A E Harris	WIA

10 SEPTEMBER 1918
M **T** W T F S S

The weather was as foul as the previous day, with the French and Americans having few combats. The RAF lost three aircraft, one pilot, and an airman wounded. Firstly a RE8 which had to force-land following damage from gunfire at 1020, then an

AWFK8 was hit by AA fire, which came down behind the front lines and smashed near Hulloch at 1400 hours. Finally a Camel responded to a wireless call near Lens. This meant that a ground station had reported a two-seater sending signals to the ground, and a fighter of 208 Squadron was sent off to intercept it, but the pilot failed to return. The Germans reported a Camel down south of Mérignies at 1545 with engine trouble.

British Casualties

Aircraft type	No.	Squadron	Crew		
RE8	D4852	4 Sqdn	2/Lt J Sharp	Safe	
			Lt S Leslie	Safe	
AWFK8	D5149	8 Sqdn	Lt E L Stacey	Safe	
			Lt W R B Mann	Safe	
Camel	F1399	208 Sqdn	Lt J P Lloyde	POW	
RE8	C2798	59 Sqdn	Lt B S Wilcox	Safe	
			2/Lt S E Rowley	WIA	*

11 SEPTEMBER 1918
M **T** W T F S S

Although on this day the Germans claimed one Allied aircraft by flak, none were lost. This was probably an Australian RE8 hit by machine-gun fire during a contact patrol, but it got back, although its crew had been wounded. However, Allied artillery fire did destroy a German balloon. The weather was again appalling, and bad weather or not, the big offensive was planned for the morrow.

British Casualties

Aircraft type	No.	Squadron	Crew		
RE8	C2728	3 AFC	Lt T L Baillieu DFC	WIA	*
			2/Lt F A Sewall DFC	WIA	

12 SEPTEMBER 1918
M T W **T** F S S

British Front

Wind and heavy rain reduced operations. No night bombing was undertaken and only one ton of bombs was dropped by day. Only one RAF machine was lost too – a 48 Squadron Bristol that left at 1715 on an OP to Menin. Jasta 35 claimed two aircraft: an AWFK8 by Leutnant Rudolf Stark, near Hermies, and a RE8 to Gefreiter Caspar Schmidt over Quéant. Stark and Schmidt overhauled the RE8 near Cagnicourt, Schmidt

Leutnant Rudolf Stark of the Bavarian Jasta 35b. In the first half of 1918 he flew with Jasta 34b and Jasta 77b. In September 1918 he scored three times and had another unconfirmed, ending the war with 11 kills. His well known book *Wings of War* (1933) has become something of a classic.

following the RE down in a series of steep spirals and seeing it hit the ground between Riencourt and Quéant, on the British side. Stark then found another two aircraft at low level, being fired on by AA and he attacked a 'Big Ack' over Havrincourt. His bullets appeared to go into the pilot's cockpit whereupon the two-seater heeled over and spun down to crash on the railway line near Hermies. Despite this, there is no information in RAF records to identify the British crews; either they must both have survived injury and their aircraft could not have been seriously damaged, or Stark's Jasta was guilty of severe optimism and overclaiming. The BF2b had to be too far north to be considered a victim of either Jasta 35 pilot – unless it was Stark's 'Big Ack'.

French Front

On this first day of the Saint-Mihiel offensive (in an area located between the Moselle and the Meuse Rivers) the weather was shocking. The Heights of the Meuse on the western face of the salient was a hilly, wooded area which extended into the area for quite a distance. The nearby Woevre plain was flat and covered with woods and lakes.

Low clouds and heavy rain, combined with strong winds made flying dangerous enough, without enemy opposition. All the French casualties were from the Division Aérienne, assigned to the operational area of the 1st American Army. Forty-five planes of the 1st Brigade d'Aviation (Groupement De Goys) dropped 9,000 kilos of bombs and fired 3,500 rounds at ground targets for the loss of two aircraft from GB5.

Forty-five Bréguets of GB5 had bombed and strafed the St Benoit, Beney and Fresnes-en-Woëvre areas, as well as attacking barracks near Vigneulles. The two aircraft from Br.29 were lost because, according to the French, they were so low; they were hit by blast from their own bombs. However, both Bréguets were claimed by German fighter pilots.

The 2nd Brigade (Groupement Duseigneur) sent out 37 aircraft which dropped 4,920 kilos of bombs and fired 1,750 rounds at ground targets. Three aircraft failed to return, including the CO of Br.13, Commandant Rocard, plus one aircraft from each of Br.128 and Br.132.

Two of the Bréguets were lost to fighters near Conflans, well to the rear of the lines – one accounted for by Leutnant Georg von Hantelmann of Jasta 15, an ex-cavalry man who was yet to turn 20, for his 7th victory, west of Conflans at 1035. The other was shot down by Jasta 64w's Unteroffizier Bader at Friauville. The others (the two GB5s and the third 2nd Brigade a/c) were lost near the lines claimed by Jasta 13 – Leutnant Kurt Hetze (the second not confirmed) and Leutnant Grimm, all over Thiaucourt. Two bombers returned with wounded gunners. Three of JGII's four Jastas were to make kills this day.

A balloon was shot down by Br.131, showing that the British were not the only bomber crews to attack balloons, although the claimants were both American, Lieutenants Carlyle L Nelson and James M Newell, serving with the French.

American Sector

One of the first sorties by the Americans, into the terrible weather, was by the 22nd Aero, whose unit insignia was a shooting star. Second Lieutenant Vaughn McCormack, one of the veterans with two victories, led off their patrol at dawn. He crashed on landing having apparently been hit by ground fire, and was killed.

The 135th Observation Squadron lost three DH4s during the day. The first was lost heading out into low cloud – in places down to 100 feet – and heavy rain at about 0500, never to return. It was hit by an Allied artillery shell and crashed in flames just north-east of Flirey, whilst supporting the 89th American Division. The crew that left at 0620 did not return either. This crew became lost in bad weather and fierce winds, finally landing in Switzerland where they were interned.

Shortly after 0600, Captain Ray Bridgeman led out another patrol from his 22nd Aero and in appalling weather near the Bois-le-Prêtre encountered a Hannover CLIII, shooting it down at 0655. The Hannover was last seen going straight down, out of control, through low clouds. Bridgeman's engine was then hit by ground fire and he had to force-land beyond the former German front lines near Remanauville. Forty-five minutes later Lieutenant Joseph Fritz Wehner of the 27th Aero attacked and damaged a balloon near Montsec.

The German balloon from Ballonzug 55, north-east of Pont-à-Mousson on the east bank of the Moselle River, was flamed at 0905. The Germans noted the attack was pressed to within 50 metres and that their observer, Leutnant Klemm, was shot through the chest and severely wounded. The American pilot was Lieutenant Frank Luke Jr, in aircraft No.21, also of the 27th Aero:

Frank Luke Jr went down in history for his rash bravery in September 1918. Between the 12th and 29th, Luke downed four German aircraft and 14 kite balloons. On the latter date he was brought down by ground fire, wounded and died from gunshot wounds from German soldiers.
His bravery earned him the DSC and Oak Leaf Cluster, and finally, the Medal of Honor.

> 'Saw three EA near Lavigneulle and gave chase following them directly east towards Pont-à-Mousson where they disappeared towards Metz. Saw enemy balloon at Marieville. Destroyed it after three passes at it, each within a few yards of the balloon. The third pass was made when the balloon was very near the ground. Both guns stopped so pulled off to one side. Fixed left gun and turned to make one final effort to burn it, but saw it started, the next instant it burst into great flames and dropped on the winch, destroying it.'

Frank Luke landed near an American balloon to get confirmation of this his first victory. He took off to return home but was forced down again by engine trouble, returning the next morning. Luke, an unknown man from Arizona, had no victories to his credit, like most of his colleagues. He was not over popular in the squadron, being a bit of a loner, but things were to change for this youngster, who had reached the age of 21 on 19 May, and who had been with the 27th since 26 July. After an unconfirmed claim on 16 August – which is why he made sure of confirmation on this occasion – Luke was to claim 18 times in September, in a meteoric career of unbelievable aggression and courage, combined with an apparent disdain for whether he survived or not. Fellow ace Ken Porter – later in a long life – remembered Luke as being 'mad'. Whatever others thought of him, and of one of his favourite retorts to fellow pilots of '...what's it matter, scared?', he was by far the best USAS fighter pilot of the war.

Major Lewis H Brereton, destined to be a general in the next war, but recently appointed the commander of the 1st US Observation Wing, and Capitaine Vallois (a senior French liaison officer), in a Salmson of the 12th Aero, were attacked at 1000. The pilot most likely to have been responsible for shooting them down was Leutnant Max Klieforth of Jasta 13, who claimed a Salmson at Thiaucourt for his first victory. Brereton's machine crashed near this town – in Allied lines – with Vallois wounded.

Mid-morning, the American fighters, who were doing a vast amount of ground strafing and bombing, encountered more opposition. First Lieutenant Charles D'Olive of the 93rd Aero claimed a Fokker between Jaulny and Viéville-en-Haye:

> 'Lieut. D'Olive states that at about 1020 Sept. 12th, between Jaulny and Viéville-en-Haye (which is slightly east of Thiaucourt) and at about 500 metres, he in company with Lieut. Cox saw EA, possibly a Fokker monoplane. Thinking Lieut. Cox had not seen the Hun, he dived and began shooting at about 350 or 400 metres. He saw tracers litter the cockpit. He had only fired 25 or 30 rounds when he turned into a cloud. He turned away to come home and just glanced backwards towards the cloud and under it saw the machine going down in a steep spin or spiral at about 250 or 300 metres. One magneto quit then and he lost sight of the Hun.'

The USAS credited D'Olive with a victory, on evidence which even the RAF would not accept at this stage of the war; the French never did. When considering American claims, the reader should be aware that the American confirmation rules were much less rigorous than the other Allies, presumably to encourage their relatively inexperienced pilots who, as they gained experience, tended to dispense with what may best be termed 'faith kills'. This is not a criticism of D'Olive, or other American pilots who would prove over the rest of the war to be as good as anyone at this dangerous profession having learnt far more rapidly than these other nations, but rather of their commanders, who encouraged this form of self-delusion that proved so costly to the RAF.

The American Day Bombardment Group lost three planes during the day. The first was the result of a brave but suicidal action by an extraordinarily brave crew. First Lieutenant Andre Gunderlach, the pilot, was a veteran of French bomber and fighter squadrons and was the flight leader of the first 10 Bréguets of the 96th Squadron standing by on their airfield. Due to bad weather, Gunderlach and his observer, Lieutenant H Pennington 'Pinky' Way, chose to go alone to bomb Bruxières, three miles over the lines near Montsec. They argued the weather was too bad for a formation.

Loaded down with bombs they left at 1045 – and almost made it. They were shot down in flames and killed near Commercy, well into Allied lines, by eight Fokkers. Feldwebel Beschow of Jasta 64w, claimed his second and final victory, near Broussey, the only Bréguet claim well inside Allied lines, although the time of the kill, in some accounts, was at 1000, but more likely 1200.

The next loss was that of Lieutenants George M Crawford and James O'Toole, who departed at 1100 for a recce over Dampvitoux in a 96th Aero DH4, although Crawford was on detachment from the 20th Aero. The mission was carried out at 50 metres, with the result that they lost their engine to ground fire, according to Crawford upon release from prison camp, and force-landed east of Pont-à-Mousson, O'Toole dying from a severe leg wound. They were also claimed by Oberleutnant

Erwin Wenig, the CO of Jasta 80b, who downed a US DH4, whose crew was captured, at Phlyn, which is east of Pont-à-Mousson.

Before the third loss, a DH4 of the 50th Observation Squadron, crewed by Lieutenants Henry Stevens and Edward Gardner, departed at 1030 on a recce mission over the US 82nd Division, who held the line on both sides of the Moselle River. They fell to Leutnant Franz Büchner, who had turned 20 in January 1918, but who had been on active service since 1914. He had flown through Bloody April with Jasta 9, staying with that unit until August 1917, scoring just one victory. By June 1918 his score was two, then the Fokker DVII arrived. He became leader of Jasta 13 on 15 June with four victories and by the morning of this day, had brought his score to 20. He would score more victories in Black September – 17 – than any other German pilot.

The 135th's third loss also came after midday, during Jasta 13's foray. Six Fokkers flew down the Moselle to the south of Metz, reportedly burnt a Spad (two-seater) – the 50th Aero DH4 – then found and shot down this 135th machine in flames near Vilcey-sur-Trey. The DH4 broke up and the observer was flung – or jumped – from the flaming wreck. The pilot was found dead in the wreckage, mercifully from a bullet in the head. This kill was also made by Büchner. The 135th received six DSCs for this day's work – to Messrs Benell, Blezer, Coleman, Hart, Morse and Suiter.

More losses came. The 12th lost a machine near Fey-en-Haye at 1210, possibly by Jasta 64w, Offizierstellvertreter Trautmann, who put in a claim for a Salmson near Flirey. The crew were unhurt and later claimed a Fokker triplane during their fight.

Franz Büchner made it three for the day by downing an 8th Observation Squadron DH4 in his green-nosed, blue-fuselaged DVII. Lieutenants Horace W Mitchell and John W Artz had taken off from Ourches aerodrome at 1330 on a counter battery mission. At 1430, having completed their task, they turned for home but were attacked by two Fokkers and a Rumpler. During the fight, their motor was hit, Artz being wounded, and forced down to be taken prisoner. After his eventual return, Artz reported:

> 'During the engagement, our engine was disabled, forcing us to land about 12 km inside the German lines, near a village. The enemy continued firing until our plane had stopped moving on the ground and we were out of it. I received a flesh wound during the attack.'

(Mitchell was later questioned about the Liberty engine which powered his DH4.)

During a rainstorm, the 1st Observation Squadron lost a Salmson 2A2 which had departed at 1400 on a recce sortie. They were attacked near the lines and came down on the right side, although the machine burst into flames on impact, the observer being killed; Harry Aldrich, the pilot, was seriously burned. They probably fell to Oberleutnant Oskar von Boenigk, commander of JGII, whose 22nd victory was a Salmson at Thiaucourt.

Several American Spad pilots were hit or staggered back with motor troubles during the day. One was Lieutenant Lansing 'Denny' Holden of the 95th, who noted in his diary:

> 'I was flying low, perhaps 800 metres, 3-4 kilometres behind the lines, when my motor dropped from 1900 revs to 1500, barely enough to keep me in the air. I turned for our lines, the motor turning slower and slower. I was gliding down;

there was nothing but shell-torn fields and woods below. I started to land when a shell hit in a trench just below me; was it Allied or German? I kept on, just skimmed over a wood and dropped to the ground on probably the one spot it was possible to alight without smashing. The field was covered with barbed wire and shell holes. I heard the rattle of a machine gun and saw something with blue move in the woods – French or German? I had expected to see American khaki. Most heavenly sight: a French poilu waved to me – I had landed 600 yards behind the front line.'

Later that day, Holden's machine was repaired and he flew it home.

A Salmson of the 104th Observation Squadron, transferring to a new base, strayed over the lines in bad weather and was shot down by ground fire on the west side of the salient. The crew remained missing until the observer Corporal A C Johnson – wounded – was discovered in a hospital abandoned by retreating Germans some time later.

The leading ace in the USAS was lost late in the day. First Lieutenant David Endicott Putnam, a Harvard graduate, was still only 19 years old despite a wealth of experience of air fighting. Born 10 December 1898, he

David Endicott Putnam flew with the French for most of 1918, but in the summer he transferred to the US Air Service, serving with the 139th Aero Squadron. His 13th 'official' victory was downed on 12 September in a fight with Fokker DVIIs, but he was himself shot down and killed in this action.

had sailed to join the French Air Service in April 1917 while still under age to join the American Aviation Service. He had joined Spa.94 in December on the Châlons front before being moved to a Morane-Saulnier monoplane-equipped Escadrille MS.156. Up to 1 June, Putnam had claimed four confirmed and eight probable victories. He then transferred to the famous Spa.38, home of Felix Madon. On 2 June – his first day with the unit – Putnam made two confirmed kills, followed three days later by one confirmed and four probables in one fight. With a score of nine confirmed and 15 probables by mid-June he joined the 139th Aero, having been commissioned into the USAS on the 10th. The aggressive Putnam had operated so far over the German lines he was often unable to get the required ground witnesses needed for a confirmed victory while with the French.

By the morning of the 12th, Putnam had run his score to 13, being the leading light of the newer, younger 2nd Pursuit Group. Near Limey at 1830, a patrol of the 139th ran into Fokkers. He was on patrol with Lieutenant Wendell A Robertson at the time, and shot a Fokker off Robertson's tail before falling in American lines, south-east of Limey, to Leutnant Georg von Hantelmann of Jasta 15, at 1835 (A). He was the 8th of von Hantelmann's eventual 25 victories. The German was also 19 and this, his second claim of the day, robbed the USAS of one of its finest officers.

At the end of the day, despite dreadful weather and fierce opposition, the French and American air crews were in complete command of the battlefield. On the ground the attack had been successful, although the Americans would suffer greatly from inexperience here as well. The cost had been low in terms of the number of sorties flown, but the American army co-operation units and their fighters had shown they could operate as a cohesive force.

During the day, the 'ordinary' Jasta 64w had made three claims and the other 'ordinary' Jastas, 77b and 80b, one each. The three component Jastas of JGII that had scored with their BMW-powered Fokkers, had made the other eight claims. This started JGII on an incredible run of 89 victories in a week for some seven losses!

As will be seen, this slaughter was costly to the French, American and British (in the IAF), but it did not in any way hinder or stop the Allied Air Services from accomplishing their tasks. As with the RAF to the north, all the crack Jagdegeschwaderen could do was to make it a Black September for their victims.

The 28th Aero lost Lieutenant George Woods to the Germans, brought down by flak (FZ69) although his loss has been variously quoted as being on the 12th, 13th, and 14th.

	A/C	KB		DES	OOC	KB
British losses	1	–	British claims	–	–	–
French losses	5	–	French claims	–		1
American losses	15	–	American claims	7		1
IAF losses	–		IAF claims	–	–	
German claims	16	–	German losses	?†		1

† Certainly no apparent personnel lost.

British Casualties

Aircraft type	No.	Squadron	Crew	
BF2b	E2527	48 Sqdn	Lt H A Cole	POW
			2/Lt C R Gage	POW

French Casualties

Bréguet XIV		Br.29	Lt G Mariage	KIA	
			S/Lt J Lavidalie	KIA	
Bréguet XIV		Br.29	Lt M de Quatrebarbes	KIA	
			Sgt Delhommeau	WIA	
Bréguet XIV		Br.13	Cmdt Rocard	MIA	
			Lt L C de Loisy	MIA	
Bréguet XIV		Br.132	Sgt C Godin	MIA	
			Sgt P Aligros	MIA	
Bréguet XIV		Br.128	Sgt E Carbone	MIA	
			Cpl L Mallet	MIA	
Bréguet XIV		Br.13	Lt Renon	WIA	*
			Lt Giquel	WIA	*

American Casualties

Salmson 2A2	3203	1st Aero	1/Lt H D Aldrich	WIA
			1/Lt D Ker	KIA
DH4	3214	8th Aero	1/Lt H W Mitchell	POW
			2/Lt J W Artz	POW
Salmson 2A2		12th Aero	Maj L H Brereton†	Safe
			Capt Vallois (Fr)	WIA
Salmson 2A2		12th Aero	1/Lt D Arthur	Safe
			1/Lt H T Fleeson	Safe
DH4	3229	50th Aero	1/Lt H L Stevens	KIA
			2/Lt F H Gardner	KIA

Aircraft type	No.	Squadron	Crew	
Bréguet XIV	4495	96th Aero	1/Lt A H Gundelach DSC	KIA
			2/Lt H P Way DSC	KIA
Bréguet XIV		96th Aero	1/Lt G M Crawford	POW
			2/Lt J A O'Toole	POW
Bréguet XIV		96th Aero	1/Lt E M Cronin	Killed
			2/Lt L C Blacker	Inj
Salmson 2A2	1143	104th Aero	1/Lt D Johnson	KIA
			Cpl A D Johnson	Evaded
DH4		135th Aero	2/Lt J W Bowyer	KIA
			1/Lt A T Johnson	KIA
DH4		135th Aero	1/Lt W C Suiter DSC	KIA
			2/Lt G E Morse DSC	KIA
DH4		135th Aero	1/Lt T J D Fuller	Interned
			1/Lt V Brookhart	Interned
Spad XIII	15137	139th Aero	1/Lt D E Putnam	KIA
Spad XIII		22nd Aero	2/Lt V R McCormack	KIA
Spad XIII		103rd Aero	Capt R C Bridgeman	Safe *
Spad XIII		28th Aero	1/Lt G B Woods	POW

† Lewis Brereton later became Lieutenant-General of the USAAF.

13 SEPTEMBER 1918
M T W T **F** S S

British Front

As in April 1917, the flyers in September 1918 had to contend with a Friday the 13th. On this second day of the Saint-Mihiel offensive there were low clouds and high winds with rain that only began to clear in the afternoon.

There was extremely limited action on the RAF front due to the weather. In fact the first action did not occur until 1050, Jasta 35b engaging DH4 bombers, claiming one – Leutnant Rudolf Stark with Vizefeldwebel Hofmann at Recourt. However, there were no RAF losses this day, except an observer in 48 Squadron being wounded. Perhaps once more, identification was poor and the DH4s were in fact Bristols. At 1500 in the afternoon, Leutnant Josef Jacobs, the highly successful air fighter and CO of Jasta 7 recently back from leave following his award of the Pour le Mérite, claimed an RE8 in the Kemmel-Bailleul area, but inside Allied lines.

At 1750, Lieutenant A E Reed of 29 Squadron claimed a black-fuselaged Halberstadt two-seater south-east of Doulemont, but again there are no known two-seater losses. The final claim of the day was a Fokker biplane to the 17th Aero, one of two that had been attacking a 13 Squadron RE8 at 1850. This may have been Leutnant Karl Plauth of Jasta 20, who was shot down but not wounded on this date. The only real success was a balloon of the British 8th Company which Leutnant Martin Demisch of Jasta 58 burnt near Monchy-le-Preux at 1840 for his 9th victory.

During the evening, however, the most successful fighter unit of the RAF in WWI, at least in terms of a victory to loss ratio, made their first claim of the month. They were 151 Squadron, specialised night fighters, flying Sopwith Camels. Flying at night they hunted German night bombers, mostly caught by searchlights. Manned by highly experienced night flyers from extensive service countering night bombing against England, 151 would score a total of 26 victories for no loss to enemy action by the war's end.

At 15 minutes past nine o'clock, Captain W H Haynes in E5142 shot down a Gotha GV near Bapaume, in flames. Haynes also had another success as his combat report notes:

> 'At 9.15, I observed EA at 7,000 ft travelling west, held in the Péronne and Somme searchlights. I closed to about 25 yards and below the EA's tail and fired two bursts of 30 rounds each. The EA immediately burst into flames and fell near Manancourt.
>
> 'I then proceeded to my patrol at Bapaume. At 9.45 p.m. I saw an EA travelling NW at 8,500 ft over Bapaume, being held in a concentration of searchlights. I was some distance away and EA turned ENE and passed out of range of the searchlights, when he turned west again. I observed EA's exhaust and followed, eventually overtaking him.
>
> 'I closed to within 50 yards and took up a position behind and below the EA's tail. I fired two bursts of 50 rounds each; the EA immediately turned to the right and went down. I could follow his course downwards by the exhaust, the sparks from which increased in number. I last saw him going down in a slow spiral about five miles NE of Bapaume. I did not see it crash.'

Haynes' first kill was witnessed by the CO of 151, Major C J Quintin-Brand DSO MC. At 2150, a Friedrichshaven GIII of Kampstaffel 1 of Bogohl 1 was shot down by Lieutenant E P Mackay in F1979 of 151, near Moislains; the crew of Leutnants Kole, Schwaderer and Gefreiter Vowinkel were all captured. Mackay's Camel was equipped with two 'speeded up' Vickers guns.

French Front

Again action was limited. On the French II Armée front, three aircraft of Br.225 were on artillery spotting duties between Conflans and Jarny. Suddenly they were attacked by a dozen Fokkers. The two Bréguets acting as protection had their controls shot away and were forced to land in the front lines, with one gunner wounded. The spotting Bréguet was reported missing, but strangely there are no matching German claims!

All other French activity were by units now attached to the Americans.

American Sector

The operational orders to the Pursuit Groups from the 1st Pursuit Wing required 'barrier patrols', layered in altitude and in multiples of four, giving a minimum strength of eight Spads. Serviceability and weather would intervene. The other hindering factor was that the 2nd Pursuit Group ordered patrols of five with the top cover from another squadron. The 3rd Pursuit Group allowed all four squadrons – the 28th, 93rd, 103rd and 213th – to strafe roads; a significant move, as will be seen.

All morning, patrols were hampered by low cloud – down to 100 metres at times – and storms. That they were flown at all is one of the advances from 1917. At 1006, the 22nd Pursuit sent out a patrol, with a DH4 of the 20th Aero bringing up the rear, to the area north of Thiaucourt. However, the 'Four' was hit by flak, or suffered engine trouble, and had to land. This experiment of a DH4 flying at the rear of a Spad formation was soon abandoned as useless, the bomber simply being unable to keep station. The 95th's patrol, 1045-1145, came back without Lieutenant Butz, who force-landed near Rampont and smashed his machine. He was unhurt although there is nothing noted as to the cause, but it was possibly ground fire. Another patrol by this unit around midday was out ground strafing, three Spads being forced down, but with no losses.

A special mission by nine Spads of the 93rd departed at 1145, returning without Lieutenant C P Nash, a member of the US Marine Corps. He was probably shot down by Jasta 13, the unit which claimed three Spads over Allamont during the late morning. One went to Franz Büchner, his 24th, another to his brother Felix, his 1st, and one to Vizefeldwebel Albert Haussmann, his 14th. The Büchner brothers also had unconfirmed claims each but obviously insufficient evidence to produce a confirmed victory. Although these are not timed, they were all in the morning.

Gustav Klaudat of Jasta 15 was also credited with a Spad at 1355 over Vionville, the first of two kills for him for the day. This was a machine from the 213th Aero, Lieutenant Frank Sidler.

If Klaudat's is included with Jasta 13's total, they total six. No other JGII claim time is before 1620 hours Allied time. Furthermore, we know what Jasta 13 and 15's pilots were doing later in the day as they nearly had a total disaster!

What occurred was this: as Leutnant Werner Neithammer wrote in *Kamp und Sieg Fines Jagdgeschwader,* both Büchner brothers, Georg von Hantelmann and Neithammer, set off by car with Leutnant Kurt Hetze to visit the front, looking for confirmation of the six claims. Near Woël, the car was strafed by a lone Spad. Evacuating the car with alacrity, the combat veterans were not silly enough to hide under the vehicle but nearby. However, on the second attack Hetze was wounded in the back, bringing his war to an end. He had five victories. The unknown Spad pilot had not only wounded one ace, but had so nearly taken out two more major aces, as well as a future ace! That would have been one of the most effective strafing attacks of the war. Unfortunately for the French and Americans, Büchner and Hantelmann in particular, would soon exact extreme revenge. It also shows the lengths German pilots went to get confirmation of aircraft shot down, and on this occasion, failed to get any and nearly lost their lives in the attempt!

At 1430, a Salmson flight of the 8th Aero headed out, one falling victim to the star turn of Jasta 18, Leutnant Hans Müller, west of Thiaucourt for his 7th victory. A second crew, Lieutenants C H Johnson and E West, returned to make a safe landing, despite being wounded. Another DH4 crew, this time from the 50th Observation Squadron, were forced to fly low because of cloud and came under intense ground fire. They continued their mission as far as six miles into German territory but the observer, Lieutenant F D Bellows, was hit and killed. Lieutenant D C Beebe brought his riddled 'Four' back and both men received DSCs – Bellows' posthumously.

It was not until 1535 that the next air action was recorded. Four Bréguets of the 96th Squadron raided Chambley, although one dropped out with engine trouble.

The others ran into Jasta 19, and although the Germans claimed three – Beaulieu-Marconnay and Leutnant Gewart at Chéry at 1720 (G), and Leutnant Scheller at Rembercourt – only two Bréguets failed to get back.

A flight of 13 Spads from the 28th Aero left on a low bombing and strafing attack at 1610 and 35 minutes later, over Jouy, were engaged by three Fokkers. Lieutenant W S Stephenson, the leader, was last seen in combat with a Fokker, a victim of either von Hantelmann (obviously after his car trip) south-west of Thiaucourt at 1707, or Vizefeldwebel Hans Christian Donhauser of Jasta 17, who claimed a Spad at about the same time.

Meantime, 10 Spads from the most experienced Pursuit Squadron – the 103rd – were attacked by Fokkers at 1700, losing Lieutenant Eugene B Jones in flames at Buvières, north of Chambley. Lieutenants Frank O'D Hunter, a 23-year-old from Georgia, and Gorman deFreest Larner, a 22-year-old from New York, who was also a veteran of seven months and two victories with the French Spa.86, avenged the loss, claiming a Fokker as out of control, apparently on fire. Larner had seen the Spad fall in flames and was then attacked by six Fokkers and an Albatros C-type. When the Fokker began to spin down, Hunter followed up the attack as the Fokker pulled up and it spun away again. Both men recieved DSCs for this action. Other US pilots claimed an Albatros DV and a Fokker, plus a Pfalz in flames. In WWII, Hunter, as a major-general, commanded the Fighter Command element of the US 8th Air Force in Europe.

Also involved in this fight was a patrol of the 93rd Aero. Seven of their Spads were in the area between 1705 and 1720, Lieutenant Charles D'Olive, from Alabama, aged 21, claimed three Fokkers; the first two were shared with Lieutenant George Furlow of the 103rd.

One of the French escadrilles aiding the Americans in the action was Spa.94, who shared a Fokker between three pilots. One was Sous Lieutenant Andre Martinot de Cordou, a 25-year-old veteran of three years of combat flying, and typical of the long serving, successful pilots that formed the backbone of the typical French Escadrilles.

Caporal Boulard of Spa.155 was shot down in flames, north of Pont-à-Mousson from 3,500 metres, his demise witnessed by the Americans of the 147th Aero. Oberleutnant Oskar von Boenigk, commander of JGII, claimed a Spad at 1715 over this location for his 23rd victory. Spa.155 claimed a Fokker over Chambley at 1750, credited as the 5th and final victory of 26-year-old Sergent Paul Montange. Vizefeldwebel Klaudat made his 2nd kill of the day at 1720, south-east of Metz. The German losses in this action were Leutnants Siebert of Jasta 15, crash-landed, and Leutnant Eugen Kelber, of Jasta 12, on only his 3rd combat flight, crashed in flames over Mars-le-Tour, probably the victim of Lieutenants L S Harding and L S Carruthers of the 93rd.

Leutnant Rudolf Rienau of Jasta 19 was shot down north of Chéry at 1900, during a fight with six Spads. He was following one Spad but was then hit from above and behind by another and his controls were shot away. He tried to keep control but finally had to bale out, but due to his delayed jump (from 550 metres), he was only claimed as 'out of control'. The victors were five Spads of the 13th Pursuit that had flown out at 1745, but did not see him jump. One US pilot would fail to return, however, Lieutenant Rob Roy Converse being shot down and captured by what he described as a black-tailed Fokker. He was the 2nd victory of Leutnant Max Klieforth

Oberleutnant Oskar von Boenigk commanded Jagdesgechwader II in September 1918, having already achieved 20 victories flying with Jastas 4 and 21. In September he claimed five Allied aircraft on the Saint-Mihiel front, to bring his wartime score to 26. He received the Pour le Mérite. A major-general in the Luftwaffe in WWII he died in a Russian POW camp in 1946.

of Jasta 19. Leutnant Oliver Beaulieu-Marconnay claimed another in Allied lines but there were no other Spad losses. Lieutenant J D Este was nearly shot down and had his engine cut out but it caught again and he survived.

IAF

The IAF bombers dropped over five tons of bombs on Ars, Metz, Mars-le-Tour and Arnaville during the day. In the morning these were flown by formations, but also by solo raiders, helped by the weather. After midday, a 104 Squadron crew claimed a Pfalz DIII out of control, south of Metz at 1300 while bombing Metz-Sablon aerodrome. The DH9s of 99 Squadron had a scrap east of the Moselle River at 1725, Leutnant Hugo Schäfer of Jasta 15 downing one near Pont-à-Mousson at 1740, one of two that failed to return. The other bomber had been tasked to bomb a bridge north-east of Ars. Its pilot was an American, Lieutenant F A Wood, with Lieutenant C Bridgett in the back.

Other crews, two of 99 and one of 104 Squadrons, had wounded on board, one observer mortally, with one machine also having to force-land in Allied lines. Vize-feldwebel Klose of Jasta 54s was credited with one kill at Pont-à-Mousson at 1650, Vizefeldwebel Kurt Delang of the same unit given the other at St Geneviève at the same time.

The night bombers lost one Handley Page (216 Squadron), with another returning from an attempted raid on Buhl airfield with a burning engine, having been hit by flak as it went over the lines. The pilot got it down with its full bomb load at base.

	A/C	KB		DES	OOC	KB
British losses	–	–	British claims	4	–	–
French losses	2	–	French claims			
American losses	8	?	American claims	15		–
IAF losses	3	–	IAF claims	1	2	–
German claims	21	1	German losses	5		–

British Casualties

Aircraft type	No.	Squadron	Crew		
BF2b	–	48 Sqdn	2/Lt G C Schofield (O)	WIA	*
DH9	D1670	99 Sqdn	2/Lt E E Crosby	KIA	
			2/Lt C P Wogan-Browne	KIA	
DH9	D3218	99 Sqdn	Lt F A Wood USAS	KIA	
			Lt C Bridgett	KIA	
DH9	D1668	99 Sqdn	Capt V Beecroft	Safe	
			Lt H S Notley	WIA	*
DH9	B9347	99 Sqdn	2/Lt T H Swann	Safe	
			2/Lt J L Hunter	WIA	
DH9	D1050	104 Sqdn	2/Lt R H Rose	Safe	*
			2/Lt T J Bond	DOW	
DH9	D3263	104 Sqdn	Lt O L Malcolm	Safe	*
			Lt H Alexander	Safe	
HP O/400	3131	216 Sqdn	Lt R W Heine	POW	
			Lt F F Jewett USAS	POW	

Aircraft type	No.	Squadron	Crew	
HP O/400	D4590	100 Sqdn	Lt E A Marchant	POW
			Lt J H L Gower	Safe *
			Lt W B Warneford	Safe
			Lt R Shillinglaw	Safe

French Casualties

Spad XIII		Spa.155	Cpl P Boulard	MIA
Bréguet XIV		Br.225	Sgt de Kermal	MIA
			S/Lt Girard	MIA
Bréguet XIV		Br.225	Sgt Metairie (M)	WIA *
Spad XIII		Spa.102	Sgt G de la Guerande	POW

American Casualties

DH4		8th Aero	1/Lt H B Rex	KIA
			2/Lt W F Gallager	KIA
DH4		8th Aero	2/Lt C H Johnson	WIA *
			1/Lt E West	WIA
Spad XIII	4413	13th Aero	1/Lt R R S Converse	POW
Spad XIII		28th Aero	Lt W S Stephenson	KIA
DH4		50th Aero	2/Lt D C Beebe	Safe *
			2/Lt F B Bellows	KIA
Spad XIII	7577	93rd Aero	1/Lt C P Nash	POW
Bréguet XIV	12006	96th Aero	1/Lt T W Farnsworth	KIA
			2/Lt R E Thompson	KIA
Bréguet XIV	4493	96th Aero	2/Lt S T Hopkins	KIA
			1/Lt B Williams	KIA
Spad XIII	15302	103rd Aero	1/Lt E B Jones	KIA
Spad XIII	–	139th Aero	1/Lt R O Lindsay	WIA *
Spad XIII	15089	213th Aero	1/Lt F Sidler	KIA

14 SEPTEMBER 1918

M T W T F **S** S

British Front

Low clouds prevailed on this front but the weather was better than the previous few days, with little rain. In consequence, aerial activity increased.

The first combat was at 0800, north-east of Vermand, between a patrol of 46 Squadron and a grey-coloured C-type. Captain Charles W Odell, who had started his second tour on 20 August, made his third victory claim and his first on a Camel. Odell was still only 19, and shared the victory with Lieutenant Nigel Bruce, an Englishman who would die in an accident on 19 September. Bruce had been with the squadron since 23 April 1918. Lieutenant Peter F Paton, a 19-year-old Scotsman, also shared in this kill. He had been with the squadron for five weeks, and 15 minutes later would burn a balloon in the same area.

The next claim was also a balloon, this time west of Quesnoy, between Armentières and Lille, to the SE5a pilot Captain Lagesse of 29 Squadron. This was at 1010, with the next combat following at 1020, by an RE8 crew of 12 Squadron. A Fokker had just burnt a balloon and was attacked and shot down by Lieutenants P F Bovington and H P Elliott at Graincourt. The Fokker fell burning, confirmed by 62nd Division troops.

Five minutes later another RE8 crew – 59 Squadron – shot down another Fokker in flames during a photo mission, described as being green, red and black:

> 'When SE of Ribecourt, a Fokker attacked us and we made a running fight at about 65 mph, continually keeping machine in turns. South of Havrincourt the Fokker did an Immelmann turn to the left at the right of our tailplane. We did a gradual turn to the right and observer opened fire into him at 20 yards' range and set his cockpit on fire. He went down in a steep dive with flames and smoke coming from the cockpit and flattened out at 1,000 ft. We saw him crash south of Marcoing with smoke coming from the wreck. Another RE8 fired from a range of about 800 yards; our machine was badly shot about.'

This was the approved RE8 defensive technique: turn and lose height at as slow a speed as possible, to force the attacker to overshoot, or pull out where the observer could shoot at it. Despite these definite claims, there are no corresponding Fokker losses this day. The cockpit fire sounds like the signal flares being hit and ignited which would certainly encourage the Fokker pilot to land quickly.

Two claims were made for RE8s during the day, one at either end of the front. To the north Leutnant Friedrich Kresse of Jasta 7 got one south-east of Ypres in Allied lines, while to the south, Leutnant Paul Baümer of Jasta 2 shot down one near Vermand. Kresse's victim was a 4 Squadron machine. It is possible that Baümer fought the 59 Squadron machine and if so, then neither side inflicted permanent damage.

To finish off the morning's activities, 84 Squadron burnt three balloons at 1030, credited to Captain Southey at Gonnelieu, Lieutenant Highwood at Bantouzelle and Second Lieutenant D C Rees, a 23-year-old South African with three years service with the Royal Engineers, but less than a month with 84, one at Bantouzelle too. Earlier in the patrol, Leutnant Fritz Rumey of Jasta 5 had picked off Lieutenant John E Reid, an 18-year-old Scotsman from Inverness, who had been out four months. He went down over Le Catelet, the German's 34th victory.

The only claim in the afternoon was once again to veteran Captain George Gates of 201 Squadron. He brought his score to 12 by downing a two-seater of FA17 crewed by Unteroffizier Erich Reinecke and Leutnant Dietgen von Salis-Marschlins, who were both killed near Villers-Plouich at 1325 (A).

The Germans were active as Unteroffizier Lohrmann of Jasta 42 downed a DH9 which fell in Allied lines at 1432, followed at 1640 by Leutnant Friedrich Noltenius of Jasta 27, flaming the 5th KBS balloon (SR135) at Vis-en-Artois. This balloon had in fact been packed with explosives, and was detonated from the ground with the intention of taking the attacker with it. Noltenius had a narrow escape as his diary records:

'I planned to take off at noon for a balloon attack but the engine ran too badly. At 1730, after new magnetos had been installed, I finally took off. There were clouds at 4,000 metres and a thin layer at 2,000 metres. At an altitude of 3,000 I flew towards the front. And then, with the engine throttled back, flew deeper and deeper into enemy territory, until I was in position behind the balloons. At the Arras-Cambrai road, near Vis-en-Artois, I clearly saw the yellow balloon.

'Enemy single-seaters were nowhere in sight. As thin veils of cloud passed below me, I started my dive. I dived in the direction of and in front of the balloon, until I was a bit lower and then pulled up to lose speed (if the prop revved too fast, there was danger of the bullets hitting the blades). As soon as I was on the same level as the balloon, I applied full throttle and flew directly towards it. At a distance of 300 metres I began to fire and closed in, firing continuously. I only wanted to press the attack home when suddenly, while I was a mere 50 metres away, a gigantic flame arose, which completely engulfed me! The shock hurled me away. I at once took course for the lines after I had discovered that the machine was still in flying condition. But what a shambles she was!

'The cloth covering had become completely slack all over the machine and billowed. Large shreds of balloon cloth hung in the struts and in the empennage. The controls acted perfectly differently. To movements of the rudder, the plane did not react at all. In addition, the plane was excessively tail heavy. In this condition I would have been unable to survive in a dogfight. Fortunately the strong western wind carried me home to our lines very quickly and I was able to land safely on our field.'

Ground fire found targets this day. A two-seater of FA26 was brought down near Langemark, Unteroffizier Böhm being wounded, Leutnant Walter Stangen killed. Second Lieutenant W A Johnston of 201 was brought down too and taken prisoner, while Major Tanner of 80 Squadron was badly shot about but got home. Also during the day, Captain E J K McCloughry of 4 AFC attacked Ennetières aerodrome from 200 feet, claiming to have destroyed two LVGs on the ground and bombing a hangar.

French Front

The weather was a lot better to the south, along the French front, with cloud banks interrupted by the first periods of sun for some days. Once again most of the French activity was in support of the Americans' offensive at Saint-Mihiel, which was drawing to a successful conclusion with the elimination of the salient. The German airmen were also more organised; as a consequence the activity was intense.

During the morning, 42 aircraft from Groupement Duseigneur of the Division Aérienne dropped 6,440 kilos of bombs on Conflans and Jonville. As they were soon to discover, bombing a railway station adjacent to JGII's airfield was a dangerous pursuit.

During the course of this expedition at 0940, a strong enemy patrol of over 20 planes attacked the formation en masse. The resulting combat lasted 35 minutes and eight German aircraft were claimed shot down. However, eight French machines were lost, four Bréguet 14 B2s from Br.132, one from Br.131 and one from Br.243.

Leutnant Hermann Becker included five September 1918 victories in his final score of 23, flying with Jasta 12. Five of these were day bombers from the 11th and 20th US Aero Squadrons.

Two escorting Caudron R.XI gunships were also shot down with another badly damaged, and of its three-man crew, one was dead and a second wounded.

The attacking Germans were from JGII, which had received 17 new Fokkers the previous day. They were supported by Jasta 65, which had been directly subordinated to von Boenigk's Circus. Leutnant Wilhelm Frickert and Vizefeldwebel Josef Hohly of Jasta 65 both accounted for Caudrons, while Felix Büchner claimed another for Jasta 13 at Conflans. The eight Bréguets went to Leutnant Hermann Becker, CO of Jasta 12, Franz Büchner, and Leutnants Grimm and Neithammer of Jasta 13, each with one, while Jasta 19 chipped in with three: von Beaulieu-Marconnay, Leutnants Rudolf Rineau and Max Klieforth also one each. The eighth kill went to Vizefeldwebel Hasenpusch of Jasta 67. It was the single biggest loss of Bréguets during the war.

At 1000, an aircraft of Sal.280 departed on a surveillance patrol over the V Armée sector and failed to return. During the afternoon, the bodies of Adjutant Giafferi and Lieutenant Arquis were found near Veil-Arcy, completely burnt. Jasta 45's Offizierstellvertreter Gustav Dörr had his 27th victory, although he claimed it as a Spad XI.

Leutnant Werner Preuss of Jasta 66 also engaged an unidentified aircraft for his 16th victory, probably Sergent Georges Fuoc of Spa.160. Lieutenant Jacques Senart, the commander of Spa.160 and a 27-year-old Parisian, claimed the newly established GC23's first kill, a Fokker, during the day in the I Armée sector, possibly in this combat.

At 1020 (G), Jasta 50 claimed two Spads at Révillon, by Leutnants Buddeberg and Maletzky. Révillon is south of the Aisne River, west of Pont Arcy. In this area Spa.152 lost Maréchal-des-Logis Alain de Freslon, and in return Sergent Couderc claimed a probable Fokker. At 1200 (G), Leutnant Walter Blume of Jasta 9 shot down a Spad at Braye, north-east of Pont Arcy, Spa.92 losing Sergent Bernon at about this time.

In the afternoon, the Gernicourt balloon was burnt at 1345 (A) followed by the Cormicy balloon five minutes later. These went down under the combined fire of Michel Coiffard, Sous Lieutenant Condemine and Caporal Lisle of Spa.154.

Things were now warming up considerably. A machine from Br.287 took off at 1400 hours on a recce flight and ran into Jasta 45's Leutnant Koennemann, who claimed a Salmson at Fismes at 1520. Then the Germans launched a series of attacks on balloons along the French and American sectors. At Mailly, south of Reims, the youngest Jasta commander ever, the 19-year-old Max Näther (he had been a Jasta commander at 18!), burnt the 76 Cié balloon at 1535, his 13th of an eventual 26 victories. He would survive the war only to be killed in January 1919 in a border war with Poland.

Before and after this time, but further south-west, near Verdun, the balloons of 25, 30 and 31 Cié were burnt between 1530 and 1538, by Unteroffizier Hans Heinrich Marwede of Jasta 67, which brought his score to four. His next claim on 3 October was filmed by an American film unit, as he burnt the 6th USBC balloon, followed immediately by him being filmed shot down and captured by the balloon's defences – a unique bit of footage. Two further balloons were shot down during the day, those of 29 and 57 Cié, one being credited to Leutnant Christiansen of Jasta 67.

Adjutant Georges Halberger and Maréchal-des-Logis Emmanuel Aubailly of Spa.153 claimed a balloon near Saint-Mihiel, but the unit lost Maréchal-des-Logis

Pierre de Villeneuve, in flames, at 1650 near Erbeviller. Oberleutnant Gottlieb Rassberger of Jasta 80b shot down a Spad in flames by Champenoux, which is about two kilometres south-east of Erbeviller.

A GC17 patrol, consisting of Sous Lieutenant Maurice Boyau, Caporal Edward J Corsi (an American) of Spa.77 and Sous Lieutenant Claude Marcel Haegelen of Spa.100, attacked and flamed a balloon near Étraye at 1745, for their 32nd, 1st and 15th victories respectively. Boyau had been flying fighters for two years with Spa.77 and was its leading pilot. This was his 18th balloon. Aged 30, he was a former captain of the French rugby team. Haegelen

Lieutenant M J-P Boyau brought his victory total to 35 in September with four balloons between the 14th and 16th. He flew with Spa.77 but after gaining his final victory he was shot down and killed by the German ace Georg von Hantelmann of Jasta 15.

was one of the big French aces of 1918, with 20 victories in that year to add to his two in 1917 flying with Spa.3, before being wounded. He had turned 22 the previous day and this was his 8th balloon. The claim was valid, for the Austrian balloon of the k.u.k. Balloonkompanie 13 was lost at 1745.

American Sector

Thirty aircraft from the 1st Day Bombardment Group departed at 0645 to bomb the Conflans rail centre, an hour or so before the French attack already mentioned. On their way back they too were intercepted. The American Liberty-engined DH4s of the 11th Squadron bombed from 3,000 metres, which was the first bomb raid by such aircraft. The squadron was engaged by pilots of Jasta 15 of JGII, the Geschwader being on its way to 80 sorties and 19 victories for this day. Two 'Fours' were shot down and in return the DH's gunners claimed two Fokkers.

Leutnant von Hantelmann got one, Vizefeldwebel Weischer the other. One of those brought down was Lieutenants F T Shoemaker and R M Groner's machine. Shoemaker got his aircraft down despite nine wounds and did not regain consciousness for five days. Groner was wounded in the leg and did not realise his pilot was wounded until the DH spiralled into a forest.

The 3rd Pursuit Group, the least experienced (with the exception of the 103rd Aero), was out early too and the 28th Aero made its first claim of the war during the 0630 patrol – a Fokker in a spin credited to the unit. Twenty minutes later two more Fokkers were claimed shot down.

The big fight of the day involved Charles Biddle's 13th Pursuit, who were out at 0715, 16-strong. Near Preny the patrol had just driven off some Fokkers from the returning 1st Bombardment Group as more Fokkers came at them, sporting the red and white fuselages of Jasta 18. Four of the Americans went down, three into captivity, one dead. In return the Americans claimed two Fokkers, one being Leutnant Günther von Büren, who had claimed one Spad before being wounded. The other three Spads were all shot down by 22-year-old Leutnant Hans Müller, bringing his score to ten.

At 0840, Leutnant Max Gossner, the 24-year-old commander of Jasta 77, burnt the 5th US Company balloon at Pont-à-Mousson, the first of three kills he would score this day. On the other side, the 27th Aero claimed a balloon destroyed at 1000 at Boinville, although it did not burn.

Twenty minutes later more Spads were in trouble north-west of Lachaussée with JGII. The Germans ran into a patrol of the 95th Aero near Hannonville, Oskar von Boenigk claiming two, and indeed, two 95th pilots were forced down. Lieutenant Sumner Sewall – a future ace – got his burning machine down, while Lieutenant John L Mitchell force-landed near Troyon-sur-Meuse.

At 1145, Vizefeldwebel Bernard Ultsch, a 20-year-old Bavarian, claimed his 11th victory – a Spad – while Gossner got his second kill of the day by claiming another. At 1340 Leutnant Müller of Jasta 18 claimed his fourth Spad of the day, down in Allied lines west of Pont-à-Mousson.

While all this was going on, US Salmsons were having trouble too. The 91st Observation Squadron lost a machine on an early patrol, and at 1100 hours three Salmsons of the 99th, on a photo mission, were attacked by nine Fokkers. The two protection machines were shot down into American lines, while the photo machine was heavily damaged, its observer, Lieutenant Raymond C Hill, badly wounded. Clarence C Kahle, his pilot, managed to get back to base but the aircraft was a write-off. Leutnant Eugen Siempelkamp, CO of Jasta 64w, claimed a Salmson at Bonzée at 1100 but was severely wounded this day, perhaps in this fight. Earlier, Oberleutnant Kohze of Jagdgruppe Nr.9 had claimed a DH4 at Pont-à-Mousson.

The 99th tried again after midday, but Gossner of Jasta 77b struck again, over the Forêt de Pertre. He shot up Captain Kenneth P Littauer and Lieutenant Theodore E Boyd of the 88th Aero, one of four protection machines for the 99th photo aircraft. Littauer, his observer severely wounded in the legs and arms, force-landed in the American lines. Littauer, the CO of the 88th, had been a member of the Lafayette Flying Corps since 1916 and had seen action with the French two-seater unit C.74. He was about to be promoted to command the 3rd US Corps Observation Group.

The 27th Aero left on another patrol at 1430, and returned two hours later, having burnt the Étain balloon at 1545. Frank Luke and his partner, Lieutenant Joseph Wehner, had separated from the patrol and attacked. Luke set the 'drachen' ablaze and was planning to attack another but aborted such an idea because of eight Fokker biplanes. Wehner had been heading for another balloon but also broke off due to heavy AA fire, joining up with Luke and the Fokkers. Wehner shot down two Fokkers, one of which he saw spin into the ground near Warcq, and then fired at an Albatros. However, none were confirmed despite far better evidence than a number of other claims that were allowed. The balloon was BZ14, with Vizefeldwebel Munchoff and Gefreiter Gasser taking to their parachutes.

At 1510, nine Spads of the 22nd Aero led by Captain Ray Bridgeman engaged 12 light-blue-fuselaged Fokkers near Mars-la-Tour. Lieutenant Ray Brooks claimed two and shared another with Lieutenant Phil E Hassinger, who was then shot down in flames. Brooks too was shot up and force-landed at Menil-la-Tour. His letter on the fight is most graphic:

> 'We were ten miles behind the lines of the infantry and my chances of escape were so slight I figured I had come to an end. I was frankly scared, but in

spite of much high tension and futile yelling at the top of my voice, I calculated by nature of my training, I suppose, to get as many of the Fokkers as possible before the inevitable.

'The only thing that saved me was that being entirely surrounded, the Germans could not shoot at me without being in their own way. A stream of white ribbons from incendiary bullets and the tracers would cut through my wings so that if I reached out my hand they were close enough to cut it off.

'Twice I tried to ram the Fokkers that had me in a direct line with their guns. One red nose "nightmare" came in from my right and endeavoured to draw me under by playing as a foil with a swoop to my level and then perceptibly below.

'I had just time to dip enough to see his features before I let him have a few incendiary bullets. I wasn't even sorry for him after that. Another I turned upon and after a short close burst, was satisfied that a second had quit, although he did not, like the first, apparently catch fire.

'Two more of the Boche, in their tactical work, happened to get in the way of my line of fire and I finally had the better feeling, finding myself with a good 2,000 metres, directly over the huge, boomerang [shaped] lake with only four of the enemy paying me too much attention to suit me, This was rather more dangerous than with a swarm, because the individuals could far better get a good shot at me where they had less chance of getting in their own way.

'A 220-hp Spad can out-dive a Fokker DVII and for 1,500 metres, with almost full motor, I spun, nose-dived, and slithered, flattening out just over the rolling country, with a fair chance over those four.'

Lieutenant Wilbert W White of the 147th Aero bagged a balloon and three Fokker DVIIs in September. On 10 October, on what would have been his last patrol before going home, he shot down a German two-seater and then, seeing a fellow pilot with a Fokker on his tail, rammed the German machine and was killed. He was recommended for the Medal of Honor but only received an Oak Leaf Cluster to his DSC.

Brooks got away and force-landed just short of his aerodrome. Hassinger was downed by von Hantelmann, claiming the Spad near Lachaussée at 1515. Brooks was claimed by Leutnant Johannes Klein at the same time and place. One of Brooks' victims was reportedly Leutnant Paul Wolff, of Jasta 13, who was captured in an intact Fokker at 1510 near the lake. Vizefeldwebel Schmuckle of Jasta 15 made his 5th claim five minutes later at St Benoît, probably Lieutenant Arthur C Kimber who was comprehensively shot up. He survived but would not out-live the month. On this day he staggered back to base, with his Spad – named 'Nick' and numbered No.12 of the Shooting Stars – having over 70 bullet holes in it.

These Spads had been engaged in opening up a safe zone for observation aircraft, and they partly succeeded, but a 24th Observation Squadron Salmson was caught at 1515, shot down into the American lines by Leutnant Gewart of Jasta 19, near Beney at 1820 (G).

Lieutenant Wilbert W White, a 29-year-old married man with two children – somewhat unusual for a combat pilot – of the 147th Aero, burnt the balloon of Ballonzug 152, east of Chambley at 1645 for his 3rd victory. Five minutes later he claimed a Fokker, for which actions he received the DSC. White would also fail to survive the war, but in a letter to his wife he wrote:

'Had a rather exciting day yesterday. I was out doing some protection work by myself and ran into three fast two-seater Boches between me and the lines. I fired and then turned tail and beat it, they after me, for a part of the lines I could get through. Went down through a little cloud and shook the three

of them and saw an enemy balloon below me so dove on that. They immediately started pulling it down and firing at me from the ground. Just then
two scout planes dove on me from the front. I pulled up and fired point blank
at the first and he went into a nose-dive. The second one, I fired on and then
dove under, crossing the lines and coming home. I put in for confirmation
on both the balloon and the plane. Hope I get them both, but I won't want
another day like that one, I can tell you that much!'

A Spad numbered '19' of Spa.94 was seen to land south of Thiaucourt by an American
balloon crew, after a fight with a German fighter, the enemy pilot being Leutnant
Bacher of Jasta 3. The Frenchman was unhurt.

During the day, Spa.95 claimed a probable two-seater at Vittonville on the Moselle
River, north of Pont-à-Mousson. Just to the north of here, the crew of Feldwebel
Deinlein and Leutnant Georg Baumann of FA(A) 199, were shot down by four
Spads, 27-year-old Baumann being killed. Among the Fokker pilots lost this after-
noon, later reported a prisoner, was Flieger Anton Kempa of Jasta 3.

That low flying was dangerous was shown by a 12th Aero Salmson. Lieutenants
S Orr and Goodale ran into a balloon cable, crashed and were killed.

IAF

The IAF's bombers continued to support the Americans, bombing Metz-Sablon
railway station twice, and Buhl aerodrome once, with 55 Squadron bombing Ehrang
railway junction. On one raid 99 Squadron was intercepted by 20 fighters and a
running fight carried on back to the lines. No.110 Squadron's brand new DH9As
bombed Boulay aerodrome. Oberleutnant Gottlieb Rassberger of Jasta 80b shot
down Second Lieutenants W F Ogilvie and G A Shipton of 99 near Pelter, who
were taken prisoner at 0900, the first of two claims for him this date.

Also during this fight, Second Lieutenant J G Dennis was severely wounded in
the stomach and signalled his observer to take over the controls, but his observer
had also been badly hit and was unable to do so. Dennis then managed to fly the
35 miles back to the aerodrome, keeping in formation and making a good landing.
He received the DFC for his courage, while he lay in hospital, hovering between
life and death, presented in person by General Hugh Trenchard, the IAF's commander. Leutnant Kandt of Jasta 18 also claimed a DH9 near Pelter which may not
have been confirmed. The bombers claimed two enemy fighters shot down.

Night bombers lost two Handley Page O/400s, one from 207, the other from
215, the latter raiding Courcelles.

	A/C	KB		DES	OOC	KB
British losses	2	–	British claims	6	–	5
French losses	15	5	French claims	9		5
American losses	12	?	American claims	12		3
IAF losses	3		IAF claims	2	–	–
German claims	48	6	German losses	6		3†

† On the Fr/US front; British front not known; two fighter pilots also wounded, fate of their aircraft
not known.

British Casualties

Aircraft type	No.	Squadron	Crew	
Camel	E4391	201 Sqdn	2/Lt W A Johnston	POW
SE5a	D6131	84 Sqdn	Lt J E Reid	POW
Camel	B7434	80 Sqdn	Maj F I Tanner	Inj *
RE8	F5905	4 Sqdn	Lt T O Henderson	WIA *
			2/Lt F Butterworth	KIA
SE5a	C9298	92 Sqdn	2/Lt L S Davis	WIA *
DH9A	D3264	99 Sqdn	2/Lt W F Ogilvie	POW
			2/Lt G A Shipton	POW
DH9A	D3215	99 Sqdn	2/Lt J G Dennis DFC	WIA *
			Lt H G Ramsey	WIA
HP O/400	C9683	207 Sqdn	Lt A Tapping	POW
			2/Lt W J N Chalkin	POW
			2/Lt J B Richardson	POW
HP O/400	C9673	215 Sqdn	2/Lt G A Harrison	POW
			2/Lt H Davies	POW
			2/Lt C Guild	POW
DH9	D5581	104 Sqdn	2/Lt G H Knight	WIA
			2/Lt F F Bates	Safe

French Casualties

Aircraft type	No.	Squadron	Crew	
Spad XIII		Spa.83	S/Lt E Gendreau	WIA *
Spad XIII		Spa.160	Sgt G Fuoc	MIA
Spad XIII		Spa.152	MdL A de Freslon	MIA
Bréguet XIV		Br.231	MdL Bernard	Safe *
			Lt Toucane	WIA
Bréguet XIV		Br.226	MdL Jus (O)	WIA *
Salmson 2A2		Sal.280	Adj Giafferi	KIA
			Lt Arquis	KIA
Bréguet XIV		Br.287	Sgt J Bonnet	Safe *
			S/Lt Jounin	KIA
Spad XIII		Spa.153	MdL P de Villeneuve	KIA
Spad XIII		GC 20	Capt R Bailly	POW
Spad XIII		Spa.65	Sgt C Descamps	WIA
Spad XIII		Spa.92	Sgt Bernon	MIA
Spad XIII		Spa. 78	S/Lt P Leroy de Boismarie	POW
Spad XIII		Spa.150	Lt P Many	MIA
Bréguet XIV		Br.132	Lt A Calbet	MIA
			Sgt E Destieux	MIA
Bréguet XIV		Br.132	Lt G de J Villele	MIA
			Cpl G Valiat	MIA
Bréguet XIV		Br.132	Cpl R Fontaine	MIA
			Cpl M Pillot	MIA
Spad XIII		Spa.26	Adj A Vincent	WIA

Aircraft type	No.	Squadron	Crew	
Bréguet XIV		Br.132	Cpl H Mestre	MIA
			Asp E Grant	MIA
Bréguet XIV		Br.131	S/Lt Teilhac	MIA
			Cpl Jacquet	MIA
Bréguet XIV		Br.131	1/Lt C L Nelson US	Safe
			1/Lt J M Newell US	WIA
Bréguet XIV		Br.243	Sgt R Landreux	MIA
			Lt Sabirini	MIA
Caudron R11		C.46	Sgt G Boeglin	MIA
			Sol E Monfils	MIA
			Sol E Ruet	MIA
Caudron R11		C.46	Cpl J Dubuisson	MIA
			Sol J Mantel	MIA
			Sol P Vincent	MIA
Caudron R11		C.46	Lt P Resel	WIA
			Sgt Maj H Lacassagne	WIA
			Sol H Poupougnac	Safe

American Casualties

Aircraft type	No.	Squadron	Crew		
DH4	32615	11th Aero	2/Lt H Shindler	POW	
			2/Lt H Sayre	KIA	
DH4	32251	11th Aero	2/Lt F T Shoemaker	POW	
			2/Lt R M Groner Jr	POW	
Salmson 2A2		12th Aero	1/Lt S Orr	KIA	
			1/Lt K C Goodale	KIA	
Spad XIII	4578	13th Aero	1/Lt C W Drew	POW	
Spad XIII	15206	28th Aero	1/Lt W B Stephenson	KIA	
Spad XIII	15241	28th Aero	1/Lt G B Woods	POW	
Spad XIII	–	213rd Aero	1/Lt I W Fish	WIA	
Spad XIII	4486	13th Aero	1/Lt H B Freeman	POW	
Spad XIII	4562	13th Aero	Lt G P V Kull	KIA	
Spad XIII	15145	13th Aero	Lt A A Brody	POW	
Spad XIII	7580	22nd Aero	1/Lt P E Hassinger	KIA	
Salmson 2A2	3325	24th Aero	1/Lt J J Goodfellow	KIA	
			1/Lt E Durrand	KIA	
Salmson 2A2	–	88th Aero	Capt K P Littauer DSC	Safe	*
			2/Lt T E Boyd DSC	WIA	
Salmson 2A2	3303	91st Aero	1/Lt P H Hughey	KIA	
			Capt K Roper	KIA	
Salmson 2A2	–	99th Aero	1/Lt C C Kahle	Safe	
			1/Lt R C Hill	DOW	
Salmson 2A2	–	99th Aero	1/Lt M W Wickersham	Safe	
			1/Lt C F Spencer	Safe	
Salmson 2A2	–	99th Aero	1/Lt J R Edwards	Safe	*
			1/Lt J Hayes-Davis	Safe	
Spad XIII	–	95th Aero	1/Lt S Sewall	Safe	
Spad XIII	–	95th Aero	1/Lt J L Mitchell	Safe	

1

2

3

1 These four pilots flew Dolphins with 19 Squadron. Lt J A Aldridge, Captain R A Del'Haye, Lt C Montgomery-Moore and Captain J W Crane (US). John Aldridge scored his 5th victory in September, Roger Del'Haye three of his nine victories in September

2 Officers of 203 Squadron, formally 3 Naval Squadron. Most were engaged during September and several of them were Canadian. Back row: left to right: Lts F T S Sehl, Fitzpatrick, Black, R Stone, C H Nelson, O P Adam, C H Lick, J D Breakey, A E Rudge. Centre: L D Bawlf, A T Whealy, Capt H F Beamish, Major R Collishaw (CO), T H Rochford, E T Haynes, Haig (armaments officer). Front: W Sidebottom, A W Carter, J E L Hunter, Bingham (adj), Townsend, N C Dixie, Duke.

3 Pilots of 32 Squadron. L to R: Lts H R Carson, W Amory, A A Callender (US), Maj J C Russell (CO), E C Spicer, M A Tancock, R W Farquhar, Farson. Alvin Callender claimed his last three victories in September, making a total of eight, but was killed the following month. Robert Farquhar, downed his 7th victory on 24 September, but he too was killed in October.

4 Lieutenants G M Comey and R S Bagby, of the Salmson 2A2-equipped 88th Aero, shared the destruction of a Hannover CLIII with another crew on 2 September.

5 No. 2 AFC Squadron flew SE5s, three of their pilots shown her are Lts J A Egan, E E Davies and J J Wellwood. Davies gained hi second of seven victories on 15 September, while Wellwood claimed two of his six this same month. Both received the DFC.

6 1st Lieutenant F Llewellyn DSC by a Salmson 2A2 of the 99th Aero Squadron. He became C Flight Commander on
19 September 019

15 SEPTEMBER 1918

M T W T F S **S**

British Front

The weather was fine for the first time in some days. As a consequence, aerial combats increased considerably. The Germans were out early, Jasta 39 launching a balloon raid in which they burnt the Quéant balloon at 0823, followed by the two at Villers, and one at Drury just minutes later. Among those lost were balloons of the 5th KBS (AR56) and 37th (SR136).

All four victories equalled the best run by a German pilot, Unteroffizier Hans Nülle gaining his 6th to 9th kills.

Captain W R Irwin of 56 Squadron was wounded by Fokkers at 0745, over Bourlon Wood, before the hostile machines left him to attack and burn a balloon. This was of the 43rd KBS, from which Lieutenants H V Williams and R H W Davidson baled out. It would appear Jasta 39 was being escorted by Jasta 34b, as at 0830 Oberleutnant Robert Greim of this unit claimed an SE5 over Hermies, just south-west of Bourlon Wood. The four balloons were just north of this position.

Fifteen minutes later, an 11-man-strong patrol of 201 Squadron met Fokkers and Pfalz DXIIs over Fontaine-Notre-Dame, Captain Reg Brading shooting down one of the latter in flames for his 12th victory. Then 84 Squadron shot down a balloon at Bellicourt at 0850. The Camels of the 148th Aero also had a fight with some Halberstadt Cs over Épinoy.

A big fight developed between 20 Squadron and Jastas 6 and 24 between 1100 and 1120, north-east of Saint-Quentin, one Bristol being lost. Oberleutnant von Wedel, CO of Jasta 24, claimed a Bristol at 1115, and Leutnant Ulrich Neckel another at 1125, both over Estrées. However, the second BF2b, with its observer wounded, force-landed inside British lines. The Bristols claimed eight Fokker DVIIs – four destroyed and four out of control, but none were recorded lost!

Four more Fokkers were claimed by 73 Squadron's Camels to the north, between Cambrai and La Folie at the same time. They lost one machine, Second Lieutenant J A Mathews being taken prisoner. Unteroffizier de Ray of Jasta 58 claimed a Camel during the day for his 1st and only victory.

Leutnant Hermann Leptien of Jasta 63 shot down a 42 Squadron RE8 at 1130, which force-landed west of Armentières. Then, just before midday, Leutnant Wilhelm Kohlbach, a 22-year-old west Prussian, who had begun flying in May 1916 as an observer, claimed a Camel at Cantaing – Sergeant R R Lightbody of 203 Squadron, while the unit was out balloon hunting. Kohlbach had been with Jasta 50 since February 1918 and on 11 August he was transferred to replace the great ace Erich Lowenhardt, head of Jasta 10, who had been killed the previous day. Kohlbach became a bomber pilot in WWII, ending that war as a major-general. He died in a British POW camp in 1947.

Jasta 58 attacked and claimed two balloons at 1305 (G), one west of Wancourt credited to Unteroffizier Kurt Pietzsch, the other to Leutnant Jeep at Vitry. The 5th KBS balloon was reported lost at 1205 (A). The next action came at 1300 (A);

Emil Thuy flew with Jasta 21 in 1917, and commanded Jasta 28 in 1918. Of his 35 victories, four were achieved during September. He received the Pour le Mérite and post-war he remained active in aviation circles, but was killed in a crash in June 1930.

Lieutenant Oren Rose of 92 Squadron shot down a Hannover CLII west of Lille. It is possible that this was an unknown pilot (who survived) and Leutnant Wilhelm Holtfort of FA(A) 236 who was killed near Armentières. Twenty minutes later, Captain H A Whistler of 80 Squadron burnt the balloon at Étricourt.

As if in reprisal, Vizefeldwebel Oskar Hennrich of Jasta 46 shot down a balloon at Bertincourt at 1440, Lieutenants G H Adams and R G A Holbrook taking to their parachutes as they left the 44th KBS balloon's basket.

Meanwhile, up on the coast, 204 Squadron's Camels got into a scrap with some of the Marine Jasta pilots around Zeebrugge, claiming two with another out of control. They lost Lieutenant R C Pattullo, who had just shared one Fokker, falling in flames after being attacked by Leutnant zur See Reinhold Poss of MFJ 4.

Just to be different from dawn aerodrome raids, at 1530 in the afternoon, during a raid lasting 15 minutes, ten SE5s of 56 Squadron attacked Estourmel aerodrome from low level. Thirty-four 25-lb Cooper bombs were dropped and around 1,820 rounds of ammunition fired. The results were claimed as one aeroplane shed destroyed, one hangar on fire, one lorry on fire and two Hannover two-seaters shot up. No. 56 Squadron lost two pilots, Captain Owen Cobb Holleran, an American, and Lieutenant L G Bowen, the former being captured. Laurence Grant Bowen was a 20-year-old Canadian, with just under a month with 56. Holleran had joined 56 on 12 April 1918, and was a 26-year-old from Atlanta. They may have been lost to fighters, as Leutnant Georg Meyer, the 25-year-old CO of Jasta 37, claimed an unidentified fighter at 1700 (G), north of Marcoing. Also claiming an SE5 was Vizefeldwebel Christian Mesch of Jasta 26, near Remy, at an unrecorded time. But most likely they were lost to ground fire.

The next action was again on the coast. Nos. 108 and 218 Squadrons were bombing Bruges when they were intercepted by pilots of MFJ 1 and 5 shortly after 1600 hours. The bombers came under heavy AA fire too, and it was thought three, having been hit, were heading for neutral Holland. However, the German Marine fighter pilots claimed three. One to Leutnant Freymadl of MFJ 1 over the Schelde estuary, the other two to MFJ 5's Flugmaat Karl Engelfried off Walcheren and Flugmeister Kutschke. 218 Squadron lost one bomber too, coming down in the water off the Schelde estuary after being hit by fighters. An escorting 204 Squadron Camel was also shot up and forced to land – understood to be by flak fire.

There was a big fight between 1700 and 1720, involving 1 Squadron's SE5s and 62 Squadron's Bristols. Several German aircraft were thought to be shot down, but only Leutnant Paul Vogel of Jasta 23b was a definite loss, coming down in Allied lines mortally wounded. Vizefeldwebel Ernst de Ridder of Jasta 27 was wounded by an SE5 pilot. Also in action at this time were the Camels of 209 Squadron, mainly against Jasta 28. Leutnant Hilmer Quittenbaum was killed, while Leutnant Emil Thuy, the CO, claimed a Camel for his 29th victory.

A number of other actions became very confused over the late afternoon. The Germans claimed victories but it is difficult to find who they might have been fighting; some claims were for types of Allied machines not even operating. Identification of types was not as easy as one might imagine. Bristols, AWFK8s, DH4s and DH9s could be and were easily misidentified. For instance, Leutnant Wilhelm Neuenhofen of Jasta 27 claimed a SE5a late in the afternoon which was probably a 20 Squadron BF2b. However, a Big Ack (AWFK8) was shot down by Leutnant Josef

Jacobs at 1810 over Passchendaele, which was a machine of 82 Squadron. It was part of a formation bombing Passchendaele railway station, being attacked by two triplanes and six DVIIs, painted black and white. A patrol of 74 Squadron were out looking for them but failed to make rendezvous. It was Jacobs' 26th victory. Another certain victory was scored by Rudolf Stark of Jasta 35b, downing the 19 Squadron Dolphin flown by Second Lieutenant G F Anderson at Cagnicourt at 1805.

Balloons were easier to identify. Jasta 5's Vizefeldwebel Karl Treiber burned the 14th KBS bag west of Fins at 1800 hours, thereby gaining his first victory, but he was to become the last ace of the Jasta. Vizefeldwebel Christian Mesch of Jasta 26 shot down the 8th KBS balloon near Boiry-Notre-Dame at 1830, kill number two for the day for him, bringing his score to 11. Another sure kill was that of Leutnant Georg Meyer, Jasta 37's star, who downed Second Lieutenant H S Smith of 60 Squadron near Bourlon at 1945 (G); that brought his score to 18.

The fighting now intensified over the last hour before sunset. Nos. 24, 29, 54, 74 and 148th were all in action and claiming kills. Even the RE8s got in on the act, a 15 Squadron crew downing a Fokker that had just attacked a balloon, while a 5 Squadron machine was forced down in Allied lines by a Fokker.

As darkness finally fell, 151 Squadron's night flyers were in action, Captain F C Broome shooting down one of the few Zeppelin Staaken Giants (Nr.31/16), flown by Leutnant Wogelmuth of Rfa 500, near Bapaume at 2220. The German pilot survived a prisoner, but the rest of his crew perished in the crash and fire. Broome's commanding officer, Major Quintin-Brand, had less luck, attacking a German bomber in searchlights, hitting one engine which covered his Camel with oil. Despite this, Quintin-Brand continued to engage but finally lost sight of the bomber over Vitry when down to 200 feet. The bomber fired a Red Light, and the Camel was surrounded by ground fire, so Quintin-Brand broke off and headed home, still smothered in thick oil.

Also this night, the RAF lost two FE2b night bombers, raiding German rear areas. All four crew men were captured, one each from 101 and 102 Squadrons.

French Front

In the VIII Armée sector, which was situated on the Vosges mountains, Lieutenant Marc Ambrogi and Adjutant Charles Mace of Spa.90 shot down a balloon at Bourdonnay at 0700. It was Ambrogi's 10th and Mace's 4th victory. Later in the day, two other Spa.90 pilots, Lieutenants Lemarie and de Ginestete, shot down the two-seater of Leutnants Friedrich Gerke and Willy Beck of FA(A) 281 over Raon l'Étape; both were killed. Then at 1130, Adjutant Jean Pezon burnt the Avricourt balloon, making it three kills for Spa.90 and five for Pezon. The Germans lost BZ26 and BZ43 on this sector this day.

At 1230, the indefatigable iron-man, Sous Lieutenant Michel Coiffard of Spa.154, in company with Sous Lieutenant Théophile Condemine and Adjutant Jacques Ehrlich, burnt three balloons, the first at Brimont, a second at Cormicy one minute later, and the third at Gernicourt at 1232. Despite the rapidity of the attack, Coiffard's Spad was badly shot up and he was forced to land near Trepail. But he had gained his 29th-31st victories, Condemine his 5th-7th and Ehrlich his 16th-18th. In all the Germans were to lose 18 balloons during this day's air fighting on the entire Western Front, although the Allies would claim 25.

Top The American ace-of-aces was Captain E V Rickenbacker from Ohio. A former racing driver, he joined the USAS and eventually the 94th Aero Squadron. He was credited with a total of 26 combat victories, six being achieved in September 1918. He was awarded the DSC and nine Oak Leaf Clusters, and the French Légion d'Honneur. Twelve years after the war he was awarded the Medal of Honor for an action that occurred on 25 September 1918. **Bottom** Lieutenant G V Daladier of Spa.93 (note the Stork badge above his medals, serving with N.73 in 1917). Gustave Daladier ended the war with 12 victories, four during September 1918. He remained in the French air force post-war.

At 1400, in the Aisne sector, the balloon of 54 Cié was flamed, its observer parachuting down. Three more were burnt in the X Armée sector, from the 28, 83 and 87 Companies, but the observers, Sergent Bosc, Adjutant Dunard and Sous Lieutenant Lemaire, all made safe descents. The balloon of 33 Cié was attacked too, but not flamed and Sous Lieutenant Aasche landed unhurt. Leutnant Hans von Freden of Jasta 50 got the 28 and 87 balloons at 1505 and 1507(A) near Juvigny. Three other claims for balloons, by Leutnants Meixner of Jasta 45, Fritz Höhn and Vizefeldwebel Arthur Korff of Jasta 60, only netted two kills, but it is not known whose is invalid. Another balloon victory this day was claimed by Leutnant Julius Fichter, a 26-year-old former artillery man, now commander of Jasta 67. He downed a balloon at Douaumont, one of the focal points of the Verdun battlefield. It was his 6th victory.

French casualties included Maréchal-des-Logis Raymond Merklen of Spa.154, killed, his Spad receiving a direct hit by flak at 1630. Five minutes later, the ace Sous Lieutenant Louis Gros of the same unit was wounded in combat with an unknown Fokker and forced to land near Lhéry, putting him out of the war.

Another confirmed balloon to the Germans was scored by Unteroffizier Bernard Bartels of Jasta 44, burning the Saint-Simon balloon at 1800(G), the first of his five victories. The French reported this balloon lost. From the French side, another of the aces, the 23-year-old Marcel Nogues of Spa.57, veteran of almost two years as a fighter pilot, admittedly interrupted by his capture on 13 April 1917 and subsequent escape, flamed two balloons. These were at Bois de Buttes at 1850 and Craonne five minutes later, but his Spad was soundly shot up by the defences and he was forced to land near Goussancourt. Another pilot was not so fortunate. Caporal Rouanet of Spa.98, attacking a balloon at Caurel, opposite the IV Armée sector, was hit and forced down east of Cernay.

American Sector

First Lieutenant Edward V Rickenbacker of the 94th Pursuit claimed a Fokker out of control near Bois de Waville at 0810, and was credited with his 8th victory.

Meantime, French units attached to the Americans went for balloons in order to blind the enemy. BZ152 was burned near Goin at 0928, Maréchal-des-Logis Sainz of Spa.94 thereby gaining his first victory. Leutnant Krawlewski baled out safely. Later in the day, near Chambley, Spa.93 burnt a balloon, shared by Lieutenant Gustave Daladier and Sergents Meyniel and Prarond. However, they lost Caporal Goujat, missing in action north-east of Pont-à-Mousson.

Also at an unknown time, Lieutenant Julien Guertiau, who had turned 33 two days earlier, claimed his 8th victory, shared with two other pilots of Spa.97. Three more victories went down to Spa.97 during the day, but the unit lost Sous Lieutenant L Martin.

The 13th Aero had a stiff fight at mid-morning, with several enemy fighters claimed shot down. One of the victorious pilots was Major Carl Spaatz, who was attached to the unit. He would later become a distinguished USAF General who would head Fighter Command of the US 8th Air Force in WWII, then command the US 12th Air Force and later command the Strategic Air Force in the Far East in 1945.

The next fight also involved another man later to command an American Air Force in WWII (5th AF), First Lieutenant George C Kenney and his observer, Second Lieutenant William T Badham, flying with the 91st Aero. They claimed a

Pfalz DIII shot down, two kilometres south-east of Gorze at 1140. Badham was one of the relatively few American observer aces, and would reach his 23rd birthday this month. From Alabama, he lived to reach 95 years.

In the afternoon at 1230, the 1st Aero, who were very aggressive users of their Salmsons, claimed an aircraft near Mamey, claimed by two crews, the pilot of one being Lieutenant William P Erwin. He was by far the most successful USAS two-seater pilot in terms of aircraft shot down, eventually gaining eight kills with his various observers, but this was his 1st. This was in fact a late confirmation, as the initial American summaries say it was not claimed. The Fokker had just burnt two balloons and as will be seen, the German pilot was not lost.

The pilot was the very active Leutnant Max Gossner, of Jasta 77, and he had destroyed the two balloons at 1325(G) near Lironville – from the 1st and 2nd US Balloon Companies, who lost theirs at 1225 Allied time. The observers, Lieutenants F R Burton and H E Dugan had both got out safely. Their ground defences claimed Gossner shot down, as well as the Salmsons having a go, but Gossner just managed to get his badly damaged machine back and down safely.

At 1250, to continue a big day for the major French aces, Maurice Boyau shared in two balloons, to bring his score to 34. These were at Foulgrey and later at La Haie-des-Allieanos at 1330, shared with three other Spa.77 pilots. Then Sous Lieu-tenant Claude Haegelen of Spa.100 and his wingman shared the Chapelet-Chery balloon – BZ55 – at 1520. A second balloon attack by Haegelen and another wingman, this time at Hannonville at 1615, brought success but in fact BZ152 was not destroyed.

Late afternoon saw the team of Frank Luke and Joe Wehner strike again. Luke burnt the balloon south of Boinville (witnessed by pilots of the 213th Aero) and a second near Bois d'Hingry, while Wehner burnt the one to the south-east of the latter location. One of these was BZ35, reported lost at 1743, another being BZ152, which again was not destroyed, although Leutnant Hoffinghoff baled out. Luke reported:

> 'I left formation and attacked an enemy balloon near Boinville in accordance with instructions and destroyed it. I fired 125 rounds. I then attacked another balloon near Bois d'Hingry and fired 50 rounds into it. Two confirmations requested.'

Very late in the evening, Luke was out again, and flamed the balloon near Chaumont at 1950. This was BZ52. Luke's score was now six in three days, a long way clear of the next American in the Saint-Mihiel battle.

During the day, JGII put up 69 sorties and claimed eight victories. Leutnant Oliver von Beaulieu-Marconnay, on his 20th birthday, claimed a Spad XIII at Petry but it was unconfirmed. Leutnant Franz Büchner of Jasta 13 claimed two Spads at Thiaucourt and Lachaussée to make his score 28, and Jasta 19's Leutnants Rienau and Scheller claimed two Spads south of Pagny. The only other Spad claim was by Vizefeldwebel Hohly of Jasta 65 at St Remy. Aside from the American Spad lost, the French lost four Spads in the US sector; the others, apart from the two already mentioned, were Adjutant Edouard Stahl of Spa.150 who fell in flames, and Sergent L Fabel of Spa.95.

Three other claims by JGII were for aircraft of the IAF.

IAF

The IAF sent nine 55 Squadron DH4s to Stuttgart, where Captain Ben Silly MC DFC led the bombing of the Daimler Works. South-east of Strasbourg, EA attacked and 55 claimed two destroyed – one in flames.

Thirteen aircraft of 99 Squadron and 12 of 104 bombed the railways near Metz Sablon. The latter unit claimed one EA but lost three of their DH9s. The Fokkers broke open the 104 formation and then picked on each DH9, attacking right back to the lines. Apart from the three who failed to get back, another just scraped over the lines after being hit in the radiator – Captain R T Gammon and Second Lieutenant P E Appleby in C6264, after claiming a Pfalz DIII destroyed. Two machines got back with wounded observers, one of whom later died.

Jasta 15 had caused all the mayhem, Leutnants Hugo Schäfer, von Hantelmann and Vizefeldwebel Theodor Weischer being the scorers. Leutnant Johannes Klein was slightly wounded.

Once again, a front-line Jasta simply burst open a bomber formation and although the targets were well within range of escorts, none were provided. By the end of September, even the RAF saw the need and 45 Squadron Camels were recalled from Italy to act as escort for IAF bombers and promised re-equipment with the keenly awaited Sopwith Snipes.

The DH9s of 110 Squadron bombed Hagenau aerodrome without loss. During their raids, the IAF's day and night bombers had delivered 21½ tons of bombs.

	A/C	KB		DES	OOC	KB
British losses	21	?	British claims	36	20	5
French losses	6	8?	French claims	13		16
American losses	1	?	American claims	13		4
IAF losses	3		IAF claims	1	–	–
German claims	42†	18	German losses	3‡		18

† Including two to flak and two that landed with engine failure. ‡ Plus two fighter pilots wounded, one two-seater crewman wounded and one killed, plus seven other airmen reported killed, six on the British front and all NCOs; units unknown.

British Casualties

Aircraft type	No.	Squadron	Crew		
FE2b (night)	A5610	102 Sqdn	Lt C B Naylor	POW	
			2/Lt H Mercer	POW	
SE5a	F6420	84 Sqdn	Lt C R Thompson	WIA	*
Camel	F6107	73 Sqdn	2/Lt J A Matthews	POW	
RE8	C2341	52 Sqdn	2/Lt J B Smith	Safe	*
			2/Lt B Shaw	WIA	
BF2b	E2512	20 Sqdn	2/Lt F E Finch	POW/W	
			2/Lt C G Russell	POW	
BF2b	F5816	20 Sqdn	Lt A R D Campbell	Safe	*
			Sgt A J Winch	WIA	
Camel	E4404	203 Sqdn	Sgt R R Lightbody	KIA	

Aircraft type	No.	Squadron	Crew		
RE8	C2649	42 Sqdn	2/Lt R M Marshall	WIA	*
			2/Lt A Mulholland	Safe	
Camel	E4391	201 Sqdn	2/Lt W A Johnston	POW	
DH9	D3107	108 Sqdn	Lt J J Lister	Interned	
			2/Lt F B Cox	Interned	
DH9	D1733	108 Sqdn	Capt W R E Harrison	Interned	
			2/Lt C Thomas	Interned	
DH9	D7336	108 Sqdn	Lt J J Macdonald	Interned	
			2/Lt G E McManus	Interned	
DH9	C2158	218 Sqdn	Lt W S Mars	Interned	
			2/Lt M E Power	Interned	
Dolphin	D5314	19 Sqdn	Lt G F Anderson	POW	
SE5a	C8866	56 Sqdn	Lt L G Bowen (USAS)	KIA	
SE5a	E1291	56 Sqdn	Capt O C Holleran	POW	
BF2b	E2525	62 Sqdn	Lt T H Bradley	KIA	
			2/Lt R H Dilloway	KIA	
SE5a	C1875	1 Sqdn	Lt W Newby	Safe	*
BF2b	D7939	20 Sqdn	2/Lt A R D Campbell	POW	
			Sgt T A Stack	KIA	
AWFK8	C8571	82 Sqdn	2/Lt H T Hempsall	POW	
			Lt J H M Yeomans MC	POW	
SE5a	E4079	29 Sqdn	Lt E F Wright	POW	
Camel	F2144	54 Sqdn	Capt G H Hackwill MC	Safe	*
Camel	E5173	54 Sqdn	2/Lt B Dixon	WIA	
RE8	C2789	5 Sqdn	Capt C F Galbraith DFC	DOW	
			2/Lt E G W Coward	Safe	
SE5a	D6981	60 Sqdn	2/Lt H S Smith	KIA	
RE8	F5894	5 Sqdn	Lt J M Bright	WIA	
			2/Lt E P Eveleigh	WIA	
Camel	E4418	204 Sqdn	2/Lt R C Pattullo	KIA	
Camel	D8221	204 Sqdn	Lt R E Hodgson	KIA	
Camel	D9496	204 Sqdn	2/Lt L P Worthington	Inj	
HP O/400	C9673	215 Sqdn	2/Lt A G Harrison	POW	
			2/Lt H Davies	POW	
HP O/400	C9683	215 Sqdn	2/Lt W J N Chalkin	POW	
			2/Lt J B Richardson	POW	
DH9	D7205	104 Sqdn	2/Lt R H Rose	POW	
			2/Lt E L Baddeley	POW	
DH9	D3263	104 Sqdn	2/Lt A D Mackenzie	KIA	
			2/Lt C E Bellord	KIA	
DH9	D3245	104 Sqdn	2/Lt G L Hall (USAS)	POW/DOW	
			2/Lt W D Evans	POW	
DH9	D532	104 Sqdn	2/Lt A A Baker	Safe	*
			Sgt N E Tonge	WIA	

Aircraft type	No.	Squadron	Crew		
DH9	D3211	104 Sqdn	Lt J Wrightman	Safe	*
			2/Lt W E Jackson	DOW	
FE2b (night)	D3783	101 Sqdn	Lt E T Stockman	POW	
			2/Lt T Payne	POW	
DH9	D3210	211 Sqdn	2/Lt J M Payne	Safe	
			Lt C T Linford	WIA	*
SE5a	D338	56 Sqdn	Capt W R Irwin	WIA	*
FE2b (night)	–	102 Sqdn	Capt R T Jones (P)	WIA	*

		French Casualties			
Spad XIII		Spa.154	S/Lt L Gros	WIA	*
Spad XIII		Spa.154	MdL R Merklen	KIA	
Spad XIII		Spa.92	Sgt H Bernon	MIA	
Spad XIII		Spa.98	Cpl J Rouanet	POW	
Spad XIII		Spa.150	Adj E Stahl	KIA	
Spad XIII		Spa.95	Sgt L Fabel	POW	
Spad XIII		Spa.97	S/Lt L Martin	MIA	
Spad XIII		Spa.93	Cpl Goujat	MIA	

		American Casualties			
Spad XIII	15221	147th Aero	1/Lt E A Love	KIA	
Salmson 2A2		1st Aero	2/Lt J W Corley (O)	WIA	*
Salmson 2A2		91st Aero	2/Lt P D Coles	Safe	*
			Capt A Tabachnik	WIA	
Salmson 2A2		99th Aero	Lt H M Sandford	WIA	*
			Lt W T O'Dell	Safe	

16 SEPTEMBER 1918
M T W T F S S

British Front

From this date, the clocks changed, and for the rest of September (and on to 6 October), Allied and German times were the same.

The weather was fine this day, which led to one of the highest claiming days of the war by the RAF – totalling no fewer than 105! With the best will in the world, this was over-claiming of at least ten times German losses!

Right on dawn, at 0515, a 13 Squadron RE8 took off to patrol the XVII Corps front and was shot down by ground fire, both men being killed. The Camels of 4

AFC started their day off at 0625 by getting into a fight with three black Fokkers, claiming two west of Lille. An hour later, in the same area, the other Australian unit, 2 AFC, covered 4 AFC who were out raiding, and encountered 15 more Fokkers – including triplanes. It is believed the German pilots were Jasta 43, the Aussies claiming one destroyed and four out of control. Leutnant Raesch, one of the leading members of the Jasta, noted in his diary:

> '...we took off with nine machines. This is the first time Jasta 43 has been up to strength. We should have formed two echelons because we ran into nine SE5s who were higher up and who dove on us. Before long, there was a tremendous amount of shooting. The moment I saw one coming at me from behind, I zoomed up, turned and attacked him on a collision course. He spun downward away from me. Burberg was in great difficulty with an Englishman sitting on his rudder, so I began firing at the scout. With my first burst, the Englishman zoomed up, then fell, but I could not follow him as we were in thick air, so I struggled along with the other seven. Victories were not forthcoming for either side.'

Later in the patrol, at 0800, 2 AFC attacked two more Fokkers, one going down out of control, another crashing into Allied lines half a mile south of Droglandt, credited to Captain Roby Manuel (who had also made a claim in the first fight). Manuel landed nearby, discovered the NCO pilot dead in the wreck and buried him. Later, Manuel reported that the pilot had been wearing a parachute, and was made to go back and dig up the German so the parachute could be inspected! This pilot is strongly suspected to be Gefreiter Kurt Brandt of Jasta 51.

Further south, 20 and 23 Squadrons got into a fight near Saint-Quentin at 0815, the Bristol boys claiming four destroyed and three out of control, the Dolphins claiming four more, one of which was also strafed on the ground after it had crashed. Back on the northern sectors, 4 AFC were engaged yet again, destroying three Fokkers over Frelinghien. The only known loss in this sector at this time was Leutnant Friedrich Kresse of Jasta 7, who fell at Houplines. But he may have been lost during a fight with 29 Squadron that followed this action – see later.

Then down by Cambrai at 0830 11 Squadron, on a recce show, ran into 25-30 Fokkers of JGIII in company with Jasta 5. Three Bristols were shot down, one by Leutnant Helmut Lange of Jasta 26, north-east of Quiévy at 0850; Fritz Rumey claimed his 35th victory west of Villers Guislain, while Bruno Loerzer got his 39th at Doignies on the Bapaume-Cambrai road.

One of those downed was the American, Lieutenant Eugene Coler. His petrol tank was pierced and the aileron controls shot away, following which Coler dived for the ground with full power on – a testimony to the strength of the BF2b – pulling out at 1,000 feet over Cambrai, where two chasing Fokkers overshot, and the Brisfit crew claimed them shot down. Coler then struggled over the lines at 150 feet, and side-slipped into the ground near Beugny. The coolness under severe strain of this experienced pilot and gunner got them out of a tricky situation.

They were probably brought down by Loerzer and Leutnant Fritz Hoffmann of Jasta 2 (his 1st and only victory; he would not survive the month), the latter also claiming a two-seater south-west of Cambrai. The other claims were well behind the German lines and Coler landed 500 metres west of Doignies. Both were claimed as DH9s although none were involved in this fight. Other Bristols, of 22 Squadron, were also shot up at this time, and Leutnant Frühner of Jasta 26 also put in a claim for a Bristol. However, two damaged 22 Squadron aircraft managed to get back over the lines.

Just after 0835, south of Linselles, 29 Squadron were in combat with Jasta 7, the SE5 pilots claiming five, while the Germans claimed three – one each to Jacobs, Unteroffizier Peisker and Vizefeldwebel Leiber. No.29 lost Second Lieutenant Peter John Alexander Fleming, a Liverpool-born 19-year-old who was captured. Jacobs described the fight as follows:

'Dawn patrol, 0735 to 0855 with eight DVIIs and one triplane. As we crossed the lines near Armentières, we saw the white puffs of flak converging on three Sopwith Camels who were pushing our way. I signalled my flight and we jumped into what turned out to be a free-for-all; whereupon, four more Camels joined the fracas and we battled them right down to the ground, when they retreated towards their home base.

'As we recrossed the lines, we were met by seven SE5s coming in from Ypres, and since our own flight was not in attack formation, the SEs picked on our stragglers. One particular fighter waltzed me down to the ground, clear back to Menin, whereupon I was joined by a couple of DVIIs who assisted me by getting on top of the Englishmen, at which point they decided to break off combat and fly home. One of my guns appeared to be hopelessly jammed during combat with an SE5 flight leader who flew brilliantly. Regaining some altitude, I was able to clear the stoppage in my port gun and soon came across an SE5 and shot off his tail causing him to drop vertically beyond the lines.'

As mentioned above, Leutnant Kresse did not return, and in fact ground observers reported a DVII falling out of formation after a fight with Camels.

It was proving a busy morning. No. 205 Squadron's DH4s were out north of Saint-Quentin at 0845 and had fights, firstly with a Hannover CLIII which was shot down in flames and then with Fokker biplanes. 205 lost a crew with two others being forced to land with dead or wounded airmen aboard. Three Jastas were involved: Leutnant Böhning of Jasta 79b claimed a DH9 north-west of Bellenglise, nine kilometres south of Saint-Quentin, which was the DH4 of Second Lieutenant Anslow who was taken prisoner, coming down with a dead gunner. Another DH4 came down in Allied lines at Germaine, which matches the claim by Leutnant Breidenbach of Jasta 44 at 0850 (although he claimed a BF2b).

Five minutes past the hour saw 201 Squadron's indefatigable George Gates destroy another two-seater, an LVG, near Hayencourt, in company with Lieutenant J M Mackay, from which both crewmen baled out safely. It must have been very galling for Allied airmen to see German airmen saving themselves in parachutes when they were not allowed to have them themselves.

DH9s of 103 Squadron, bombing targets near Lille at 0900, were attacked by Jasta 20 when over Lomme. Leutnant Karl Plauth, a 22-year-old from Munich, shot down one for his 7th victory since arriving at the unit on 14 June. 103 lost another aircraft on this raid. Fifteen minutes later, Leutnant Holle of Jasta 31 claimed another DH9 north-east of Douchy, which in fact was a DH4 crew of 25 Squadron, returning from a photography mission to Maubeuge, west of Valenciennes. No. 62 Squadron also got into a fight with Fokkers while escorting DH9s of 49 Squadron north-east of Douai. They claimed three of the German fighters but lost one machine, possibly to Leutnant Paul Baümer of Jasta 2 Boelcke, north-east of Henin-Liétard – his 26th victory.

Pilots of 29, 19, 87 and 79 Squadrons had scraps mid-morning, then at 1030 1 Squadron were in a fight while escorting 98 Squadron on a bomb raid. Lieutenant Howard Kullberg shot down one in flames but was chased back to the lines by five others, having been wounded in the leg in three places, although he landed safely. Kullberg's combat career was thus ended, with a score of 19, a DFC and bar, but the worst was yet to come, as by a stupefying piece of bureaucracy, he was arrested for possessing a camera while on active service!

No.98 Squadron claimed three fighters shot down but lost one bomber and had another shot up. Leutnant Otto Löffler of Jasta 2 claimed both, one north of Ave-luy and one north-east of Arras, bringing his score to 11. Leutnant Emil Thuy of Jasta 28w claimed an SE5a at an unknown time and location which may well have been Kullberg, as his unit was operating in this area.

Up on the Channel coast, 210 Squadron lost Second Lieutenant Edward Burleigh Markquick, an 18-year-old, born in Calcutta, India, after just ten days with the squadron. He went down north-west of Bruges at 0915, in a fight with MFJ 3, the victim of Vizeflugmeister Hans Goerth.

At 1110, near Zeebrugge, 210 Squadron flew another patrol, claiming two Fokkers but losing Second Lieutenant Jack Arthur Lewis, a 25-year-old from Bristol. He too was a novice, having been with the unit for just a month. Leutnant Theo Osterkamp, the acting CO of the Marine Feld Geschwader, claimed two Camels at Coxyde, while Leutnant Wilhelm of MFJ 4 got another off Zeebrugge. At 1135, Captain T W Nash of 204 Squadron blasted a balloon south of Ostende, bringing his score to five. This 26-year-old Londoner would raise this to eight before being killed in action on 23 October.

British two-seaters did not fare well, 35 losing a Big Ack to AA fire just before noon, then two DH9s of 57 Squadron were shot down, one falling in German lines, the other crash-landing in the front lines with a dead pilot. Jasta 23b got them; Unteroffizier Kleinschrodt over Denain, near Valenciennes, and Leutnant Heinrich Seywald, a 23-year-old from Regensburg, the Staffelführer, west of Cantin; his 6th and final kill. No. 57 Squadron claimed four!

At about this time Leutnant Noltenius of Jasta 27 had a long fight with an RE8 and had to withdraw after the British crew put ten bullets into his radiator. During the day he was apparently credited with a two-seater for his 8th victory. It is possible that this was the second 103 Squadron machine, but more likely it was a

Lieutenant H. A. Kullberg from Massachusetts, flew with 1 Squadron in 1918, and downed his 19th and final victory on 16 September, his 18th went down on the 3rd. He received the DFC.

late confirmation of this RE8, although no other RE8s were lost other than the one at dawn.

Fritz Rumey of Jasta 5 added two kills to his score at 1230 and 1235, recording a Camel and an SE5 down. Lieutenant J R Montgomery of 3 Squadron was the Camel pilot, killed two miles west of Cambrai at this time.

It was over an hour before more clashes came, 41 and 84 Squadrons seeing combat, while 70 Squadron lost a pilot on a balloon strafe at 1430, presumably to ground fire. Then 22 Squadron's Bristols met Jasta 37 over Quesnoy Wood. The BF2b crews claimed two enemy fighters but lost one with another being forced down inside British lines. The latter machine, flown by Lieutenant T W Martin and Sergeant M Jones, had their aileron controls shot away, and the Brisfit side-slipped down to 2,000 feet. In order to steady it, Jones climbed out onto the wing to use his weight to help level it out. It worked and they were able to get down without injury. Jones was later awarded a merited DFM. Leutnant Georg Meyer and Unteroffizier Gengelin were the victors, although their claims were for a 'scout'.

More fighting involved 79, 201, 87 and 88 Squadrons, in the latter's case two Fokkers colliding during an attack by Lieutenant Ken Conn, north-east of Habourdin aerodrome, near Lille. Then 56 and 3 Squadrons fought Jasta 26 south of Havrincourt Wood; two Fokkers were shot down, one falling in flames minus its wings. Two Allied machines were claimed by the Germans, a Camel by Vizefeldwebel Mesch at 1755 and an SE5 to Leutnant Macard at 1800. The latter was Second Lieutenant Noel Frederick Bishop, an 18-year-old from Worthing, who fell to his death east of the wood. No.32 Squadron dived into this fight later and claimed more Fokkers. The SE5 of Lieutenant M A Tancock lost its air pressure in the middle of this fight but he got back over the lines and crash-landed. He may well have been claimed by the Germans.

At unknown times during the day, Bruno Loerzer and Leutnant Klimke of Jasta 27 claimed an SE5 and a Camel respectively, while Leutnant Rudolf Stark, CO of Jasta 35b, was shot up and wounded in the leg, but not seriously enough to put him in hospital.

Camels of 46 Squadron and then 85 Squadron's SEs were in fights during the afternoon, the latter in company with 203's Camels. All scored victories. One went to Captain Cyril Crowe MC of 85, recently demoted from squadron commander by court martial, following a car crash. He was driving back from a party at another base when he hit a tree and two senior fellow pilots were killed. It seems rather stupid to demote such a vastly experienced air fighter as Crowe, despite the serious consequences of the crash, but it happened, and now he was just a flight commander. Crowe had come out with and been a founder member of 56 Squadron in April 1917. His recent command had been 60 Squadron but after a month he was again promoted to major, and took over 85.

Flieger Siegfried Braun of Jasta 23b, was shot down in flames in a Pfalz DXII, over Cantin at 1850. This location is too far north for 46, 203 or 85 Squadrons, as Cantin lies on the Douai-Cambrai road, some ten kilometres north of their locations. The only other claims at this time were for two Fokkers by another ten-strong recce patrol of 11 Squadron, flying over Cambrai at 1850. One was claimed north and the other south of the town. Given the rather imprecise RAF combat reports that tended to mention where fights started but not always where they finished, it would appear Braun was one of the flamers credited.

Back on the Channel coast, just on 1900, 204 rounded off the day for the RAF by claiming no fewer than 11 victories in 15 minutes, during a fight that started at Blankenberghe. Three were LVGs and eight Fokkers. All three two-seaters were destroyed, one falling in the sea, while all the Fokkers, bar three, were out of control.

An interesting fact is that of the nine RAF pilots claiming victories in this fight, only one would survive the war, that man being John Raymond Chisam, a 19-year-old who joined 204 on 25 August. From September to the end of the war, this squadron suffered the highest losses of any RAF fighter squadron. Their opponents were the Marine Feld Jastas and probably the Marine two-seater units. In this fight, MFJ 1 lost Vizeflugmeister Horst Sawatski and Flugmaat Nake – both wounded – and the ace, Leutnant zur See Heinrich Wessels, shot down and mortally wounded.

Josef Jacobs of Jasta 7 made the final kill of the day:

Josef Jacobs ended the war with 48 victories, achieved from 1916 to 1918. By 1918 he had been commanding Jasta 7 for some months and continued to do so, using as his personal choice, the Fokker DrI triplanes, of which he had more than one! In September 1918 he added nine victories to his tally. He was a recipient of the Pour le Mérite and after the war remained in close association with flying and sport.

'During the 1830-1935 evening mission, we observed a few fighter squadrons in the far distance. In the haze I could make out a few observation balloons, so I first flew north into enemy territory and then dived south on to a balloon. When I was within 200-300 metres range, the observer parachuted to earth, and I fired 40-50 rounds from my guns, then immediately turned back towards my lines. As I looked over my shoulder, I could observe six to eight spots in the balloon, glimmering from tracers, and suddenly it exploded in flames. Being well satisfied, I curved back to the front under very little enemy anti-aircraft fire. This was my 28th victory.'

Jacobs' victim was the 5th Company balloon, situated at Poperinghe, which was burned at 1935 that evening.

French Front

The weather on this part of the front was windy but clear, giving good visibility. Half the French casualties were on the American part of the front, despite the winding down of the Saint-Mihiel offensive. The French lost three missing, plus two airmen wounded, while on the rest of their front they lost two killed, two missing and one taken prisoner.

A patrol of Spa.90, in the VIII Armée sector, that comprised Marc Ambrogi, Adjutant Jean Pezon and Caporal Rivière, flamed a balloon near Cirey. This was evidently BZ141 which was destroyed at 1010 by three Spads between Juvigny and Cirey. The observer baled out but on the return flight Rivière was hit by fire from Flakzug Abteilung 10, south-west of St Ludwig, force-landed and was taken prisoner. Also in the sector, the French claimed a probable victory over an aircraft. This must have been the two-seater of FA 10, which was attacked by two Spads, and crash-landed.

Further balloon attacks were mounted from both sides. Shortly after 1100, a patrol of Spa.77 went for one near Harville, flamed by Maurice Boyau and Aspirant Cessieux. They were then engaged by seven German aircraft which cost the French Air Service one of its greats. Boyau evaded the initial pass, then went to assist Caporal Walk of his patrol, but was then reportedly hit by ground fire, falling in flames. Cessieux was badly wounded but made it back to force-land in friendly territory, and Walk too was forced down. Their attackers were Jasta 15, von Hantelmann and Vizefeldwebel Klaudat both claiming Spads, south-west of Conflans and at St Hilaire, the latter between the lines. Both locations are near Harville, and it would appear Hantelmann claimed Boyau, the Frenchman having just achieved his 35th victory.

In the IV Armée sector, the balloon of 50 Cié of the French balloon service was set on fire by two aircraft at 1130. For once the observer did not survive, despite taking to his parachute, for he was hit in the head by a bullet and killed. The balloon was apparently attacked by Jasta 47 but the name of the claimant is unknown.

At 1650, in the V Armée sector, Adjutant Lemeteyer of Spa.12 was seen to fall into enemy lines following a fight, and later in the day, at 1815, a patrol from GC22 engaged three German aircraft, which were quickly joined by 15 more. There are three known claims in this area, one by Offizierstellvertreter Gustav Dörr of Jasta 45, who claimed a Spad near Fismes for his 28th kill, and two to Jasta 72, Leutnants Gustav Frädrich and Herbert Mahn.

Near Soissons, a French two-seater was forced to land by four Fokkers, crewed by Lieutenants Seillere and Guillet. Locations for Jasta 72's victories are not known, nor if they were single- or two-seater Spads. Dörr's claim was for a Spad VII, but probably a XIII.

Other air fights during the day netted victories for Spa.57 and Spa.87, Spa.38 and the veteran Sous Lieutenant René Pelissier, a 32-year-old from Versailles, commander of Spa.175 since the start of September after two years' active service. He gained his 6th and final victory in the Saint-Mihiel region. Two pilots of Spa.93 shot down an LVG north-east of Juvelize at 1025, Lieutenant Gustave Daladier gaining his 9th victory and Adjutant Pierre Delage his first. Delage would have a meteoric career as a fighter pilot. He would achieve seven victories by 4 October, on which date this 31-year-old from the Dordogne region would be killed in action.

On the Aisne front a Bréguet XIV was shot down in flames, possibly by ground fire.

American Sector

As the ground fighting lessened in the salient area, so did the American activity, the Americans only losing one fighter and four bombers. The fighter pilot lost was Lieutenant Robert M Stiles of the 13th Pursuit, who had three victories. He departed with the 0545 patrol and was last seen south of Metz at 0720, shot down by Feldwebel Hoffmann of Kest 3. Lieutenant Murray Guthrie – a future ace – lost his engine in this action and was lucky to get back over the lines, force-landing near Dieulouard.

At 1115, Lieutenant George F Fisher of the 49th Aero claimed a Rumpler for his second victory. This may have been Vizefeldwebel Padberg and Leutnant Springorum of FA(A) 279, shot down but not harmed. Otherwise, Spa.100 (Haegelen and Sergeant Peuch) and Spa.93 have valid claims for a two-seater, if they misidentified their LVG. Also making a claim for a two-seater, was Lieutenant Louis Charles Simon Jr of the 147th Pursuit, in the vicinity of Hadonville at 1245. He left his patrol with engine trouble, but was then attacked by three Hannovers. This was at 4,000 metres and by the time he had despatched one and got back over the lines, he was down to 400.

The 96th Bombardment Squadron sent out a flight of seven aircraft at 1650 to bomb Conflans. Two planes dropped out before the lines were reached, then another, not being able to keep up, fell out and bombed Hadonville. The four others which reached the target were engaged in combat on the return trip, three going down in flames, while the fourth crash-landed behind German lines. They had been attacked by Jasta 19 whose pilots claimed four Bréguet bombers just before 1800 in the

Conflans-Briey area, two falling to Beaulieu-Marconnay to bring his score to 19, the other two credited to Leutnant Rudolf Rineau and Gefreiter Felder.

The American day bombers had suffered another 'bloody nose', and for the same reasons all the day bombers were suffering: the formations were too small, they went out unescorted, and whenever quality German pilots got in amongst them, heavy casualties ensued. Remarkably the US 8th Air Force in WWII were to suffer similar problems at the beginning of their war over France and Germany in 1943. Does no one study history or does each generation have to learn the hard way?

Unfortunately for the squadrons of the US 'First Team' of the American Day Bombardment Group in 1918, things were only going to get worse – far worse!

Late in the evening, the pair of Frank Luke and Joe Wehner struck again. This 27th Aero deadly duo shared the balloon near Reville at 1903, the flames of which consumed the observer's parachute and he was killed. They then burnt the Romagne balloon at 1940, and the pair finished off their activities by Wehner burning the Mangiennes balloon at 1945. Both men landed in the dark at their aerodrome, with the aid of flares. It brought Wehner's score to four and Luke's to eight.

IAF

The Handley Page bombers had been out during the night of 15/16 September, 97 Squadron having one of its machines damaged, and it crashed on its way back from a raid on Mainz railway centre pre-dawn.

The IAF day bombers had another busy day, dropping a total of thirteen-and-a-half tons of bombs and firing 4,120 rounds of ammunition. No. 55 Squadron sent five planes to raid Mannheim, leaving at 1220. On the way, one DH4 flown by Second Lieutenants W E Johns and A E Amey, became separated from the flight after a flak splinter punctured their main fuel tank, and they had to run for home, pursued by Fokkers. They were shot down, Amey being killed in the air, by Vize-feldwebel Ludwig Prime of Jasta 78 and Leutnant Georg Weiner of Jasta 3 at Alt-Eckendorf, north-east of Zabern at 1330. Prime lost the disputed kill to Weiner, the latter thereby gaining his 7th victory. The other 'Fours' had a running fight with 15 enemy fighters after bombing but all got home.

Following 55 in were 11 DH9s of 110 Squadron, who bombed soon afterwards. The leader of the formation had aborted after take-off with engine trouble, and the lead flight descended to 13,000 feet from 17,400, at which height they had bombed. Flak hit two of them, causing the pilots to leave the formation; one crew was killed, the other came down into captivity. A third DH was shot up, its observer killed, but the pilot got back. Kest 1a, the victors of the week before, failed on this occasion to get sufficient height to engage, the laurels going to Jasta 70, who claimed both DH9s that had been separated: Leutnant Anton Stephen and Feldwebel Metzger were the claimants. Jasta 70's CO, Oberleutnant Hans Schlieter, was slightly wounded in the encounter, 110 claiming one Fokker driven down damaged.

During the night of 16/17 September, 24 aircraft, representing all the IAF's night bombing squadrons, set out to bomb Metz, Frescaty, Boulay, Trier, Merzig, Frankfurt and Cologne. The night was a disaster for 215 Squadron, which lost four Handley Pages. Two crews were interned in Holland and Luxemburg, 100 Squadron lost one; the newly arrived 115 Squadron lost one too, the crew landing in Switzerland. Another 216 aircraft was damaged as it landed back at base, while two of 115 Squadron had already been damaged in crashes near their bases, but without casualties. According to the Germans, they used 173 searchlights to illuminate the raiders, while anti-aircraft guns fired 16,063 shells.

	A/C	KB		DES	OOC	KB
British losses	20	1	British claims	60	42	2
French losses	9	1	French claims	3		3
American losses	5	–	American claims	3		3
IAF losses	11		IAF claims	–	1	–
German claims	49	2	German losses	4†		?

† Three fighter pilots killed and eight wounded.

British Casualties

Aircraft type	No.	Squadron	Crew		
HP O/400 (night)	C9758	97 Sqdn	Lt H Cooper	WIA	
			2/Lt A Hinder	KIA	
			2/Lt O F Bendall	Safe	
RE8	F5977	13 Sqdn	2/Lt J J Elder	KIA	
			Lt A Ostler MC	KIA	
BF2b	C946	11 Sqdn	2/Lt J C Stanley (USAS)	POW	
			2/Lt E J Norris	POW	
BF2b	C878	11 Sqdn	2/Lt L Arnott	KIA	
			2/Lt G L Bryers	KIA	
BF2b	E2215	11 Sqdn	Lt E S Coler MC (US)	WIA	
			2/Lt E J Corbett	WIA	
DH4	D9250	205 Sqdn	2/Lt F F Anslow	POW/W	
			Sgt L Murphy	KIA	
DH4	D8429	205 Sqdn	Lt E D Danger	WIA	
			2/Lt A G Robertson	KIA	
DH4	B7964	205 Sqdn	2/Lt G C Matthews	WIA	*
			2/Lt H S Mullen	WIA	
BF2b	E2244	62 Sqdn	2/Lt R H Stone	POW	
			2/Lt N F Adams	POW	
BF2b		62 Sqdn	2/Lt C H Moss (P)	WIA	*
DH9	C2221	98 Sqdn	Lt W V Thomas	Safe	*
			Sgt C H O Allwork	Safe	
DH9	D3267	98 Sqdn	2/Lt F J Keble	POW	
			2/Lt C H Senecal	POW	
DH9	D3254	103 Sqdn	Capt F A Ayrton	POW	
			2/Lt B P Jenkins	DOW	
DH9	D489	103 Sqdn	2/Lt W H Cole	KIA	
			Sgt S Hookaway	KIA	
SE5a	E6002	29 Sqdn	2/Lt P J A Fleming	POW	
BF2b	F5824	22 Sqdn	Lt T D Smith	Safe	*
			2/Lt S C Barrow	Safe	
BF2b	C978	22 Sqdn	Lt L N Caple	Safe	*
			Lt G S Routhier	Safe	
DH4	A7788	25 Sqdn	Capt R L Whalley	KIA	
			2/Lt E B Andrews	KIA	
DH4	D8378	25 Sqdn	Lt C Brown	Safe	
			Lt E W Griffin	KIA	*

Aircraft type	No.	Squadron	Crew		
Camel	F1962	54 Sqdn	Lt J C MacLennan	Safe	*
Camel	B7271	210 Sqdn	2/Lt E B Markquick	KIA	
AWFK8	D5146	35 Sqdn	Capt J E Phillips	KIA	
			2/Lt C V Hepburn	KIA	
Camel	E5173	54 Sqdn	2/Lt B Dixon	WIA	*
Camel	D1946	54 Sqdn	2/Lt B H Matthews	Safe	*
Camel	D3357	210 Sqdn	2/Lt J A Lewis	KIA	
Camel	F5958	3 Sqdn	Lt J R Montgomery	KIA	
Camel	E1597	70 Sqdn	Lt J Glen	KIA	
FE2b (night)	A5610	102 Sqdn	Lt C B Naylor	POW	
			Lt H Mercer	POW	
BF2b	E2519	22 Sqdn	2/Lt W Kellow	KIA	
			2/Lt H A Felton	KIA	
BF2b	D8089	22 Sqdn	Lt T W Martin	Safe	*
			Sgt M Jones	WIA	
SE5a	B8499	56 Sqdn	2/Lt N F Bishop	KIA	
AWFK8	–	2 Sqdn	2/Lt R P Powell (P)	WIA	*
DH4	F2634	57 Sqdn	Lt G Anderson	KIA	
			Sgt J S Macdonald	WIA	
DH4	F7597	57 Sqdn	Lt P W J Timson	WIA	*
			2/Lt I S Woodhouse	Safe	
DH4	A7987	57 Sqdn	2/Lt J P Ferreira	KIA	
			2/Lt L B Simmonds	KIA	
SE5a	B8427	1 Sqdn	Lt H A Kullberg DFC (US)	WIA	*
DH9	B7603	211 Sqdn	Capt W D Gairdner	Safe	*
			2/Lt H M Moodie (O)	KIA	
Camel	E1479	148th Aero	Lt G C Dorsey (USAS)	WIA	*
DH4	F5712	55 Sqdn	2/Lt W E Johns	POW	
			2/Lt A E Amey	KIA	
DH9A	E8410	110 Sqdn	Sgt A Haight	KIA	
			Sgt J West	KIA	
DH9A	F997	110 Sqdn	Lt H V Brisbin	POW	
			Lt R Lipsett	POW	
DH9A	E8434	110 Sqdn	Lt K B H Wilkinson	Safe	*
			2/Lt H M Kettener	WIA	
HP O/400 (night)	C9658	215 Sqdn	Lt H R Dodd	KIA	
			2/Lt E C Jeffkins	POW	
			2/Lt A Fairhurst	POW	
HP O/400 (night)	D4566	215 Sqdn	Lt H B Monaghan	POW	
			Lt H E Hyde	POW	
			2/Lt G W Mitchell	POW	
HPO/400 (night)	C9727	215 Sqdn	2/Lt C C Fisher	Interned	
			2/Lt R S Oakley	Interned	
			2/Lt C J Locke	Interned	
HP O/400 (night)	D9684	215 Sqdn	2/Lt J B Lacy	POW	
			2/Lt R Down	POW	
			Lt C N Yelverton	POW	

Aircraft type	No.	Squadron	Crew	
HP O/400 (night)	D9689	115 Sqdn	Lt R L Cobham	Interned
			Lt E G Gallagher	Interned
			2/Lt E E Taylor	Interned
HP O/400 (night)	D8302	100 Sqdn	Lt F R Johnson	POW
			Lt R C Pitman	POW
			2/Lt F H Chainey	POW
HP O/400 (night)	C9662	216 Sqdn	Lt B Norcross	POW
			2/Lt R H Cole	DOW
			Sgt G Hall	POW

French Casualties

Aircraft type	Squadron	Crew		
Bréguet XIV	Br.?	Sgt Gros	MIA	
		Lt Carré	MIA	
Spad XIII	Spa.12	Adj E Lemeteyer	KIA	
?	?	Sgt Garin	Safe	
		Lt Fargeaud	Safe	
?	?	Lt Seillere	Safe	*
		S/Lt Guillet	Safe	
Spad XIII	Spa.?	Sgt Rouanet	MIA	
Spad XIII	Spa.77	Asp H Cessieux	WIA	*
Spad XIII	Spa.77	S/Lt M Boyau	KIA	
Spad XIII	Spa.77	Cpl R Walk	POW	
Spad XIII	Spa.93	Cpl A Goujat	KIA	
Bréguet XIV	Br.229	Sgt Foiny	MIA	
		Cpl K Becker	MIA	
Spad XIII	Spa.90	Cpl Rivière	POW	
Voisin XB2	F114	Mdl G Ravault	POW	
		Adj Deaux	POW	
		S/Lt Bombezin	KIA	

American Casualties

Aircraft type	No.	Squadron	Crew		
Spad XIII	–	13th Aero	1/Lt R M Stiles	KIA	
Spad XIII	–	13th Aero	1/Lt M K Guthrie	Safe	*
Bréguet XIV	4494	96th Aero	1/Lt C P Anderson	KIA	
			1/Lt H S Thompson	KIA	
Bréguet XIV	4875	96th Aero	1/Lt N C Rogers	KIA	
			2/Lt K A Strawn	KIA	
Bréguet XIV	4726	96th Aero	1/Lt R C Taylor	KIA	
			1/Lt N A Stuart	KIA	
Bréguet XIV	12005	96th Aero	1/Lt C R Codman	POW	
			2/Lt S A McDowell	POW	
DH4	–	20th Aero	1/Lt A F Seaver DSC	Safe	
			1/Lt J Y Stokes DSC	Safe	

1 Sopwith Dolphin of 19 Squadron, C4129.
Lt L H Ray claimed his 3rd victory in this machine
on 16 September.

2 SE5a D6940, that flew with 29 Squadron in
1918. Lt C M Wilson gained his 8th and final
victory in it on 16 September, having claimed
three more with it in August. Lt E G Davies
destroyed two balloons with it on 29 September.

3 Sopwith Camel D1922, shot down on
1 September. Lt H V Fellows (an American) of
73 Squadron taken prisoner.

4 Camel F2137, flown by Captain D R MacClaren
from Ottawa. He ended the war with 54 victories,
the last nine in this machine, and seven during
September 1918. He received the DSO,
MC & Bar, DFC.

5 Three pilots of Spa.154. Sous Lieutenant Paul
Barbreau, eight victories, Sergent Abbott, and
Jacques Ehrlich. Ehrlich achieved his final four
balloon victories in mid-September bringing his
score to 19, although he was brought down
following his last victory, on 18 September, to
become a prisoner. Just over a week later he was
commissioned as Sous Lieutenant.

6 Four pilots of the 95th Aero. Ted Curtis, Harold
Buckley, Alex McLanahan, John Mitchell. Curtis
downed his 3rd victory on 27 September and
achieved six in all. Buckley claimed four of his five
victories in this month. Buckley later wrote the history
of the 95th. Curtis made Major-General in WW2.

17 SEPTEMBER 1918
M T W T F S S

British Front

Today was another fine one, with the activity on the front being described by the RAF communiqué as 'normal'. Early on, the recce DH4 of 25 Squadron was intercepted on the way to Maubeuge. Lieutenant C Brown did return at 0830, but his observer, Lieutenant E W Griffin, was dead in his cockpit.

In trying to keep the German Air Service down, two RAF squadrons continued the increasing practice of bombing enemy airfields with an attack on Émerchicourt, beginning soon after dawn. Ninety-one bombs were dropped and the aerodrome and area well strafed by 64 and 209 Squadrons, although they lost one aircraft each to ground fire. No. 22 Squadron provided top cover for the raid. The attack awoke Leutnant Noltenius of Jasta 27, who noted that it achieved practically nothing. However, Jasta 36 had a tent burnt down, lost a triplane, a DVII and a Fokker E.V monoplane on the ground – not bad for practically nothing!

Two SE5s of 84 Squadron failed to return from an early sentry duty patrol. Both were NCO pilots, sent out alone, Sergeants A Jex and F S Thompson. Jasta 5 got at least one of them, Leutnant Fritz Rumey gaining his 38th victory at 0905 near Rumilly, but it is not recorded who claimed the other. Shortly before 1000, 40 Squadron's Lieutenant Arthur T Drinkwater, an Australian from Melbourne, opened his score on his second tour with a Fokker south-east of Cambrai. Drinkwater had earlier flown DH4 bombers with 57 Squadron in 1917. However, No.40 lost Second Lieutenant F W King south of this location, being brought down wounded inside German lines to Leutnant Hans Boes of Jasta 34b.

Captain Fred Lord of 79 Squadron downed a Fokker over the River Lys at 1010, seeing it go down with its prop stopped, crashing near the bridge on the south-west edge of Comines. The pilot, however, must have survived as no German fatalities are known.

Bristols of 11 and 88 Squadrons had fights mid-morning, as did 2 AFC's SE5s, while a 59 Squadron crew returned badly shot up by Fokkers. No. 25 Squadron were also in a fight, one DH4 having to force-land on its return to base. Another DH4 from this squadron failed to return from another show, and was probably the victim of Leutnant Frommherz of Jasta 27, after it had been crippled by a pilot from Jasta 2 Boelcke.

At midday 46 Squadron were in a fight with German fighters, making claims, while 57 Squadron, on another raid, lost a machine to flak near Wahignies at 1310. Another aircraft lost to ground fire was a 24 Squadron SE5, ground strafing near Vermand. Meantime, Fritz Rumey of Jasta 5 added a second kill for the day by downing Lieutenant J E Smith of 60 Squadron. As the afternoon wore on, Leutnant Noltenius set off for another of his balloon attacks. He reported:

> 'The sky was perfectly cloudless. At 4,000 metres I crossed the lines and flew deep into enemy territory, with the engine throttled back. I had a bad time

fighting the violent wind. Finally I was on a level with the balloon, dived vertically, and then raced for the balloon. I did not close in very hard as immediately my guns jammed. On turning away I saw two observers jump. Then I went much closer for a second attempt, but still the balloon did not burn. I followed through with a third attack but departed quickly as the flak became uncomfortably heavy. Fortunately the balloon eventually ignited, a fact I only learned on landing.'

This was his 9th victory, scored at 1530 over the 20th KBS balloon, SR151, which exploded in flames at 2,000 ft.

There was more activity late in the day, beginning on the Channel coast. Off Zeebrugge a German seaplane was shot down by a 217 bomber crew at 1825. A few minutes later, south of Ostende, 210 Squadron had a scrap, losing Second Lieutenant John Edward Harrison, 22, who had been on the squadron just 17 days. He fell to Flugmaatrose Gerhard Hubrich of MFJ 4, his 4th victory.

Further south, 74 Squadron and 22 Squadron both had fights and claimed victories, while the 17th USAS unit also downed a Fokker but had one Camel forced to land with its controls shot away. A Camel was claimed by ground fire near Neuve Chapelle at 1805.

Jasta 5 were back in action at 1915, meeting 46 Squadron near Bourlon Wood. Lieutenant Harold Toulmin MC, aged 21, another new arrival with just 17 days on the squadron, was killed, while Second Lieutenant Cronan Edmund Usher-Summers was made a prisoner. They were brought down by Rumey and Josef Mai. This made Rumey's score a round 40, three on this day, and six in two days. Mai's kill was his 26th.

It is interesting to reflect on the German reluctance to recruit NCOs into their officer corps, despite awards, experience and victories. The famed trio of Jasta 5 – Rumey, Mai and Otto Könnecke – had all been senior non-comms. Rumey was commissioned in July 1918 when his score was 25; Mai in September 1918 after 23 victories; and Könnecke in June 1918 after 21 kills. Between them they would bring down 110 Allied aircraft in the war and Rumey and Könnecke received the 'Blue Max', and Mai was recommended for it, but not before any of them had been commissioned.

That night, 151 Squadron struck again, claiming three night raiders. At 2052, Lieutenant E P Mackay shot down an AEG GV of Kampfstaffel 4, five miles southeast of Estrées-en-Chaussée, killing Gefreiter Otto Kurth, with Leutnants Gerlach and Tillmans taken prisoner.

Then at 2241, Major Brand attacked a machine later identified as a Friedrichshafen GIII, which blew up in mid-air, while Captain D V Armstrong shot down another

Friedrichshafen in flames east of Bapaume. This was a bomber of Kampfstaffel 5, who lost Leutnants Max Scharf, Josef Freck, and Unteroffiziers Paul Nöller and Paul Kagelmacher – all killed at Pronville. Both had originally been claimed as Gothas.

The Germans lost another aircraft this night, reported as a DFW, crewed by Leutnant Nolte and Flieger Geiger, who were taken prisoner. They were of Kampfstaffel 8 and whether this loss had anything to do with Brand's or Armstrong's claims is not clear.

The night bombers were out, 101 Squadron's FEs running into trouble. One machine was hit by ground fire and had to come down 15 miles behind the German lines. The crew destroyed the machine and then managed to reach the lines on foot and get back. A second FE was also hit and force-landed in the front lines, both men scrambling to safety, but only the engine of their pusher was later salvaged.

French Front

The weather on this front was reported as cloudy in the morning, fine in the afternoon. The fighting let up considerably, but still cost the French flyers three men killed, two wounded and three balloons burned.

Sous Lieutenant William Herisson of Spa.75, a 24-year-old veteran from Nîmes, claimed a two-seater over Vailly at 1800 hours, shared with Sergent Le Tilly, and also a Fokker during the day, shared with Sergent Baralis. These brought Herisson's score to 11. Leutnant Hans Siemann of FA(A) 227 was killed at Braisne on this day, possibly one of the two-seater crew.

In the X Armée Sector, the balloon of 33 Cié was flamed, apparently by Vizefeldwebel Artur Korff of Jasta 60, his 7th victory. Adjutant L Flament parachuted safely. The other two balloon losses were on the Aisne front, but with no recorded claimants, perhaps they were hit by artillery fire.

The French lost two-seaters, one being Caporal Dubourg and Adjutant Huart, killed over Nesle. The other was a Bréguet flown by Maréchal-des-Logis Kienne, killed, and Sergent Sauton, wounded, of Br.269, brought down in the front lines by flak fire. The other French combats occurred on the American sector.

American Sector

Balloons were attacked by Spa.100, Caporal Maufras failing to return from going for the balloon at Hattonville, but he came down in French lines and returned the next day. Sous Lieutenant Haegelen and Lieutenant Poulin shared the balloon at 1615.

In the 19 Armee sector, Leutnant Georg Weiner of Jasta 3 claimed a Bréguet XIV for his 8th kill, over Falkenberg during the morning. This aircraft, from Br.111, Groupe de Bombardement VI, crewed by Sous Lieutenant E de Carnell and Sergent A Puel, came down north-east of Commercy.

The first American loss occurred at first light. The 24th Aero sent out a Salmson at 0515, and it probably fell to Leutnant Franz Büchner of Jasta 13, for he scored his 29th victory near Dampvitoux on this day.

The other high scoring German pilot on this front, von Hantelmann, of Jasta 15, gained his 15th victory at 1510, north of Gorz. The American pilot was Lieutenant Waldo Heinrichs of the 95th Pursuit. This unit had flown out seven-strong at 1430 to hunt for balloons and got into a fight with Fokkers over the Lac-de-Lachaussée, Heinrichs later giving this graphic account:

'An explosive bullet hit me in the left cheek and knocked out 16 teeth, breaking both my jaws and then tearing through the windshield, breaking it also. I remember spitting out teeth and blood and turned for our lines. Pulled a "reversement" and came out underneath the chap who was firing at me from behind. Two more explosive bullets hit me in the left arm, tearing through and breaking the left elbow. Two broke in the right hand and nearly took off the right small finger. Another hit me in the left thigh, one in the left ankle and one in the right heel. Two more hit me in the leg. Saw my left arm hanging broken by my side.'

Despite these terrible injuries (he'd been wounded in ten places) Heinrichs managed to crash-land – and survived a prisoner. The 95th had just been re-equipped with Marlin guns, most of which jammed in this fight, the 95th being lucky to only lose just one man. These .30 guns were gas-operated, a modification of the Colt-Browning gun, intended to replace the British Vickers guns. In France their cloth feed belts gave a good deal of trouble in wet weather, which led to a number of jams.

At 1655, between Éply and Waville, Feldwebel Hans Popp, a 24-year-old from Hof and a member of Jasta 77b, was killed, shot down by seven Spads. These were probably the 103rd Aero pilots, who claimed four Fokkers in a long fight in the Bayonville area.

	A/C	KB		DES	OOC	KB
British losses	14	–	British claims	16	13	–
French losses	4	3	French claims	3		1
American losses	3	–	American claims	4		–
IAF losses	–		IAF claims	–		–
German claims	13†	2	German losses	6		?

† Three to flak.

British Casualties

Aircraft type	No.	Squadron	Crew		
DH4	D8378	25 Sqdn	Lt C Brown	Safe	*
			Lt E W Griffin	KIA	
SE5a	D6030	64 Sqdn	2/Lt W W Chrieman	POW	
Camel	E4382	209 Sqdn	2/Lt J E Walker	KIA	
BF2b	D8062	88 Sqdn	Lt F Jeffreys	Safe	*
			Lt F W Addison	Safe	
SE5a	C6480	84 Sqdn	Sgt A Jex	POW	
SE5a	C9069	84 Sqdn	Sgt F S Thomson	POW	
DH4	A7820	25 Sqdn	Lt R Dobson	Safe	*
			2/Lt A G Grant	WIA	
SE5a	E4053	40 Sqdn	2/Lt F W King	POW/WIA	

Aircraft type	No.	Squadron	Crew		
BF2b	D8088	11 Sqdn	Capt A Morrison	Safe	*
			Sgt R Allen	Safe	
RE8	F5971	59 Sqdn	Lt A Ibbotson	Safe	*
			2/Lt W J Carruthers	Safe	
DH4	A8031	25 Sqdn	Lt J H Latchford	Safe	
			2/Lt J Pullar	Safe	
SE5a	B8412	24 Sqdn	2/Lt W J Miller	KIA	
DH4	F6133	57 Sqdn	2/Lt W A Wilson	POW	
			2/Lt H H Senior	POW	
SE5a	C9297	60 Sqdn	2/Lt J E Smith	KIA	
Camel	D9513	17th US	2/Lt J A Ellison	Safe	*
BF2b	E2218	62 Sqdn	2/Lt R A Boxhall	Safe	*
			2/Lt L Miller	Safe	
Camel	F2130	46 Sqdn	Lt H Toulmin MC	KIA	
Camel	F6226	46 Sqdn	2/Lt C E Usher-Summers	POW	
Camel	F3931	210 Sqdn	2/Lt J E Harrison	KIA	
Camel	E1405	210 Sqdn	Lt I C Sanderson	WIA	
FE2b (night)	C9834	101 Sqdn	Capt H W Stockdale	Evaded	
			2/Lt N C Shergold	Evaded	
FE2b (night)	F5863	101 Sqdn	Lt A W Allen	Safe	
			Lt E H Clarke	Safe	
DH4	D8421	205 Sqdn	Lt H F Taylor	Safe	
			2/Lt H S Millen	WIA	

French Casualties

Bréguet XIV	3.314	Br.269	MdL Kienne	KIA	
			Sgt Sauton	WIA	
?		?	Cpl Dubourg	KIA	
			Adj Huart	KIA	
?		Esc.255	Asp Mokel (O)	WIA	*
Bréguet XIV		Br.111	S/Lt E de Carnell	MIA	
			Sgt A Puel	MIA	
Spad XIII		Spa.100	Cpl Maufras	Safe	

American Casualties

Salmson 2A2	1150	1st Aero	Lt W B Cowart	KIA
			2/Lt H W Dahringer	KIA
Salmson 2A2	–	24th Aero	1/Lt W L Bradfield	POW
			1/Lt A L Clark	POW
Spad XIII	15199	95th Aero	Lt W H Heinrichs	POW/WIA

18 SEPTEMBER 1918

M T **W** T F S S

British Front

Cloudy weather returned on this day and the RAF noted decreased activity by the Germans. On the ground, however, activity increased greatly. The British Army attacked from where their line joined the French line, just north of Saint-Quentin, to Épehy, about 11 miles to the north. Three Corps, comprising eight divisions, attacked. The centre Corps, the Australians, gained the most success, going 'over the top' at 0520. They took positions overlooking the Hindenburg Line's main defences, opposite Bellicourt. Intense fighting occurred along this section of the front, which also reflected where most of the aerial activity took place.

A balloon was shot down at La Barrière, in the Belgian coastal area, by 213 Squadron's Camels. It was shared between First Lieutenant D S Ingalls, an American navy pilot, and Lieutenants H C Smith and G S Hodson. It fell burning onto a balloon hangar and burnt it and neighbouring hangars as well. This was George Hodson's first claim of his second tour, bringing his score to five. This 19-year-old Englishman from Surrey would end his career as an air marshal.

Single-seaters were out looking for ground targets, but one SE5a of 92 Squadron was brought down by ground fire at Wingles at 1030, its pilot taken prisoner. At 1140, bombers of 103 Squadron lost a DH9 north-west of Lille to flak fire. Unteroffizier Sowa of Jasta 52 claimed his 4th victory here, which was contested by flak gunners.

At exactly the same time, Leutnant Garsztka of Jasta 31 scored his 2nd victory, an SE5a in flames at Lempire. This in fact was a Camel of 46 Squadron, Lieutenant H C Saunders being shot down in flames east of Hesbecourt at 1150, which is just south of Lempire. Yet another novice pilot had been lost. Like Toulmin, killed the day before, Herbert Saunders had joined 46 on the last day of August. An ex-infantry man, this Canadian was an old man, in pilot terms, being 33 when he died. A few minutes later Garsztka claimed a DH9 over Saulcourt. His aircraft identification was off again, as his victim was a 35 Squadron 'Big Ack' which went down in flames. The observer either fell or jumped from the burning two-seater at 2,000 feet, and although the pilot was alive when he came down, he died of burns.

At 1215, the Dolphins of 23 Squadron encountered Fokkers over Lihaucourt. Captain James Pearson, an American from New Jersey, claimed one in flames and another out of control, bringing his score to eight. Pearson survived the war and passed away in January 1993, the last known US ace to die.

The next combats were after 1400, 40 and 80 Squadrons having fights with DVIIs. Leutnant Hans Böhning, the commander of Jasta 79b, shot down a balloon north of Vaux for his 17th victory, this being the 22nd KBS balloon, from which Lieutenant Lindsay and Corporal Burgess baled out. At 1510, Leutnant Noltenius burnt another, his 10th victory. He wove his way through clouds, burnt the balloon and returned, damaged in the propeller by ground fire. This was the 8th KBS balloon – AR37 – lost at 1512 according to the balloon casualty report.

The Germans, fully aware of the ground activity, were responding by taking out these observation balloons. Eight minutes after AR37 went down, Leutnant Carl Degelow, commander of Jasta 40s, burnt the 36th Company balloon at Poperinghe, his 14th victory. Another went down at 1540 at Tincourt, near Saint-Quentin, by Vizefeldwebel Treiber of Jasta 5, which was the 14th KBS balloon.

The final fight of the day was at 1730. Captain Dudley Lloyd-Evans MC of 64 Squadron claimed two Fokkers east of Havrincourt Wood, one destroyed, one out of control. These brought his score to eight and he received the DFC this month, and became tour expired. He was to win a bar to his DFC flying in Mesopotamia in 1920.

All claims this day had been for Fokkers apart from one LVG C, by Howard Burdick, of the 17th US Aero at Rumilly – in flames. This happened at 1100, one of two LVGs located and pursued. Burdick's fire knocked out the gunner of one, shortly before the machine caught fire and crashed. The second LVG was hit and the observer dropped into his cockpit following attacks by Lieutenants George Vaughn and Glenn Wicks.

Rumilly is just south of Cambrai, opposite the German 2 Armee area. This Armee reported one two-seater casualty, Unteroffizier Hoppe and Leutnant Buchwald of FA 17 both wounded, although noted as hit by ground fire! A two-seater of FA 207 may also have been hit this day; the observer, Leutnant Hans Stanger, is recorded as the observer. In two different sets of records, he is noted as being killed on both the 18th and 25th of September – with different pilots! It is possible, of course, that his pilot on the 18th, Flieger Fackart, survived being shot down with Stanger on the 18th, Stanger then being killed a week later.

Captain J W Pearson from New Jersey, flew with the RAF in 23 Squadron, flying Dolphins. He received the DFC for his 11 victories, two of which he scored on 18 September 1918.

French Front

The French only suffered two air casualties this day, but both were important men. For the second time in three days, a balloon attack went wrong. In the V Armée sector a patrol from Spa.154, consisting of Adjutants Jacques Ehrlich and Paul Petit with Sergent Charles Peillard, attacked a balloon near Brimont at 1805. They had a difficult time and had to make three passes before they flamed it. It was Ehrlich's 19th, Petit's 6th and Peillard's 2nd victory.

By this time they were very low, and instead of trying to regain altitude, they raced for the lines. They were met by 11 Fokkers and as a result of the combat, Ehrlich and Petit were both shot down and taken prisoner. Petit was badly wounded and died in captivity.

Surprisingly, it is not known which German unit was involved, and it is open to question whether they were credited to ground fire, for balloon defences on this day were credited with two victories, with other flak units accounting for seven more. However, German fighter pilots were credited with 21 kills, including balloons, the authors only having found a corresponding 18.

The only other French claims of the day were a balloon by Aspirant Bonneau of Spa.48, and a two-seater shared on the American sector, near Jonville, by pilots of Spa.89 and Spa.23, at Belrupt. Leutnants Wilhelm Babetz and Willi Thormann of FA(A) 247 were lost at Froidmont, which may relate to this action.

American Sector

Action was more intense – especially in terms of casualties – on the American part of the front, primarily due to another comprehensive slaughter of American day bombers. All the action took place well into the afternoon, no doubt due to weather, as occurred on the French front.

At 1405, Lieutenants Lansing C Holden and W H Taylor of the 95th Aero, departed on a voluntary patrol and ran into a formation of five Fokker biplanes. During the combat, Bill Taylor, who was eager to avenge the loss of his friend Heinrichs on the previous day, was shot down in flames over Dampvitoux, victim of Franz Büchner – his 10th victory in six days and his 30th overall. It would prove a good day for Büchner.

At 1610, the 139th Aero encountered some Pfalz Scouts over Pagny-sur-Meuse, claiming two shot down, shared by seven pilots. However, it would prove a sad day for the 27th Aero. The team of Luke and Wehner departed on a balloon strafe at 1600 hours and located two at Labeuville, west of Mars-la-Tour, both bursting into flames at 1645. The second of these Luke hit at an altitude of just 30 metres. However, the pair were immediately attacked by Fokkers and Wehner, in trying to cover his friend during his second balloon attack, was shot down in flames. Luke then claimed two of the Fokkers at St Hilaire, and later joined in on an attack on a Halberstadt C over Jonville. This latter machine was also attacked by Spa.89 and 23, and it crashed into the American lines, possibly a machine lost by FA 36, brought down in combat with six Spads at Maas-Ost (Leutnants Karl Höhne and Ernst Schulz). Landing back, Luke credited Wehner with a share in the two balloons, which brought his dead friend's score to six.

Luke's five claims in about ten minutes took his total to 13, but he was distraught over the loss of Joe Wehner. He fell at Vionville at 1645, brought down by Georg von Hantelmann – his 16th victory. One of the balloons destroyed was from BZ112. Details of Fokkers lost only show one Jasta 13 pilot, Leutnant Erich Kampfe, being shot down this day and he took to his parachute. He was wounded by ground fire on his way down, and died of his wounds on the 20th in a hospital in Metz.

The American 11th Bombardment Squadron sent ten DH4s on a mission to bomb Mars-la-Tour, following twenty minutes behind the 20th Bombardment Squadron's similar force. This had meant in the past that the earlier raid stirred up the opposition and the second unit across was invariably the one hit. Why this somewhat bizarre tactic persisted is unclear, but on this occasion, the 11th suffered the almost inevitable consequences.

Three of the DH4s had fallen out before the lines were crossed but the other seven pressed on in cloud. One became separated, leaving just six to bomb Conflans, as they were unable to locate Mars-la-Tour. At 1720, near Conflans, 11 Fokkers of Jasta 12 found them and attacked. These were joined soon afterwards by elements of Jasta 6, part of JGI. As if the presence on the front of JGII was not enough, JGI was beginning to move down opposite the Americans, and Ulrich Neckel's Jasta 6 had just arrived. By coincidence, Neckel had been a long time member of Jasta 12, so may have joined in their patrol.

Two DH4s went down in flames straight away, followed shortly afterwards by another. Eventually, just Lieutenants Vincent P Oatis and Ramon H Guthrie returned to base, two more bombers having fallen during the running fight home. The Germans overclaimed by one, pilots being credited with six in all: Leutnant Hermann Becker got two (victories 15 and 16), both west of Conflans, Leutnant Besser one at Conflans, which blew up when it hit the ground, killing an Austrian soldier. Leutnant Alfred Greven got one south-west of Conflans, as did Flieger Wilke. Neckel downed his – which was his 26th victory – also at Conflans. The sole returning US crew claimed one Fokker shot down between Olley and Moulette.

Late in the evening, patrols were sent out by the 2nd Pursuit Group to strafe near Mars-la-Tour, and several combats took place. Lieutenant David McClure, 213th Aero, who had three victories, failed to return. Jasta 13's Franz Büchner shot down two Spads, one being flown by what he described as a skilled pilot, but who finally went down near Chambley at 1725.

	A/C	KB		DES	OOC	KB
British losses	4	–	British claims	5	4	1
French losses	2	–	French claims	2		2
American losses	9	–	American claims	11		2
IAF losses	–		IAF claims	–	–	–
German claims	30†	4	German losses	4		?

† Nine to ground fire (possibly including two Bréguets and a Salmson in the C Abteilung area, listed as cause unknown). Only 18 fighter pilot claims found.

British Casualties

Aircraft type	No.	Squadron	Crew		
SE5a	D6971	92 Sqdn	Lt C M Holbrook	POW	
DH9	D5572	103 Sqdn	2/Lt T M Phillips	KIA	
			2/Lt R E Owen	KIA	
RE8	C2490	3 AFC Sqdn	Lt D F Dimsey	Safe	*
			2/Lt R F C Machin	KIA	
Camel	D9405	46 Sqdn	Lt H C Saunders MM	KIA	

Aircraft type	No.	Squadron	Crew	
AWFK8	F7395	35 Sqdn	Lt M C Sonnenberg	DOW
			2/Lt J Clarke	KIA
SE5a	C5357	40 Sqdn	2/Lt L C Band	WIA
FE2b	C9834	101 Sqdn	Capt H W Stockdale	Evaded
			2/Lt N C Shergold	Evaded

French Casualties

Spad XIII	7921	Spa.154	Adj J L Ehrlich	POW
Spad XIII	15060	Spa.154	Adj P A Petit	POW/DOW

American Casualties

DH4	–	11th Aero	1/Lt E T Comegys	KIA
			2/Lt A R Carter	KIA
DH4	–	11th Aero	1/Lt L S Harter	KIA
			1/Lt M Stephenson	KIA
DH4	–	11th Aero	1/Lt J C Tyler	KIA
			1/Lt H H Strauch	KIA
DH4	–	11th Aero	1/Lt R F Chapin	POW
			2/Lt C B Laird	POW
DH4	–	11th Aero	1/Lt T D Hooper	POW/WIA
			1/Lt R R Root	POW/WIA
Spad XIII	7555	27th Aero	1/Lt J F Wehner	KIA
Spad XIII	4512	95th Aero	Lt W H Taylor	KIA
Spad XIII	15186	213rd Aero	Lt D M McClure	POW

19 SEPTEMBER 1918
M T W **T** F S S

British Front

On the ground, the British Army continued to attack the Hindenburg Line. The weather was overcast with a high wind. Consequently the level of air fighting reduced drastically. Indeed, the RAF only made two claims prior to noon.

The first of these was by the New Zealander, Captain R B Bannerman, who raised his personal score to ten by shooting down a Fokker DVII east of Houthulst Forest at 0735, being seen to break up in the air. Far to the south, 73 Squadron shot down another at 1040.

Late in the morning, 5 Squadron lost an RE8 on the Arras front, its pilot being killed, the observer wounded but lucky to fall into Allied lines, although the RE was wrecked. Unteroffizier Paul Hüttenrauch of Jasta 7 claimed an AWFK8 during the day, which is probably this incident. Identification, as noted before, was often poor among both sides, evidenced by another RAF loss in the afternoon. However, a 10 Squadron Big Ack was attacked by three DVIIs over Voormezeele at 0905, while directing fire for five 9.2 guns. The observer fired at them and they withdrew.

At 1600, a significant event occurred. Jasta 11 claimed a Bristol Fighter near Bellenglise, right in the middle of the battle area. This was the last claim against the RAF made by its nemesis of Bloody April and many battles since. Leutnant Julius Schulte-Frohlinde's 3rd claim was in fact not a Bristol but an RE8 of 3 AFC, supporting the Australian infantry. Its crew were killed, having taken off at 1515.

Late afternoon saw bombers of 57 Squadron intercepted after a raid on Havrincourt. The five DH4s had just turned north off the target as eight Fokkers came down on them. Two of the German machines were thought to have been shot down, with one DH4 being shot up too, having to make a forced landing at Selis on the way home.

At 1810, the veteran commander of 54 Squadron, Major R S Maxwell MC, made his 8th claim, a C-type out of control east of Havrincourt Wood. Maxwell was out on a solo patrol/special mission. He spotted a lone DFW at 13,500 feet north of Saint-Quentin and drove it down at 1730. Continuing on, he then saw another DFW over Bourlon Wood, attacked and reported it had fallen out of control. Twenty-eight-year-old Gefreiter Paul Milkowski and his observer, Leutnant Robert Müller, 25, of FA(A) 224, were killed in action, crashing near Gonnelieu, which is due east of Havrincourt Wood. This is one of the very few 'out of control' claims made in September for which any victim can be identified.

Josef Jacobs of Jasta 7 claimed his 29th victim at 1900, a Camel at an unknown location – neither is the victim known, although 70 Squadron were attacked by a fighter while low-bombing, but suffered no losses. The only RAF Camel lost was that of Lieutenant N Bruce of 46 Squadron, killed in collision with one of his colleagues – who survived. However, the Germans only recorded two claims for the day, and neither of the two Jasta 7 pilots really scored. In his diary, Jacobs recorded Hüttenrauch downing a Big Ack for his 4th victory, which clearly didn't crash if it was the already mentioned 10 Squadron machine. Jacobs' own victory is noted as having crashed, the pilot 'soon abandoned the aircraft' – which seems to indicate the pilot clambered from the wreck (?) and had come down on the British side of the lines.

Camel C3380, of 54 Squadron. Major R S Maxwell MC shot down a DFW two-seater flying it on 19 September 1918.

French Front

The weather was equally as bad on both the French and American fronts, with low cloud and rain. The French lost one aircraft during the day, Caporal J Fonteile in a Spad of Spa.89 being reported missing. He was lost to balloon defence units, who claimed two aircraft shot down.

The French made one claim, at about 0900. It was for a new type of two-seater that had a white fuselage with red wings and tail, brought down by a patrol of Spa.150, which crashed near Rezonville. (German losses this day recorded Leutnant Lorenz, a pilot with FA241, as wounded.)

Some movements took place on the 19th, as GC12 (Spa.3, 26, 67 and 103) – the famed Cigognes (Storks) Group – moved from Lisle-en-Barrois in the II Armée Sector to La Noblette in the IV Armée, in preparation for the offensive being planned in the Meuse-Argonne Sector.

American Sector

The only action of note this day was the loss of First Lieutenant John W Ogden of the 213th Aero. He got himself lost in bad weather and landed by mistake on a German aerodrome, being taken prisoner. Lieutenant Fred Philbrick of the 28th fell in flames over Chambley.

	A/C	KB		DES	OOC	KB
British losses	5	–	British claims	2	3	–
French losses	1	–	French claims	1		–
American losses	1	–	American claims	–		–
IAF losses	–		IAF claims	–		–
German claims	3		German losses	4		–

British Casualties

Aircraft type	No.	Squadron	Crew		
RE8	F6045	5 Sqdn	Lt H W Driver	KIA	
			2/Lt R Greenyer	WIA	
RE8		9 Sqdn	2/Lt J Turnbull (O)	WIA	*
Camel	F2172	46 Sqdn	Lt N Bruce	KIFA	
Camel	C8342	46 Sqdn	2/Lt A A Partridge	Inj	
RE8	E120	3 AFC	2/Lt J C Peel	KIA	
			Lt J P Jeffers	KIA	

French Casualties

Spad XIII	4720	Spa.89	Cpl J Fonteile	MIA

American Casualties

Spad XIII	15304	213th Aero	1/Lt J W Ogden	POW
Spad XIII	4600	28th Aero	1/Lt F Philbrick	KIA

5

6

7

1 Georg von Hantelmann, one of the youngest of the German aces, he scored 12 of his 25 victories in September, including David Putnam on the 12th and Jo Wehner on the 18th, plus Maurice Boyau, the French ace, on the 16th.

2 Franz Büchner of Jasta 13, on the occasion of his 30th victory, which he achieved on 18 September 1918, one of three Spads he downed that day.

3 Leutnant Julius Buckler flew with Jasta 17 from 1916 till the end of the war, in which time he accounted for 36 Allied machines. He took command of his Jasta on 22 September. He was wounded five times during the war and received the Pour le Mérite.

4 Frank K. Hays flew with the US 13th Aero where he won the DSC for his six victories, three being claimed on 13 September. He is seen here wearing his DSC medal.

5 René Fonck by his Spad fighter, with the 'Stork' marking denoting this to be of Spa.103.

6 Night bombing by aircraft of the Independent Air Force operated mainly with Handley-Page O/400s, such as the one here.

7 Day bombers came in the shape of the DH9 and the DH9A, both depicted here.

British Front

The weather remained wet, with low clouds and continuing high winds. Unlike the previous two days, the Germans were out in force, consequently combats were far more frequent, with the RAF alone totalling over 40 claims.

Two two-seaters were attacked early, one by 24 Squadron, the other by a Dolphin of 79, the latter north of Habourdin, an aerodrome on the outskirts of Lille. An hour after these actions, at 0750, 88 Squadron's Bristol crews fought a number of Fokkers, claiming three, but this appears to have been an action with Jasta 56, who only lost Leutnant Helmut Gantz, severely wounded, and he died the next day in hospital.

At around the same time near Marcoing, Jasta 27 got into a bitter fight with a number of British single-seaters; 60 and 201 Squadrons were the main units involved. Hermann Frommherz got a Camel for his 23rd kill, while Noltenius and Neuenhofen also shot down fighters, the former over Marcoing for his 11th victory, the latter at Proville, for his 8th. No. 60 Squadron lost Lieutenant G F Caswell to Fokkers north of Marcoing at this time and 201 lost Lieutenant J P Mill at Seranvillers. The third was possibly Lieutenant E B Larrabee of 24 Squadron, who failed to return from a patrol that left at 0600. Noltenius called this the hardest fight of his life, whilst a young flight commander from 201 was also impressed. Noltenius recorded:

'We took off at 0700 when we saw flak bursts appear in the sky. At first we did not see any planes. We flew at an altitude of 4,000 metres and it was atrociously cold. We then proceeded more towards enemy territory and gave the flak a chance to bang away at us. This alerted the Englishmen and before long a Sopwith formation of seven machines arrived overhead. We turned home in order to lure them a bit farther over our territory, but Neuenhofen attacked immediately.

'The Englishman spun instantly with Neuenhofen in pursuit. I closed in too, pulled up and fired. The Englishman I had attacked also spun down with me behind him. When I got rather close, I fired and now the dogfighting really started, which was not made any easier by the fact that another Englishman sat on my neck. The Englishman carried a pennant as squadron marking, a ribbon of black and white stripes about the fuselage, just in front of the vertical tailplane. He also had a white "C" on the top wing.

'He flew brilliantly. Spinning had no doubt been only a trick meant to lure me into following him and be killed then. He fired at me from all angles. However, often enough I sat behind him and forced him lower and lower. Finally, with barely 100 metres altitude left, he tried to escape over the lines as the wind had carried us deep into our territory.

'This proved to be his undoing. I now had a good chance and his aircraft rammed into the ground. This was in my memory, the most exciting fight of my life as a fighter pilot. If the wind had not been unfavourable to the

Englishman, things might have turned out the other way. My peculiar technique of side-slipping permitted me to escape over and over again, though he tried loops and everything in the bag and even though his plane was the more manoeuvrable one. But the Fokker was faster and he was unable to escape when he tried to fly home. He was wounded and taken prisoner of war.'

Later, Captain Ronald Sykes DFC wrote of this fight:

'Our flight of five Camels met 12 Fokkers at 5,000 feet, south-east of Cambrai and chased them well east, well into enemy territory. They then turned and must have opened their throttles of new, more powerful engines; to our surprise they easily climbed above us and we had to turn west into the misty air under a cloud. They came through the cloud and started a dogfight. In the streams of mist, identification was difficult but I fired into several "black crosses" as they crossed close ahead.

'A Camel levelled up and looked round again; a misty shape just astern was just starting to go down in flames; I dived below the mist to identify it but all I could see was the top column of black smoke, so I zoomed up and joined a formation of three dim shapes but had the shock of my young life when I got up close and saw their black crosses. They had not seen me so I fired into the nearest one and then pulled up and changed direction in the cloud and dived down into clear air.

'I could see three Camels a long way off going west and no Fokkers but I felt there could be a lot of them above me in the streamers of mist. Did a lot of violent evasive action to avoid being a sitting target. Then "archie" started and I knew the Fokkers had gone and it was safe for me to fly for the other three Camels which were in clear air towards the lines.

'It was Lieutenant Mill who had been shot down, and much later when the infantry advanced through the area, we found his shallow grave beside the remains of his Camel near Seranvillers.

'The Fokkers were in strange green and buff colours, and our Intelligence reported that they belonged to a Circus and had the 185 BMW engine which normally used full throttle only at high altitude; we did not meet them again.'

There are some interesting points to this fight. Firstly, although Noltenius had correctly described the tail markings of 201 Squadron – the black and white stripes – Mills was lost in Camel 'H' and was killed. Noltenius would appear to have picked up one of the SE5s as both these pilots were captured. Also, Sykes reported green and buff Fokkers – almost certainly a misreporting of the SE5s. Possibly involved was Leutnant Georg Meyer of Jasta 37, who took his tally to 20, north of Hermies at 0800. This may have been Larrabee.

Caswell was lost to a blue Fokker at Cantaing at 0740. Also wounded in this fight was a new member of 60 Squadron, who described the fight in his autobiography, published shortly after his death on 4 October 1981. Second Lieutenant Henry Frederick Vulliamy Battle was at the tail of the 60 Squadron formation as they dove away from the eight attacking Fokkers. Battle was hit in the left posterior, but got away into the clouds and managed to land at the friendly aerodrome of 59 Squadron at 0825. His month of active service was over but he would retire an air commodore OBE DFC.

There followed a period of fights and overclaiming by the RAF. No. 218 Squadron claimed three out of control victories during a bombing raid up north, near Bruges at 0920, then between 1000 and 1030 a patrol of 20 Squadron, reinforced by a Flight of 84, was engaged in a fight with up to 20 Fokkers near Saint-Quentin. The RAF communiqué noted that this fight handicapped the RAF due to the strong westerly wind blowing the combatants deeper into German territory. However, the two units claimed no fewer than nine destroyed with a further three out of control. Two of these went to 84, the rest to the Brisfit crews.

In fact this fight was with Jasta 5, who in turn claimed two of the two-seater Bristols. Oberleutnant Otto Schmidt, Staffelführer, got one in flames at Fresnoy-le-Grand at 1037 (his 14th), Unteroffizier Leicht the other over Croix Fonsommé at 1040, also in flames. In the event, 20 Squadron only lost one – in flames. Jasta 5 did not lose a single pilot on this date – nor, it seems, any Fokkers.

The whole problem of fighting over German territory, often at high speed and in a twisting, turning dogfight, in which the Fokkers often dominated, was of reporting what had actually happened. It has to be remembered that the fighter pilot's *raison d'être*, apart from defending the Corps and bombing aircraft, was to shoot down German machines. Equally, the fighter squadrons existed to score victories.

The RAF treated each combat within a fight as a separate entity. Each pilot in the main wrote his own report of the combat, or certainly dictated it to the recording officer who then had it typed up. No one seemed to look at the fight as a whole. By 1918 some squadron commanders and some Wing staff were cutting down on claims by finally looking at the fight as a whole. Colonel Louis Strange was one. However, as the combat reports were passed along, any report with 'disallowed' written on it was still counted back on the squadrons. No change was made to the squadron copy of the report, nor was any revised total noted in the records changed.

Thus, when awards for medals went forward, a pilot with (say) four destroyed and two out of control claims would be put up for a DFC. (At this stage, some brigades had set out six claims as a minimum for a medal.) One of the 'OOC' claims may have been made three months previously – and subsequently disallowed at Wing. From reading all the extant combat reports and War Diaries and other records available, it is obvious to the authors that no one checked this! So a pilot (or a gunner/observer) could get a claim credited towards his medal which had long since been disallowed. However, the two major reasons for overclaiming were as follows: firstly, no ground witnesses were necessary, and no signed air witnesses were required, although quite often another pilot might add his confirmation to a report of a brother officer if he had seen something; secondly, the extremely scant debriefing that followed combat meant little assessment. If two squadrons were in a fight, then double claiming was absolutely certain. It is also evident that often a pilot would see a burning machine hit the ground, but far from being a German, it was one of their own machines, one blazing mass several hundred feet below looking much like any other.

The pilots themselves, with some exceptions, were not liars. They believed what they were accurately claiming. With the insular arrogance of the British Military, which continued into WWII, the British were sure that the Germans were lying about their losses. They were also amazed at the French system not 'trusting' their pilots and crews, by requiring ground witnesses. Their pilots were trusted, and that was that!

The RAF operated 90 per cent of its time over the German lines. It did not have the benefit of counting wrecks. When 151 Squadron claimed, it was nearly totally accurate because it was the only RAF unit that operated under 'German' conditions.

Also, the RAF was completely lacking in any sensible form of overall assessment of results. A failed infantry attack failed. The bodies were there, the ground was not taken. Better efforts would be made next time. In the air there was no system of deciding whether a fight was a failure or not. The evidence was not there – unless they took a massive loss e.g. six out of eight machines failing to return. It took camera guns and a stricter assessment system before RAF claims became very accurate later in WWII. As for the Germans, they overclaimed as well, as evidenced by the usual two claims for one loss in big fights. When the front lines were more or less static, things improved, but fighting over a fluid battle-front, confirmations became less strict.

The 'victorious' RAF pilots, if they knew what they were doing, did not follow their 'victims' down, as even watching them overlong was dangerous. They would have been twisting and turning, checking for danger from behind, above, underneath and each side, and only then might they make a quick check to see if their recent spinning target was still going down. What their eyes may have picked out then could have been almost any machine, their's or someone else's, and if near the ground, in low mist or haze, any number of pilots would return home and put in a combat report for an enemy aircraft shot down. It happened with the bombers too, and the two-seater Bristols.

With half a dozen gunners in a formation of, say, DH4s, being engaged by a gaggle of Fokkers, each firing back desperately before they themselves might be hit, and seeing one Fokker spin away – often just getting out of the way when perhaps the odd bullet or two started hitting their machine – any number of the six gunners might claim a victory. And in the confines of their own little world, wholly concentrating on staying alive and getting that Fokker away from them, they might not be totally aware of all that was going on around them in that instant.

It would be very similar in WWII, during the huge daylight battles fought above Germany by the American 8th Air Force bombers. Attacked by scores of Me 109s or FW190s, a box of four-engined B-17s or B-24s might have up to 30 gunners blazing away. If two German fighters went down, more than a dozen gunners would return reporting a kill.

Should anyone suspect that the Germans in WWI had any reason to hide losses, let it be said that apart from being totally against strict policy there was no reason, and certainly it was very difficult to fabricate even if some unit commander thought it desirable. Each Kofl (Kommandeur der Flieger) – the officer in charge of all flying units assigned to a particular Armee – had to receive accurate reports from each unit each day and there is no defensible reason for any Kofl to try and hide casualties. Those casualties, especially aircraft losses, would have to be made good by the AFP (Armee Flug Park) – aircraft supply depot. The AFPs would have to order replacement machines and crews from FEAs (Flieger Ersatz Abteilung) – aviation replacement units – in order to maintain front-line operational strength. Therefore, how would it be possible for a Kofl, or all Kofls, to turn in false reports to Kogenluft (Kommandierenden General der Luftstreitkräfte) – generals in command of the German Army Air Service – and/or Idflieg (Inspektion der Fliegertruppen) – inspectorate of military aviation? The answer, of course, was that it was not possible. Therefore, although the Germans did keep as meticulous records as the British – certainly in aircraft – their methods of accounting for personnel casualties were little different from the Allies. Most surviving Jasta records appear to be extracts, so one cannot write up one side's losses with the same enthusiasm as 'victories'. A lot of Jastas do not appear to have any non-fatal casualties listed, especially late in the war!

Everyone says from time to time how thorough and meticulous Germans were, how rigid in military matters and so on, so why should anyone doubt their losses. The only reason has to be that with so many aircraft claimed by Allied units and so few apparent recorded losses, there has to be a discrepancy in those records. But the plain truth is, there isn't. The Allied air forces were simply claiming too many victories, i.e. they were not shooting down the number of hostile machines they thought, or would like to think. They had to believe this or the losses sustained were not worth it. And again, this was the first air war in history; who would think that anyone would have the slightest interest in statistics after the war? The winners would win and the losers would lose and that would be sufficient.

To balance the argument, it has to be said that some German claims do not check out, despite the equally meticulous German method of assessing confirmations. Each claim had to have two independent witnesses and be agreed by Kogenluft; yet even so, occasionally the system failed – even with someone as well known as Manfred von Richthofen – but not as much as on the Allied side.

At 1050, a DH9 was claimed in flames south-east of Montigny by Leutnant Karl Odebrett of Jasta 42 – an experienced pilot, whose 14th kill this was – yet there is no known loss to match it. Leutnant Hans Böhning, CO of Jasta 79b, was also wounded further north-east, over Soriel, reportedly in a fight with another DH9. It ended his war, with a record of 17 victories; he was to die in a sailplane gliding accident in 1934. The only DH9 casualty this day was a 205 Squadron machine on a bomb raid, whose pilot was mortally wounded. He got his machine back but died of his wounds. 205, who had just started to receive DH9As, were operating from Proyart, midway between Amiens and Saint-Quentin.

Whilst this fight was on, the day's activities were hotting up on the Channel coast. Two Fokkers were claimed at 1015 by 65 Squadron south-west of Bruges. Five minutes later 204 Squadron also became involved, claiming six Fokkers, between Dixmude and Ostende, but losing two Camels with another pilot forced to land. The Marine pilots of MFJ 1 and 2 shot them down, one going to Leutnant P Becht at Beerst, while Leutnant Max Stinsky got his south-east of Pervyse – in Allied lines. Leutnant Theo Osterkamp claimed another at Praet Bosch and Vizeflugmeister Karl Scharon got a fourth at Pervyse. One too many – a double claim.

Just before 1100, Carl Degelow of Jasta 40 brought his score to 15 by shooting down a 48 Squadron BF2b at Annappes, but this was the last fight of the morning.

At 1455, the 148th American Squadron, still fighting on the British front, were in action, First Lieutenant Elliott White Springs shooting down a Fokker north of Cambrai, but the unit lost Harry Jenkinson. They had been out on an intended balloon strafe. Leutnant Noltenius claimed a Camel at Aubigny-au-Bac at 1445 and left us this graphic account:

> 'We now played a nice game with them. We kept approaching them rather closely while over there, but moved away smartly when they came too close. Then one of them came too close and Klimke rushed into the attack, pursuing him downwards. The fight ended when the Camels disappeared in the clouds. I had to remain upstairs and kept a careful watch. Now I saw another Sopwith turn in our direction, planning to catch Klimke from the rear. I attacked him head-on and shot well from this position. Thereupon, he turned away, but not tightly enough. I positioned myself behind him and after aiming carefully, fired. Though the distance between us was nearly 400 metres, the plane broke into flames after a short burst. It carried two pennants.'

The next fight was a huge affair between JGIII and three squadrons of the RAF. This occurred from the south to the north of Cambrai and slightly to the west. No. 87 Squadron Dolphins made three claims, all destroyed over Noyelles. Lieutenant Leslie Hollinghurst was attacked by a Fokker while accompanied by Captain A W Vigers MC and was comprehensively shot up, but got away and then shot one down off the tail of Lieutenant D C Mangan. In return, Mangan claimed the one that had shot up Hollinghurst, while Captain H A R Biziou claimed a third.

The SE5s of 85 Squadron were also involved, Lieutenant J W Warner claiming a Fokker in flames east of Bourlon Wood at 1530. The main involvement, however, was from 203 Squadron, who had all three of its flights out on this patrol. They claimed five Fokkers, all near Hayencourt, one destroyed and another breaking up, from which the pilot baled out. They lost two Camels.

The fight had been with Jasta 26, who indeed claimed two Sopwith Camels – credited to Leutnant F Brandt at Écourt for his 9th, at 1540, the second to Leutnant Otto Frühner, east of Cagnicourt at 1545, for his 27th. However, his Fokker was then hit and he baled out, landing safely but injured sufficiently to keep him out of the war. Second Lieutenant W H Coghill had claimed the machine from which the pilot parachuted, so this was yet another case of a youngster getting his first kill, by downing a high-scoring and highly experienced fighter pilot; although there is a suggestion that Frühner may have collided with a Camel first, for he reported that he had been rammed by a crashing Camel which caused his wings to break off. This was not the case, for he was hit by Coghill. Leutnant Schneider was also shot down in this fight and survived, but it is not certain if he went down to 87, 85 or 203 Squadron.

Leutnant Paul Baümer of Jasta 2 Boelcke claimed a Camel east of Rumaucourt, reportedly at 1550. None were lost at this time but an hour later, at 1650, Lieutenant D C Ware of 209 Squadron was shot down in flames near here – over Écourt, by a Fokker. In return, 209 claimed a Fokker out of control.

That night 151 Squadron struck again. At 2135, Captain F C Broome shot down an AEG bomber seen in the moonlight; it fell in flames at Tincourt, in Allied lines, north-west of Saint-Quentin. Leutnant Karl Schneider, Vizefeldwebel Johannes Schnabel and Flieger Walther Fischer were all killed at Jeancourt, which is a couple of kilometres from Tincourt. Both Schnabel and Fischer were just short of their 18th birthdays, no doubt a sign of how manpower in Germany was in short supply.

French Front

During the day there was little fighting on this front and only two claims were made. A Bréguet bomber crew claimed one, and a fighter patrol of GC14 another. The Germans recorded losses on this front, Flieger Wilhelm Sudmeyer killed in action at Bouriers, Flieger Karl Porzelt at Saint-Avold and Luftsch Johann Semken killed in action at Montigny – the latter a balloon man.

That evening, Unteroffizier Eddelbuttel and Leutnant Huss of FA276 took off at 2210 and were hit by ground fire and forced to come down in French territory. However, they managed to regain the German lines on the 22nd.

That night the French lost three bombing aircraft. Jasta 73 claimed three night-flying Voisins, credited to Franz Kirchfeld, Offizierstellvertreter Werner Schluckebier and Leutnant Fritz Anders, the Staffelführer. Jasta 73 specialised in night sorties, Fritz Gerhard Anders becoming the first WWI German night ace. Groupement Pouderoux reported three bombers lost, one coming from GB1.

The 1st Brigade d'Aviation was ordered to change its sphere of operations to the area between Montfaucon and the Moselle River, covering part of the French II Armée and all of the American 1st Army front. The 2nd Brigade was to cover the area between Prunay and Montfaucon, covering the rest of the II Armée and IV Armée fronts.

American Sector

Nothing to report.

IAF

All five HP Squadrons made raids this night, to Boulay, Frescaty, Morhange and Buhl airfields, Thourout railway station, Mannheim and the gas works at Karlsruhe. At least one night fighter was encountered, but this was shot down in flames by Lieutenant E J Whyte, gunner to Lieutenant Firby, which won him the DFC. German AA fire claimed one bomber shot down in flames over Metz, and another crashed on landing but without crew casualties.

	A/C	KB		DES	OOC	KB
British losses	13	–	British claims	30	13	–
French losses	3	–	French claims	3		–
American losses	–	–	American claims	–		–
IAF losses	–		IAF claims	–		–
German claims	21		German losses	4†		–

† Possibly two or three more.

British Casualties

Aircraft type	No.	Squadron	Crew		
SE5a	E4072	24 Sqdn	Lt E P Larrabee (USAS)	POW	
BF2b	E2183	88 Sqdn	Lt A Williamson	Safe	*
			2/Lt K C Craig	Safe	
Camel	C125	201 Sqdn	2/Lt J P Mill	KIA	
SE5a	D6945	60 Sqdn	2/Lt H F V Battle	WIA	*
SE5a	F5472	60 Sqdn	Lt G F C Caswell	POW	
SE5a	E4000	29 Sqdn	Lt C G Ross DFC	Safe	
BF2b	E2260	48 Sqdn	Lt M R Mahony	POW	
			2/Lt J N Keir	POW	
BF2b	E2158	20 Sqdn	2/Lt A R Strachan	KIA	
			2/Lt D M Calderwood	KIA	
RE8	F6007	9 Sqdn	Lt C Dotzert	Safe	*
			2/Lt K S Hill	WIA	
Camel	B6319	204 Sqdn	2/Lt D F Tysoe	WIA	*
Camel	D8205	204 Sqdn	2/Lt C L Kelly	KIA	
Camel	D3387	204 Sqdn	2/Lt E G Rolph	POW	
Camel	F6192	148th Aero	1/Lt H Jenkinson	KIA	
Camel	E4409	203 Sqdn	2/Lt M G Cruise	KIA	
Camel	E4377	203 Sqdn	2/Lt G C Milne	POW	
Camel	F5986	209 Sqdn	Lt D C Weare	KIA	
RE8	D4866	59 Sqdn	Lt W C Christian	Safe	
			2/Lt W G Brown	WIA	*
RE8	–	21 Sqdn	2/Lt F L W Dowling	WIA	*
			2/Lt W Cooke	Safe	
DH9	F6119	205 Sqdn	Lt W V Theron	DOW	*
			2/Lt J J Rowe	Safe	
HP O/400 (night)	C9732	215 Sqdn	2/Lt A C G Fowler	KIA	
			2/Lt C C Eaves	KIA	
			2/Lt J S Ferguson	KIA	
HP O/400 (night)	D4589	115 Sqdn	Lt Firby	Safe	*
			Lt C A Bonar	Safe	
			Lt E J Whyte	Safe	
HP O/400 (night)	D5424	115 Sqdn	3 crew	Safe	*

French Casualties

Voisin XB2 (Groupement Pouderoux)	GB1	Two crew	MIA	
Voisin XB2 (Groupement Pouderoux)	GB1	Two crew	MIA	
Voisin XB2 (Groupement Pouderoux)	GB1	Two crew	MIA	

British Front

The weather continued to be bad, with a good deal of cloud and a very strong wind. Considering the losses sustained during this month, how much more severe they might have been if fine weather had kept both sides active in the air!

In the early hours of the morning, one of the RAF's night bomber crews put up a good show. Lieutenant H R Hern of 148 Squadron, whilst gliding down to bomb Seclin aerodrome, was caught in a heavy barrage of 'flaming onions' and tracer, being wounded in the shoulder at 1,000 feet. In spite of this wound he dropped his bombs with what was described as good effect. On the way back, against heavy head winds, he was again subjected to much ground fire. His observer, Lieutenant A A Tutte, seeing his pilot was in a fainting condition, climbed onto the top of the FE's gondola and held the 'joystick'. Being in front of the pilot, he would, of course, be facing backwards. At the same time, he forced some brandy down his pilot's throat. In this situation, and in spite of fainting three times, Hern and Tutte returned safely and Hern landed without further damage. Both men received the DFC.

On this night of the 20th/21st, eight FEs of 83 Squadron bombed Bazuel aerodrome, the bombers meeting sporadic gunfire from around Cambrai. Meantime, two other aircraft of the squadron flew night recce sorties but Major D A MacRae, acting CO of C Flight, and his observer were hit by ground fire, which punctured the fuel tank. He was forced to land near Montigny Farm. It was only his second sortie in France but this 33-year-old Canadian survived and continued with 83 until the war's end. He had previously been with Home Defence units.

The Dolphins of 79 Squadron shot down two two-seaters early on, Captain R B Bannerman sending his down to crash south-west of Hollebeke at 1015, Lieutenant

Below Another nice picture of an SE5a (E5965), this one with 2 AFC Squadron. Lt G J Cox was lost in this aircraft on 21 September to become a prisoner of war.

Top right Three Sopwith Dolphin pilots with 79 Squadron. Captain R B Bannerman DFC (NZ), Lt C L Lindberg, and Captain F W Gillett (US). Seven of Bannerman's victories were scored in September, while seven of Gillett's fell the same month. Both received the DFC.

H M S Parsons sending another down east of Oostaverne 20 minutes later. On the debit side, Carl Degelow of Jasta 40s knocked down an RE8 of 7 Squadron at St Julien, north of Ypres at 1045, which went down in flames. The Germans also noted the arrival of an SE5a of 2 AFC, Lieutenant George Cox having to force-land near Armentières after his engine was knocked off its mountings by an unknown object.

Shortly after noon, Jasta 7 found and attacked DH9s of 108 Squadron over Zarren, on the Dunkirk front. Josef Jacobs claimed two, but only one was confirmed, Leutnant Karl Plauth of Jasta 20 getting the second at Staden. The 'Nines' claimed one Fokker out of control.

Other than some scraps by Dolphins of 79 and 19 Squadrons, there was little activity until the evening. At 1745, 84 Squadron claimed two Fokkers north-east of Saint-Quentin, and at 1810, Captain W E Shields of 41 Squadron forced two Fokkers to collide, one being seen to crash, the other spinning down out of control.

Above Paul Bäumer initially served with Jasta 5 in 1917 before moving to Jasta 2. By the end of March 1918 he had been credited with 18 combat victories. Following a crash in May he returned to the front and by early October his score had risen to 43. Sixteen of these had been accounted for during September 1918, including three on the following dates: 21, 27 and 29 September. He received the Pour le Mérite following his 20th victory. He died in a flying accident in 1927.

Then Captain W R 'Wop' May of 209 Squadron got into a fight, and although he claimed a Fokker, his own machine was damaged sufficiently for it to be written off upon his return to base. Lieutenant G Knight also added a victory to his score of the previous day. This fight took place at 1835 over Écourt St Quentin, both claims being out of control. However, Vizewfeldwebel Ernst de Ritter of Jasta 27 was shot down unhurt during this encounter. For once the Germans overclaimed, for they reported two Camels shot down, one by Frommherz, the other by Leutnant Klimke, but only May was shot up.

Five minutes later, to the north, near Lille, the RAF lost one of its legends – fortunately as a prisoner. Captain Sidney 'Timbertoes' Carlin was lost in a fight with Jasta 29. Unteroffizier Westphal got him east of La Bassée for his 2nd victory. In return 74 claimed four, two being out of control, but Jasta 29 had no losses.

To the south, JGIII encountered bombers. North of Fontaine Notre Dame, which 57 Squadron had just bombed, the formation was attacked by up to a dozen Fokkers. In a fierce fight, one DH4 was brought down, although three were claimed. Surprisingly, these three were credited to the usually reliable Paul Baümer of Jasta 2 Boelcke, his victories 28 to 30, east of Bourlon Wood, east of Lagnicourt and east of Morchies. However, there was a 205 Squadron DH9 shot up some time during the afternoon, its observer wounded, but the time and location are uncertain. The DH gunners reported shooting down one Fokker out of control, while the whole formation got a share of a red Fokker with a yellow tail – in flames. The only recorded casualty was the 17-victory ace Leutnant Rudolf Klimke of Jasta 27 who was wounded three times in the shoulder at this time, in combat with two-seaters, so it seems pretty certain one of the Fokker pilots was him. (There is a suggestion, however, that he was wounded in a fight with BF2bs.)

Another two-seater DH4 of 205 Squadron however, was lost at 1735, falling to Josef Mai of Jasta 5 – his 27th victory – at Le Catelet, although the German records note this to be an hour later; but this, along with other noted records, may be due to historians forgetting that German time was no longer one hour ahead of Allied time at this period.

A German two-seater crew of Schlasta 2, Vizefeldwebel Niemeyer and Unteroffizier Kappel, claimed an RE8 north-west of Épehy at 0945, but no RE8s feature on the loss reports. However, two AWFK8s on contact patrol work returned with wounded observers, and although one was supposedly hit by ground fire, it would not be the first time AWs would be mistaken for RE8s, despite the size difference!

During the day, the Germans had extensively overclaimed, something they were prone to do when operating near a battle front in bad weather. Obviously the confirmation system broke down when aircraft fell into a battle area or inside Allied lines. However, they never overclaimed as much as the RAF!

That night the real professional operators of the RAF struck another three times (and, it must be said, the only RAF unit that had one-on-one fights over their own lines with thousands of witnesses!). No.151's commander, Major Brand, shot down a Friedrichshafen GIII at 2126 near Gouzeaucourt. Nine minutes later, to the south of this location, he shared an AEG with Lieutenant J H Summers, a post-war member of the Royal Australian Air Force. Then Lieutenant A A Mitchell struck again, with a Gotha north of Péronne, also at 2135. One of the crews brought down came from Bombenstaffel 23, Bogohl 7 – the AEG – crewed by Vizefeldwebel Wilhelm Gudemann and Leutnant Werner Schmidt, who fell at Proyart. Bogohl 7 also lost Unteroffizier Wilhelm Lansberg killed and Gefreiter Bosche wounded, coming down near Sailly. A third crew, Leutnant Delte and Flieger Stocker, also of Bogohl 7, were wounded. In fact, all three aircraft were probably AEGs.

French Front

A patrol from GC 16 was engaged in combat with 14 Fokkers at 0800 over Cerney, losing Spa.151's Sergent Frederic Claudet, in flames. The only claims for Spads were by Jasta 18, but all were at 1900 or later in the evening. One assumes someone got the time wrong. Nine machines of Jasta 18 attacked Spads over the Facq Woods and Vizefeldwebel Richard Schleichardt, formally of Jasta 15, gained his 3rd and final kill, in Allied lines at this time. This was followed five minutes later by two more Spads, one to Leutnant Hans Müller, his 12th, and one to Leutnant Erich Spindler, his 2nd and last victory, both falling over the Combres Heights. Sergent Millot of Spa.65 was reported wounded.

A recce sortie by three aircraft of Br.221 in the VIII Armée sector was attacked at 1000 hours by five hostile machines. During the combat, the Bréguet of Sous Lieutenant Bernard and Sergent Darbonnens was hit and the rear man wounded, but they got back.

Groupe de Combat 11 commenced operations in the IV Armée sector, located at Frencheville, about 15 km south-east of Châlons.

American Sector

At 1750, First Lieutenant Herbert R Hall of the 95th Aero claimed a Fokker at 2,000 metres over Doncourt. This was evidently another misidentification or the aircraft type was recorded wrongly, as a two-seater of FA2 was lost at St Hilaire, in the Armee Abteilung 'C' sector, and Doncourt is about three kilometres to the south-east. This was the only US claim of the day.

This FA2 machine was flown by Unteroffizier Gerhard Schlueter and Leutnant Erwin Sklarek, who were both killed. Another two-seater was lost on this same front, Flieger John and Leutnant Eduard Reichenwaller of FA 46 being killed over Bray. This may relate to a French claim for an aircraft shot down by Sous Lieutenant Cousin of Spa.163, in a combat over Tahure, or a claim made by a patrol from an unknown escadrille.

IAF

IAF bombers dropped a total of fifteen-and-a-half tons of bombs and fired off 7,810 rounds of ammunition at hangars, searchlights, AA batteries, trains and other targets. No. 216 Squadron bombed factories at Rombach, 207 Squadron bombed the airfields at Metz and Frescaty. 115 Squadron attacked Morhange and Leiningen railway stations, while 215 raided the blast furnaces at Hagondange, which were heavily defended by flak. One HP of 216 lost an engine and crashed on landing, injuring the pilot, whose 29th and final operation this turned out to be.

	A/C	KB		DES	OOC	KB
British losses	8	–	British claims	14	6	–
French losses	2	–	French claims	2		–
American losses	–	–	American claims	1		–
IAF losses	–		IAF claims	–	–	–
German claims	14	–	German losses	6		–

British Casualties			
Aircraft type	No.	Squadron	Crew	
FE2b (night)	F5853	83 Sqdn	Lt D D A Greig	Evaded
			2/Lt W A Armstrong	Evaded
RE8	F5976	7 Sqdn	Lt W G Allanson	KIA
			2/Lt W Anderson	KIA
SE5a	E5965	2 AFC Sqdn	2/Lt G Cox	POW
DH9	D5759	108 Sqdn	2/Lt H L McLellan	KIA
			2/Lt F X Jackson	KIA
DH9	D3092	108 Sqdn	2/Lt D A Shanks	KIA
			Sgt R Sear	KIA
Camel	D9599	209 Sqdn	Capt W R May	Safe
DH4	F5827	57 Sqdn	2/Lt O McI Turnbull	KIA
			Lt D F V Page	KIA
DH9	A8089	205 Sqdn	2/Lt A N Hyde	KIA
			2/Lt W W Harrison	KIA
DH9	F1015	205 Sqdn	Lt W H Clarke	Safe
			2/Lt W Tunstall	WIA
SE5a	D6958	74 Sqdn	Capt S Carlin MC	POW
AWFK8	D5137	8 Sqdn	Lt G L Ballantyne	Safe
			2/Lt A B McDonald	WIA

Aircraft type	No.	Squadron	Crew		
AWFK8	F7383	35 Sqdn	Lt H C Heintzman	Safe	*
			2/Lt A E Harris	WIA	
HP O/400	–	215 Sqdn	2/Lt A C G Fowler	KIA	
			2/Lt C C Eaves	KIA	
			2/Lt J S Ferguson	KIA	
FE2b	–	148 Sqdn	Lt H R Hern	WIA	
			2/Lt A A Tutte	Safe	

French Casualties

Spad XIII		Spa.151	Sgt F Claudet	KIA	
Spad XIII		Spa.65	Sgt P Millot	WIA	
Bréguet XIV		Br.221	S/Lt Bernard	Safe	*
			Sgt Darbonnens	WIA	

22 SEPTEMBER 1918
M T W T F S **S**

British Front

Low clouds and rain storms returned to the British end of the front, whilst the weather was good in the morning on the French front, later turning to rain.

The Camel pilots of 4 AFC were on patrol early, and three, flown by Lieutenants P J Sims, T C Cox and T H Barkell, were at 6,000 feet preparing to dive-bomb Armentières railway station. Suddenly above them appeared 13 Fokker DVIIs of Jasta 30, who immediately dived. For the second time in the month the Australians had been caught, and once again their patrol was nearly wiped out. Sims got away safely but Cox was forced to land near Sailly. Barkell was nearly lost, as he was attacked by four Fokkers. The first he avoided by a half-roll and turn, which took him on to the Fokker's tail, claiming this shot down out of control. He then claimed another in the same fashion but was hit by the others, one of which followed him down to 100 feet, where he crash-landed in British lines near Neuve-Église. The Aussies timed the fight at 0820, while Jasta 30's CO, Leutnant Hans-Georg von der Marwitz, reported his 12th victory south of Neuve-Église at 0815, and Leutnant Friedrich Bieling reported his 1st victory at Ploegsteert Wood at 0820.

Prior to this, Vizefeldwebel Karl Bohnenkamp of Jasta 22s claimed two Camels shot down at 0750 north of Épehy – inside Allied lines. It is not known to which unit these Camels belonged (Épehy is way down south from 4 AFC's area), there being no corresponding British losses.

The next fight took place at 0840. Pilots of the 17th US Aero, escorted by Dolphins of 87 Squadron, ran into Jasta 34 and elements of JGIII. Once again Leutnant Noltenius was involved. His diary records:

'At 0700 hours the whole Geschwader took off. We climbed to great altitude – no activity at all. Finally, six machines – two-seaters – made an appearance.

George A. Vaughn Jr from New York, achieved seven victories with the Royal Air Force, flying SE5s with 84 Squadron. Moving to the 17th Aero he brought his score to 13, three of them in September. He too received both the US and British DFCs. Two of his September victories were over Leutnant Fritz Noltenius of Jasta 27, who survived, and Karl Bauernfeind of Jasta 34, who did not.

Staffel 26 went after them. It did not take long and soon enemy single-seaters appeared, coming towards Albert. We flew over enemy territory; from our side a squadron of Sopwiths approached. We dived on them at once but I remained higher up because I saw another Sopwith formation approaching. I flew in front of their leader in order to make him attack me. He promptly dived vertically for me and I turned towards him firing at once. Then another Fokker wedged himself between the Sopwith and me and the dogfight continued.

'Alternately, Mesch, Neuenhofen and I were behind him. Finally Neuenhofen got close enough, kept behind him and forced him down for good. I kept a bit higher up because the cloth covering of the top wing had torn off and several ribs were broken in the hectic dogfight. The kill was credited to Neuenhofen. Frommherz too shot down one.'

First Lieutenant George Vaughn of the 17th, reported:

'Whilst on OP at 0845, I dived vertically on EA which was circling over a machine of our formation at 7-8,000 feet and fired at him from a range of 80 yards. He dived steeply past others of our machines below, and I could not observe results, since I turned to engage another EA, which I shot down and which was observed to crash by Lieut. Dixon.'

Vaughn was then shot up himself but got back using his emergency fuel tank. Dixon saw Vaughn's Fokker burst into flames and crash; Vaughn was awarded the American DSC for this action. The Americans lost two pilots: Lieutenant Theose E Tillinghast became a prisoner (but later escaped), while Lieutenant Gerald P Thomas was killed. Howard Knotts also claimed a Fokker, which he last saw suspended upside down in a tree! Lieutenant Glen Wicks also claimed a Fokker destroyed west of Rumilly. Sixty years after the war, the noted aviation historian Jon Guttmann showed Vaughn Noltenius's account of the fight, and he immediately recognised himself as the German's opponent.

In all the Germans claimed four kills, the other two by Leutnant Franz Brandt of Jasta 26 and Bruno Loerzer, JGIII's leader, the latter's 41st victory. During the fight, Captain H A R Biziou of 87 Squadron claimed two aircraft destroyed over Bourlon Wood at 0840. Jasta 34b lost Leutnant Karl Bauernfeind, killed south-west of Cambrai – in flames – presumably the victim of George Vaughn.

More fights took place around 0900, Vizefeldwebel Belz of Jasta 1 claiming an RE8 at 0855; none were lost although a 53 Squadron machine returned shot up by ground fire, while 87 Squadron's Captain A W Vigers and Lieutenant Ross MacDonald shared a Rumpler destroyed at 0910. Nos. 64 and 24 Squadrons also made claims for Fokkers during the morning. However, the latter unit lost an SE5, its pilot having both petrol tanks shot through, forcing him to land between the trenches. Lieutenant W C Sterling regained the Allied lines but his fighter had to be abandoned.

Second Lieutenant J G Gunn of 56 Squadron was lost near Hamel at midday to Fokkers, Leutnant Thuy of Jasta 28w claiming his 31st victory near Vitry, not far from Hamel. Also Bruno Loerzer claimed another single-seater during the day, possibly Lieutenant D A Nevill of 41 Squadron, missing over Comines soon after 1300.

At 1325 a 12 Squadron RE8 crew beat off the attentions of some Fokkers. Lieutenants H J Evans and C A Stubbings put up a stout show against a succession of attacks, Stubbings firing at each as it came in. The last Fokker to dive zoomed up, looped, then fell upside down and was seen to crash.

Other than the Jasta 34b loss, the only other recorded German casualty was Leutnant Krayer of Jasta 45, who was wounded on this day, the unit operating on the French front.

French Front

Adjutant Charles Mace shot down two balloons to claim his 2nd and 3rd victories. The first was at 1004 near Geline, the other three minutes later at Juvelize. These balloons were BZ62 and BZ36, both lost in this area by a lone Spad. Caporal Taillor of Spa.124 also reported downing a Fokker on this day.

The Germans claimed a Bréguet south of Flavy le Martel at 0956, Leutnant Karl Odebrett of Jasta 42 seeing it come down inside French lines. This was possibly the Bréguet of Br.123, in which the US observer was wounded (1/Lt E M Powell). Vizefeldwebel Hünninghaus claimed a Spad near Pont Arcy while Oberleutnant Oskar von Boenigk, leader of JGII, claimed an American Salmson near Conflans. None were reported lost.

American Sector

The only American activity was the moving from the Toul area to Vivincourt, 50 km south-south-east of Verdun, of the 1st Army Observation Group. They were preparing for the Meuse-Argonne offensive, due to start on the 26th.

	A/C	KB		DES	OOC	KB
British losses	5	–	British claims	8	6	–
French losses	–	–	French claims	–	2	–
American losses	–	–	American claims	–		–
IAF losses	–		IAF claims	–	–	–
German claims	13	–	German losses	2		2

British Casualties					
Aircraft type	No.	Squadron	Crew		
Camel	E1592	4 AFC	Lt T C Cox	Safe	*
Camel	E7191	4 AFC	Lt T H Barkell	Safe	*
Camel	F2157	17th Aero	1/Lt T E Tillinghast	POW	
Camel	F5969	17th Aero	2/Lt G P Thomas	KIA	
Camel	F6034	17th Aero	1/Lt G A Vaughn	Safe	*
RE8	C2506	53 Sqdn	2/Lt J P Sharpe	Safe	
			2/Lt S A Bird	Safe	
SE5a	E6012	24 Sqdn	Lt W C Sterling	Safe	
SE5a	C8864	56 Sqdn	2/Lt J G Gunn	POW	
SE5a	F5453	74 Sqdn	Lt F J Hunt	Safe	*
SE5a	C9133	41 Sqdn	Lt D A Nevill	POW	

23 SEPTEMBER 1918
M T W T F S S

British Front

This Monday was a day of more strong winds, overcast sky and some rain. The RAF communiqué described enemy aircraft activity as slight, and most of that occurred late in the evening.

The Camel-equipped 3 Squadron lost a pilot to Fokker DVIIs at 0800, Second Lieutenant Stuart H Richardson, a Londoner, who would have turned 19 on the 28th, and who had been on the squadron for just one month. A comrade of his, Lieutenant Albert McManus, an American, left this sad account of how a novice's mistake was usually fatal:

> 'Just came in from a dawn show which I was leading. There were 18 machines in three layers of six machines each, about 2,000 feet above each other. My flight was the lowest, at about 7,000 feet. The two hours were almost up when I saw nine Fokkers about ten miles north-west of us, and also a two-seater about a mile east. I had a go at the two-seater, to drive him east, and then I turned to run out from the Fokkers. One of my pilots, a new chap, cut right through the formation and in under the Fokkers, who immediately attacked. They were firing explosive bullets at him, and he didn't even try to get away but just flew straight until one of the explosive bullets hit his petrol tank which burst into flames. The flames immediately went out, but burst out at three distinct times during his fall. He must have lost his head, for he was on our side of the lines and could have spun down to the ground and got away. It just made me sick, for it is the first time that I've lost a man, and he just made himself a gift to those Huns. If he had stayed with me he'd have been all right, for the rest of us were not even fired upon.'

Also shot down, but force-landing safely, was Lieutenant Martin Giesecke of the 17th Aero, who was unhurt. Both were possible victims of JGIII, or another Jasta. Leutnant Noltenius of Jasta 27 claimed a two-seater in flames inside German lines and another was claimed by Leutnant Frommherz, but neither were confirmed and perhaps they were given to another unit. No other German claims appear to have been made during the day that fit the time or location, as total claims for the day were nine, plus a balloon. There is also the possibility that one of the German claims listed on the 22nd was actually for the 23rd.

An RE8 of 13 Squadron then attacked a DFW two-seater, which was circling over a downed Camel. Lieutenant G S Bourner dived on it, fired, then turned to let his observer, Lieutenant F A D Vaughn, fire as well. The enemy machine fell to the ground and burst into flames at 0835, near Sains-lès-Marquion.

The next action was over the Belgian coastal plain. A patrol of 213 Squadron drove down a Fokker out of control six miles east of Dixmude, but was disallowed by Wing HQ. In fact, they had accounted for Flugmaatrose Karl Schiffmann, of MFJ 2, who was killed by Camels at Ichtegem, which is due east of Dixmude. In the afternoon, a DH9 of 211 Squadron went down to flak over Bruges, and landed in Holland.

Oberleutnant Hasso von Wedel, of Jasta 24s, reported shooting down an SE5a at 1620 near Villers Outreaux, but there was no such loss. An hour later, at 14,000 feet north of Bourlon, an LVG crew from FA(A) 228 were shot down, crashing near Sailly, under a kilometre north-east of Bourlon. Vizefeldwebel Paul Färber and Sergeant Leopold Bach were both killed – victims of the deadly Captain George Gates of 201 Squadron, whose 14th victim spun straight in after a burst from his guns.

During the day, the 42 Squadron crew of Second Lieutenants G C Upson and A N Thomson, whilst on a photography sortie, were attacked by eight Fokker biplanes, one of which hit their fuel tank, dousing Upson with petrol. The observer fired 30 rounds at this Fokker when his Lewis gun was hit and put out of action. However, another crew saw the Fokker go down and crash. At 1715, another 42 Squadron RE, crewed by Second Lieutenants D A Newson and G E M Browne, was brought down in flames by a Fokker. This was probably Leutnant Hermann Leptien, CO of Jasta 63, who made his 7th and final claim of the war, south of Fleurbaix at 1710.

The bulk of the actions came in two intense fights in the evening. The first was between six Dolphins of 87 Squadron and 14 red and black Fokkers at 1745, although one was described as having black and white checks. In the first encounter they claimed one Fokker destroyed and two out of control, and 25 minutes later in another scrap the Dolphin pilots claimed three more, two out of control, while Lieutenant Leslie Hollinghurst reported the pilot of his Fokker either baled or jumped out. Lieutenant F W Goodman was shot up, wounded, and forced to land near Sailly. Leutnant Fritz Rumey of Jasta 45 claimed a Dolphin south of Barelle at 1815 – his 41st kill.

The Bristols of 20 Squadron encountered a formation of DVIIs north-east of Saint-Quentin at 1815 and over the next 15 minutes claimed six of them, four destroyed and two out of control, whilst losing one, with another observer wounded. This fight was with Jasta 24s, whose Vizefeldwebel Kurt Ungewitter claimed his 4th victory at Levergies at 1825. Jasta 24s recorded no losses.

That evening, 102 Squadron sent out its FE2 bombers at 1940 hours. One machine was hit by AA fire, its crew being forced down at Épehy, between the front line and the support trenches. Both men scrambled into the British trenches, but their machine was shelled and destroyed.

French Front

There was not much activity on this front either. Leutnants von Beaulieu-Marconnay of Jasta 19 and von Hantelmann of Jasta 15 are reported to have claimed on the 23rd or 25th. It is believed the 25th was the correct date. A Spad (two-seater!?) claimed by Vizefeldwebel Hans Christian Donhauser of Jasta 17 at 1255 believed to have been a Salmson 2A2 of Sal.28 – the only French loss this day. However, Caporal Stanley of Spa.23, whilst attacking a German two-seater, was hit by return fire. Making a forced landing in the front lines he smashed his aircraft but it is not certain if it was a total loss.

A balloon was reported shot down by Leutnant Oldenberg of Jasta 22s at Atilly at 1620, while the only French claim was an EA downed by Lieutenants Denis and Beucler of Sal.40, near Mont-sans-Nom.

	A/C	KB			DES	OOC	KB
British losses	4	–	British claims		10	6	–
French losses	1	1?	French claims		1		–
American losses	–	–	American claims		–		–
IAF losses	–		IAF claims		–	–	–
German claims	5	1	German losses		2†		–

†Apart from those already mentioned, German casualties also included one Feldwebel, one Gefreiter and two Fliegers as being killed this date, units unknown.

British Casualties

Aircraft type	No.	Squadron	Crew	
Camel	F6029	3 Sqdn	2/Lt S H Richardson	KIA
Camel	H7275	17th Aero	Lt M Giesecke	Safe
RE8	C2300	42 Sqdn	2/Lt D A Newson	KIA
			2/Lt G E M Browne	KIA
Dolphin	D3741	87 Sqdn	Lt F W Goodman	WIA *
BF2b	E2562	20 Sqdn	Lt J Nicholson	KIA
			2/Lt B W Wilson	KIA
BF2b	E2467	20 Sqdn	Lt E A Britton	Safe *
			Sgt R S Dodds	WIA
FE2b (night)	A6521	102 Sqdn	Capt P M McSwiney	Safe
			Lt E R Canning	Safe
BF2b	E2363	11 Sqdn	2/Lt C Johnson	Safe *
			Sgt G H Hampson	WIA
Camel	F2174	80 Sqdn	2/Lt F A Fairburn	KIA

French Casualties

Salmson 2A2		Sal.28	Cpl Latil	MIA
			Sgt Saloman	MIA
Spad XIII		Spa.23	Cpl A H Stanley	Inj
Spad XIII		Spa.95	S/Lt B Schroeder	WIA *

24 SEPTEMBER 1918
M **T** W T F S S

British Front

As the weather improved to being fair with some cloud according to the RAF, it was described as being magnificent by Friedrich Noltenius. In consequence there was a marked increase in aerial activity. During the day the RAF were to claim 96 aircraft and balloons; the Germans admit to losing six aircraft, whilst claiming 26 Allied aircraft and seven balloons in return.

Still aggressive despite their near disaster of the 22nd, 4 AFC Squadron were about early again, in pairs. Captain E J K McCloughry claimed a DFW C east of Lille at 0625, followed by a Fokker ten minutes later, both destroyed, taking his victories to 21. The Fokker's colleagues, however, wounded the Australian but he just managed to regain the Allied lines before force-landing. Soon afterwards, George Jones added another Halberstadt two-seater to the squadron's bag, this time near Lens. Jones and his fighting partner, Lieutenant V H Thornton, attacked it at 3,000 feet, with Jones getting east of the Germans, thereby cutting off their retreat to safety. Jones then attacked from underneath after which the observer was last seen hanging out of the Halberstadt. Going in for the kill, Jones finished it off. Offizier-stellvertreter Ernst Hanisch and Leutnant Richard Biermann, of FA 19, crashed at Henin-Liétard and were killed.

At 0700, 40 Squadron got into a fight with Jasta 58. Captain G J 'Ben' Strange, the younger brother of the 80 Wing Commander Lieutenant Colonel Louis Strange MC DFC, was seen to shoot down one Fokker in flames, the patrol being awarded another in flames (to Second Lieutenant G S Smith) with two more out of control. Leutnant Martin Demisch was seen to shoot down an SE5a at Abancourt at 0730, his 10th victory – which was Ben Strange – but was then shot down himself and killed, most likely by Smith.

The Americans of the 148th Aero were involved in the first large-scale fight of the day, running into seven Fokkers near Bourlon Wood, reinforced by up to 40 more. They claimed seven shot down, but had three of their Camels lost, coming down inside Allied lines but without injury to the pilots. This fight had started at 0728, the two bottom sections of Henry Clay's 'C' Flight being engaged by blue-tailed Fokkers; the two other sections then joined in. Lieutenant E H Zistell was wounded after shooting down two Germans and crash-landed, unconscious, near Bapaume. Lieutenant Larry Callahan also force-landed.

The scrap would appear to have been with Jasta 36, whose machines sported blue tails, and then Jasta Boelcke, for whom Leutnant Paul Baümer claimed a Camel at Sailly for his 31st victory. No. 148, after their reverses earlier in the month, were deliberately beginning to fight in teams. Whilst the Americans could still be said to be relatively inexperienced, the capacity to learn and use their brains to develop advanced tactics was perhaps only equalled by the Australians. Colonel Strange had the two Australian Flying Corps fighter squadrons in his 80 Wing (2 and 4 AFC), and bemoaned the lack of any organised tactics before or during the fight by 40 Squadron, which had resulted in the death of his brother.

Around this time, further to the east of Cambrai, 57 Squadron's DH4s were returning from an attack on Beauvais aerodrome, escorted by 62's Bristols. They ran into 30 more Fokkers, with 62 claiming four but losing Lieutenants N N Coope and H S Mantle – both POW – and had another Brisfit shot up, with yet another being forced down before it reached base. Another pilot, Captain W E 'Bull' Staton MC DFC, having just gained his 25th victory, the unit's most successful air fighter, was wounded, putting an end to his WWI career. No. 57's gunners, meantime, claimed another three shot down. The Germans claimed three Bristols: Vizefeldwebel Robert Wirth of Jasta 37, south of Beauvais at 0830; Leutnant Lehmann of Jasta 59 reported one down in Allied lines at Boursies; while Leutnant Hans Jebens of the same staffel scored one at Bantouzelle.

There was a good deal of SE5 action at this time. 56 Squadron claimed victories over Sailly, although they had one pilot wounded and forced down. No. 32 Squadron also had a pilot forced down about 0930. The Germans claimed several: Leutnant Rumey, his 42nd victory, and Otto Schmidt his 15th, both from Jasta 5. Oberleutnant Krafft of Jasta 59 scored his 2nd at Inchy – time unknown – probably Lieutenant D S Atkinson of 32 Squadron.

A balloon strafe mounted by 84 Squadron netted three balloons at 0915, while covering aircraft downed a Fokker between Estrées and Gouy. This signalled an intense period of combats. No. 88 Squadron engaged Fokkers near Habourdin aerodrome, the experienced crews of Captain Alan Hepburn/Second Lieutenant H G Eldon and Captain Charles Findlay/Second Lieutenant A B Radford each claiming one at 1010. Vizefeldwebel Peter Stenzel of Jasta 14 was shot down at Fort d'Englos, which is exactly in this location.

Twenty minutes later 2 AFC claimed an Albatros C-type out of control then further to the north, 74 Squadron claimed two Siemens-Schuckert DIV rotary-engined scouts out of control. This was one of the few specific instances of Siemens-Schuckerts being claimed and identified by British pilots. As this patrol continued, they scored a destroyed by downing a Rumpler two-seater near Lille at 1045.

Just before this, at 1040, the last fight of the morning had started, north-west of Havrincourt. It was the second big fight of the day for the Americans, this time the 17th Aero who claimed seven Fokkers; one in flames, four crashed, and two out of control. This fight was with JGIII at least, as Jasta 27's diarist, Noltenius, reported a fight at this time, during which Vizefeldwebel Schmidt was severely wounded in the knee.

The only other claims of the morning were three DH9s by Jasta 20 and another by Jasta 22s. The former three were in a fight in the La Bassée area, with Leutnant Karl Plauth getting the first at 1040 – his 9th victory – and Leutnant Hans Johannes Gildemeister the second at Lorgies. The third went to Leutnant Joachim von Busse also at Lorgies, for his 8th victory. No. 103 Squadron lost two 'Nines' but the survivors made no claims, although Leutnant Bruno Hobein was wounded during the day, possibly in this action. Vizefeldwebel Karl Bohnenkamp got the Jasta 22s DH9 far to the south at Vermans, just west of Saint-Quentin, in Allied lines, but at the exact same time. The only two-seater lost near here in the morning was an 8 Squadron 'Big Ack' which left its base at Foucaucourt at 0620 for a contact patrol and never returned.

More balloon attacks occurred late morning/early afternoon. Vizefeldwebel Oskar Hennrich of Jasta 46, the unit's chief balloon-buster, claimed one for his 14th victory at 1120, between Étricourt and Manancourt. Then 84 Squadron made their second balloon-busting run at 1350, claiming a further four – all at Cambrai.

The two ex-RNAS Camel units operating on the Belgian coast had a heavy engagement at 1440. 210 Squadron claimed seven Fokkers and 213 four more,

NCO pilot Oskar Hennrich of Jasta 46, gained nine of his 20 kills in September, including three balloons on the 24th.

for one casualty. This was Captain S C Joseph DFC of 210, who was wounded and forced to land. He was claimed by Leutnant zur See Curt Wilhelm of MFJ 4, at Pervyse – in Allied lines – at 1415. In all, the Camel pilots claimed eight destroyed and three out of control. Despite these claims, the German Marines reported no losses at all! The idea that it was the inexperienced newcomers that were optimistically over-claiming can be discounted here, as all these claiming pilots were experienced – indeed, all were aces!

Four o'clock saw the next combat, Bristols of 20 Squadron claiming two Fokkers destroyed and two out of control south-east of Saint-Quentin. Ten minutes later Jasta 46 struck at the Allied balloon lines near Fins, Hennrich burning his second gas bag of the day at 1612, another falling to Leutnant auf der Haar, also near Fins. The RAF reported Lieutenant J L King and 2AM B C Holmes baling out of their 1 KBS balloon at 1615. This was closely followed by the loss of the 32nd KBS balloon at 1616, from which Second Lieutenant A E Hopkins and Corporal R B Stewart also baled out safely.

About this time, 49 Squadron lost three DH9s to intense fighter attack while they were trying to bomb Aulnoye railway junction, far to the east of Cambrai. They had left at 1450 and during the day, in this vicinity, the Germans claimed three DH9s and a DH4. The only timed claim was at 1730, by Leutnant Josef Mai of Jasta 5, his 28th victory falling at Beauvais. The others went to Jasta Boelcke's Paul Baümer, south-west of Clary, and Otto Löffler, west of Cambrai, while the 'Four' went to Oberleutnant Hans Helmut von Boddien. This veteran of Jasta 11 was now commander of Jasta 59, and it was his 2nd victory of the day, bringing his score to five. In addition, 49's returning machines carried one wounded pilot and two wounded gunners.

Another 'Nine' was shot down up north, Leutnant zur See Paul Achilles downing a 108 Squadron machine at Werckem at 1620. Another DH bomber, from 211 Squadron, force-landed in Holland, brought down by AA fire.

From 1700 onwards, as evening set in, there were three actions in the Cambrai area at one time involving DH9s of 18 Squadron and their escorting Bristols of 22 Squadron. Also in the action was 32 Squadron, who reported that while on patrol between Cambrai, Le Cateau and Bohain they observed the running fight nearing Cambrai from the east.

Captain Andrew Callender led 32 north to Le Cateau and swung in behind seven Fokkers which were following the bombers and attacked from the east with his lower formation. The Fokkers were taken by surprise and scattered. Callender attacked the leading machine which had a streamer on its rudder, claiming it shot down, believed crashed, on the northern edge of Bourlon Wood. Finding himself under a fight between Fokkers and 'Nines' he attacked three of the Germans over Marquion, one of which went down in a steep spiral, apparently out of control and last seen at 5,000 feet over Havrincourt.

Other pilots claimed three Fokkers as out of control north of Cambrai – all timed between 1705 and 1710 – while an 18 Squadron crew claimed two Fokkers in flames, over Marquion at 1715. Prior to this the escorting Bristol crews had been in action: Captain S F H Thompson and Sergeant Ronald M Fletcher, the top crew active in 22 Squadron, claimed a Fokker over Cambrai at 1700. Fletcher was the second highest scoring Bristol observer – this was his 26th victory – and the most successful

NCO gunner in WWI. It was also Thompson's 29th victory. The Bristols also reported a further three Fokkers shot down.

This fight was with JGIII, who reported no losses. Also involved was Jasta 44, Vizefeldwebel Becker claiming a British two-seater at Metz-en-Couture, south of Cambrai, which went down on the Allied side at 1725.

Two two-seaters were downed by Captain Roy King of 4 AFC east of Ploegsteert at 1720, while on the coast ten minutes later, Lieutenant David Ingalls, the American navy pilot flying with 213 Squadron, claimed a Rumpler flying east over Nieuport at 13,000 feet. His report continued:

> 'Camels pursued and engaged EA over St Pierre Capelle. Lt Ingalls USNRF, fired 200 rounds at 100 yards range. Lt Hodson 100 rounds at 200 yards range. Both pilots followed the EA down to 6,000 feet when machine was observed to fall in flames.'

One of Ingalls' letters home added some detail, which shows just how curt combat reports could be:

> 'This was the closest shave I had, therefore it is interesting to me. We flew along the lines at 15,000 feet for some time, got disgusted and started for home, as it was getting dark. As we left the lines, I saw "Archie" over La Panne and there picked up a machine heading towards Ostende on our side of the lines. I fired my guns to attract Hodson's attention and set out in pursuit, for Archie on our side of the lines meant a Hun... The Hun was an old Rumpler, the slowest I ever saw, and he kept on, so I dove under him and came up from below. But he was so slow that I overshot and could not train my guns on him. So I dove again and tried once more. He would turn one way to give his observer a shot and I would try to keep under him, making a bigger circle, so his observer could not shoot. A few seconds and I tried to come up beneath him again. His machine was too slow again and I almost overshot, but succeeded in firing a few rounds from just beneath.
>
> 'Nothing happened, so I dropped and continued working for a good position, completely fed up at not being able to get one. On a turn he very nearly got me, for before I could make the outside circle, his observer fired about ten shots, the tracers all going by between the struts on my left side. We were only ten yards off at the time and I could see the two Huns perfectly in their black helmets, and it was rather fascinating to be so close. All the time we were getting further over the lines and I was getting madder. So I gave up the careful, cautious tactics, got straight behind him and kept firing for probably 100 rounds.
>
> 'At last a big puff of smoke came up like an explosion and I felt fine. I turned and dove down to the ground to chase myself home. When way over the lines and not high enough to be safe from Archie, the stunt is to race along just over the ground at about 200 to 300 feet. I had not seen Hodson anywhere.'

Ingalls' Camel was none the less damaged by ground fire and he only just got back to base. The 1st Marine Feld Flieger Abteilung lost Leutnant Emil Melcher in this action.

Twenty minutes later, the SE5s of 41 Squadron claimed a Fokker destroyed west of Comines with another out of control. Captain C Crawford was shot down and taken prisoner at 1800, downed by Leutnant Carl Degelow, north of Zillebeke Lake, the 17th victory for this CO and leading ace of Jasta 40s. Another SE5a was claimed south of Ypres at the same time by Vizefeldwebel Maack of Jasta 63 – in Allied lines – but none are reported forced down.

Ten minutes after 6 o'clock, 59 Squadron's Captain D H M Carberry took his total to at least five, the second highest for an artillery observation pilot. He and Lieutenant J B V Clements were doing a recce to Gonnelieu at 1,200 feet when they saw two Halberstadts behind the enemy lines 300 feet higher. One hundred rounds from Carberry's front gun into one of them resulted in some return fire but the two-seater spun down and crashed near Lateau Wood.

The German lost a two-seater crew on the Somme this day, noted as a ground-fire casualty. Vizefeldwebels Hermann Hoos and Richard Wagner of Schlasta 15 were both captured.

At 1820, 2 AFC entered their second combat of the day. Fifteen SEs, in three flights of five, were west of Lille at 17,000 feet; then over Habourdin, 11 Fokkers were encountered in two layers. Captain Eric Simonson led a flight on to the top five, with the other ten going for the lower six. Later some Pfalz Scouts attempted to intervene. Total claims by the Australians came to eight. (It is possible the Jasta 14 loss occurred in the fight rather than with 88 Squadron earlier.)

The last fight of the day occurred as darkness approached, at 1845. 204 Squadron attacked a formation of Fokker biplanes and triplanes in the Pervyse to Dixmude area. One triplane and five DVIIs were claimed for the loss of Second Lieutenant T Warburton, brought down and captured by Josef Jacobs of Jasta 7, who generally led his unit in a black triplane, even at this late stage of the war. Jacobs noted in his diary:

> 'As we flew towards Ypres, three Camels started gliding after us and I pulled my flight up slowly in the direction of Dixmude, and, sure enough, they opened their engines to cut us off. I stood my triplane on its nose and the highest flying Camel dropped down erratically as my guns stuttered. I kicked rudder and went after him while a couple of my chaps fired bursts across his nose to prevent him from getting away. I finally caught him again, just above the ground, and the Englishman defended himself to the last and did not want to capitulate, but he suddenly banked around and started to land near Moorslede, but turned over when his wheels hit some shell holes. The pilot, Lieutenant Warburton, was unhurt and taken prisoner. I had a look at his machine that evening which was completely wrecked. The chap must have had incredibly good luck not to have been injured.'

Jasta 7 had set out seven-strong and all returned, so what was considered a six-to-one victory for 204 was actually a one-to-nil loss! Jacobs was probably the only ace still in a triplane. He liked the Tripe better than a DVII, and he had a good reason for inspecting the downed Camel. His main problem was the supply of suitable rotary engines for his Driedekker and he had a standing arrangement with front-line troops to send back any rotary engines they should find undamaged in crashed British aircraft. A case of champagne would be their reward and suffice it to say Jacobs generally obtained a replacement engine for his black machine, with its Nordic 'God of the North Wind' insignia painted on the fuselage.

That night, the CO of 65 Squadron, Major Hugh Champion de Crespigny, together with one of his pilots, Lieutenant Maurice Newnham, attacked Gontrude aerodrome between 2200 and 0030 hours, despite strong winds and a rain storm, one of the earliest examples of night intruder sorties by single-seaters.

This night too, FE2 bombers were out; one 101 machine taking off at 2125 failed to return, its crew being brought down, wounded and taken prisoner. A 102 Squadron FE headed off at 2330 but its engine was hit by ground fire and the pilot had to force-land at Sailleaumont; the observer was injured but the FE was salvaged.

French Front

Sous Lieutenant d'Estainville of Spa.87 burnt the Bourgogne balloon at 0745.

Two French aces added to their scores, Sous Lieutenant Charles Marie Joseph Léon Nuville, a 29-year-old with 22 months on Spa.57, claimed his 12th at 1215, a two-seater down at Cernay-en-Dormies, in company with Maréchal-des-Logis Imhoff. Four hours later, Capitaine Henri Hay de Slade, CO of Spa.159, gained his 15th by downing an EA north of Suippes. French pilots also scored five probables during the day.

Jasta 44s claimed a French two-seater in the morning, probably Sous Lieutenant Bouillane and Sergent Junot. They were wounded when their Bréguet, along with two others, was in action with 10 EA on the Picardie sector. (Unit not recorded.) The Bréguet was claimed by Offizierstellvertreter Bansmer at 1050, in French lines, south-west of Attigny. Another two-seater victory went to Vizefeldwebel Friedrich Poeschke of Jasta 53. At 1100 he shot down a Salmson 2A2 of Sal.263 at Besine, which crashed south of Somme-Py, although he in fact claimed a Spad XI.

Pilots of Spa.78 claimed a two-seater in the area of Xammes at 1133. The action began at 4,700 metres, the German spinning down to 400, when another 100 rounds were fired into it. The crew were Vizefeldwebel Fittgen and Leutnant Konnigs of FA 37.

Balloons were again the target of the German pilots during the day. Unteroffizier Heinrich Haase of Jasta 21s shot down the balloon of 75 Cié south of Braisne at 1350, but Leutnant Wilhelm Meyer of Jasta 47 was lost to ground fire while attacking a balloon at 1630, being taken prisoner. The French balloon of 45 Cié was damaged by French defensive fire during this attack. Either Meyer or Leutnant Wember of Jasta 61 were, however, credited with this balloon, or another that was lost in this area. At 1810, Adjutant Couillard of 43 Cié jumped successfully for the fourth time, after the attentions of Vizefeldwebel Max Kuhn, also Jasta 21s, south of Fismes, at 1815.

American Sector

The front was still fairly quiet as the build-up for the 26th continued. At 1530, a patrol from the 22nd Aero claimed a two-seater near Woel. A C-type of FA 29, crewed by Vizefeldwebel Wilkens and Leutnant Rudolf Kaehne, fell near Briey in the Armee Abteilung 'C' Sector, Kaehne certainly being killed.

Jasta 15's acting commander, Leutnant Johannes Klein, shot down a Spad at 1615, and Offizierstellvertreter Gustav Dörr also claimed a Spad near Soissons at 1900, but no corresponding losses have been found. However, Lieutenant E L Moore of the 49th Aero seems to have been slightly wounded on this date.

	A/C	KB			DES	OOC	KB
British losses	14	–		British claims	52	37	7
French losses	2	4		French claims	4	–	1
American losses	–	–		American claims	1		–
IAF losses	–	–		IAF claims	–		–
German claims	26	7		German losses	6†		?

† Possibly at least two more, 17 Armee reporting four men killed, units unknown.

British Casualties

Aircraft type	No.	Squadron	Crew		
SE5a	E4054	40 Sqdn	Capt G J Strange	KIA	
AWFK8	B8837	8 Sqdn	Lt W F R Robinson	KIA	
			Lt J H Roberts	KIA	
Camel	E7160	4 AFC	Capt E J K McCloughry	WIA	*
BF2b	E2515	62 Sqdn	Lt N N Coope	POW	
			2/Lt H S Mantle	POW	
BF2b	D7899?	62 Sqdn	Capt W E Staton MC DFC	WIA	*
			Lt L E Mitchell	Safe	
SE5a	F5488	56 Sqdn	Lt F A Sedore	WIA	*
SE5a	D6983	32 Sqdn	Lt D S Atkinson	Safe	
DH9	F5842	103 Sqdn	Lt H C Noel	KIA	
			Sgt L C Owens	POW	
DH9	D2877	103 Sqdn	Lt C Hebner	KIA	
			2/Lt D Davenport	KIA	
DH4	F6165	18 Sqdn	Lt R C Bennett	Safe	*
			2/Lt A Lilley	Safe	
DH9	D3251	211 Sqdn	2/Lt J Olorenshaw	Interned	
			2/Lt R L Kingham	Interned	
DH9	D7208	108 Sqdn	2/Lt J M Dandy	POW	
			Sgt C P Crites	POW	
DH9	E8869	49 Sqdn	Capt E D Asbury	KIA	
			2/Lt E J Gillman	KIA	
DH9	F6098	49 Sqdn	Lt C C Conover	POW	
			2/Lt H J Pretty	POW	
DH9	E658	49 Sqdn	Lt H J Bennett	POW/DOW	
			2/Lt R H Armstrong	POW	
DH9	D1097	49 Sqdn	2/Lt E C Moore (USAS)	WIA	*
			2/Lt L Eteson	WIA	*
DH9	D3265	49 Sqdn	2/Lt J F Higgins	Safe	
			2/Lt L C Belcher	WIA	*
BF2b	E2363	11 Sqdn	2/Lt C Johnson	Safe	*
			Sgt G H Hampson	WIA	*
SE5a	E4074	41 Sqdn	Capt C Crawford	POW	
Camel	C6620	4 Sqdn	Lt D T Warburton	POW	
Camel	B7232	204 Sqdn	Lt O J Orr	Safe	*
Camel	D8147	210 Sqdn	Capt S C Joseph DSC	WIA	*

Aircraft type	No.	Squadron	Crew		
HP O/400	–	207 Sqdn	2/Lt J M Mackinnon (O)	WIA	•
BF2b	–	22 Sqdn	Capt G McCormack (O)	WIA	•
FE2b (night)	D9922	102 Sqdn	2/Lt W Lloyd-Williams	Safe	•
			Lt O Reilly-Patey DFC	Inj	
FE2b (night)	D9921	101 Sqdn	Lt B H Kelly	POW	
			2/Lt J W Brown	POW	

French Casualties

Bréguet XIV		Br.?	S/Lt Bouillanne	Safe	?
			Sgt Junot	KIA	
Salmson 2A2		Sal.263	Sgt Delporte	KIA	
			S/Lt Burfin	KIA	

American Casualties

Spad XIII		49th Aero	1/Lt E L Moore	WIA	?

25 SEPTEMBER 1918
M **T** **W** T F S S

British Front

An overcast sky with rain in the morning reduced aerial activity. A patrol of 64 Squadron made the first encounter at 1740, a C-type out of control near Bourlon Wood – possibly Vizefeldwebel Adolf Martens and Leutnant Hans Stanger of FA(A)207, who were reported lost near La Ferrières, although further south than Bourlon. (See also comment on 18 September RE: Stanger.)

There were no other reported actions until 1745, 213 Squadron losing three Camels in a fight with Marine units. No. 213 did claim one Fokker in return but Vizeflugmeister Alexandre Zenses of MFJ 2 got his 8th victory, Paul Achilles of MFJ 5 his 4th and 5th.

A couple more Fokkers were claimed by 208 and then 85 Squadron around 1800, while over Fresnoy, 27 Squadron's bombers ran into Jastas 34b and 31, losing two aircraft. Robert Greim scored his 24th victory by downing one south of Escaufort at 1815, Unteroffizier Brungel the other at Busigny, at 1825. No. 27 did claim one Fokker destroyed and three out of control. The one destroyed was seen to spin into the ground between Bohain and Ponchaux; of the 'OOCs', one disappeared in low cloud after falling like a leaf, another – a most persistent German pilot firing from under the DH9's tail – also went down, confirmed by 148 Squadron as out of control, while the last out of control was finally observed to pull out and land in a field.

In fights between 1800 and 1830, 20 Squadron claimed no fewer than eight Fokkers between Cambrai and Saint-Quentin, 22 claiming two more between Cambrai and Bourlon Wood. Amidst this, 25 Squadron's bombers were in action against Fokkers, claiming one over Bohain and two more over Ponchaux. Gefreiter Franz Wagner of

Jasta 79b was killed in action at Preselles Ferme, by either 25 or 22 Squadron, while Leutnant Fritz von Braun claimed a Bristol down at Villers-Guislain.

There were no DH4 losses reported, although earlier in the day 25 Squadron's Captain S Jones had to force-land at Haute Avesnes at 1130 with a wounded observer. Jones left the machine ticking over while he arranged for the wounded man to be taken to hospital. He then instructed two orderlies to load the rear cockpit with ballast but the throttle accidentally opened, the aircraft moved forward, ran 50 yards and turned over. The damage needed to be repaired at No.2 ASD.

On the half-hour, Major Geoffrey Bowman MC and bar burnt a Rumpler north-east of Ypres for his 30th victory, possibly a crew lost from Schusta 24. Bowman had first spotted some Fokkers over the Roulers-Menin road but was then attracted to the two-seater by white AA bursts. He wrote:

> 'I fired 40 rounds from both guns at close range and EA burst into flames. I turned back to the lines and after about half a minute, saw the flames die down. I turned back towards the EA, who was then flying nose-down, due north, and not burning very well. I fired again at long range without effect. At 2,000 feet over Houthulst Forest, owing to bad visibility, I could not see if he crashed. EA burnt slowly the whole way down.'

The former naval units were in action during the next half hour, with 204 Squadron reporting two Fokkers colliding while attacking Lieutenant C J Sims south-west of Ostende. No. 213 then lost its fourth pilot of the day, Second Lieutenant G Iliff giving Leutnant Franz Piechulek of Jasta 56 his 11th victory at Kortemarck at 1850.

The only other loss this day was an RE8, shot down by ground fire at 1620. The crew force-landed in the front lines, and although the crew were safe, the machine had to be abandoned.

The final action of the day came an hour before midnight over Arras. Lieutenant T R Bloomfield of 151 Squadron shot down an AEG of Bogohl 6, although he reported his kill as a Gotha. As he attacked he could see pamphlets being thrown out of a bottom trap door. Opening fire, the machine almost immediately caught fire and fell burning between Montenescourt and Agny, exploding when it hit the ground. Leutnant Reinhold Lampe, Feldwebel August Platte, Unteroffizier Karl Rühlicke and Gefreiter Adolf Mörch were all killed.

French Front

Two Spad fighters were shot down early in the day. At 0805, Leutnant Rudolf Fuchs of Jasta 77b claimed his first victory over Arnaville; Caporal Abeles of Spa.88 was reported missing in the area. In the same area, Sergent Millot of Spa.65 was attacked by three Fokker triplanes. He spun vertically and force-landed, his Spad riddled with bullets but he appears not to have been claimed.

To the north of the French line, Vizefeldwebel Karl Treiber of Jasta 5 claimed a Spad two-seater south of Saint-Quentin at 1800, which was probably the Bréguet lost this day. In the II Armée area, a Salmson of Sal.47 broke up in the air during a fight with six Fokkers, falling in German lines at Hageville, shot down by Leutnant Friedrich Hengst of Jasta 64w. Only one German aircraft was claimed by the French, Adjutant Priollaud of Spa.159 shooting down one over Ornes during the day.

The Germans also got a night victory. This was scored by Leutnant Fritz Anders of the night-fighting Jasta 73, over Moronvillers, the location where a Farman of F. 114 was lost. Anders had been a pilot since 1912, and this was his 2nd kill of the month, and his 5th night kill. It was also his 7th overall – and last.

American Sector

First Lieutenant Eddie Rickenbacker of the 94th Aero claimed a Fokker and a Halberstadt two-seater near Billy, and north-east of Verdun in the morning. Then at 1002, the 139th destroyed a Rumpler near Damloup.

Jagdgeschwader Nr.I began offensive operations on the front this day, Jasta 10's Leutnant Justas Grassmann burning a balloon at 0950 near Pont-à-Mousson. The US 10th Balloon Company lost its gas bag near Jezainville, five kilometres from Pont-à-Mousson, the observer, Lieutenant J W Lavers, taking to his parachute.

IAF

After some days of inactivity, the IAF set out on long-range bombing raids today. Twelve aircraft of 55 Squadron took off at 0815 to bomb the munitions factories south of Kaiserslautern, attacking at 1010 with nine 230-lb and six 112-lb bombs. On the return trip they were engaged by 12 enemy fighters, later reinforced as the danger period near the lines was entered. No. 55 claimed two destroyed and two out of control, but lost four. Three fell to Jasta 70, including one in Allied lines; Leutnant Anton Stephen crashed one at Albertsweiler, Vizefeldwebel Lemke one at Bergzabern, and Vizefeldwebel Krist one at Brumath. The other went down near the target area at 1010, under the guns of Leutnant von Beaulieu-Marconnay, the Jasta 19 pilot's 20th victory.

Then 11 aircraft, the modern DH9A machines of 110 Squadron, set out to bomb railway works at Frankfurt, flying in two formations. The first was led by Captain A Lindlay, the other by Captain A C M Groom. The squadron dropped one-and-a-half tons of bombs at midday, but during the five-hour 40-minute sortie, four bombers were shot down, despite the gunners claiming to have sent down five fighters out of control. Among those lost was the first formation leader. The survivors landed at base with one dead and two wounded gunners.

The first two losses were at 1115 and 1120, on the outward journey, Gefreiter Meyer of Jasta 3 sending his victim down south-east of Sarralbe, swiftly followed by Jasta 15's Leutnant Georg Hantelmann's kill south of Metz. The last two, well on the return journey, went to Jasta 78b, Leutnant Richard Schmidt, at Zabern at 1430, and Vizefeldwebel Prime near Buhl airfield at 1500.

In fact, Buhl airfield was also the target assigned to five aircraft of 99 Squadron. They too were engaged, one DH being badly shot up, the crew eventually crash-landing in Allied lines, two miles short of their base at Azelet, south of Nancy.

IAF bombers really needed escorts, but most of their German targets were simply out of range of any fighter types. They would have been happy to meet short-range escorts as they returned to the lines, but of course there was no way of knowing when or where the bombers would re-appear. Even if a spot and approximate time were arranged, a running fight with German fighters would invariably split up the bombers and alter their courses and ETA home.

	A/C	KB			DES	OOC	KB
British losses	7	–		British claims	15	7	–
French losses	5	–		French claims	1		–
American losses	–	1		American claims	4		–
IAF losses	8	–		IAF claims	2	7	–
German claims	22	1		German losses	4?†		?

† Personnel casualties suggest at least two or three more may have been lost.

British Casualties

Aircraft type	No.	Squadron	Crew		
DH4	A8051	25 Sqdn	Capt S Jones	Safe	*
			2/Lt J Pullar	WIA	
DH4	D3163	27 Sqdn	2/Lt C B Sanderson	POW/DOW	
			Sgt J Wilding	POW	
DH4	E8857	27 Sqdn	2/Lt A V Cosgrove	KIA	
			2/Lt S C Read	KIA	
RE8	F5892	59 Sqdn	Lt J Stanley	Safe	
			2/Lt J W Elias	Safe	
Camel	C66	204 Sqdn	2/Lt T Warburton	POW	
Camel	B7232	204 Sqdn	Lt O J Orr (USAS)	Safe	
Camel	B7252	213 Sqdn	Lt C P Sparkes	POW	
Camel	D8216	213 Sqdn	Lt L C Scroggie	KIA	
Camel	D3360	213 Sqdn	2/Lt J C Sorley	KIA	
Camel	E4385	213 Sqdn	2/Lt G Iliff	KIA	
BF2b	E2252	20 Sqdn	Capt T C Traill	Safe	
			Lt R Gordon-Bennett	WIA	
DH4	D8413	55 Sqdn	2/Lt A J Robinson	KIA	
			2/Lt M R Burnett MM	KIA	
DH4	D8386	55 Sqdn	Lt W G Braid	Safe	
			2/Lt G S Barber	KIA	
DH4	D8356	55 Sqdn	2/Lt J B Dunn	KIA	
			2/Lt H S Orange	KIA	
DH4	D8388	55 Sqdn	2/Lt P G Pretty	POW	
			2/Lt G R Bartlett	POW	
DH4	F5714	55 Sqdn	Lt G B Dunlop	POW	
			2/Lt A C Hayes	POW	
DH4	D8392	55 Sqdn	2/Lt H Wood	WIA	*
			2/Lt J D Evans	Safe	
DH4	–	55 Sqdn	2/Lt C Turner	Safe	*
			2/Lt J T L Atwood	KIA	
DH9A	F992	110 Sqdn	Lt L S Brooke	KIA	
			2/Lt F Proven	KIA	
DH9A	E9660	110 Sqdn	Lt C B E Lloyd	POW	
			2/Lt H J C Elwig	POW	
DH9A	F1030	110 Sqdn	Capt A Lindley	POW	
			Lt C R Cross	POW	

Aircraft type	No.	Squadron	Crew		
DH9A	E8422	110 Sqdn	Sgt H W Tozier	KIA	
			Sgt W Platt	KIA	
DH9A	F1000	110 Sqdn	2/Lt C M B Stevenson	Safe	*
			Lt H J Cockman	WIA	
DH9A	E8420	110 Sqdn	2/Lt N N Ward	Safe	
			Sgt W H Neighbour	KIA	
DH9A	F993	110 Sqdn	Lt R P Brailli	Safe	
			Lt F R Casey	WIA	*
DH9	D3270	99 Sqdn	2/Lt H E King	Safe	*
			2/Lt J M Oliphant	WIA	

French Casualties

Bréguet XIV		Br.?	Adj Fabiani	MIA	
			S/Lt Lormail	MIA	
Farman		F.114	Lt P Bizard	MIA	
			Capt Garnier	MIA	
			Asp Rives	MIA	
Spad XIII		Spa.88	Cpl P Abeles	MIA	
Spad XIII		Spa.65	Sgt Millot	Safe	
Salmson 2A2		Sal.47	Sgt Chauffeur	KIA	
			MdL Alby	KIA	

American Casualties

Spad XIII		93rd Aero	1/Lt H B Merz	WIA

26 SEPTEMBER 1918
M T W **T** F S S

British Front

The weather which was fine during the previous night, continued fine during this day. There was good activity on the British Front, but the main feature of the day was the opening of the Meuse-Argonne offensive on the French and American sectors. It was not, however, until mid-morning that the air actions began for the RAF.

The first big fight was timed between 1030 and 1100 hours, on the coast north-east of Ostende to Blankenberghe. Camels of 65 and 204 Squadrons were in combat, giving direct or indirect escort to DH4s of 202 Squadron. No. 204 claimed two destroyed and four out of control for the loss of two, to MFJ 5 pilots Flugmaats Karl Engelfried and Christian Kairies, one at Wenduyne, the other at Neumunster. The latter pilot's victory was over the very aggressive Canadian ace Lieutenant W B Craig, from Smith Falls, Ontario, who was killed. Since mid-August he had scored eight victories and was about to receive the DFC. One DH4 also went down, this last being seen at 16,500 feet over Ostende, being chased by five enemy fighters, the kill going to Leutnant zur See Freymadel. No. 65 also lost a Camel, credited to

Vizeflugmeister Sawatski of MFJ 1, also over Ostende, and flown by Lieutenant W R Thornton who was taken prisoner.

During the latter half of the morning, 87 and 65 Squadron both claimed two-seaters, while 74 Squadron shot down a Fokker biplane. No.48 Squadron also got one of eight Fokkers that engaged them over Menin, although the Bristol crew then had their engine shot out and they had to force-land. On the German side, Vizefeldwebel Karl Bohnenkamp of Jasta 22s claimed a Camel down in Allied lines north-west of Ronnsoy as his 12th victory, but there is no obvious corresponding loss.

A big airfield strafe took place soon after lunch, Camels, SE5s and BF2bs of 203, 40 and 22 Squadrons going for Lieu St Amand, 12 km north-east of Cambrai. The SE5s went in first, dropping their 25-lb bombs on hangars and huts, one of the former catching fire, while several huts were destroyed. No. 203 followed them down, setting fire to three more hangars and bombing a fourth. Living quarters were also strafed. A DFW two-seater was also set on fire. Major Ray Collishaw, the Canadian ace and CO of 203, attacked a fighter he saw taking off and shot it down in flames. Later he brought down another enemy machine. Lieutenant D Woodhouse also spotted some mounted troops on a nearby road and shot them up, inflicting several apparent casualties. In all 88 bombs fell on the target, and five aircraft were destroyed by 203, two more by the escorting Bristols.

The Camels did not have it all their own way: Second Lieutenant W H Coghill, having successfully engaged one Fokker, was hit and wounded by another. Two more Camels were shot up, one pilot force-landing in the front line. Lieutenant N C Dixie got into the front trenches but his Camel was shelled. These were probably among the claims of JGIII, Bruno Loerzer getting his last two kills of the war at this time, bringing his score to 44. Ernst Bormann of Jasta 2 also claimed a Camel around this time, north of Cambrai, and if it was not one of 203's machines it may have been a Dolphin of 23 Squadron that was last seen over Bellicourt at 1145. 203 lost another Camel during the day, Lieutenant F J S Britnell DSC being brought down by ground fire while on contact patrol. His engine seized and he too plunged into the front-line trenches, surviving, but his fighter was lost. 'Duke' Britnell was an ace, having accounted for his 8th victory this very day.

During the afternoon, the 148th Aero had a big fight east of Bourlon Wood, and Fritz Rumey of Jasta 5 scored his 43rd victory over a Bristol Fighter of 'L' Flight at Gouzeaucourt. At 1433, Vizefeldwebel Christian Mesch of Jasta 26 claimed a Dolphin west of Saint-Quentin, but this was more probably a Bristol Fighter of 20 Squadron, time and location fitting. He was not the first German pilot to confuse the double-bays of the Dolphin (overlooking the wing-stagger) with the BF2b.

More combats abound. No. 80 Squadron fought Jasta 31 at 1740, each claiming one, but it was a Camel that came down in flames north-west of Saint-Quentin, accounted for by Leutnant Sylvester Garsztka for his 5th victory (although he claimed an SE5). At 1805, Jasta 5 attacked DH4s of 57 Squadron, two falling, one to Rumey – his 44th victory – while Karl Treiber gained his 4th kill, all scored this month, with two more to come. Another of the bombers, flown by Captain A Newman and Lieutenant E G Pernet, claimed a Fokker in flames south-east of Cambrai but Pernet was wounded. The DH force-landed in Allied lines, and so did another DH, also badly shot about. 46 and 208 Squadrons also had scraps with Fokkers in the early evening.

Hauptmann Bruno Loerzer gained most of his victories with Jasta 26, and in early 1918, commanded JGIII. Ending the war with 44 victories, the final ten were achieved during September. Awarded the Pour le Mérite, his post-war career embraced flying and the Luftwaffe. In WWII he rose to the rank of Generaloberst.

Balloons were attacked and destroyed by Jasta 46, one falling to Vizefeldwebel Oskar Hennrich at 1645 – his 17th victory – and one to Unteroffizier Fröhlich at 1745, his first of two kills. Both balloons were at Liéramont, the first belonging to 6-15-5, the second to 14-14-5.

During the day, two Jasta 37 pilots were wounded, Vizefeldwebel Robert Wirth and Leutnant Mappes. It is difficult to know by whom but the fights with 22 and 203 might provide the most probable source.

French Front

Dawn saw the beginnings of a clear and beautiful day, the day the French/American offensive began. A feature of the Allied plan was to capture and disrupt the German rail system, making it difficult for them to bring up supplies and reinforcements, and to hinder any sort of retreat. The main cross-railway line ran from Metz through Montmédy-Mezières-Hirson to Valenciennes, although the vital section was the Metz-Mezières line. If this could be cut or disrupted between these two points before the Germans could withdraw from France and Belgium, then the ruin of the German army would be accomplished. Thus the mission of the French/American forces was to cut this vital rail line, while the Germans knew they must hold it to stop a catastrophe. The task was given to the French IV Armée and General Pershing's 1st US Army.

The chosen ground was difficult for the attackers; it was, after all, a forest, and a hilly one at that. At 0200 hours, 3,800 guns opened fire on the German trenches and positions to their rear for the ritual, but not always effective, softening-up process. The French and Americans went 'over the top' at 0530.

Attacks were to continue along this front for the 47 remaining days of the war. The number of aircraft Colonel Mitchell had at his disposal had dropped recently to about 800, 600 of which were American.

The air war was very much more sophisticated by this stage of the war. As an example, the French bombers deliberately bombed German airfields commencing at 0130, to try and keep the German fighters on the ground. The specialist night-bombers of GB7 acted as path-finders with volunteer crews from the three Groupes de Bombardements of Escadre 12. GB's 5, 6 and 9 bombed various airfields. Three crews of GB5 hit St Loup, three more from GB6 went for Attigny while three others of GB9 bombed Leffincourt.

The French Air Service was active all along the front. The Division Aérienne was assigned to cover the attack, with Escadre de Combat No.1 covering the IV Armée, while No.2 covered the right flank and attacked observation balloons between Samogneux and Manheulles.

To the east of Reims, Groupement Ménard pilots (Champagne sector) claimed three balloons north of Somme-Py, Saint Hilaire and north of Cerny, one each for Spa.93, 97 and 37. One was shared with Adjutant Georges Lienhard, at 32 years of age a veteran of air operations in Italy, but who had only come to Spa.37 at the end of May 1918. He would score three victories this day to make him an ace.

In the afternoon, another ace, Adjutant Armand Berthelot of Spa.15, shot down a DFW two-seater north of Montfaucon. However, a Spad was lost in the IV Armée sector. Sergent Roger Caillet of Spa.89 was killed in combat, falling near Souain. Vizefeldwebel Alfons Nägler of Jasta 81 claimed a Spad near Suippes, about six kilometres south of Souain, while Unteroffizier Karl Hoffmann of Jasta 60 claimed another at 0900 near Massiges.

Three balloons were also shot down by the Germans on the IV Armée front. The 21 Cié lost a balloon from which Sous Lieutenants Vallier and Defleury baled out. The 19 and 30 Cié balloons were also lost. Leutnant Fritz Höhn of Jasta 60 got one at 1215 by Minaucourt; Leutnant Hermann Häbich of Jasta 49 another at 1540 in the same area, while Leutnant Hans von Freden of Jasta 50 claimed his at Perthes at 1755.

Escadre 12's bombers of GB5, escorted by protection units R.239 and R.240, attacked Medeah during the day and were attacked by Fokkers. The Caudron RXI crews of the latter unit shot down two for the cost of a wounded R.239 pilot, Sergent Meynadier, whose aircraft was also damaged. Also active was GB13, whose force of 54 Bréguets, protected by eight Caudron RXIs from C.46, dropped 9,520 kilos of bombs in the area from Manre to Challeronge, mainly on railway targets. The formation engaged in 11 combats during which Br.132 and C.46 each claimed a Fokker.

In the II Armée sector, Lieutenant Hayer and Caporal Chausden of the two-seater Spa.215 were shot down in combat with eight enemy fighters but neither was hurt. Leutnant Blume of Jasta 9 claimed a Spad two-seater at Tahure around 1215, which was probably this crew. However, Gustav Dörr of Jasta 45 also claimed a Spad at Fismes at 1300 – his 30th kill – so he too may have been responsible. An earlier Spad two-seater went to Jasta 60's Leutnant Höhn at 0830, at Somme-Py. Without knowing the exact time the Spad came down, any one of these three may have been the victor. A single-seat Spad of Spa.315 crash-landed after a combat near Belfort. Caporal Boutin was injured, and may have been the victim of Leutnant Wilhelm Frickart of Jasta 65, his 9th victory.

On the main IV Armée front, the French claimed four balloons and ten aircraft, six of the latter going to one man, the highly successful, albeit controversial, Lieutenant René Fonck of Spa.103. This action was basically concentrated along the west, or left edge of the offensive, where it overlapped the combats of Ménard 's units.

Spa.12 started the day by burning two balloons, the aristocrat Capitaine Armand Jean Galliot Joseph de Turenne, its 27-year-old commander, sharing them with two of his pilots. De Turenne had opened his score back in November 1916 and by now was one of the foremost leaders of the French fighter arm. The balloon, shot down over St Geneviève at 0800, took his score to 14. The next balloon went down 20 minutes later, to Sergent Saxon (an American) and Caporal Haller north of Somme-Py.

Late in the morning, an aircraft from Spa.103, flown by Fonck, who had been on leave since mid-August, his score standing at 60, climbed away from his airfield. Fonck spotted five Fokkers at 1145 and attacked. He bounced the outside rear machine, whose pilot saw him coming and tried to warn the others, but was shot down, along with the rear Fokker. The Frenchman reported these two crashed at St Marie-à-Py and St Souplet, following which, never one to lose an advantage, Fonck broke off the action. Soon afterwards, he saw a Halberstadt two-seater being shelled by French AA. He dived on it, firing at the observer who was killed straight away. The pilot dived so violently to get away – he failed – that the body of his observer was flung out before it crashed at Perthes-les-Hurles, at 1210. FA(A) 233 lost Unteroffizier Richard Scholl and Leutnant Eugen Anderer, both killed, over Perthes.

Mid-afternoon, Lieutenant George W Eypper, an American serving with Spa.98, shot down a two-seater north-east of Bouconville. Sous Lieutenant Marcel Nogues of Spa.57 – who had been captured in April 1917 but escaped – gained his 13th and final victory by sharing a balloon north-east of Somme-Py at 1645. Five minutes later, the Sechault balloon, more to the east than the claims so far, was flamed by Sergent Kaminsky of Spa.124.

Later in the evening, a four-man patrol of Spa.103 set out, led by Fonck. In the same area were the pilots of Spa.26, led by Capitaine Joseph de Sevin and aircraft of Spa.165. De Sevin was 24 and had been a fighter pilot since 11 November 1915, rising from Caporal to Capitaine, while gaining 11 victories and 13 probables. Fonck flew above his three companions, acting as cover. Eight Fokkers attacked the three, and as Fonck was diving to the rescue, de Sevin joined in, as did three more Fokkers. Soon he and Adjutant Brugère of Spa.103 were below the Fokkers and in deep trouble. Fonck claimed two of the Fokkers east of Souain as he tried to extricate them. Unfortunately, de Sevin was last seen spinning down out of control. Fonck then claimed another Fokker north-east of Somme-Py. This is interesting in itself, as these combats are usually described as being with a Fokker, then with two two-seaters! Spa.165 also claimed a Fokker over Souain at 1755, credited to Sergent Gaudry – his first.

Upon his return, Fonck was credited with all three, bringing up his second six-in-a-day claim. He was bemoaning the fact that his guns had jammed, otherwise he would have got more, and also regretting the demise of de Sevin, when the missing man walked in from a crash-landing. The Fokker he claimed himself was also one of those claimed by Fonck, so de Sevin did not receive credit for his victory. This was somewhat embarrassing for the French, as de Sevin was highly respected, and a Capitaine, and not likely to be a liar! As the news of the six for Fonck had already been released, the other side of the story was kept quiet!

This fight had been with Jasta 50, for whom Leutnant Maletzky claimed a Spad at 1800 at Perthes, followed by another at 1810 at Le Mesnil. The latter was de Sevin. The Jasta lost Vizefeldwebel Weinmann, who was captured, and was the victim of either one of the French aces.

Meanwhile, at 1800 Spa.37 and Spa.3 combined to down another Fokker south of Tahure, although the former unit lost Lieutenant Boby de la Chapelle, who died, possibly as a result of this fight. In this general area during the day, Sous Lieutenant Arthur Coadou, the acting commander of Spa.88, crashed a two-seater into Allied lines for his 4th victory, while Sous Lieutenant Pierre Gaudermen, shared an EA west of Ville-sur-Toube with two other members of Spa.68. Paris-born Gaudermen, at the advanced age of 35, was on his way to becoming an ace, now having gained his 4th kill. Jasta 50 was once more in action, Leutnant Hans von Freden claiming a Salmson near this same locality at an unknown time, bringing his score to 11.

The last French claim of the day also involved two aces, the first being de Turenne, whose second claim of the day was a C-type, also at Ville-sur-Toube, at 1845, shared with pilots of Spa.91 and 89. It was also the 5th victory of Adjutant Emile Regnier, whose Médaille Militaire citation specified that this victim was a two-seater in French lines, and that Regnier was severely wounded in the fight. De Turenne was wounded as well, and there are sufficient reports to indicate that their opposition may well have been a Fokker rather than a two-seater. Also, it is possible that Spa.68 and 88 were involved in this victory.

Despite the dubious nature of some of Fonck's claims on this day, his overall performance far outstrips other top-scorers, British Empire's Bishop and the American, Rickenbacker. Many of the latter's claims were out of controls, probably out of control and forced to land, often while he was out alone – just like Fonck and especially Bishop! Fonck's, because of the stricter French confirmation system, were at least visible (supposedly) from the ground. Upon reflection, it seems all three were overcome by ambition, especially as the number two men for all three countries – Mannock (not forgetting McCudden), Georges Guynemer and Frank Luke – were very accurate claimers.

Max Näther spent 1918 with Jasta 62. He scored a total of 26 victories before his 20th birthday, six of which were claimed in September.
He was shot down and killed in early 1919 during the border conflict with Poland.

American Sector

The ground offensive began as the troops came out of their trenches at 0530. The east end of the attack was against the heights on the Meuse River; to the west, the Argonne Forest. In the middle was a ridge with the three German strongpoints of Montfaucon, Gunel and Berricourt. The offensive ground to a halt on the 29th, after three days of bitter fighting. However, more attacks continued into late October, at which time the German army cracked.

After some days of quiet, resting up for the coming offensive, and changing bases, the Americans went full out on the opening day of the assault. The majority of fighter opposition came from JGII, who had another good day – in the sense of shooting down the opposition – although they barely interrupted the American and French Air Services' work. Major Harold Hartney's 1st Pursuit Group was assigned to burn German balloons and keep the front clear of German two-seater recce aircraft. Top cover for these operations was to be provided by the 2nd and 3rd Pursuit Groups.

Thus the day began with an organised balloon strafe, netting two destroyed and two damaged, one by the 94th Aero (near Nantillois at 0552) the other to the 27th Aero (near Lisson at 0553). Less than an hour later, the 27th destroyed the Romagne balloon, at 0634. In this half hour, three more balloons were damaged and forced down.

The 94th and 95th Aeros had had early skirmishes with Fokkers, with two claimed shot down; one by Rickenbacker, who had damaged his propeller when the interrupter gear failed. Then, shortly after 0700, another wave of combats began, the 28th and 22nd Aeros each claiming victories over Fokkers. At 0710, Leutnant Max Näther of Jasta 62 claimed a Spad at Bezonvaux (his 14th victory), while exactly an hour later Jasta 8's Vizefeldwebel Wilhelm Seitz, an original staffel member, claimed a Spad for his 11th victory in the same vicinity. Both Spads were from the 13th Aero. Flying with them was the future General, Major Carl Spaatz, still gaining combat experience while attached to this outfit.

He reported shooting down a Fokker out of control and damaging another near Damvillers, and was chasing a third when he was attacked by two others. Spaatz was saved from this predicament by Captain Charles Biddle and two other pilots who forced the Fokker down out of control. However, the 13th lost two pilots, Lieutenants T P Evans and Van H Burgin, both brought down and captured.

Lieutenant John Sperry of the 22nd Aero, who had already claimed one Fokker in an earlier fight, scored a second – in flames – near Étain at 0820, described as having a green nose and white tail. Vizefeldwebel Robert Massbacher of Jasta 77b was shot down in flames over Allied lines this day, but despite being wounded, managed to get back over the German side to crash-land. He may have been Sperry's victim.

Between 1015 and 1100, the American day bombers set out on a series of support raids. For the 20th Bombardment Squadron it was to be a tragic day, as they lost five bombers, although they claimed three fighters shot down. The chief killers were Jasta 12, who for the second time in a week obliterated an American bomber formation.

The 96th Aero was the first off, sending eight planes to Dun-sur-Meuse, two of which aborted. The other six, led by First Lieutenant David Young, dropped their bombs on the town but were attacked on the return journey. Two fighters were claimed shot down – one awarded to all six crews – the second, a Pfalz, to Lieutenant Paul J O'Donnell, gunner to Lieutenant Harold J Forshay. O'Donnell was then hit and killed.

The second formation off was from the 11th Aero, but it was soon apparent they had not recovered from the mauling of the 18th, as their formation broke up and the leader aborted. One crew, Lieutenants W W Waring and S H G Norris, then joined up with the next formation along – that of the 20th Aero.

This absurd tactic of the American Bomb Group, of sending out very small formations in close succession to the same target, went wrong yet again, although the plan had been to meet up over Vitry. They didn't. The 20th's flight of seven was hit soon after crossing the lines and two planes went down right away, with another crippled and starting to lag behind. The 11th Aero crew dropped back to protect it and both crews made it back, with Waring and Norris claiming a Fokker near Damvillers. Three more bombers went down, while the observer in another was killed. The consolation of a Fokker shot down, credited to the 20th as a whole, was little reward.

The pilots of Jasta 12 claimed five DH4s. Leutnant Hermann Becker claimed two (17th and 18th), Vizefeldwebel Otto Klaiber got his 1st, Leutnant Besser his 2nd and Leutnant Alfred Greven his 2nd too. This last was Lieutenants Guy B Wiser and Glenn C Richardson, who were captured, with Richardson leaving this account:

'Left Moulin at 9 o'clock in the morning in a heavy ground fog. The flight consisted of eight DH4s with orders to bomb Dun-sur-Meuse. We were to meet three other flights from our group at Vitry and proceed over the lines. We failed to meet the other three flights and continued on over, reaching the lines at about 1030 at an altitude of 13,000 feet... We were attacked by five Fokkers who kept well to the rear and down. We all opened fire and one Fokker went down and the other four withdrew. At this time we were running parallel to the lines for some reason or other, which we have never ascertained, probably due to a lost sense of direction.

'Almost immediately, 12 more Fokkers attacked from the front and above. The leader dived through our formation attacking our flight leader. I fired one drum of ammunition and then had a jam in both guns. I had jams with each magazine and did not succeed in getting two shots in succession from that time on. I noticed three of our machines go down in flames and then turned to see our engine smoking and steaming as though on fire. I received a shot in the leg which was a flesh wound only but caused my leg to grow numb.

'Turning toward the front, I noticed the reserve tank was shot and a spray of gasoline hit me in the face. At this time we were running engine full on and trying to make the lines but at an altitude of 8,000 feet our propeller stopped dead, necessitating a slow glide. Three Fokkers hung to our tail firing all the way down until we reached 500 feet. We had been side-slipping to present as difficult a target as possible and we pulled out of the last slip at about 200 feet and glided to the ground, landing without smashing on the field which turned out to be the aerodrome of the 12th German Aero Squadron.'

The base was Giraumont. The two Americans were entertained by JGII pilots, led by Greven, and in 1961, Wiser and Richardson were shown a series of photos taken on that occasion. For the other Americans, fate was not so kind. Six were killed and two others also captured. At least one was seen to jump from 13,000 feet, to avoid the dreadful fate of being burnt alive. First Lieutenant Merian C Cooper also reported on his experiences on his return from prison camp:

'My observer ... was shot through the neck. The shot came out through his shoulder and knocked him into his cockpit. I received a graze across the head, which stunned me. Although severely wounded and bleeding heavily, my observer endeavoured to carry on the fight, but collapsed. As my engine was hit and I was unable to keep up with the formation, I was surrounded by enemy airplanes. Just at the instant of kicking into a spin in order to make myself as poor a target as possible, my engine caught fire. I believe that was due to the gas line or carburettor being hit and petrol spurting out onto the hot exhaust pipe. My plane on fire, I fell one or two turns into a spin, during which time my hands and face were burned. By putting the plane into a nose dive and opening the throttle wide, I was able to burn out the gas in the engine and extinguished the fire.'

Cooper force-landed, the victorious German pilot landing alongside, and looking after them.

Late in the morning, at 1140, a patrol of the 139th Aero claimed the first two-seater of the day – a DFW over the Bois de Consenvoye – shared between six pilots. However, this patrol then lost three pilots killed during an engagement with Jastas 13 and 15. Vizefeldwebel Albert Haussmann of Jasta 13 got his at Bertincourt, Leutnants von Hantelmann and Hugo Schäfer of Jasta 15 sending theirs down at Étain, at 1215. Leutnant Johannes Klein of Jasta 15 also claimed one south of Metz but this was not confirmed.

From midday there was some intense air action. At 1210, the 13th's Lieutenant William Stovell claimed a blue and red-nosed Fokker, with a checkerboard wing, near Havrincourt. During this patrol, Lieutenant A C Kimber ran out of luck. A direct hit from an artillery shell obliterated his Spad as it dived down to strafe. An hour later, a German two-seater investigating the centre of the ground attack was shot down by two pilots of the 49th Aero, and at 1350 two other pilots of the 49th claimed a Fokker near Étain but lost Lieutenant Irving J Roth, who was probably shot down by Jasta 8's Vizefeldwebel Rudolf Francke, who gained his 15th kill at this time and vicinity.

Also during the day, Lieutenants David C Beebe and Milton K 'Micky' Lockwood of the 50th Observation Squadron were forced to land their DH4 near Daucourt aerodrome after a fight with six Fokkers. They were probably claimed by Leutnant Näther, whose 26th victory, and second of the day, was reported as a Salmson at Abancourt, which is due north of where they crashed. A Salmson of the 1st Observation Squadron took off at 1330 but was shot down near Varennes, evidently going down under the guns of the unrivalled killer of American aviators, Franz Büchner. He claimed a Salmson for his 34th victory five kilometres north of Varennes; he would end this day with four kills.

It was now the Germans who attacked French and US observation balloons. At 1415, Leutnant Haebler of Jasta 68 burnt two at Aubréville and Réchicourt. The first was the French 39 Cié, the second the US 8th Company gas bag, from which First Lieutenant C J Ross and Second Lieutenant H D Hudnut parachuted. Unfortunately, Ross waited too long to jump, and pieces of the burning balloon fell onto his parachute, setting it on fire, plunging Ross to his death. His companion landed unharmed.

An hour later, Max Näther with Leutnant Breidenbach burnt two more balloons at Thierville, just north of Verdun. These were the 9th and 3rd US Balloon Company balloons, from which Lieutenants S V Clarke, S E White, H P Neibling and G C Carroll all baled out safely. Soon afterwards, at 1630, the 95th Aero burnt the Reville balloon, shared between Lieutenants Harold R Buckley and Alex McLanahan. Frank Luke of the 27th Aero was also out after balloons, with a new partner, Lieutenant Ivan A Roberts, but they ran into Fokkers. Luke sent one down out of control but he did not see it crash and then he had gun problems. The last he saw of Roberts was of him fighting over Consenvoye; he did not return, a victim of Franz Büchner, who claimed his 34th kill over this location.

Top Captain H W Cook with Major R McK Chambers of the 94th Aero. Harvey Cook downed two balloons in September, ending the war with seven victories, while Reed Chambers also scored his first two victories in this month, ending the war also with seven victories. They are standing in front of a captured Fokker DVII.
Bottom Franz Büchner spent most of his war with Jasta 13 from 1917, becoming its leader in June 1918. He scored 40 victories, including 17 in September 1918, mostly on the American front. On the 26th he shot down four US aircraft. At his throat can be seen the Pour le Mérite.

Büchner was in action again at 1756, the 94th getting into a fight with Jasta 13. Although the 94th were credited with a Fokker, Lieutenant Alan Nutt was shot down, followed by Lieutenant Alan B Sherry. His shot up Spad crash-landed in no man's land, where he remained until the following day. This brought Büchner's score to 36. In the fortnight since the 12th, he had claimed 14 victories – mostly Americans. The day ended with Lieutenant Harvey W Cook of the 94th burning a balloon near Grandham at 1848. At unknown times and locations, Jasta 72s claimed a total of five victories during the day, two to Leutnant Herbert Mahn, and one each to Leutnants Gerold Tschentschel, Gustav Frädrich and Ernst Schultz. The victory types are also unrecorded. The Americans lost a Salmson of the 91st Observation Squadron, but this was to AA fire.

Overall, the Americans would be well pleased with this day's efforts. The most experienced 1st Pursuit Group suffered only three losses while doing its job. The 2nd Group did suffer some heavy casualties, but these lesser experienced units soon learnt. The 3rd Group made some claims for no losses. Unlike Saint-Mihiel, only a couple of observation aircraft were attacked by the Fokkers, which barely interrupted their important work. The bombers, as usual, bled. For the Germans, some of the lesser Jastas performed well, but none equalled the performance of the three JGII units that engaged the Americans. At least 13 victories for no loss, but also for no result!

IAF

Seven aircraft of 99 Squadron left at 1505 on a bombing mission to Metz. They were intercepted by 40 enemy fighters from Jastas 3, 4, 77b and 15 at least. Fighting their way to the target, six were able to drop their loads, causing fires in the railway junction. There was persistent fighting all the way back, with gunners claiming two fighters destroyed and another out of control. Five DH9s were brought down in the general area south of Metz, west of the Moselle River. Two more crews were forced to come down in crash landings inside Allied lines, both with dead gunners aboard. Leutnant Ernst Udet of Jasta 4, the highest scoring pilot alive in France, who started the day with a score of 60, was wounded in the thigh during this action.

Claims by the opposition are so numerous it is difficult to paint a picture of what actually occurred. A complicating factor is the loss of a DH9 from 104 Squadron, ten of which left on a mission, five aborting, the one being lost to Fokkers while bombing the same general target. German claims were as follows:

Oberleutnant Ernst Udet is a well-known WWI ace with a long career at the front. By the early summer of 1918 he commanded Jasta 4 within the Richthofen Geschwader, having already served in Richthofen's old unit Jasta 11. By September he had a score of 60 victories, to which he added two DH9 bombers on 26 September. The holder of the Pour le Mérite, he survived the war and remained a popular figure in the flying world. He became a Generaloberst in the Luftwaffe in WWII, but unable to contend with the political in-fighting, committed suicide in November 1941.

1615	Leutnant Heinz Graf von Gluczewski-Kwilicki	Jasta 4	SE of Kemnat
1710	Leutnant Ernst Udet	Jasta 4	Montengingen
1715	Vizefeldwebel Seidel	Jasta 3	SE Frescaty – u/c
1715	Leutnant Richard Kraut	Jasta 4	Buch
1720	Leutnant Ernst Udet	Jasta 4	S of Metz
1720	Leutnant Johannes Klein	Jasta 15	Verny, S of Metz
1725	Leutnant Max Gossner	Jasta 77b	Mannigen
1727	OfStv Bernard Ultsch	Jasta 77b	Kubern
1730	Vizefeldwebel Agne	Jasta 77b	Grosspunach
1730	Vizefeldwebel Schaflein	Jasta 77b	Pullingen
?	Leutnant Joachim von Ziegesar	Jasta 15	Pont-à-Mousson – u/c

Given the times, it would appear Jasta 15 accounted for the 104 Squadron aircraft, with Leutnant von Ziegesar losing the claim, while the rest were the 99 Squadron losses. To some extent it depends if the two bombers that came down in Allied lines were observed from the German side and allowed, for this would make seven DH9 losses for seven claims, the Jasta 3 victory being in some doubt. However, in some records, Jasta 4 do not receive credit for any of their four claims. Perhaps this was because the famous element of the Circus had just arrived and the Kommander der Flieger of the 19th Armee boosted the morale of Jasta 77b, who had seen some action during September but little beforehand since June 1918.

All four of Jasta 77b's victories are recorded as coming down inside German lines, generally near the sites for Jasta 4. The Germans called such disputes 'strittig' or 'contested' – and had a procedure for settling them. The result of this dispute is not known. If there was any suggestion of Jasta 4's claims being over-ruled in favour of Jasta 77b, perhaps thoughts were revised when it was realised that the now wounded Udet would have increased his score to 62 if his victories were confirmed. Being universally recognised as having scored 62 kills in the war must indicate that they, at least, were upheld. In any event, one of the 99 Squadron gunners had put Udet out of the war, for he saw no further action before the Armistice.

	A/C	KB		DES	OOC	KB
British losses	16	–	British claims	18	10	–
French losses	5	1	French claims	12		7
American losses	17	3	American claims	22		5
IAF losses	5	–	IAF claims	2	1	–
German claims	58	9	German losses	?†		?

† No figure has been found; personnel casualties indicate 15 airmen of all ranks killed, one taken prisoner, at least one wounded and at least one Jasta 68 pilot down in flames but unhurt.

British Casualties

Aircraft type	No.	Squadron	Crew	
Camel	E1552	65 Sqdn	2/Lt W R Thornton	POW
Camel	D3374	204 Sqdn	Lt W B Craig DFC	KIA
Camel	C75	204 Sqdn	Lt G E C Howard	KIA
DH4	A7632	202 Sqdn	Lt F A B Gasson	KIA
			2/Lt S King	KIA
Dolphin	H7243	23 Sqdn	Lt E Fulford	POW
Camel	D9632	203 Sqdn	Lt N C Dixie	Safe
Camel	D9611	203 Sqdn	Lt F J S Britnell	Safe
Camel	D9640	203 Sqdn	2/Lt W H Coghill	POW
BF2b	E2163	'L' Flt	2/Lt C A Harrison	POW
			Lt J A Parkinson	POW
DH9	D1016	107 Sqdn	2/Lt H Gill	Safe
			2/Lt J Thompson	Safe
BF2b	E2155	20 Sqdn	2/Lt L G Smith	DOW
			2/Lt E S Harvey	KIA
Camel	D8168	208 Sqdn	Capt A Storey	WIA
Camel	F1975	80 Sqdn	2/Lt H Walker	KIA
DH4	F6187	57 Sqdn	Lt F G Pym	POW
			Sgt W C E Mason	POW
DH4	D8149	57 Sqdn	Lt P W J Timson	KIA
			Lt A N Eyre	KIA
DH4	D8424	57 Sqdn	Capt A Newman	Safe
			2/Lt E G Pernet	WIA
DH9	D5742	218 Sqdn	2/Lt J T Aitken	DOW
			2/Lt G F Hibbert	POW
DH9	D3271	218 Sqdn	Capt J F Chisholm DSC DFC	Interned
			Sgt H J Williams	Interned

Aircraft type	No.	Squadron	Crew	
RE8	C2800	3 AFC	Lt G M Deans	Safe
			Lt T H Prince	WIA
DH4	–	25 Sqdn	2/Lt C W Blasdale (O)	WIA
RE8	–	5 Sqdn	Capt G N Moore (P)	WIA
RE8	–	52 Sqdn	Lt W E C Coombs (P)	WIA
DH4	D7232	104 Sqdn	Lt O L Malcolm	KIA
			2/Lt G V Harper	KIA
DH9	D5573	99 Sqdn	2/Lt L G Stern	KIA
			2/Lt F O Cook	KIA
DH9	D3213	99 Sqdn	2/Lt W H C Gillet	POW
			2/Lt H Crossley	POW
DH9	E632	99 Sqdn	Lt S C Gilbert	KIA
			2/Lt R Buckby	KIA
DH9	C6272	99 Sqdn	2/Lt C R G Abrahams	KIA
			2/Lt C H Sharp	KIA
DH9	B9347	99 Sqdn	Capt P E Welchman MC DFC	POW
			2/Lt T H Swann	POW
DH9	B9366	99 Sqdn	2/Lt H A Boniface	Safe *
			2/Lt S McKeever	KIA
DH9	D544	99 Sqdn	Lt H D West	Safe *
			2/Lt J W Howard	KIA

French Casualties

Aircraft type	No.	Squadron	Crew	
Salmson 2A2		Sal.16	Sgt H Lemaire	WIA *
			Lt Champagnet	Safe
Salmson 2A2		Sal.16	MdL R Neveux	WIA *
			S/Lt Guinard	Safe
Spad XIII		Spa.37	Lt E B de la Chapelle	DOW
Spad XIII		Spa.89	Sgt R Callinet	KIA
Caudron RXI		R239	Sgt Meynadier (P)	KIA *
Bréguet XIV		Br.234	Brig G Delage	WIA
			Asp Patouret	WIA *
Bréguet XIV		Br.234	S/Lt Richaud	KIA
			Lt Sacquin	WIA
Spad XI		Spa.213	Lt Hayer	Safe
			Cpl Chausden	Safe
Spad XIII		Spa.315	Cpl E Boutin	Inj
Bréguet XIV		Br.9	Capt Schlumberger	WIA *
			Asp Pacquet	WIA
Spad XIII		Spa.26	Capt J M X De Sevin	Safe *

American Casualties

Aircraft type	No.	Squadron	Crew	
Salmson 2A2	5229	1st Aero	1/Lt J F Richards II	KIA
			2/Lt A F Hanscom	KIA
Spad XIII	15195	13th Aero	1/Lt T P Evans	POW
Spad XIII	15102	13th Aero	2/Lt V H Burgin	POW
Salmson 2A2	7519	24th Aero	1/Lt C W Higgins (O)	WIA

Aircraft type	No.	Squadron	Crew	
DH4	32792	20th Aero	2/Lt D B Harris	KIA
			2/Lt E Forbes	KIA
DH4	32819	20th Aero	1/Lt R P Matthews	KIA
			2/Lt E A Taylor	KIA
DH4	32915	20th Aero	1/Lt P N Rhinelander	KIA
			1/Lt H C Preston	KIA
DH4	32492	20th Aero	1/Lt M C Cooper	POW
			1/Lt E C Leonard	POW
DH4	32286	20th Aero	2/Lt G B Wiser	POW
			1/Lt G C Richardson	POW
DH4	32584	20th Aero	1/Lt S C Howard	Safe *
			1/Lt E A Parrott	KIA
Spad XIII	–	22nd Aero	1/Lt A C Kimber	KIA
Spad XIII	7519	27th Aero	2/Lt I A Roberts	KIA
Spad XIII	–	49th Aero	1/Lt I J Roth	KIA
Salmson 2A2	–	91st Aero	1/Lt A E Kelly	KIA
			1/Lt F B Lowry	KIA
Spad XIII	4504	94th Aero	1/Lt A Nutt	KIA
Spad XIII	–	94th Aero	1/Lt A B Sherry	Safe
Bréguet XIV	–	96th Aero	2/Lt H J Forshay	Safe *
			2/Lt P J O'Donnell	KIA
Spad XIII	7515	139th Aero	1/Lt H A Garvie	POW
Spad XIII	15129	139th Aero	1/Lt H R Sumner	KIA
Spad XIII	15153	139th Aero	1/Lt H A Petree	KIA
DH4	–	50th Aero	2/Lt D C Beebe	Safe *
			2/Lt M K Lockwood	Safe

27 SEPTEMBER 1918
M T W T **F** S S

British Front

The weather was fine, but cloudy. While the French and American attack had gone forward on a 20-mile front the previous day, the very low level of experience of the American troops had led to severe fighting and no immediate breakthrough. Significantly, no German reserves were being moved to that part of the front.

On this morning, General Sir Henry Horne's 1st Army and General Sir Julian Byng's 3rd Army both launched attacks following a day-long bombardment by the overwhelmingly superior artillery of the British army against the Woton and Hindenburg Lines. The 1st Army attacked between Épehy and Saint-Quentin, while the 3rd Army launched itself across the Canal du Nord, due east of Cambrai. The German army began to fall back on the whole front, from Lens to Armentières to the north again, to avoid being cut off. Four-to-five-mile penetrations were made on this first day, with the front getting to within three miles of Cambrai. Meantime, further north, the British 2nd Army, in co-operation with the Belgians, were preparing to attack on a front from St Eloi to Dixmude.

As would be expected, the RAF was highly active over the battle fronts, and the German Air Service responded making another day of heavy air combat. There would be plenty of targets for the Germans, for the four RAF Brigades in action – I, III, V and IX – mustered over 1,000 aircraft. The more southern battle opened along a 13-mile front between Sauchy Lestrée and Gouzeaucourt, with the Canadian Corps assigned to spearhead the attack, with 8 Squadron's Big Acks used once more as tank support, as well as contact and artillery work.

There was much ground attack and support by both fighters and Corps aircraft, resulting in a number of casualties. On the 1st Army front there were five squadrons allocated exclusively to ground-attack work – 40, 54, 64, 203 and 209. The 3rd Army had one squadron assigned – 201 – but others were given roving commissions to fly both air and ground patrols. The first three RAF losses were caused by ground fire between 0645 and 0700. Camels of 70, 73 and 201 were brought down. The latter, flown by Lieutenant W A W Carter, actually came down in German territory with his fuel line cut; with the fighting going on about him, he managed to get back to the British side. In fact he took back a wounded soldier, and when coming across two unescorted German prisoners, got them to help him!

The Dolphins of 19 Squadron had a series of fights between 0715 and 0735, claiming several Pfalz and DVIIs. North-west of Cambrai, Lieutenant Lewis Ray attacked three triplanes, and claimed all three shot down – one destroyed and two out of control! Then 22 Squadron's Bristols fought a two-seater and some Fokkers, claiming the former and three of the latter. At 0800, the DH4s of 18 Squadron ran into Jasta 57, losing one machine, with another crashing on landing back at base. Leutnant Johannes Jensen claimed a DH9 at Féchain, north-west of Sancourt, but the Staffelführer, Paul Strähle, was hit a glancing blow to the head, from either 18 or 22 Squadron, being forced to land at Aniche aerodrome.

Balloons were yet another obvious target at the start of an attack, 3 Squadron destroying three, the last one having been hauled right down to the ground. Two LVGs were also shot down. However, engaged by Fokkers, they lost Lieutenant Theodore R Hostetter, a 20-year-old American from a well-known New York brewery family, who had been just nine days at the front. Lieutenant Jeff Wood, a 22-year-old lad from York, with six weeks on the squadron, became a prisoner. German pilots scoring victories over Camels at this time were Jasta 2's Leutnant Hermann Vallendor, two, north of Bourlon Wood and at Marquion at 0825, Ernst Bormann and Unteroffizier Karl Fervers, also of Jasta 2, north of Cambrai, while Oberleutnant Robert Greim, CO of Jasta 34b, got a Camel south of Masnières at 0815, seven kilometres south of Cambrai. This fight probably overlapped with the 19 Squadron fight. However, 73 Squadron lost a Camel in flames to ground fire over Bourlon Wood, possibly claimed in the above fight.

At 0800, 56 Squadron's SE5s dived on eight Fokkers over Cambrai and claimed five. Lieutenant George Osborne Mackenzie, a 25-year-old Canadian from Ontario, with four weeks on the squadron, was last seen with three fighters on his tail near Bourlon Wood at 0820. He was probably the victim of Paul Baümer of Jasta 2, who claimed two SE5s in this area at an unknown time. Jasta Boelcke's Leutnant Fritz Heinz was killed in action over Awoingt, probably in this fight.

On the half hour, 98 Squadron had two DH9s shot up, one coming down to crash-land in a shell hole at Grévillers, the other staggering back for repair. Vize-feldwebel Fritz Senf of Jasta 59 shot down a DH9 at Goeulzin for his first victory. For the following half hour, 29 and 84 Squadrons downed balloons, a 4 Squadron RE8 force-landed after hits from ground fire, 79 Squadron claimed a two-seater over Armentières and Paul Baümer shot down a DH4, most likely one lost by 25 Squadron during a recce of the Mons area.

At 0915 the first actions of a new British type at the front began – 43 Squadron's Sopwith Snipes. No. 107 Squadron were bombing Bohain railway station, escorted by 1 and 43 Squadrons, and near Bertry and Brévillers, Fokkers were engaged. No. 1 Squadron claimed one destroyed and one out of control, while Captain C F King and Lieutenant C C Banks, the leading aces of 43, shared another out of control, the first Snipe 'victory', following which Lieutenant R S Johnston claimed a second.

The SEs of 40 Squadron joined combat with Jastas 1 and 27 at 0930, over Oisy-le-Verger. Three SEs went down, and another pilot crash-landed near Cambrai wounded. Jasta 1 claimed two – Leutnant Raven von Barnekow, Unteroffizier Gustav Borm, one each, while Leutnant Hermann Frommherz, Jasta 27, got two.

Bombers of 27 Squadron, escorted by SEs of 32, attacked Émerchicourt at 0945. Lieutenants C M Allan and C E Robinson were attacked by a Fokker which dived and zoomed under them but Robinson got in a burst, hitting the Fokker's petrol tank. The fighter burst into flames, turned over, spinning down on fire. Although the Fokker had shot their controls away they got down without injury. No.32 Squadron, in turn, claimed six Fokkers, four destroyed (one in flames!) and two out of control. Oberleutnant Hans-Helmut von Boddien, CO of Jasta 59, was wounded by DH9s in this fight, and Leutnant Hans Jebens jumped over Bouchain from a flaming Fokker, but his parachute failed to deploy.

The Bristol Fighters of 20 Squadron were in action at 1030, claiming four Fokkers shot down for the loss of Lieutenants F E Turner and C E Clarke over Fontaine Notre Dame. This was the victory of Offizierstellvertreter Friedrich Altemeier of Jasta 24s, the 17th kill of this high-scoring NCO, who would end the war with 21 victories.

An RE8 crew had a lucky escape mid-morning. Lieutenants R E Britton and B Hickman of 13 Squadron were attacked by eight Fokkers, Hickman being wounded early in the fight although he believed he shot down one Fokker. Britton was then wounded too, and in trying to avoid further damage went into a spin, landing in German territory. With the Fokkers withdrawing, Britton managed to take off again and got back to base, although he fainted and crashed trying to land. There are no German claims for an RE8 this day, and one can imagine some frustrated pilot and intelligence officer trying in vain to locate the 'downed' two-seater. More successful was Leutnant Richard Ruckle of Jasta 33, who claimed a Bristol at Busigny at 1130, 62 losing a machine east of Saint-Quentin; happily the crew were captured.

Just before midday, up on the coast, 65 Squadron were in a fight over Ghistelles, claiming four Fokkers but losing Second Lieutenant R O Campbell. Leutnant Franz Piechulek of Jasta 56 gained victory no. 12 – a Camel – north-west of Thorout, which is the only claim all day north of Ypres, although it was timed an hour later (in error?).

Between midday and 1300 the Camels of 54 Squadron lost a pilot – at 1210 – and had another pilot shot up. Two Camels were claimed by Jasta 5's two stars Rumey and Mai at this time. Mai probably got Lieutenant P McCraig (victory 29), who was killed, Rumey the other (his 45th), but as he was killed this day, he was probably credited with the kill rather than any detailed investigation being gone into.

Just before 1300, 19 Squadron were in action again, claiming two Pfalz DIIIs, during an escort mission to DH4s near Aubigny-au-Bac. However, 19 lost one of its aces, Captain Cecil Gardner, shot down into Allied lines near Bapaume, severely wounded, dying on the 30th. Unteroffizier Gustav Borm of Jasta 1 claimed a Dolphin at Bourlon Wood at 1300 (his second kill of the day), which fits very well.

In the following half-hour, 18 Squadron crews on recce sorties were engaged by fighters. Second Lieutenants J K S Smith and A Lilley being shot up and wounded. Lieutenants R Johnson and A Toes failed to return, no doubt the victims of Leutnant von Barnekow, who claimed a DH4 at Sailly at 1300. Another two-seater – this time a BF2b of 88 Squadron – also failed to return from a scrap around 1400. One DVII was sent down out of control, but Vizefeldwebel Fritz Classen of Jasta 26 secured his 8th victory north-west of Abancourt (south of Brunemont on the Sensée Canal).

The RAF had a casualty break until around 1600, but then lost three more BF2bs of 22 Squadron, one being crewed by Captain S F H Thompson MC DFC and Second Lieutenant C J Tolman; Thompson was the highest scoring ace Brisfit pilot of the war to be killed, falling near Cambrai. The other two crews were taken prisoner, although one pilot died. Claimants were Vizefeldwebel Oskar Hennrich of Jasta 46, at Neuvilly at 1600; Oberleutnant Otto Schmidt of Jasta 5, at Cattenières at 1550 (his 16th victory); and one to Carl Degelow of Jasta 40s, west of Valenciennes. In the past, Degelow is noted as having downed an 88 Squadron crew (see Classen above), but they were killed, and Degelow reported his victims were captured, one of three BF2bs he attacked. It would seem the other two Bristols evaded south of Valenciennes, and ran into Jastas 5 and 46, who were part of the same Jagdgruppe. Degelow got Lieutenants G J Smith and G B Shum, while either Hennrich or Schmidt got Thompson. Only this morning, Thompson had brought his score to 30. The third crew were noted as being interned, but where they could have got to if correct, is unknown.

As already mentioned, the great German ace Fritz Rumey was killed on this day, apparently baling out of his crippled DVII but having his parachute fail. At 1720, four Fokkers were claimed over Cambrai, three to Lieutenant Frank Lucien Hale, one destroyed and two out of control. It has often been thought that Rumey was killed in a collision with Lieutenant G E B Lawson of 32 Squadron, who was credited with two Fokker DVIIs this day, but both were claimed at 0930, and Rumey, as already noted, claimed a Camel at 1208. Did Hale, a 23-year-old American from Syracuse, New York, shoot down Rumey? He noted in his combat report:

'On the second OP of the day, ten Fokkers at 9,000 feet over Cambrai seen attacking DH9s of 27 Squadron. SE5s went to assist, Hale firing 25 rounds into one from point-blank range. It fell over, out of control, into clouds 4,000 feet below. He was then attacked himself by one who shot him up from the tail. With a climbing turn and a half roll, Hale came out on the enemy's tail, firing one burst of 150 rounds at point-blank range. This machine turned over on its back and was observed to be still falling 2,000 feet below, on its back and completely out of control, side-slipping and spiralling. Another DVII attacked, and Hale put himself into a spin, going into clouds at 5,000 feet, came out underneath and flew west. He then saw a Fokker DVII below. He fired from 500 feet overhead directly into the enemy aircraft, which held its course and was firing into the SE5s. At 50 yards Hale then fired both guns, 75 rounds, and saw tracer going in. The enemy dived, zoomed to stalling point, fell on its back and went down on one wing, then the other, helplessly out of control; at 2,000 feet it was still falling.'

By 1745, 32 had lost Second Lieutenant C A Cawley, taken prisoner after possibly shooting down a Fokker. Jasta 2's Leutnant Gerhard Bassenge claimed an SE5 at Noyelles, just south-west of Cambrai, while Vizefeldwebel Fritz Classen of Jasta 26 claimed one south of Sailly, just west of the city. Jasta 37 had two fighter pilots wounded on the 2 Armee front this day, Leutnant Mappes and Vizefeldwebel Robert Wirth.

As the late afternoon progressed, the 17th Aero, 210 and 11 Squadrons all saw combat. At 1800 hours 57 Squadron bombed a HQ north of Cambrai and got into a scrap with Fokkers, the gunners claiming two DVIIs out of control – one splendidly coloured black underneath, yellow with red spots on top wings and a grey fuselage. Three DHs were shot up, three men wounded, one bomber force-landing near 13 Squadron's base, another force-landing at 62 Squadron's aerodrome.

At this same time, Second Lieutenant E G Robertson of 85 Squadron was last seen east of Saint-Quentin in combat with two Fokkers, probably being shot down by Ernst Bormann of Jasta Boelcke, who claimed a fighter at Saint-Quentin, although he recorded it as a Camel, not an SE5a.

German flak gunners claimed three aircraft shot down during the day, and in the north the Belgian Willy Coppens flamed yet another balloon over Leflinghe – his 31st victory.

It becomes increasingly difficult to tie up German losses as 1918 progressed due to gaps in the records, especially concerning times and locations. The Germans certainly seemed to lose a number of men and machines this day, other than those already mentioned, and some would have been on the French front. Jasta 31 had Leutnant Holle wounded, while another 17 Armee front casualty appears to have been a Marine two-seater crew, Flugmaat Richard Arfendt and Leutnant Wilhelm Kreitz who were killed at La Lovie, the nearest British victory being that of Ken Unger of 210 Squadron downing a Halberstadt 'south-east of Nieuport'. Other losses are listed as: Fliegers Gustav Dunkel and Fritz Schuster at La Briquette; Vizefeldwebel Gerhard Meyer and Vizefeldwebel Christian Volquartzen killed at Hachy; Leutnant Eugen Wild killed at Rethel; Leutnant Josef Heckenberger, killed; Gefreiter Heinrich Brinker, killed at Tournai.

French Front

Escadre de Combat No.2 was assigned to cover the American attack between Dun-sur-Meuse and Abaucourt. Despite the assumed activity, there was little real action until the evening due to early rain and low cloud. At 1655, Leutnant Hans von Freden of Jasta 50 shot down a balloon by Minaucourt for his 12th victory, the IV Armée's 31 Cié balloon being burnt at exactly this time.

In turn, Spa.77 burnt a German 'drachen' south-east of Étain, shared between Sergent Edward J Corsi, an American, and Maréchal-des-Logis Thévenod. They were then attacked by three Fokkers that had been guarding the balloon, Thévenod being brought down and killed. Leutnant Max Näther of Jasta 62 claimed a Spad at Montezville, 12 km north-west of Verdun, between Étain and the lines, to bring his personal score to 17.

A number of enemy machines were claimed downed by various units – Spa.163, Spa.124, Spa.95, Spa.89 and Spa.100 – then during a bomb raid, Escadre de Bombardement 12 sent out a huge force of 86 Bréguet XIVs, escorted by 14 Caudron RXI 'gun-ships', escorted by aircraft of GC19. They bombed troops, and convoys between Attigny and Somme-Py. Fokkers tried to intervene, the French gunners claiming two, but two Bréguet crews were wounded and got back. One of the Bréguets may have been claimed by Vizefeldwebel Alfons Nägler of Jasta 81, who reported a Bréguet shot down north of Tahure. The same Jasta claimed a Spad near Ville, by Vizefeldwebel Averes.

Other claims by the Germans were by Leutnant Korff, also north of Tahure, followed by a Spad two-seater near Marfaux by Leutnant Fritz Höhn at 1820 (the other Bréguet that was hit?). Two Spad pilots returned wounded during the day, one at least having been hit by ground fire.

American Sector

The battle front was covered in clouds in the morning, with rain continuing until 0900, but it cleared in the afternoon, although low clouds persisted until 1700. Again little action took place until the late afternoon.

Observation aircraft were out, one observer being wounded by a Fokker as the 91st Squadron were engaged, although they claimed a Fokker in flames near Crépon. Then the 99th Aero lost a Salmson, brought down by AA fire with a wounded observer.

Once again the Germans appeared to be overenthusiastic in claiming Spads. Two were reported shot down by Leutnant Hans Korner of Jasta 19, near Pagny, with Vizefeldwebel Prime of Jasta 78b sending down another near Herbéviller five minutes later. In turn, the 147th Aero claimed a Fokker near Montfaucon; another, with a red nose and blue tail, was shared by two more pilots.

The 95th Aero was involved in the final fight of the day, claiming two Rumplers. The first was at 1814 near Brieulles, the second at 1825 near Fléville, although First Lieutenant Thomas F Butz had to make a forced landing after this fight.

	A/C	KB		DES	OOC	KB
British losses	28	–	British claims	28	30	6
French losses	1	1	French claims	6		1
American losses	1	–	American claims	5		–
IAF losses	–		IAF claims	–		
German claims	43†	1	German losses	6/10‡		?

† Three to flak. ‡ Total personnel casualties were at least 17 killed, and six wounded.

British Casualties

Aircraft type	No.	Squadron	Crew		
Camel	D9460	70 Sqdn	2/Lt P M Wallace	POW	
Camel	F1917	73 Sqdn	Capt W H Hubbard DFC	Safe	
DH4	A7899	18 Sqdn	Lt R C Bennett DFC	POW	
			Lt N W Helwig DFC	POW	
DH4	F6005	13 Sqdn	2/Lt C C A Daniel	Safe	*
			2/Lt H F Lee	WIA	
Camel	E4375	201 Sqdn	Lt W A W Carter	Safe	
SE5a	F5495	56 Sqdn	Lt G O Mackenzie	KIA	
SE5a	F5482	56 Sqdn	Lt J A Pouchet DSM	Safe	*
Dolphin	E4501	19 Sqdn	Capt C V Gardiner	DOW	
Camel	F6117	3 Sqdn	2/Lt J A Wood	POW	
Camel	F2158	3 Sqdn	Lt T R Hostetter	KIA	
DH9	D7334	98 Sqdn	Lt E A R Lee	Inj	*
			2/Lt E G Banham	WIA	
DH9	D1106	98 Sqdn	Lt P Fish	Safe	
			Lt G Richmond	Safe	*
DH4	A8031	25 Sqdn	Lt H D Hazell	KIA	
			2/Lt D B Robertson	KIA	
SE5a	E1350	40 Sqdn	2/Lt C M G Morton	KIA	
SE5a	B8442	40 Sqdn	Lt N D Willis	POW	
SE5a	C9135	40 Sqdn	2/Lt P B Myers	KIA	
SE5a	E1345	40 Sqdn	Lt R Mooney USAS	POW	
BF2b	C944	62 Sqdn	2/Lt P S Manley	POW	
			Sgt G F Hines	POW	
Camel	D9472	73 Sqdn	2/Lt W A Brett	KIA	
RE8	F6011	59 Sqdn	Capt L M Woodhouse MC DFC	KIA	
			Lt W S Peel MC	KIA	
RE8	D4939	13 Sqdn	Lt R E Britton	WIA	*
			2/Lt B Hickman	WIA	
BF2b	E2566	20 Sqdn	2/Lt F E Turner	KIA	
			2/Lt C E Clarke	KIA	
DH4	A7887	18 Sqdn	2/Lt A Lilley	Safe	
			2/Lt J K S Smith	Safe	*
Camel	E1549	65 Sqdn	2/Lt R O Campbell DCM	KIA	
DH9	E669	108 Sqdn	2/Lt A S Jones	KIA	
			Sgt N Richardson	KIA	
Camel	B6421	54 Sqdn	Lt P McCaig	KIA	
Camel	F2135	54 Sqdn	2/Lt J M Stevenson	Safe	*
BF2b	E2153	88 Sqdn	Lt C Foster	KIA	
			Sgt T Proctor	KIA	
BF2b	D8089	22 Sqdn	2/Lt G B Shum	KIA	
			Lt G J Smith	POW	

Aircraft type	No.	Squadron	Crew		
BF2b	E2243	22 Sqdn	2/Lt C H Wilcox	POW	
			Lt J R Drummond	KIA	
BF2b	E2477	22 Sqdn	Capt S F H Thompson MC DFC	KIA	
			2/Lt C J Tolman	KIA	
SE5a	B8355	32 Sqdn	2/Lt C F Cawley	POW	
DH9	D5749	103 Sqdn	2/Lt W S Marchant	Safe	
			2/Lt H S Crees	WIA	
DH4	A8085	57 Sqdn	2/Lt G J Dickins	WIA	*
			2/Lt A H Aitken	Safe	
DH4	A8086	57 Sqdn	2/Lt F deM Hyde	Safe	*
			Lt E H Eyres	WIA	
DH4	F6114	57 Sqdn	Lt E M Coles	Safe	*
			2/Lt C Wilkinson	WIA	
SE5a	H7249	85 Sqdn	2/Lt E G Robertson	KIA	
Camel	E4407	210 Sqdn	2/Lt H E Light	Inj	
RE8		12 Sqdn	Lt C R Pithey DFC	WIA	*
			Lt H Rhodes DFC	WIA	
RE8	–	52 Sqdn	Lt J W H Scales (P)	WIA	*
AWFK8	–	8 Sqdn	Lt A R Robb	Safe	*
			2/Lt S F Blackwell	WIA	
BF2b	–	62 Sqdn	2/Lt R F Hunter (O)	WIA	*

French Casualties

Spad XIII		Spa.100	Sgt H Gantois	WIA	*
Spad XIII		Spa.77	MdL Thévenod	MIA	
Spad XIII		Spa.60	Lt Cuvelier	WIA	*
Bréguet XIV		Br.108	Lt R Metayer	WIA	*
			Asp R Mullet	WIA	
Bréguet XIV		Br.111	Sgt/Maj C Leteneur	WIA	
			Asp A Etchberry	WIA	
Bréguet XIV		GB4	Lt Delephine	KIA	

American Casualties

Salmson 2A2		91st Aero	1/Lt W F Baker	Safe	
			2/Lt R S Jannopulo	WIA	
Salmson 2A2	1156	99th Aero	1/Lt J E Eaton	Safe	
			1/Lt E R Case	WIA	
Spad XIII		95th Aero	1/Lt T F Butz	Safe	

British Front

Low clouds and rain predominated in the morning, clearing in the afternoon. In fact the weather was foul and was responsible for some heavy casualties. The Fourth – and last – Battle for Ypres opened on this day. General Sir Herbert Plumer's 2nd Army and the Belgian army's attacks were great successes. By nightfall the Germans had been cleared out of Houthulst Forest and at the end of the next day, all the territory lost in April 1918 had been regained. This also meant all the territory gained at such a frightful cost the previous autumn was regained too. Crews of 7, 10 and 53 Squadrons did much valuable work in this sector.

One of the reasons for this success was that the German army had run out of men, and increasing sections of them were not prepared to fight any more. Another reason was the dominant RAF which enabled all attacks in this month to be surprises. While the air forces' efforts in WWI, of all sides, need to be taken in context, there is no doubt that by 1918 Allied air-to-ground attack especially was making its impact on German troops. These were mainly carried out by the RAF, but it became increasingly obvious to the German soldier that he was constantly being buzzed, bombed, shot up and generally harassed by enemy fighters, while the Allied two-seaters, now protected far better than hitherto, were able to range artillery on them almost with impunity.

This same strafing, and the day bombing, often met good and accurate ground fire as witnessed this morning, for soon after dawn, 202 Squadron lost three crews during an attack on a dump at Engel, and no Jasta pilots claimed DH4s this day. Also a 204 Camel pilot failed to return while strafing near Thorout. No. 29 Squadron had three of its SE pilots fail to return, all ending up as prisoners.

Air fighting began around 0700, the RE8 team of Carberry and Clements knocked down a Halberstadt over La Vacquerie valley, but Lieutenant J A Fenton of 209 Squadron was lost south of the Scarpe River at 0745, possibly by Unteroffizier Fervers of Jasta Boelcke. An RE8 was also shot down by Unteroffizier Jeckert of Jasta 56, over Moorslede, which was a 7 Squadron loss.

Fighters and ground fire caused other losses, plus at least one to weather during this early morning period. No. 203 Squadron tangled with Jasta 2 at 0830 losing Sergeant W N Mayger MM, down in flames to Leutnant Gerhard Bassenge, although he claimed an SE5a. There were also more multiple losses. No.41 Squadron lost five SE5s at this time, mostly to ground fire and the weather, although Josef Jacobs was credited with two SE kills at this time, his 33rd and 34th victories. No. 65 Squadron lost no fewer than six Camels with another force-landing, to ground fire and weather. Three pilots were taken prisoner, two more being interned in Holland. At 0900, 213 Squadron lost three Camels, with another force-landing at Moeres aerodrome after an encounter with fighters and ground fire.

Towards midday, Leutnant Piechulek of Jasta 56 claimed a DH bomber, which was either a 211 Squadron machine, lost while raiding Staden, or a 217 Squadron machine that failed to return; 217 also had a DH4 shot up but it got back. As the afternoon progressed and the weather improved, there were constant combats going on all along the front, with claims and losses difficult to tie up. One fight at 1230 was between 204 Squadron and MFJ 2, the Camel pilots claiming three Fokkers but having one machine force-land, Lieutenant E R Brown being injured. Two German pilots claimed him – Alexandre Zenses for his 9th victory, and Theo Osterkamp for his 27th, both at 1230, both at Woumen.

At 1430, Engel was again raided, 202 losing another machine to this target, but this time to fighters, Flugmaat Nake of MFJ 1 making his first victory claim. German fighter pilots had more success during the afternoon. Leutnant Ernst Baumgartel of Jasta 56 shot down an SE5a near Ypres at 1240, into Allied lines, while a few minutes later, Leutnant Josef Raesch of Jasta 43 shot down another SE5, which fell east of Ypres in German lines. Colours seen on the Fokkers seem to indicate Jasta 56, but Captain E C Hoy DFC of 29 Squadron was brought down at this time to become a prisoner. Hoy had brought his own score to 13 the previous day, and Raesch now had a score of four which would rise to seven by the end of the war.

Combats now came thick and fast and it is difficult to match opposing units. Those that can be included a scrap between 210 Squadron and MFJ 4 south-east of Nieuport at 1745. However, in the general area were Camels of 70 Squadron, Dolphins of 79 and some two-seaters, said to be Bristols by the Germans but probably the DH4s of 218 Squadron. There might also have been some French Spads about, from Spa.62 (see later). No. 70 Squadron lost a Camel north of Gheluwe, but while both sides claimed a number of victories, few aircraft were actually lost.

Shortly afterwards, Marine pilots engaged two-seaters, Theo Osterkamp claiming a Bréguet XIV near Pierkenshoeck at 1810, possibly a Belgian machine lost this day. The two Belgian losses were Warrant Officer Robert J M M Cajot and Lieutenant Alfred T M Bricoult, of 2 Escadrille, who came down at Cortemarck in a Bréguet XIV A-2 to be taken prisoner, and Sous Lieutenant Jean M A G de Roest d'Alkemade and Lieutenant Charles G N F Coomans of 7 Escadrille, flying a Spad XI, who came down near Clercken (Houthulst), although they were apparently hit by flak. Robert Cajot, in WWII, was the CO of the Belgian detachment at the Franco/Belgian school at RAF Odiham, England, having escaped from his native country in July 1940.

Leutnant Bargmann of MFJ 2 shot down a DH9 at Beerst at 1815, perhaps the other Belgian aircraft that failed to get home? With the heavy fighting on this northern part of the front, it is not surprising that further German claims were made, Carl Degelow of Jasta 40s shooting down a Camel here, his 19th victory, Flugmaat Pfeiffer of MFJ 3 another Camel at Woumen at 1815, and this appears to have been Lieutenant R M Bennett of 204 Squadron. From Beckenham, Kent, Bennett at 18 years of age was probably the youngest British ace to die in action. Another claim was for a Spad, to Vizefeldwebel Krebs of Jasta 56 at Kastelhoek – again possibly the Belgian Spad XI. However, the French lost two Spads in the VI Armée Sector, Caporaux Gerard and Gaulhiac of Spa.62. The other claim was an SE5a by Unteroffizier Eduard Binge of Jasta 16, his 4th and final victory of the war.

French Front

The weather here was bad all day, with low clouds and strong winds. Once again, the first job was to try and blind German observations of the battle area by balloon observers, and during the day the French burnt four German 'drachens'. At 0845,

Lieutenant J C Romatet gained his 5th victory on 28 September, a balloon, and had seven victories by the Armistice. After his 5th victory he was awarded the Legion d'Honneur. To the left is Capitaine R P Fonck, the French ace-of-aces, credited with 75 victories. During September 1918 he achieved seven victories flying with Spa.103 of Les Cigognes Group. As noted by their medals, both men won the Légion d'Honneur, Medaille Militaire and Croix de Guerre with numerous Palmes. Fonck, indeed, became a Commandeur of the former.

at Orfeuil, Sous Lieutenant Jean Charles Romatet, the 25-year-old Corsican CO of Spa.165, got his 5th victory, sharing the balloon with two of his pilots. Then at 0900, the incomparable Michel Coiffard burnt his 23rd balloon (victory 31) south of Semide. Half an hour later, Spa.163's Sergent Onillon flamed the Challeronge balloon. Finally, at 1115, the American, Sergent James Connelly, also of Spa.163, claimed the 4th, bringing his own total to six. This too was floating above Challeronge, on the west end of the assault area.

In the IV Armée sector, Sal.252 lost a crew to Fokkers, Sergent Bal and Sous Lieutenant Nouvellon being killed as they crashed into French lines. Then a Bréguet of Br.9 failed to return, crewed by Caporal Moser and Sous Lieutenant le Comte des Floris.

Three French two-seaters were claimed by the Germans. Vizefeldwebel Friedrich Poeschke, Jasta 53, shot down his 4th victory at Somme-Py, at 1145, while Leutnant Gustav Frädrich and Vizefeldwebel Karl Arnold each claimed 2A2s near Manre. Two observers were wounded by ground fire on this sector, but whether either were involved with enemy fighters is not known. However, Adjutant Montel and Sergent Pautrat of Br.123 were reported missing this day, which may have been the third.

Groupe de Combat 13 engaged in five combats between 1330 and 1530 in the Somme-Py to Manre area, claiming one destroyed and two probables. Adjutant Marcel Laurent Henriot, a 22-year-old from Saulnat in the Haute-Saône region of France, and who had been with Spa.65 since March, claimed his 6th and final victory north of Somme-Py. Sergent Dambet, also of Spa.65, claimed his 1st. The Escadrille lost Sergent Milhau.

The Germans brought down two Spads: Leutnants Ernst Schulz and Herbert Mahn of Jasta 72s both reported Spads down at Ardeuil, two kilometres north of Manre. Sergent Bourgeois was injured during the day, possibly as the result of combat. Also operating on this front was Spa.124, their Russian GC21 staff commander, Capitaine Paul d'Argueff, bringing down two two-seaters, one at 1010 over Manre, the other at 1520 at Sechault, to bring his score to 13. In between, Lieutenant Henri Berge, the CO of this unit, claimed a probable north of Forges Woods at midday. At 1645, Lieutenant Henri de Sevin, commander of Spa.151, got his 2nd victory over Somme-Py.

Lieutenant René Fonck of Spa.103 claimed a two-seater north-east of Somme-Py at 1030 to bring his score to 67. A patrol of Spa.31 also reported a Fokker biplane down north of Bois de Buoc at 1145, while on the German side Unteroffizier Boness of Jasta 53 claimed a Spad at Somme-Py at 1150.

American Sector

On the front of the Meuse-Argonne offensive, the French and Americans kept up the pressure. The Germans reacted in the air, starting at 0815, with Leutnant Fritz Höhn of Jasta 60 returning the compliment by flaming a balloon near Tahure.

Lieutenant Weiss jumped from the burning 67 Cié gas bag. Then at 0850, Höhn returned to burn the American 6th BC's balloon at Béthelainville, from which First Lieutenants H F Gossett and G R Nixon baled out safely.

However, the Americans claimed three balloons at this time too. The first at 0600 went to First Lieutenant Eddie Rickenbacker, near Sivry-sur-Meuse. Six minutes later another 94th Aero pilot, Harvey Cook, flamed a balloon near Cléry-le-Petit. Frank Luke got the third – near Bétheniville at 0609 – the pilot's 14th victory.

The 22nd Aero were busy in combat shortly between 0840 and 0900, claiming six Fokkers. One of the Fokkers was that probably flown by Unteroffizier Karl Hoffmann of Jasta 60, who was killed in combat over the Argonne Forest during the day. At 0915, the 139th Aero claimed three Pfalz DIIIs over Cléry-le-Petit, then a Rumpler over Forges at 1030 by a flight commander of the 27th Aero, Jerry Vasconcells.

During the day, the specialist night observation 9th Aero was caught in daylight. Two of their aircraft had been joined by a Salmson of 88 Aero, then proceeded to patrol. Over the front they were attacked by five Fokkers north-east of Montfaucon. The DVII pilot that came in on Second Lieutenants Harry A Dolan and Basil D Woom scored with his first burst, shooting away the aileron contols and sending the DH4 down in a spin to crash-land; the crew were shaken but unharmed.

Second Lieutenant Lee D Warrender and First Lieutenant Harry C Crumb were wounded, Warrender through the neck, Crumb through the abdomen – they crashed in no man's land. Crumb was severely wounded and told his pilot to leave him and save himself; he later died of his wound. The accompanying Salmson was shot down in flames, but surprisingly, the crew of Second Lieutenant H E Loud and Captain C T Trickey survived, though wounded, and Loud later succumbed.

Franz Büchner shot down the Salmson, his 37th kill, while Leutnant Werner Niethammer, also Jasta 13, reported downing a Salmson near Pagny, and Leutnant Oliver von Beaulieu-Marconnay of Jasta 19 reported downing a Spad two-seater for his 23rd kill, both most probably misidentification of the DH4s.

At 0950, the balloon of the 1st US Company was attacked by seven Fokkers south of Dannevoux. One Fokker was brought down by the protective fire of the nearby 2nd Balloon Company gunners, Vizefeldwebel Heinrich Brobowski of Jasta 53 being captured. The balloon was damaged but not destroyed, although First Lieutenant S I Howell sensibly baled out.

A lull followed until the afternoon. Several combats and claims occurred, involving the 147th, 213th, 93rd and 103rd Aeros. Another DH4, this time from the 50th Observation Squadron, was shot down by ground fire late in the day, having taken off at 1552. The crew were rescued safely from in front of the lines.

The last victory of the day went to Frank Luke at 1550, a Hannover CLIII near the Bois d'Apremont, bringing the American's score to 15. Bad weather then closed in, ending combat for the day.

	A/C	KB		DES	OOC	KB
British losses	33	–	British claims	24	7	–
French losses	7	1	French claims	8		4
American losses	4	–	American claims	20		3

	A/C	KB		DES	OOC	KB
Belgian losses	2	–	Belgian claims	–		–
IAF losses	–	–	IAF claims	–	–	–
German claims	33†	2	German losses	5‡		?

† At least two by flak. ‡ At least five, with an additional five airmen reported killed, which may or may not have resulted in lost aeroplanes; one of the airmen being from FA205.

British Casualties

Aircraft type	No.	Squadron	Crew	
SE5a	F5456	29 Sqdn	Lt B R Rolfe	POW
SE5a	F5480	29 Sqdn	Lt D A O'Leary	POW
SE5a	D6947	29 Sqdn	2/Lt W L Dougan	POW
DH4	N5962	202 Sqdn	Lt R Ringrose	KIA
			2/Lt H Hollings	KIA
DH4	A8025	202 Sqdn	Capt A V Bowater	POW
			Lt D L Melvin	POW
DH4	A8066	202 Sqdn	Lt C R Moore	POW
			2/Lt E Darby	POW
DH4	A7924	217 Sqdn	1/Lt J E Gregory USAS	KIA
			2/Lt E Martin-Bell	KIA
Camel	H7288	65 Sqdn	2/Lt W J Brooks	KIA
Camel	F1542	65 Sqdn	2/Lt D M John	Interned
Camel	B7864	65 Sqdn	Lt F Edsted	Interned
Camel	D8145	65 Sqdn	Lt J C Malcolmson DFC	POW
Camel	E1487	65 Sqdn	Lt J McM Maclennon DFC	POW
Camel	D8158	65 Sqdn	2/Lt R C Mitten	POW
Camel	F5937	209 Sqdn	Lt J A Fenton	KIA
Camel	D8187	204 Sqdn	Lt R M Bennett	KIA
RE8	C2530	7 Sqdn	2/Lt H M Matthews	WIA
			2/Lt C Fletcher	KIA
Camel	F3220	203 Sqdn	Sgt W N Mayger MM	KIA
Camel	E7199	70 Sqdn	Sgt A C Hall	POW
SE5a	B7900	64 Sqdn	2/Lt A T Sheldrake	KIA
SE5a	E4048	41 Sqdn	Lt A F Smith	POW
SE5a	F5484	41 Sqdn	2/Lt H C Telfer	POW
SE5a	F5506	41 Sqdn	2/Lt W Mitchell	POW
SE5a	E4061	41 Sqdn	Lt P B Cooke	POW
SE5a	C8887	41 Sqdn	2/Lt H B Hewat	POW
Camel	D3326	213 Sqdn	2/Lt A Fletcher	POW
Camel	D3372	213 Sqdn	Lt P C Jenner	POW

Aircraft type	No.	Squadron	Crew	
Camel	F3948	213 Sqdn	Lt W A Rankin	POW
DH9	E8936	211 Sqdn	2/Lt W J Johnson	POW/DOW
			Sgt W E Jones MM	POW
Dolphin	F6020	79 Sqdn	Lt R J Morgan	POW
AWFK8	D5152	10 Sqdn	Lt C F J Lisle	WIA
			2/Lt M de Verteuil	Safe
RE8	D6741	7 Sqdn	2/Lt W K Rose	WIA
			2/Lt A E Jenkins	KIA
RE8	E273	7 Sqdn	2/Lt G A J Henry	DOW
			2/Lt A Westall	WIA
SE5a	C9294	56 Sqdn	Lt D W Grinnell-Milne	Safe
Camel	D8175	70 Sqdn	2/Lt J S Wilson	KIA
DH9	D5622	108 Sqdn	2/Lt P L Phillips	Safe
			2/Lt P S McCrea	Safe
DH4	A7849	202 Sqdn	Lt A M Stevens	KIA
			2/Lt W H L Halford	KIA
Camel	D8218	204 Sqdn	2/Lt E R Brown	WIA
Dolphin	C8115	87 Sqdn	2/Lt D A Thomson	POW
SE5a	C1914	29 Sqdn	Capt E C Hoy DFC	POW
DH9	D5654	218 Sqdn	2/Lt T M Steele	POW
			2/Lt G Gedge	POW
DH9	C1206	218 Sqdn	2/Lt F Nelson US MCR	WIA *
			2/Lt L L Barr	DOW
DH9	D5712	218 Sqdn	1/Lt E R Brewer USMC	WIA
			Sgt H B Wersheimer USMC	WIA
DH9	E8881	218 Sqdn	Lt H D McLaren DFC	Safe
			Sgt G Barlow	WIA
RE8	C1036	4 Sqdn	Lt R H Schroeder	Safe *
			2/Lt B R Jones	KIA
RE8	–	7 Sqdn	2/Lt S Kennan (O)	WIA *
AWFK8	C8643	82 Sqdn	Lt J Sangster	WIA *
			2/Lt L J Skinner	WIA
Camel	–	3 Sqdn	2/Lt R L McLeod	WIA *
RE8	–	13 Sqdn	2/Lt J Nicole (P)	WIA *
SE5a	F854	56 Sqdn	Lt J C Speaks	WIA
DH4	–	27 Sqdn	2/Lt C M Allan (P)	WIA *
Camel	–	70 Sqdn	Lt C L Frank	WIA *

French Casualties

Spad XIII		Spa.62	Cpl Gerard	MIA
Spad XIII		Spa.62	Cpl Gaulhiac	MIA
Bréguet XIV		Br.282	Sgt Roux	Safe *
			Asp Bertrand	WIA
Spad XIII		Spa.65	Sgt R Milhau	MIA

Aircraft type	No.	Squadron	Crew	
Spad XIII		Spa.65	Sgt Bourgeois	Inj
Bréguet XIV		Br.123	Adj Montel	MIA
			Sgt Fautrat	MIA
Salmson 2A2		Sal.252	Sgt Bal	KIA
			S/Lt Nouvellon	KIA
Bréguet XIV		Br.9	Cpl Moser	POW
			S/Lt H le Comte des Floris	POW
Bréguet XIV		Br.269	Lt Gilles (O)	KIA
Bréguet XIV		Br.55	Lt L Mailloux (O)	WIA *

		Belgian Casualties		
Bréguet XIV A-2		2ème Esc	WO R J M M Cajot	POW
			Lt A T M Bricoult	POW
Spad XI		7ème Esc	S/Lt J de R d'Alkemade	?
			Lt C G N F Coomans	?

		American Casualties		
Spad XIII	–	27th Aero	1/Lt P V Stout	WIA
Salmson 2A2	–	88th Aero	2/Lt H E Laud	DOW
			Capt C T Trickey	WIA
DH4	–	50th Aero	1/Lt F McCook	Safe
			2/Lt M K Lochwood	Safe
DH4	–	9th Aero	2/Lt H A Dolan	Safe
			2/Lt B D Woon	Safe
DH4	–	9th Aero	2/Lt L D Warrender	WIA
			1/Lt H C Crumb	DOW
Spad XIII	–	28th Aero	2/Lt L P Moriarty	WIA

29 SEPTEMBER 1918
M T W T F S **S**

British Front

The weather began fine in the morning, with overcast, cloudy conditions settling in during the afternoon. This day saw yet another sector of the German front being attacked; the fourth day in a row this had occurred. This time, General Sir Henry Rawlinson's 4th Army smashed straight through the main Hindenburg Line positions near Bellicourt, called the Battle of the Saint-Quentin Canal. The main thrust went in between Bellenglise and Venduille. This resulted in pushing the Germans into a retreat which would not stop until the end of the war. On other sections of the front, Passchendaele was retaken by Allied troops, while the Belgians recaptured Dixmude.

As luck would have it, on this front, captured German documents enabled the British commanders to know the exact location of every German machine-gun position, trench mortar and battery, as well as ammunition and supply dumps, telephone and signals centres.

The day's first action took place near Estourmel at 0730, seven of 87 Squadron's Dolphins encountering 11 Fokkers. Lieutenant Hollinghurst claimed one down out of control for his 10th victory, but the unit lost the veteran Canadian Ross Mac-donald, although by whom is difficult to discover as no Dolphins were noted as claimed this day. At this same time, Captain J D Breakey of 203 Squadron, engaged on a low-bombing patrol, saw a lone LVG two-seater and attacked. Firing 150 rounds into it, the LVG climbed steeply, stalled and crashed near the Sensée Canal. This is believed to be a machine from FA33, who lost two aircraft this day.

On the hour Camels and Fokkers clashed near Wijnendaele Wood. 210 Squadron claimed eight, one German pilot being seen to jump. The Camel boys lost one pilot, Second Lieutenant John F Stafford, a 22-year-old American from Fall River, Mas-sachusetts. He was probably on his first sortie, as he had only arrived four days earlier! MFJ 1 pilots claimed victories – Vizeflugmaat Hackbusch, Leutnant Freymadl and Flugmaat Reiss, all timed at 0820. Vizefeldwebel Krebs of Jasta 56 claimed an SE5a at Westroosbeke at 0815 although none were lost. (It is just possible the MFJ claims fit losses the day before!)

At 0830 an RE8 was shot down by Unteroffizier Ludwig Jeckert of Jasta 56 near Zonnebeke. The only RE8 crew downed had left their base at 0730, a 6 Squadron machine, but as they were operating from Moslains, well south of Cambrai, it could not have been them. They were most probably brought down by ground fire when operating north of Saint-Quentin.

Bombers of 211 Squadron were in action at 0810 over Roulers and 1 Squadron's SE5s had a fight at 0845. At this latter time too, 11 Squadron's Bristols were in action against DVIIs south-east of Cambrai, one falling to Josef Mai of Jasta 5, on fire, east of Caudry at 0850 – the German's 30th victory.

Over Busigny at this same moment, 27 Squadron were fighting Fokkers after bombing the place. One DVII came up under the tail of two of them and was

SE5a C8841 of 1 Squadron. Lt D C Pegg shot down a Fokker DVII in it on 15 September, but Lt L N Elworthy was brought down flying it on 29 September, shot down by Karl Odebrett of Jasta 42, to become a prisoner.

promptly shot down, bursting into flames and breaking up. However, one DH9 was shot down in turn by Vizefeldwebel Treiber, also of Jasta 5, north of Caudry.

More bombers were out an hour later, escorted by 1 Squadron's SE5s. The fighters claimed two DVIIs but one SE also went down, victim of Leutnant Karl Odebrett of Jasta 42, who notched up his 16th kill at Bohain. A 3 Squadron Camel force-landed just behind the front at 0945 after a low patrol and a fight with Fokkers. Paul Baümer of Jasta 2 claimed two Camels this day at unknown times, and this may have been one of them.

Just prior to 10 a.m., 84 Squadron went on one of their famous balloon strafes, reporting no less than five 'drachens' burnt, north of Villers-Outréaux (two), Beaurevoir, L'Espagne and north of Montbrehain. One SE5 failed to return, the South African Second Lieutenant D C Rees – probably the SE brought down by Vizefeldwebel Oskar Hennrich of Jasta 46 at Villers-Outréaux at 1020. Three more balloons fell to 29 Squadron at around the same moment, further north, near Comines and Armentières. However, Lieutenant R G Robertson had to force-land near Ypres after being hit by ground fire.

Towards 1030, 20 Squadron were in a fight with Fokkers, putting in claims of six victories north of Saint-Quentin, but they too lost a machine and an ace pilot – Lieutenant N S Boulton and Second Lieutenant C H Case. It has been noted elsewhere that they were brought down by Mai of Jasta 5, but the times do not agree. Jasta 2 claimed two Bristols at undisclosed times – possibly three as Baümer is noted as having downed an RE8 which may have been another type. However, 22 Squadron lost two Bristols mid-morning. The main possibility is that the 20 Squadron BF2b was the 20th victory of Offizierstellvertreter Friedrich Altemeier of Jasta 24s, at Montbrehain, north of Saint-Quentin.

This really is the problem with these last September days: there is so much confused fighting over several overlapping sectors of the front, that it is difficult to have any understanding of who was fighting who. This even applies to aircraft brought down on the Allied side – a rare occurrence. Captain C W Cudemore of 64 Squadron is a case in point. He saw a formation of four Fokkers apparently flying protection to balloons and attacked, shooting down one out of control. The second Fokker he went for fell away and crashed north-west of Sailly, inside British lines, where it burst into flames. This may have been Leutnant Fritz Hoffmann of Jasta Boelcke, killed west of Cambrai.

The fight which cost 22 Squadron two machines occurred between 1130 and midday, and they probably went down to Baümer and Unteroffizier Karl Fervers. A difficulty now is that the surviving German records are not so good as in earlier months and years of the war. For instance, 211 Squadron lost two DH9s with another two shot up at this same time, but there are no apparent claims. Jasta 7 were in the area, and may have been the unknown Jasta, for it is understood that some pilot scores are missing for this unit. Combats abound in this late morning period, with 41, 70, 92, 213 and the 148th Aero all seeing action.

At 1220, 218 Squadron lost two bombers to fighters; Leutnant Willi Rosenstein of Jasta 40s claimed a two-seater at 1240, and Leutnant Kohlpoth of Jasta 56 another at Beythem at 1230. As the morning had been, so too was the afternoon: massed combats and air fights. And it was not always the inexperienced pilots who were caught out. At 1315, Captain E B Drake of 209 Squadron was lost over Cambrai, probably to ground fire. Drake was 20 and came from Weymouth, and had been in the RNAS since October 1916. The Camels of 43, 203 and 209 had been ground strafing the crossings over the Sensée Canal, west of Hem Lenglet, to the north of Cambrai. This dangerous yet exhilarating task would claim many more lives before the war's end. Another pilot gaining experience but lost this day was Lieutenant Francis R Christiani, an American with 84 Squadron. He had gained four victories during this month, but was last seen over Montbrehain.

Another experienced pilot was Captain R C L Holme MC of 29 Squadron. His SE was also hit by ground fire, and although he staggered back to the lines, he had to crash-land in some shell holes and was lucky to get into front-line trenches. Age and experience did not necessarily go hand-in-hand. However, experience was necessary when in action against the aces. Two pilots of 46 Squadron, Second Lieutenants A M Allan and N F Moxon, were 21 and 28 respectively, the former from Toronto, the latter from London. The common factor was that they had both been on the squadron three weeks. This day they were both shot down and taken prisoner – possibly to the vastly experienced Paul Baümer of Jasta Boelcke, who downed his two Camel victories this day over Sailly and Bourlon Wood.

It happened on both sides too. During the day, the Staffelführer of Jasta 51 was brought down and taken prisoner after an attempted attack on a balloon. Hans Eberhardt Gandert, who had eight victories, had commanded his unit since the previous December. Yet experience was obviously necessary, and one who had it was Willi Coppens; this day he shot down a balloon, again at Leffinghe – victory No.32. However, during this day he flew near to a British RE8 and was continually fired on by the observer, despite Coppens trying to show the British crew his Belgian roundels and the fact that they were well inside British lines. The RE8 eventually landed at Proven airfield, so it was probably a 7 Squadron machine. Coppens' more than a little upset, landed too and protested. The observer inspected Coppens' machine, finding one bullet hole in the left wing, a second through the tailplane!

French Front

The weather was still atrocious, with more high winds and low clouds. The French lost four aircraft. Capitaine Paul Reverchon, the commander of Spa.31, failed to return from a patrol near Orfeuil, on the IV Armée front, just after 0945. Sous Lieutenant Robert Waddington was also shot up and force-landed, but after claiming a Fokker for his 12th and final victory. Reverchon was shot down by Leutnant Hans von Freden, of Jasta 50, at Somme-Py at 1000, the German's 13th victory.

Unteroffizier Otto Bieleit of Jasta 66 shot down what he thought was a Bréguet north of Jouy, which was in fact a Spad XI of Spa.42 flown by Sergent Kalley and Lieutenant Kervadoe. However, a Bréguet of Br.282 was forced to land in French front lines after a combat.

Up on the northern Flanders front, a Spad two-seater of Spa.34 was engaged by Theo Osterkamp, commander of MFJ 2, west of Zarren, although he reported the machine as a Bréguet (Germans often failed to distinguish between Bréguets, Spad XIs, Salmsons and DH4s). Both crew members were wounded but got their aircraft down inside Allied lines; however, Osterkamp had his 29th victory. On the Reims front French fighter pilots also claimed eight probable victories.

American Sector

The previous evening JGII had moved west to get fully in front of the main direction of the Allied offensive. Jastas 12 and 13 went to Charmois, while 15 and 19 moved into Stenay, just north of Charmois.

A Salmson of the 12th Observation Squadron was brought down by ground fire between Fléville and Cornay, north of Varennes. The pilot, First Lieutenant Wistar Morris, was killed, the observer, Cassius H Styles, captured. His later account stated:

> '...we had gone to the front again for a reconnaissance, and having sufficient gasoline, had gone well over the lines to look at Fléville. While there we saw a German battery of field artillery, crossing an open field west of the Aire River. We attacked them with our machine guns and put two of the four guns and their horses out of commission. One gun tumbled into the river. As a machine gun was set up to fire at us, we silenced it with a couple of bursts from our guns. When there were no more soldiers in sight, we again returned to HQ and made another report.
>
> 'Then we left to go home, but as we had more gas than we needed, we decided to take another look at Fléville. When we reached there, we saw a good number of soldiers around the second cannon we had shot up and started firing on them. After a few bursts we were hit by a machine gun hidden in some bushes. We crashed and a few minutes afterwards, Lt Morris died, although first aid was given him by some German soldiers.'

Two-seater fought two-seater at 0455. Lieutenants William P Erwin and Byrne V Baucom in their Salmson 2A2 of the 1st Aero Squadron did battle with a Rumpler two-seater at 150 metres, sending it down north of Fléville. This aggressive observation pilot would achieve eight victories in WWI, while Baucom scored three.

The 93rd Pursuit claimed a victory at 1625. Three Spads teamed up to down an Albatros two-seater near Chaumont; Leutnant Karl Metzler of FA(A) 287 was killed near this location. Ten minutes later, Fokkers were encountered, the Americans claiming four shot down for the loss of one. First Lieutenant Roswell H Fuller crashed near Damvillers about 1635, brought down by Unteroffizier Bader of Jasta 64w, whose victim, he reported, fell south-west of Chaumont, although the time was noted as 1720.

The half hour around sunset of this day saw the end of the remarkable career of the determined, intense, relentlessly aggressive – and abnormally brave – Frank Luke Jr. Luke had set out at 1622 to go for three balloons along the Meuse River, near Dun-sur-Meuse. Ground observers saw him burn all three – the BZ95, 64 and 35 balloons – but then saw him no more.

Apparently he had started at the Meuse and headed east, burning the balloon at Dun, then at Brière Ferme, and the last at Milly. Here he was hit by the defences of Leutnant Mangel's BZ35, suffering a chest wound. He then headed for the small village at Murvaux, passing over it, heading east, circled, and turned back west, landing in near darkness on a slope west of the village, just 50 yards from a creek.

He got out of his Spad and started to crawl towards the stream in order, it must be assumed, to drink, as his type of wound induces a raging thirst. Knowing that the Germans would be looking for him, he fired one round from his revolver, in order to attract attention, before slumping over dead. The later stories about shoot-outs on the ground are simply not true; Luke's career does not need such embellishments. After his last three victories, bringing his score to 18, the end had come to an American warrior of the highest order. And his country awarded him their highest award for bravery and courage, the Medal of Honour, Luke having already been the recipient of the Distinguished Service Cross with Oak Leaf Cluster.

More Spads were lost this evening. First Lieutenant T A Gabel of the 49th Pursuit failed to return, last seen in the vicinity of Souilly at 1730. Just before 1800, a flight of three Spads of the 95th departed to patrol the Dun-sur-Meuse area. One dropped out, leaving First Lieutenants Lansing Holden and Granville O Woodard to continue. At about 1855, they attacked and burned two balloons but were then bounced by four Fokkers. Leutnant Rudolf Rienau of Jasta 19 shot down Woodard, who was taken prisoner. Holden left a letter in his own, somewhat disjointed, style describing these events:

'Woody and I went over just above the clouds. We hunted for perhaps half an hour before I spotted two balloons, almost on the ground. Somehow I had a hunch that everything wasn't all right – they weren't shooting at us. We circled for some time – luckily. Four German planes appeared between us and the lines; it was another trap. I climbed into the scattered clouds; that was the last time I saw Woody. Then they opened with the hottest "archie" fire I ever went through. I waited for developments – it was almost dark – and I was at about 2,500 metres, too dark to see the balloons till one burst into flames – Woody must have gotten it. I don't know if he had seen the German planes coming; he never came home. I won't forget him in a hurry, he was one of the most modest, all around good fellows I have met over here.

'It was so dark by this time that the Huns must have gone. The gunners, I don't think, saw me till I started shooting – the balloon was only 100 metres up. I waited as patiently as I could till I was very close, then fired [but] my guns jammed! They were shooting machine guns and "flaming onions". I was so mad it didn't faze me. I just got the hammer and started fixing the guns. I got the guns fixed and was turning to fire again when up she went. Can you picture that great sausage wrapped in flames in the dead of night?'

The other American loss this day was a Salmson of the 99th Aero, brought down by flak fire near Romagne. Lieutenants John W McElroy and Howard T Kinne were killed.

	A/C	KB		DES	OOC	KB
British losses	22		British claims	37	20	9
French losses	2		French claims	6		1
American losses	6		American claims	7		5
IAF losses	–		IAF claims	–		
German claims	29	1	German losses	4†		3?

†At least four, but probably more, as a further 10/12 airmen of mostly unknown units were reported killed in action, including one from FA287. Leutnant Gerold Tschentschel, an ace of Jasta 72, was also severely wounded this day on the French front.

British Casualties

Aircraft type	No.	Squadron	Crew	
Dolphin	C4155	87 Sqdn	Lt R M Macdonald	POW
DH9	D3172	27 Sqdn	2/Lt H S Thomas	KIA
			2/Lt T Brown	KIA
DH9	D482	211 Sqdn	2/Lt J L McAdam	Safe
			2/Lt T W Kelly	KIA
BF2b	E2509	62 Sqdn	Lt R H O'Reilly	KIA
			2/Lt L E Mitchell	KIA
RE8	D4734	6 Sqdn	2/Lt S H Scott	KIA
			2/Lt A C J Payne	POW
BF2b	F5814	11 Sqdn	2/Lt T T Smith	KIA
			Lt J L Bromley	KIA
Camel	F6175	3 Sqdn	2/Lt A W Tinham	Safe
Camel	D9664	210 Sqdn	2/Lt J F Stafford (USAS)	KIA
SE5a	C8841	1 Sqdn	Lt L N Elworthy	POW
BF2b	E2266	22 Sqdn	Lt E Adams USAS	KIA
			Sgt G H Bissell	KIA
BF2b	E2517	22 Sqdn	Lt C W M Thompson	POW
			Lt L R James	POW
Camel	H7274	80 Sqdn	2/Lt R Bramwell	KIA
BF2b	E2561	20 Sqdn	2/Lt N S Boulton	KIA
			2/Lt C H Case	KIA
SE5a	C9293	84 Sqdn	2/Lt D C Rees	KIA
DH9	D3093	211 Sqdn	2/Lt A G White	KIA
			2/Lt J B Blundell	KIA
DH9	D565	211 Sqdn	Lt W H Mooney USAS	POW
			2/Lt V A Fair MC	DOW
Camel	F6188	80 Sqdn	Capt H J Welch	KIA
Camel	E4376	209 Sqdn	Capt E B Drake	KIA
RE8	F5872	59 Sqdn	Capt T S Symons DFC	KIA
			2/Lt F W Chadwick	KIA
DH9	E8883	218 Sqdn	Lt H P Brummell	POW
			Sgt R S Joysey	POW
DH9	D3272	218 Sqdn	2/Lt J L Pritchard	KIA
			2/Lt A E Smith	KIA
RE8	C2693	5 Sqdn	2/Lt E A Harrison	Safe
			2/Lt E M Patterson	Safe
Camel	F5960	46 Sqdn	2/Lt A M Allan	POW
Camel	D6572	46 Sqdn	2/Lt N F Moxon	POW
SE5a	D6982	84 Sqdn	2/Lt F R Christiani (USAS)	KIA
SE5a	D6942	29 Sqdn	Capt R C L Holme MC	Safe
AWFK8	C8643	82 Sqdn	Lt J Sangster	WIA
			2/Lt L J Skinner	WIA
RE8	–	6 Sqdn	2/Lt W M Anderson (O)	WIA *
AWFK8	D5144	8 Sqdn	2/Lt G A Ballantyne	Safe *
			2/Lt J B Ballantyne	WIA

Aircraft type	No.	Squadron	Crew		
DH9	E8419	205 Sqdn	Lt H G Kirkland	WIA	
			2/Lt C O'N Daunt	KIA	
RE8	C2610	3 AFC	2/Lt S H Deamer	WIA	*
			Lt P R Fullerton	Safe	
DH9	C1212	27 Sqdn	2/Lt C E Robinson (O)	WIA	*
DH9	D7324	103 Sqdn	Capt J Austin-Sparkes	WIA	*
			2/Lt J B Russell DFC	WIA	
DH9	–	206 Sqdn	2/Lt A G Squire (O)	WIA	*

French Casualties

Spad XI		Spa.34	MdL de Bellencourt	WIA	*
			Lt F de Bussy	WIA	
Spad XIII		Spa.31	Capt P Reverchon	KIA	
Spad XIII		Spa.31	S/Lt R Waddington	Safe	*
Spad XIII		Spa.26	Adj G Naudin	WIA	*
Spad XI		Spa.42	Sgt Kalley	MIA	
			Lt Kervadoe	MIA	
Bréguet XIV		Br.8	Adj Coudreau (P)	WIA	*

American Casualties

Salmson 2A2	–	12th Aero	1/Lt W Morris	DOW	
			1/Lt C H Styles	POW	
Spad XIII	7613	93rd Aero	1/Lt R H Fuller	KIA	
Spad XIII	–	13th Aero	1/Lt E R Richards	WIA	*
Spad XIII	7642	49th Aero	1/Lt T A Gabel	KIA	
Spad XIII	7984	27th Aero	1/Lt F Luke Jr DSC	DOW	
Spad XIII	–	95th Aero	1/Lt G O Woodard	POW	
Salmson 2A2	1225	99th Aero	1/Lt J W McElroy	KIA	
			1/Lt H T Kinne	KIA	
Salmson 2A2		1st Aero	1/Lt C G Johnson	Safe	
			1/Lt A W Duckstein	WIA	

30 SEPTEMBER 1918
M T W T F S S

British Front

Unlike the last day of Bloody April, the last day of Black September ended in a whimper compared to some other days. This was due in part to the continued bad weather, which was even worse than it had been of late; it was all low cloud and heavy rainstorms.

The RAF made no claims at all during the day, but lost three planes – all late in the day. As always the poor two-seater crews had to be out trying to locate the front-line troops or to range artillery. They had not been slaughtered as much as in April 1917, but Leutnant Heinrich Henkel of Jasta 37 caught an RE8 of 12 Squadron flying a patrol for VI Corps over Crevecoeur at 1700 hours and shot it down. Lieutenants T H Jacques and F N Billington became victory No.5 for Henkel, who would gain three more in October. An hour later, Second Lieutenant L S Davis on an OP with 92 Squadron became the 6th and final victory of Leutnant Sylvester Garsztka of Jasta 31 over Lehaucourt.

The final casualty inflicted on the RAF was to a Bristol crew of 48 Squadron, wounded by ground machine-gun fire this date.

On the German side, FA(A) 207 lost a crew at Aubencheul-au-Bac, probably to ground fire, killing Unteroffizier Hermann Geithner and Leutnant Johann Schwartz.

For the ground troops, the war would go on, but for the Royal Air Force, at least Black September was finally over.

French Front

In the IV Armée sector, Caporal Heine and Caporal Gerain of Spa.164 attacked an enemy aircraft at 1823 over Challeronge, the German falling in what was described as a damaged condition. Then Heine was shot down and killed near the Bois de Cernay, the victim of Vizefeldwebel Alfons Nägler of Jasta 81, who claimed a Spad at Ville, which is just south of here. Leutnant Hans Rolfes of Jasta 45 crash-landed on this day, possibly a victim of this air fight. Rolfes had downed his 17th victory just the day before. He had just been placed in command of Jagdgruppe Ost (Jastas 9, 21, 45 and 66), although he retained command of Jasta 45, which he had formed and led since December 1917.

Leutnant Hermann Habrich and Leutnant Franz Ray, both of Jasta 49, the latter being the Staffelführer, each claimed a Spad at Somme-Py and Manre at 1820 for their 5th and 17th victories respectively. The problem sometimes is that the Germans tended to note a Spad victory without mentioning if it was a single- or two-seater. The problem too was that their identification of a Spad XI could be for a Salmson, DH4 or a Bréguet, as mentioned before. As no single-seaters appear to have been lost, it is possible they were two-seaters. One known loss was a Salmson of Sal.106, flown by Adjutant Couderc and Sous Lieutenant Zuber, who crashed and had their machine written off near Mont Murat, neither man being injured. Another casualty was a Bréguet of Br.123, which failed to return.

The only confirmed claim of the day was by Spa.163, a two-seater shot down near Cerny at 1823 shared by three pilots, one being an American member of the Lafayette Flying Corps, David S Paden.

American Sector

The Americans ended the month with just one loss, a Salmson 2A2 of the 104th Aero, which was forced down in German lines where the crew were taken prisoner. With no German making a claim, they either fell victim to ground fire or mechanical failure. One Spad pilot, First Lieutenant Irwin W Fish, of the 213th Aero, was wounded during the day, probably by ground fire.

	A/C	KB			DES	OOC	KB
British losses	2	–	British claims		–	–	–
French losses	3	–	French claims		1		–
American losses	1	–	American claims		–		–
IAF losses	–	–	IAF claims		–		–
German claims	7	–	German losses		?†		–

† Total unknown but other than those mentioned above, an observer in FA241 was wounded by ground fire, Leutnant Georg Schlenker, leader of Jasta 41 with 14 victories, was severely wounded, while 11 other airmen were reported killed, although not all may have been due to combat.

British Casualties

Aircraft type	No.	Squadron	Crew		
RE8	C2442	12 Sqdn	2/Lt T H Jacques	KIA	
			Lt F N Billington	KIA	
SE5a	C9298	92 Sqdn	2/Lt L S Davis	KIA	
BF2b	–	48 Sqdn	2/Lt W S Rycroft	WIA	*
			2/Lt H C Wood	WIA	

French Casualties

Spad XIII		Spa.164	Cpl L Heine	KIA	
Salmson 2A2		Sal.106	Adj Coudero	Safe	
			S/Lt Zuber	Safe	
Bréguet XIV		Br.123	Adj A Montel	MIA	
			Sgt M Pollet	MIA	
Bréguet XIV		Br.207	Capt M Morize	WIA	

American Casualties

Salmson 2A2	1038	104th Aero	Capt E R Haslett	POW	
			1/Lt R E Davis	POW	
Spad XIII		213th Aero	1/Lt I W Fish	WIA	*
Salmson 2A2	–	9th Aero	2/Lt M F Saunders (P)	POW	

Summary and Conclusions

What does the intense aerial combat of September 1918 tell us of the changes in aerial warfare since the previous April 1917? Firstly it was a much larger affair, with the sizes of the main protagonists being at least twice that of before. It was also a good deal more specialised.

April 1917 had seen the RFC introduce specialised night-bombing squadrons to add to the standard artillery observation, reconnaissance, bombing and scout squadrons. This had expanded into strategic bombing by day and night, tactical bombing day and night, long-range recce flights, specialised long-range recce squadrons, night-fighter squadrons, fighter squadrons and fighter squadrons doubling as ground-attack and close-support units. These last units – particularly the Sopwith Camel squadrons – signalled the rise of the fighter-bomber, which ended up dominating close-support work in WWII and into more modern times. The Independent Air Force was about to introduce the dedicated long-range single-seater fighter escort to bombers. This was No.45 Squadron, back from Italy, which saw out the war waiting for long-range Snipes in order to begin this duty. Most of the tactical bomber raids were escorted. The IAF were not, and suffered accordingly.

The French had long-range multi-crewed and multi-gunned escort fighters (Caudron RXIs) for their bombers. They had also, perhaps, advanced the furthest of the Allies in using concentrations of fighters, kept in large multi-squadron combinations, to be used to support offensives. In the Groupe de Combats of the Division Aérienne were the best of the Spad units.

The RAF did not copy this. Except for transfers of units between more active and less active fronts, the only Wing that approached the French in terms of mobility was the Headquarters Wing. Most RAF fighter squadrons stayed on the same army front. When they fought in Wings they combined fighter recce and fighter squadrons and, except for No.61 Wing – the mainly ex-RNAS Wing based at Dunkirk – which was all Camel-equipped, always mixed up the different types of fighters with the concept of each type being the best for low level, medium escort and high cover work. Squadrons on a front were reinforced for major offensives by having units added to the Wing, but the RAF never developed tactical groupings at Wing level that fought and trained together. The Wing was mainly administrative and not operational. Louis Strange's 80 Wing was different and would have become the more common style, as it had begun in August 1918 deliberately to use large formations to match the German Circuses. This did not happen all the time, as 4 AFC's loss of four or five Camels showed.

Where the RAF totally excelled, especially in April 1917, was in the performance of the Corps (or Army Co-operation) organisations where the observation squadrons of RE8s and AWFK8s operated fairly freely over the German lines, providing aerial photographic coverage, total mapping requirements and complete capacity for artillery co-operation for the army. They had also begun ammunition drops to forward troops, smokescreen laying and dedicated tank support while maintaining their low level contact patrol work.

April 1917 had seen the slaughter of the fighter and recce squadrons of Nieuports and Sopwith ½ Strutters on the Arras sector, during which the fighter squadrons had not been able to stop the depredations of the Jastas on the BE2s. September 1918 saw perhaps one day when JGII had some impact on a small section of the front, in interfering with the RE8s. Mostly they did not. Few RE8 units lost more than three or four machines for the month, and some of them were to ground fire, and all operated more or less how they chose. The RAF's September 1918 casualties had shifted to the fighter-bombers and the day bombers of both the tactical and strategic kind. In the main, the Bristol F2b fighter-recce units carried out their tasks with low casualties, although both 11 and 48 Squadrons did lose a number of machines, but it was nothing near the level of the Strutter units of Bloody April.

The Americans were able to contribute fully to the Allied cause for the first time during September 1918. Given their late arrival in the war, and some of the obvious difficulties of operating in a service that was a part of the Signal Corps, it is perhaps surprising that they did so well. The reason their fighter pilots did was that their tactical leadership was drawn from the Americans (and Harold Hartney, a Canadian), who had current modern operational experience with the French, embracing the Lafayette Flying Corps, and the British.

They also introduced a high level of teamwork to their efforts like the French, matched the British aggression, but only when needed, and introduced far more commonly than the RAF the operation in patrols of large numbers and multi-squadrons. Their Pursuit Groups were the equivalent of Groupes de Combat, rather than RAF Wings, i.e. operational units of single types of fighters that were coordinated to achieve specific tasks. They also operated as fighter-bombers.

In day bombing, the Americans took a lot longer to learn, primarily handicapped by a level of incompetence at the Bombardment Group level, matched only by the bravery of the crews. No escorts were provided until massacres forced them to do so (a lesson re-learnt in WWII!). Sending flights of under twelve across the lines in separate formations, to bomb the same target, separated by small time differences resulted in three disasters during the month. If the Jastas did not get the first small group, they would effectively eliminate one of the following formations.

The American observation and recce squadrons, given the low level of experience, were very good at their work and extremely aggressive. Overall, despite significant casualties, by the end of September the Americans could operate effectively against the best that Germany could offer. Their equipment was very good, but their aircrew were far better than any other air service. This was because the best and brightest – mainly highly educated young men of high physical standards – had gravitated to the USAS. This was no different from the other services, except the Americans had not had theirs killed off over the previous three years of mass casualties on the Western Front. Physical standards were, perhaps, too strict, as many a good pilot in the other services would have failed the medicals, but overall the Americans had an extremely motivated group of men who were bursting to fight, confident they would beat the Germans, in order to get the war ended. It was also the first and only chance many would have of seeing Europe and being part of what was still, for many, the great adventure. There were also no inborn class hang-ups as with the British and French; all aviators were officers. Such enthusiasm was tempered somewhat in the French Air Service and the RAF by their more realistic and experienced view on the hazards of operations against a dangerous foe.

The numbers of the 'colonials' in the RAF also aided its capabilities. Large numbers of Canadians, Australians, Americans, South Africans and New Zealanders served in the RAF, in roughly the listed order in terms of numbers. The Americans were also present in the French Air Service.

The German Air Service had also been reorganised since Bloody April. They had concentrated on night bombing, particularly of tactical targets by 1918. Indeed, on one raid on No.1 Aeroplane Supply Depot on 23 September, a total of 41 airmen were killed, with four more missing and 114 wounded. The two-seater Schlachtstaffeln had been expanded to carry out ground attack and other support tasks. Their effectiveness appears to have been very low. It is hard to find in Allied army unit records any major inconveniences caused by their activities. The Australians, for example, took more notice of the night bombing and would lose more men in any one of their major assaults than by aerial attacks for the whole war. Aside from doubling the manpower needed, a two-seater's performance was always less than the fighter opposition. Another 50 Jastas equipped with Fokker DVIIs, that had a prime ground-attack role, and dual-fighter role – such as was undertaken by the Camels, SE5s and Spads – would have been far more effective.

The German reconnaissance crews were doing their best, and were operating on their lone high altitude sorties all the time, but did not manage to detect the major Allied attack buildups of the month. They did suffer casualties, particularly when climbing and descending, as their aerodromes were within range of RAF fighter patrols. The German artillery co-operation flyers also suffered during the month and were beginning to suffer from severe shortages, particularly petrol, as indeed the other sections of the service were. They carried on with their tasks as they had all through the war, but were now under constant harassment.

The German fighter force had doubled in early 1918 to 80 Jastas and nine Kests. They were the only arm of the German Air Service that could really impact on the Allied air services. The quality of their equipment had improved over the summer of 1918 with the arrival of the Fokker DVII, and most of the Jastas were at least partially equipped with this type, or the slightly less efficient Pfalz DXII. There were still numbers of Albatros DV and Pfalz DIII fighters in service, mainly with the newest Jastas, or those on very quiet parts of the front, and small numbers of Fokker triplanes were still operating. In addition there were also five Marine Feld Jastas available, operating in the north, which were well equipped, well trained and successful.

The Germans grouped 12 of their leading Jastas into three Jagdgeschwader – more commonly known to the Allies as Flying Circuses. The impact these units had, being a mere 15 per cent of the whole fighter force, was tremendous and they inflicted casualties out of all proportion to their numbers. By September, JGI 'Richthofen' was a shadow of its former self having absorbed most of the pressure from the Amiens battle of August 1918. Oskar von Boenigk, an alumnus of JGI in the summer of 1917, led JGII, and in September 1918, the 40-odd Fokkers of this group claimed over 100 Allied planes, mainly American, for minimal losses. Despite this impressive performance, the star turns of September were the four (three after 4 September) Jastas of JGIII, claiming 129 RAF aircraft during the month: the staff scored 11, Jasta 2 got 46, Jasta 26 got 33, Jasta 27 got 32 and Jasta 36 nine (the latter disappearing from the scene after the 4th, having been reduced to three serviceable aircraft). The three other BMW-powered Fokker-equipped units inflicted heavy casualties on the RAF. Jasta scores for September were:

Jasta	1	6	Jasta	23	8	Jasta	47	–	Jasta	70	5
Jasta	2	46	Jasta	24	5	Jasta	48	–	Jasta	71	–
Jasta	3	6	Jasta	26	33	Jasta	49	9	Jasta	72	12
Jasta	4	2	Jasta	27	32	Jasta	50	14	Jasta	73	5
Jasta	5	37	Jasta	28	6	Jasta	51	–	Jasta	74	–
Jasta	6	5	Jasta	29	5	Jasta	52	2	Jasta	75	–
Jasta	7	14	Jasta	30	2	Jasta	53	6	Jasta	76	–
Jasta	8	3	Jasta	31	10	Jasta	54	4	Jasta	77	12
Jasta	9	9	Jasta	32	–	Jasta	56	12	Jasta	78	3
Jasta	10	2	Jasta	33	3	Jasta	57	2	Jasta	79	4
Jasta	11	8	Jasta	34	5	Jasta	58	12	Jasta	80	7
Jasta	12	11	Jasta	35	6	Jasta	59	6	Jasta	81	9
Jasta	13	27	Jasta	36	9	Jasta	60	18	Jasta	82	–
Jasta	14	–	Jasta	37	11	Jasta	61	2	Jasta	83	2
Jasta	15	24	Jasta	39	17	Jasta	62	7	MFJ	1	9
Jasta	16	3	Jasta	40	7	Jasta	63	4	MFJ	2	11
Jasta	17	4	Jasta	41	–	Jasta	64	9	MFJ	3	5
Jasta	18	10	Jasta	42	5	Jasta	65	5	MFJ	4	6
Jasta	19	22	Jasta	43	1	Jasta	66	8	MFJ	5	9
Jasta	20	9	Jasta	44	4	Jasta	67	9	Stab JGI		–
Jasta	21	6	Jasta	45	26	Jasta	68	5	Stab JGII		5
Jasta	22	8	Jasta	46	15	Jasta	69	–	Stab JGIII		11

Note: Jastas 25, 38 and 55 were not operating on the Western Front; some Jastas would have scored more than shown here, while some which have no victories noted may well have scored some but records are incomplete for this late period; while Jastas 2 and 5 did well as they had done in April 1917, Jasta 11 was a shadow of its former self in terms of kills.

This list shows a total of 721 Allied aircraft and balloons brought down for the month of September. To these scores must be added the claims of Flak units, infantry ground fire and successes by two-seater crews of the *Flieger Abteilungen und Schutzstaffeln*. This latter figure could be shown in the region of 715 aircraft and 87 balloons (total victories claimed – 802).

Numbers are always difficult to agree or reconcile, and the September figures are just as difficult. However, although they cannot be totally accurate, the following figures of what we know will give an indication of the combat losses. These indicate:

RAF aircraft lost	373 (incl. 37 IAF)
French aircraft lost	100
USAS aircraft lost	87
Total	**560**

Thus with some 715 German claims, there is something like 155 more claims than losses, but obviously some aircraft seen to fall inside Allied lines were counted but not actually lost to the Allied cause.

Again we can break down the Allied aircraft types lost:

British			
Camel	109	RE8	24
SE5	74	AWFK8	13
DH9/9A	54	HP O/400	12
BF2b	38	Dolphin	9
DH4	32	FE2b	8

French			
Spad XIII	42	Voisin	4
Bréguet XIV	32	Caudron R11	2
Salmson	9	Farman	1
Spad XI	4	Others	6

American			
Spad XIII	37	DH4	21
Salmon 2A2	20	Bréguet XIV	9

Personnel Casualties

	Killed	Missing	POW	Wounded	Inj	Interned	Evaded
British	209	67	301	163	7	22	2
French†	49	87	3	62	3	–	–
American‡	76	4	37	25	1	2	1
Totals	**334**	**158**	**341**	**250**	**11**	**24**	**3**

† Obviously a number of the missing were in fact captured. ‡ But not including USAS men serving with either the British or French.

The RAF, in turn, claimed prodigious quantities of Fokkers shot down, which did not match even slightly the actual German losses. Even though it is difficult to know exactly their losses, fighter pilots dead, wounded, and prisoners are known, and even if one trebled this figure to cover lost machines from which pilots parachuted or survived crashes, it still falls very short of the claims. This has led to the idea among students of WWI aviation that the German fighters were inflicting a severe defeat on the RAF, which only the over optimistic claims of the RAF refuted. This is total rubbish. While JGIII and other units inflicted large casualties, their impact on the RAF's activities was minimal. No RAF squadron was stopped from operating. The most that was achieved was in modifying the way in which these activities were carried out.

According to 'our' figures, the Allies claimed:

RAF	521 aircraft destroyed plus 353 'out of control' (total 874)
IAF	11 aircraft destroyed plus 12 'out of control' (total 23)
French	98 aircraft destroyed (there were also some 50 probables)
USAS	135 aircraft destroyed (but including probables)
Total	765 plus 365 'OOC' by the RAF/IAF = 1,130 (plus KBs): (1,180 if one adds French probables)

German losses, as we have said already, are hard to determine. Those that seem fairly certain, total in the region of 107-plus for September 1918, but even if we are 100 per cent wrong/underestimating, that would still only make it 214! (A possible 11 claims for every German loss.)

The question might be asked, did the RAF commanders at HQ have any idea that their fighter pilots were overclaiming, to the extent that they appeared to destroy each month the total number of enemy fighters their intelligence gatherers, however primitive their sources might or might not have been, reported the Germans had available? Yet still they had sufficient men and machines to come up and inflict enormous losses on the Allies. (Shades of '... the last 50 Spitfires...' in the latter half of the Battle of Britain in 1940!) Did these same WWI commanders and intelligence people believe that the Germans 'had' over 1,000 aircraft on the Western Front to shoot down, which must mean that, in total, the Germans had to have somewhere in the region of at least 6,000 aircraft opposing them in the first place?

As for the German Jastas, the quality varied greatly. Jasta 5 was certainly the next most successful unit, and most of the other Jastas achieved something. But their impact was minimal and would become more so as their lack of fuel supplies restricted operations. They were also running out of pilots – few of the Jasta ever being at full strength – and their successes often depended on one or two quality pilots in each Jasta. Some Jastas operating on both the RAF and French/American fronts achieved little. Even if they were vastly outnumbered, the defensive posture, lack of aggression and an avoidance of losses meant that a considerable proportion of the German fighter units were basically wasting petrol!

The lack of accurate German casualty records (aircraft), especially of unwounded pilots, make assessment of claims by the RAF difficult, as has already been said. However, one point of note is that the Jastas, throughout their entire period of service, never destroyed an RAF aircraft on its aerodrome, whereas considerable numbers of German aircraft were lost in attacks on theirs. Jasta 40, for example, did not operate until mid-September because their machines had been destroyed on the ground by 80 Wing on 17 August. Power projection, as it is now called, belonged entirely to the Allies.

The Germans, despite a number of historians defending them vigorously, also overclaimed, although not in the same proportions; but that is, in the perspective of the aerial war, irrelevant. The RAF, in its basic roles of army support and co-operation, was basically doing precisely what it wanted to do or was asked to do. Every now and then, three or four times a month on average, a large fight would ensue when they were engaged by the Germans, and more often than not the RAF were severely dealt with. We think the point has been made that despite its lack of numbers in comparison, the German Jastas were by no means defeated, either in September or in the final six weeks the war had to run. Fuel and numbers were on the decline, but their morale was still as high as in the spring of 1917.

The Aces

The current fashion amongst a school of the 'serious' historians is to decry the role of the aces, and state that they received undue publicity and recognition for achieving very little.* This idea too is rubbish. To use the RAF as an example: their main striking arm in the battle for aerial supremacy, i.e. the capacity to carry out their roles and prevent the Germans from doing theirs, was the fighter force. In April 1917, the RAF fighter force was simply unable to achieve this due to a number of factors. One of these factors was that the average fighter unit had one or two experienced pilots per flight and a number of these were very much less experienced than the German Jasta leaders.

By September 1918 this had changed. It is important to remember that the tactical leadership of the RAF was vested in the captains – the flight commanders, who led the three flights in each squadron. Some squadron commanders flew, others did not, but the major day-to-day tactical decisions rested with the flight commanders.

In April 1917, the RFC and RNAS had 23 fighter units in the field (counting single-seater and the FE2 units), and of these 23 squadron commanders only one was an ace – Mulock of 3 Naval. Of the 78 flight commanders at the start of the month, 21 were or would become aces during April – roughly 25 per cent. By September 1918, the RAF had 32 fighter squadrons (single-seater and BF2b units). Of the 43 squadron commanders, 19 were aces; this is over 40 per cent. Of the 126 flight commanders (on 1 September three were vacant positions), 104 were aces – over 80 per cent. In addition, the average flight would have at least one more pilot who would become the next flight commander in it, or would be ready for a posting to a vacancy elsewhere and they too would almost without exclusion be aces. While it is acknowledged that by 1918 surviving pilots had had the opportunity of raising their status to ace due to the passage of time, the fact remains that on average about 25 per cent of pilots on strength at any one time in 1918 were aces. Therefore, aces are represented in command positions over three times more than the percentage of pilots they made up.

In April 1917 too, the fighter arm of the British was being led by a large percentage of inexperienced men, undoubtedly brave but often not tactically astute and not provided with sufficient support of trained men to raise the experience level of their units. There is also the factor that promotion was in many instances on length of service rather than proven ability, which was about to change. Following the subsequent story of these units during 1917 is to follow the story of the slow building

* History terms an ace as a pilot with a score of five victories or more, despite acknowledging that, with over-claiming, a number of recognised aces would not fall into such a category; but we would not even contemplate a change to the long established historical precedent.

up of experience in the squadrons, and leadership provided by those pilots with the gift of being able to become an ace.

By September 1918, the conclusion can be drawn that the tactical fighter leaders of the RAF were aces. This small percentage of pilots, perhaps 10 per cent at any one time, not only did the vast majority of the scoring, they were doing the vast majority of leading as well. Therefore, the significant role played by aces in the RAF's operational capacity should not be minimised. The idea that teamwork and the good solid average pilot were the backbone of the RAF rather than the aces is simply a misunderstanding of what was involved. Aces were the prime motivators of teamwork and leadership. The lone wolf aces, of whom in reality there were very few, had been replaced by leaders of tactical teams called flights. The RAF's tactical commanders were confident, experienced men, well aware of the risks and managing to project the confidence that they were totally capable of dealing with the German fighters.

Of course, this was not always true; aces would die during the month as would the novice pilots, but their loss would not lower the leadership and experience level of the squadron. It must be acknowledged too that there were a number of valuable and experienced pilots who proved good leaders, but who did not have the ability to shoot straight – or get the deflection right. This happened in both world wars, just as some with the ability to shoot well and bring down enemy aircraft simply had no head for tactical leadership (but these were usually the exception). There were too the pilots who would survive months of active service and score no victories, but survive, so they had to be good, solid pilots, accumulating vast experience from what was happening. There are no records, diaries or other memoirs the authors have seen that indicate anything other than that the RAF was confident it could handle the Germans in aerial combat. What terrified most of them was ground fire when strafing – and burning in the air!

The Corps and bomber crews were doing valuable work, but they were able to do this work to the extent they did only by the presence of the fighter pilots. The Fokkers were generally 'blotted-up' in attacking the fighters. It was when the fighters were not present (the IAF and long-range raids by the RAF day bombers) that they suffered. Remember that almost all RAF fighter squadrons were involved in extensive ground-attack duties as well; the significance of the fighter pilots increases again.

One of the biggest errors the British RFC/RAF command made in WWI was in failing to establish any real process of authenticating the claims made by their pilots. This led them to vastly overrate their success against the German Air Service and their victory to loss ratio. (But as mentioned earlier, it seems logical to assume someone must have realised the estimated German strength was not being destroyed with such regularity.) This led to no attempt being made to improve this situation or to eradicate a complacency about their methods that would have dire consequences in WWII. The RAF's failure officially to recognise the identities of their leading pilots, unlike the French and the Germans, contributed to this malaise. By 1918 decorations to fighter pilots were awarded, in the main, on the basis of victories but no system was in place to check what resulted. *The Times of London* newspaper in 1918 published the communiqués each side put out at the end of each month, listing the claims and losses of each air force. The paper, its readers and the RAF simply assumed the Germans were liars to admit to so few losses. Combined with the abysmal decision not to supply their airmen with parachutes, all the RAF managed to do was to live, as one of the songs their cynical pilots often sang put it, '... in a world of illusion'.

The French were much more realistic and in general made by far the most accurate claims. However, in the English-speaking world, the achievements of the French Air Service have always been underrated. One reason was undoubtedly the far lower casualties sustained, and lower total claims than the British!

As for the Americans, they also failed to set up a realistic claims system, although many of the early claims mirrored the French system, but at least they made their pilots famous. They too were to forget some of the lessons of the war over the peace, but the one lesson that should not have been lost on the rest of the world but by the Germans and the Japanese in WWII, and by others since was never, ever, to underestimate the quality of the men the Americans could put into their fighting aeroplanes. Frank Luke, Joe Wehner, Wilbur Wright, Ray Brooks, and the men of the Day Bombardment Group were as good as any, despite a lot less experience. The other way in which the American contribution to the air war has also been underestimated is the number of them that were in the RFC, RNAS and RAF.

The RAF Fighter Squadron in September 1918

The following section attempts to provide a view of the background of the fighter pilots that made up the RAF on 1 September 1918. It is by way of a sample, not scientifically selected, but rather selected on the basis of what units have reasonable officers' records still available to the historian, mainly retained in the Public Record Office, London. This analysis covers the records of Nos.1, 4 AFC, 29, 46, 56, 84, 204 and 210 Squadrons. They are split evenly between SE5a and Camel units, the former being 1, 29, 56 and 84. On 1 September, the strength of these units varied between 21 pilots (210 Squadron) and 30 pilots (204).

Nationality

The following table indicates what country the pilots came from, based on where their next of kin or bank was located.

	1	4 AFC	29	46	56	84	204	210	Total
English	11	–	7	13	6	4	8	11	**60**
Scottish	–	–	–	1	4	3	3	–	**11**
Welsh	1	–	–	–	2	1	–	–	**4**
Irish	2	–	–	1	–	–	1	–	**4**
Canadian	5	–	5	8	9	4	12	4	**47**
Australian	–	28	–	1	–	–	–	1	**30**
American	3	–	5	1	5	4	1	5	**24**
South African	3	–	6	1	–	8	1	–	**19**
New Zealander	–	1	–	–	–	–	–	–	**1**
West Indian	–	–	1	–	–	–	–	–	**1**
Unknown	–	–	–	–	–	–	2	–	**2**
Totals:	**25**	**29**	**24**	**26**	**26**	**24**	**28**	**21**	**203**

From this, the English contributed about a third of the RAF; and with the rest of the British Isles added in, about 40 per cent. Allowing for the distortion caused by the presence of an Australian unit, the Canadians and Americans were the next biggest component. In particular the Canadians predominated in the two former RNAS squadrons. The South Africans tended to be concentrated in one or two units, the largest two groups in the RAF being 29 and 84.

Age of the Pilots on 1 September 1918

	1	4 AFC	29	46	56	84	204	210	Total
18	1	–	–	3	1	1	2	1	**9**
19	4	–	6	12	3	5	7	5	**42**
20	5	2	4	2	3	1	3	2	**22**
21	2	3	3	3	2	5	5	1	**24**
22	1	2	1	1	2	–	3	3	**13**
23	5	7	2	–	2	4	6	3	**29**
24	2	2	4	–	4	4	–	–	**16**
25	2	3	1	1	7	1	1	5	**21**
26+	3	6	3	3	2	3	1	1	**22**
Unknown	–	4	–	1	–	–	–	–	**5**
Totals:	**25**	**29**	**24**	**26**	**26**	**24**	**28**	**21**	**203**

From this can be drawn the inference that 19-year-olds predominated in 1918. These would be men that had enlisted as soon as they were old enough, and took about ten months to train. The Australians were older, which is explained by the large majority of the AFC's pilots being ex-army men who had been overseas since 1915-16. But the spread of men in their early twenties indicates the idea that the majority of pilots being under 20 is incorrect. However, as a word of warning, the RNAS units tended to be a good deal younger, and this sample may not be typical.

Length of Service
The following table illustrates the length of service of pilots in these units, in months.

Months	1	4 AFC	29	46	56	84	204	210	Total
0-1	8†	7	4	11‡	13	15†	14	2	**74**
1-2	2	9	5	5	3	–	1	1	**26**
2-3	7	2	4	–	2	–	3	10	**28**
3-4	4	3	4	3	3	3	2	3	**25**
4-5	4	1	–	3	2	1	3	–	**14**
5-6	–	2	3	2	1	2	2	2	**14**
6-7	–	3	2	–	1	2	–	1	**9**
7-8	–	–	1	1	1	–	–	1	**4**
8-9	–	–	–	–	–	–	1	–	**1**
9-10	–	2	1	1	–	–	–	–	**4**

Months	1	4 AFC	29	46	56	84	204	210	Total
10-11	–		–	–	–	–	–	–	–
11-12		–	–	–	–	–		–	–
12-plus	–	–	–	–	–	1§	2	1§	4
Totals:	**25**	**29**	**24**	**26**	**26**	**24**	**28**	**21**	**203**

† Includes one pilot on second tour as a flight commander. ‡ Includes two pilots on second tour as flight commanders. § Both men were the squadron commander.

* Hickey (aged 21), a Canadian, had operated with 4 Naval/204 RAF from August 1917 and was still in action on 3 October, the date he collided with another pilot and was killed. He had 21 victories. Tonks (aged 20), from London, England, also joined 4 Naval/204 RAF in August 1917, and was rested from operations on 13 October 1918. He had 12 victories but died in a crash in July 1919.

The largest number of pilots had less than one month's experience. There are two reasons for this: firstly, the large number of casualties during August, and secondly, those pilots who had arrived over the quiet winter months of early 1918 had completed their tours in July and August. The pilots that counted were the ones with two to six months' experience. All units had at least eight of these. The longest serving pilots (as distinct from the commanders) of all these men were Captains C R R Hickey and A J B Tonks of 204 Squadron.*

The average tour lasted between six and eight months. Another reason for the high number of pilots that had arrived on some units in July 1918, was the spreading influenza epidemic beginning to decimate Europe, which would continue well into 1919. Also, the Australians had received a number of RAF pilots to maintain strength during June and July and many of these had left in August.

The Claims

This table analyses what scores pilots who were on these units on 1 September had on that date.

	1	4 AFC	29	46	56	84	204	210	Total
0	16	14	5	11	18	14	14	6	**98**
1	–	6	3	6	3	1	2	2	**23**
2	2	2	3	3	1	2	4	3	**20**
3	1	–	5	3	1	2	2	2	**16**
4	1	1	1	–	–	–	2	2	**7**
5-9	1	2	3	2	2	2	2	3	**17**
10-19	3	3	4	–	1	2	2	3	**18**
20-29	1	1	–	–	–	–	–	–	**2**
30-39	–	–	–	–	–	–	–	–	**–**
40-49	–	–	–	–	–	1	–	–	**1**
50-plus	–	–	–	1	–	–	–	–	**1**

This table shows that at any one time, over 45 per cent of pilots had not scored. Another 30 per cent had scored between one and five times, while just about 25 per cent were aces!

The really big scorers are few and far between. Only four of the 203 Squadron pilots had over 20 claims. Of these, Captain R T C Hoidge of 1 Squadron had just started his second tour; Captain A H Cobby of 4 AFC ended his tour on 4 September; Captain A W Beauchamp-Proctor of 84 Squadron had also just started a second tour; while Captain D R MacLaren of 46 Squadron was just rolling along towards the end of his first year of combat.

Although not analysed here, it is apparent that the average fighter pilot who survived operations took two to three months to score. Under a month was exceptional – these men were either very aggressive, burned a balloon, shared in a kill, or were just plain lucky. It was not uncommon for a pilot to fly a whole tour without scoring. The import of this is that the fighter pilot's job was to shoot down the opposition. Nevertheless, those pilots who generally survived a tour would show themselves as sound pilots, perhaps good patrol members, or did not have the overall ability to shoot well. Even in WWII, there were any number of successful fighter pilot leaders with small scores, but whose experience and ability were unquestioned.

The Casualties

This table shows what happened to our sample of the 203 pilots on strength on 1 September 1918. Casualties are defined as either killed or missing in action, prisoners of war, and accidents that were either fatal or resulted in the pilot leaving the unit. Posted means the pilot was posted out of combat, tour expired or ill, or promoted to another unit. In the case of some Americans, they transferred to the USAS.

	1	4 AFC	29	46	56	84	204	210	Total
September	1	5	6	7	10	6	9	5	**49**
October	2	1	3	4	5	1	10	4	**30**
November	–	3	1	–	–	–	–	–	**4**
Posted	2	6	8	6	6	7	4	4	**43**
End of War	20	14	6	9	5	10	5	8	**77**
Totals:	**25**	**29**	**24**	**26**	**26**	**24**	**28**	**21**	**203**

Approximately a quarter of these pilots became casualties in September, not including those that arrived during the month and were lost that same month. Another third survived to the end of the war, while just over 20 per cent were posted. Roughly 30 per cent of the pilots on strength were turned over during the month. No.1 Squadron would only suffer three losses in combat of the 35 pilots on strength. This was mainly because they had by far the fewest combats of the units in this sample. Nos. 56 and 204 Squadrons had by far the most casualties. No.56 lost many pilots ground strafing and also lost one or two in fights for the rest of the war. No.204 lost some in September, but had two really bad days in October, losing more than four Camels at a time. Most of 4 AFC's casualties came in two fights, on 5 September and 4 November, both at the hands of JGIII.

Given the 50 per cent or so of pilots that were either posted or lasted to the end of the war, the RAF fighter pilots were surviving quite well, relative to earlier periods such as Bloody April. However, it indicated that one in two RAF pilots at this late stage of the war was going to be lost in action or accidents. The air war was not easy, flying unarmoured, slow aeroplanes strafing troops, or in combat with Fokkers, especially when not equipped with parachutes.

Training

By 1918 the RAF had established a reasonably sophisticated training system. A trainee pilot would be taught to fly, then taught aerobatics and other advanced flying before specialising in single-seaters. Then the neophyte fighter pilot went to fighting schools, to be taught combat tactics and air gunnery. On arrival in France, he would spend about a week at a depot – perhaps less in times of high battle casualties – awaiting a vacancy at the front. Most squadrons then tried to initiate the novice slowly, showing them around the front and allowing them to settle in.

Allowing for this advance on earlier times, the dangers for the novice were still immense. Squadron commanders, especially Major W E Young of No.1 Squadron for example, were pushing for training units on quiet sectors of the front to break in these tyros, instead of sending them into combat in the intense areas. This was how the RNAS had done it in 1917 and early 1918, using Nos. 11 and 12 Naval Squadrons in the Dunkirk area as early examples of operational training units.

The Lessons Learnt – Only to be Forgotten

The major lesson learnt from this study is that history repeats itself. At the outbreak of WWII, the RAF had seemingly forgotten most of what its fighter pilots had learnt through bitter experience. This new generation of fighter pilots would die under-trained, never having been taught to shoot properly, nor had they the right combat tactics. It was well into the war before the same basic processes were introduced. And it was well into 1941 before fighter-bombers were rediscovered. Army co-oper-ation, as it had been used in WWI, had totally disappeared, because no aeroplane built for the task could survive the flak and fighters.

Despite the emergence of large formations of aircraft in 1917-18 – a wing for the Allies, Jagdgeschwader for the Germans – WWII's early conflicts were fought by the RAF, in flight or squadron strengths, inevitably overwhelmed by the continued employ-ment of large numbers of fighters by the Germans. Between the wars, the RAF, at least partially to justify their independent service status, promoted the role of the strategic bomber. Despite the losses sustained by unescorted day bombers of the IAF in 1918, the policy followed in the early WWII days was for unescorted day bombers, deemed to be able to fight their way to a target. Even more amazing was that while Bomber Command thought this policy would work, Fighter Command was just as sure they would be able to stop German bombers reaching British targets.

The lessons that unescorted day bombers would be extremely vulnerable were ignored, and even in 1942 the Americans experienced losses when unescorted. Tactical day bombing was only able to operate successfully when escorted.

The big loss, however, was of almost all capacity to support the army at a tactical level, something the Germans developed with their Stuka dive-bombers. It was not until well into 1942 that the Desert Air Force re-learned the value of ground attack, and remembered how well the RAF had done in 1918 by ground strafing and bombing with fighters.

However, the Germans too lost their way a little between the wars. While they improved their army support capacity it was at the cost of strategic bombing, producing only medium-range bombers. Whilst they developed long-range escort fighters (as the British and French tried to do) such as the Me 110 for these medium bombers, they could not survive against single-seat fighters, and their own single-seaters lacked the range to escort with any hope of success.

However, the main reasons why they lost the air war in WWI were repeated in WWII. They had insufficient numbers of day fighters; quality and quantity will defeat quality any time. The Germans also underestimated the Americans. Germany's training system and operations broke down under the strain of a lack of resources and increasing fuel shortages. The extraordinary resilience and quality of their veteran pilots was just not enough. Another generation later, the equivalent of Paul Baümer, Fritz Rumey, Franz Büchner, Georg von Hantelmann, etc. had to try and beat off overwhelming numbers in defence of the Fatherland. That both generations did not succeed was not because of lack of courage and dedication of the Jasta pilots in WWI nor the Geschwader pilots of WWII.

This brings the authors to the final conclusion they hope readers will draw from this book. We have tried to show how and why the Allied Air Forces suffered the largest number of losses in what was a difficult month during the final year of this conflict. The Germans lost the air war, but it took many lives of brave yet frightened young French, American and British aviators to achieve this, just as it took many youngsters on the ground to overcome the Germans in the land battles.Any denigration of their German opponents in the air only devalues this sacrifice. German fighter pilots were as good as any, and perhaps more so. Their strategic and tactical circumstances – outnumbered and with much longer tours of duty – resulted in them having many opportunities for combat. That resulted in a good deal of aces scoring victories, and the differential in aces' scores would be vastly greater in WWII.

The German Air Service fought to the last. It took the best of the Allied world to triumph in both wars. The cost of victory in WWII would have been a great deal less if the RAF had remembered some of the basic lessons learnt at such a high price in WWI.

Appendix 1

RAF Victory Claims

Time	Pilot/Crew	Sqdn	Vic No	E/A	Location	How
				1 September 1918		
0740	Lt L E Taplin	4 AFC	7	Balloon	Fromelles	DF
0745	Lt R King	4 AFC	14	Balloon	Le Grand Riez	DF
0750	Lt W E G Mann	208	8	DFWC	S Scarpe River	DF
0815	Capt G C Dixon	40	6	two-seater	SE Henin-Liétard	OOC
0830	Lt F E Luff	74	3	Balloon	Menin	DF
0925	Lt J W Wright	4 AFC	1	Fokker DVII	SE Bailleul	OOC
1025	Capt E C Hoy	29	6	Balloon	NE Armentières	DF
1125	Lt R F McCrae	46	4	Fokker DVII	E Brie Bridge	OOC
1320	Lt F W Gillet	79	4	LVG C	NE Armentières	D
1330	Lt G K Runciman &	62	3	Fokker DVII	NE Cambrai	OOC
	Sgt H H Inglis	62	1			
1330	Lt A W Blowes &	62	3	Fokker DVII	E Cambrai	OOC
	2/Lt H S Hind	62	3			
1345	Sgt D E Edgley &	57	3	Fokker DVII	Cambrai	DF
	Sgt N Sandison	57	2			
1345	Sgt D E Edgley &	57	4	Fokker DVII	Cambrai	OOC
	Sgt N Sandison	57	3			
1345	Lt F O Thornton &	57	2	Fokker DVII	Cambrai	DF
	2/Lt F C Craig	57	3			
1350	2/Lt F J Hunt	74	1	Balloon	NE Armentières	DF
1400	Lt E M Coles &	57	3	Fokker DVII	Cambrai	OOC
	Sgt J Grant	57	5			
1430	Lt M A Tancock	32	1	Albatros DV	Doignies	D
1810	Capt E C Hoy	29	7	Fokker DVII	NE Armentières	OOC
1815	Lt A E Reed	29	15	Fokker DVII	W Armentières	OOC
1830	Lt E Swale	210	10	Fokker DVII	E Ypres	OOC
1850	Capt G K Cooper	208	6	Fokker DVII	Écoust-Saint-Quentin	OOC
1900	Lt H A S Molyneaux	56	2	Fokker DVII	S Riencourt	OOC
1910	Capt A Hepburn &	88	8	Fokker DVII	E Becelaere	DF
	Sgt E Antcliffe	88	6			
				2 September 1918		
0630	Capt R C B Brading	201	9	Fokker DVII	Heudicourt	OOC
0715	Capt R C B Brading	201	10	Fokker DVII	Lagnicourt	D
0715	Lt R Sykes	201	5	Fokker DVII	Lagnicourt	D
0915	Lt H H Beddow &	22	9	Fokker DVII	Arras-Cambrai Road	D
	2/Lt T Birmingham	22	7			
0915	Lt I O Stead &	22	5	Fokker DVII	Arras-Cambria Road	OOC
	2/Lt W A Cowie	22	4			
1005	Lt M D Sinclair	60	2	LVG C	Bruhemont	D

Time	Pilot/Crew	Sqdn	Vic No	E/A	Location	How
1015	Major F I Tanner	80	4	two-seater	S Cartigny	D
1015	Lt J Collier	80	1	two-seater	S Mons-en-Chausée	D
1115	Lt F G Gibbons &	22	9	Fokker DVII	Haynecourt	D
	Sgt G Shannon	22	2			
1115	Capt S F Thompson &	22	26	Fokker DVII	Haynecourt	D
	Sgt R M Fletcher	22	23			
1115	Lt F G Gibbons &	22	10	Fokker DVII	Haynecourt	D
	Sgt G Shannon	22	3			
1130	Sgt A S Cowlishaw	64	2	Fokker DVII	Marquion	D
1150	1/Lt F E Kindley	148 US	5	Fokker DVII	S Rumaucourt	D
1150	1/Lt C T McLean	148 US	2	Fokker DVII	Buissy	D
1150	Lt W B Knox	148 US	1	Fokker DVII	S Rumaucourt	OOC
1200	Capt W H Farrow	64	10	Fokker DVII	Aubencheul	OOC
1435	Capt G C Dixon	40	7	Fokker DVII	Écoust Saint-Quentin	OOC
1900	Lt L E Taplin	4 AFC	8	Halb C	E Aubers	OOC
1910	1/Lt O P Johnson	60	1	Albatros DV	Marquion	D
1930	2/Lt W S Rycroft &	48	1	Fokker DVII	N Menin	OOC
	2/Lt H L Ward	48	1			
1930	Lt H A Cole &	48	2	Fokker DVII	Menin	OOC
	2/Lt J W London	48	1			
1930	Lt J B Cowan &	48	1			
	Lt T L Jones	48	1			
1945	Lt J B Cowan &	48	2			
	Lt T L Jones	48	2			

3 September 1918

Time	Pilot/Crew	Sqdn	Vic No	E/A	Location	How
0630	Capt W A Southey,	84	11	Rumpler C	S Manancourt-Nurlu Rd	D
	Lt Wilson,	84	1			
	Lt Miller &	84	1			
	Lt F R Christiani	84	1			
0630	Lt S E Searson &	5	1	DFW C	Barelle	DF
	Lt T K Green	5	1			
0645	Capt W A Southey	84	12	Balloon	Fins	DF
0700	Lt M G Burger	54	2	Hannover C	Moeuvres	D
0700	Lt C W M Thompson &	22	4	Pfalz DXII	Sailly-Sallisal	D
	2/Lt G McCormack	22	1			
0705	Lt L E Taplin	4 AFC	9	Balloon	La Plouich	DF
0710	Capt W R Irwin	56	10	Fokker DVII	Étaing	D
0710	Capt W R Irwin	56	11	Fokker DVII	Haynecourt	D
0710	Lt H P Chubb	56	1	Fokker DVII	Étaing	D
0710	Lt H A S Molyneaux	56	3	Fokker DVII	Étaing	OOC
0730	Capt D Lloyd-Evans	64	5	Fokker DVII	Brebières	OOC
0910	Capt J I Morgan	70	5	Fokker DVII	S Roulers	OOC
0910	Lt S T Liversedge	70	10	Fokker DVII	S Roulers	D
0910	Lt McPhee	70	1	Fokker DVII	S Roulers	OOC
0910	Lt J A Spilhaus	70	1	Fokker DVII	S Roulers	OOC
0930	2/Lt C R Thompson	84	4	Balloon	S Poeuilly	DF
0935	Lt J A Glen	70	1	Balloon	Warneton-Deulemont	DF
1010	Capt J E Doyle	60	7	Fokker DVII	Inchy	D
1055	Capt J L M White	65	13	Fokker DVII	Engel	OOC
1100	Capt J L M White	65	14	Fokker DVII	Engel	OOC
1110	Lt H E Browne	65	4	Fokker DVII	Engel	OOC
1110	2/Lt R O Campbell	65		Fokker DVII	Engel	OOC
1150	Lt R C Pattullo	204	1	Fokker DVII	Dixmuide-Ypres	OOC

Time	Pilot/Crew	Sqdn	Vic No	E/A	Location	How
1150	Lt B E Barnum	204	2	Fokker DVII	Gheluvelt	OOC
1150	Lt R M Gordon	204	7	Fokker DVII	Gheluvelt	OOC
1150	Capt F I Lord	79	6	Fokker DVII	Armentières	DF
1310	Capt G B Gates	201	9	Hannover C	Moeuvres	DF
1315	Lt A S Compton	54	2	Hannover C	E Moeuvres	DF
1325	Lt F W Gillet	79	5	Balloon	Armentières	DF
1425	Capt W E G Mann	208	9	Fokker DVII	Marquion	OOC
1520	Lt L G Bowen	56	1	Fokker DVII	Roisel	OOC
1530	Capt W A Southey	84	13	Balloon	N Fins	DF
1600	Capt G B Bailey & Lt A Ostler	13 13	1 1	Fokker DVII	Inchy-Moeuvres	D
1600	Capt G B Bailey & Lt A Ostler	13 13	2 2	Fokker DVII	Inchy-Moeuvres	D
1645	Lt H R Carson	32	1	Fokker DVII	Douai	OOC
1715	Lt C R Pithey & Lt H Rhodes	12 12	10 11	LVG C	Lagnicourt	D
1720	Lt C O Stone	2 AFC	1	Fokker DVII	NW Cambrai	OOC
1720	Lt F R Smith	2 AFC	5	Fokker DVII	NW Cambrai	OOC
1745	Capt H P Lale & 2/Lt R J Ralph	20 20	13 13	Fokker DVII	S Havrincourt Wood	OOC
1745	Lt P T Iaccaci & Lt A Mills	20 20	15 10	Fokker DVII	Havrincourt Wood	D
1745	Lt G E Randall & Lt G V Learmond	20 20	4 3	Fokker DVII	S Havrincourt Wood	OOC
1750	Lt C R Oberst & Lt R Gordon-Bennett	20 20	1 2	Pfalz DIII	Havrincourt Wood	D
1750	Lt C R Oberst & Lt R Gordon-Bennett	20 20	2 3	Pfalz DIII	Havrincourt Wood	OOC
1810	Lt W S Jenkins	210	6	Fokker DVII	Lille	OOC
1815	Lt E J Jacques & 2/Lt N P Wood	27 27	1 1	Fokker DVII	SW Valenciennes	D
1820	Lt H A Kullberg	1	18	Fokker DVII	Avesnes-le-Sec	D
1830	Capt H A Patey	210	11	Fokker DVII	NE Roulers	DF
1830	Lt E Swale	210	11	Fokker DVII	Courtrai	D
1830	Capt S C Joseph, Lt C W Payton, Lt Hughes, Lt Lewis & Lt I C Sanderson	210 210 210 210 210	12 5 2 1 6	Fokker DVII	Menin-Courtrai	D
1830	Capt H J Larkin	87	9	Fokker DVII	Épinoy	OOC
1830	Capt A W Vigers	87	9	Fokker DVII	Épinoy	D
1830	Capt H J Larkin	87	10	Fokker DVII	Épinoy	OOC
1830	Capt A W Vigers	87	10	Fokker DVII	Épinoy	OOC
1830	Capt W E Staton & Lt L F Mitchell	62 62	23 5	Fokker DVII	SE Marquion	D
1845	Capt G E Gibbons & Lt T Elliott	62 62	13 7	Fokker DVII	N Cambrai	OOC
1845	Capt G E Gibbons & Lt T Elliott	62 62	14 8	Fokker DVII	N Cambrai	OOC
1845	Lt L N Hollinghurst	87	6	Hannover CLIII	Masnières	D
1845	Lt E J Stephens	41	6	Fokker DVII	S Vitry	D
1900	Lt L E Taplin	4 AFC	10	Balloon	Herlies	D
1925	Capt G B Gates	201	9	Albatros C	E Metz-en-Couture	DF
1930	Capt E C Hoy	29	10	Fokker DVII	N Comines	D

4 September 1918

Time	Pilot/Crew	Sqdn	Vic No	E/A	Location	How
0555	Capt E J K McCloughry	4 AFC	18	Balloon	Erquinghem	DF
0605	Lt O B Ramsey	4 AFC	1	Balloon	La Bassée	DF
0630	Lt M D Sinclair	60	3	Fokker DVII	Paillencourt	D
0630	Lt O P Johnson	60	2	Fokker DVII	Épinoy	DF
0630	Lt G M Duncan	60	6	Fokker DVII	Cambrai	D
0645	Lt G C Whitney	148 US	1	Fokker DVII	Marquion	OOC
0700	Capt R N G Atkinson &	206	4	Balloon	Frelinghein	DF
	2/Lt W T Ganter	206	2			
0710	Lt R King	4 AFC	15	LVG C	Erquinghem-le-Sec	D
0710	1/Lt H R Clay	148 US	5	Fokker DVII	S Sains-lès-Marquion	D
0710	1/Lt C Bissell	148 US	2	Fokker DVII	SW Marquion	D
0714	1/Lt H R Clay	148 US	6	Fokker DVII	Marquoin	D
0715	1/Lt C Bissell	148 US	3	Fokker DVII	W Marquoin	OOC
0715	Capt A H Cobby	4 AFC	29	Fokker DVII	Wattignies	OOC
0745	Capt S Carlin	74	9	Balloon	NW Armentières	DF
0750	Capt G W F Darvill &	18	8	Fokker DVII	Cantin	DF
	Lt W Miller	18	5			
0750	Capt G W F Darvill &	18	9	Fokker DVII	Aubigny-au-Bac	D
	Lt W Miller	18	6			
0805	Lt F S Gordon	74	6	Balloon	S Roulers	DF
0815	Lt D H S Gilbertson &	70	5	Fokker DVII	Escaillon	D
	Lt J S Wilson	70	3			
0815	Lt K B Watson	70	3	Fokker DVII	Escaillon	DF
0900	Capt E C Johnson &	88	11	Fokker DVII	Seclin	DF
	Lt W I N Grant	88	2			
0900	Lt C Foster &	88	3	Fokker DVII	Seclin	OOC
	Lt B R Smyth	88	6			
0915	Capt E C Johnson &	88	12	Fokker DVII	Phalempin	OOC
	Lt W I N Grant	88	3			
0930	Capt C Findlay &	88	9	Fokker DVII	S Don	D
	2/Lt C T Gauntlett	88	1			
0930	Capt E C Johnson	88	13	Fokker DVII	Provin	OOC
	& Lt W I N Grant	88	4			
0930	Lt K B Conn &	88	9	Fokker DVII	Provin	OOC
	Sgt C M Maxwell	88	1			
0930	Lt C Foster &	88	4	Fokker DVII	Provin	OOC
	Lt B R Smyth	88	7			
0930	Lt R Schallaire &	62	2	Fokker DVII	Marcq	D
	2/Lt R Lowe	62	2			
0930	Capt G F Gibbons &	62	15	Fokker DVII	Abancourt	D
	2/Lt T Elliott	62	10			
0930	Capt G F Gibbons &	62	16	Fokker DVII	Cambrai	OOC
	2/Lt T Elliott	62	11			
0930	Capt W E Staton &	62	23	Fokker DVII	Marquette	OOC
	Lt L E Mitchell	62	6			
0940	Lt G F Manning &	48	1	Fokker DVII	W Armentières	D
	2/Lt P A Clayton	48	2			
0940	Lt V E Knight	2 AFC	1	Fokker DVII	SE Douai	OOC
0945	Lt F L Hale	32	2	Fokker DVII	N Cambrai	DF
0950	Lt F L Hale	32	3	Fokker DVII	SE Arras	OOC
0950	2/Lt F T Scott &	107	2	Fokker DVII	La Sentinelle	DF
	Sgt W J Palmer	107	2			

Time	Pilot/Crew	Sqdn	Vic No	E/A	Location	How
1000	Lt A B Agnew &	12	1	Fokker DVII	Moeuvres-Inchy	D
	2/Lt A E Chadwick	12	1			
1000	Capt A MacGregor &	57	4	Fokker DVII	Bourlon Wood	OOC
	Sgt J Grant	57	6			
1010	Lt W Hubbard	3	10	Fokker DVII		D
1010	Lt A W Franklyn	3	6	Fokker DrI		D
1010	Lt S D Lavalle	3	1	Fokker DVII		D
1010	Lt D J Hughes	3	4	Fokker DVII		POW
1015	Lt F M Tudhope	46	4	Fokker DVII	Pronville	OOC
1040	Capt T F Hazell,	24	38	Balloon	Bernes	D
	Lt W A Southey &	24	22			
	2/Lt A L Bloom	24	1			
1045	Capt T F Hazell	24	39	Balloon	Gouzeaucourt	D
1045	Lt A D Shannon &	11	2	Fokker DVII	E Cambrai	OOC
	2/Lt C E Spinks	11	1			
1045	Lt E N Underwood &	11	1	Fokker DVII	E Cambrai	OOC
	2/Lt G S Turner	11	1			
1045	Lt C R Smythe &	11	3	Fokker DVII	S St Hilaire	DF
	2/Lt W T Barnes	11	3			
1110	Lt O J Rose	92	7	Halb C	Quiéry-Douai	D
1235	Lt A E James	4 AFC	1	Balloon	SE La Bassée	DF
?	Lt F E Hyatt &	5	1	Fokker DVII	NW Épinoy	OOC
	Lt R Greenyer	5	1			
1255	Lt A H Lockley	4 AFC	1	Balloon	S Armentières	DF
1330	Lt C B Seymour &	11	1	Fokker DVII	Douai-Cambrai	OOC
	Sgt W J Gillespie	11	1			
1330	2/Lt S W Highwood &	84	4	Balloon	Douvieux	DF
	2/Lt C R Thompson	84	5			
1345	Lt R C Bennett &	18	4	Fokker DVII	Bailleul	OOC
	2/Lt A Lilley	18	1			
1615	Capt A T Whealy	203	27	Fokker DVII	Trescault	D
1715	Lt D J T Mellor &	205	2	Fokker DVII	Roisel	OOC
	Sgt W J Middleton	205	6			
1815	Capt A Morrison &	11	3	Fokker DVII	Douai	D
	Sgt R Allen	11	3			
1825	2/Lt L Arnott &	11	1	Fokker DVII	Auberchicourt	OOC
	Sgt C W Cooke	11	1			
1930	Major K L Caldwell	74	20	Fokker DVII	S Lille	D
1930	2/Lt F J Hunt	74	2	Fokker DVII	S Lille	OOC

5 September 1918

Time	Pilot/Crew	Sqdn	Vic No	E/A	Location	How
0625	Lt A H Lockley	4 AFC	2	Balloon	Pérenchies	DF
0630	Lt L E Taplin	4 AFC	11	Balloon	Pérenchies	DF
0655	Lt C L Childs	70	1	Fokker DVII	E Ploegsteert Wood	DF
0950	2/Lt S W Highwood	84	5	Balloon	S Poeuilly	DF
0950	2/Lt C R Thompson	84	6	Balloon	S Poeuilly	DF
1015	Sgt A S Cowlishaw	64	3	Fokker DVII	NE Cambrai	D
1015	Sgt A S Cowlishaw	64	4	Fokker DVII	NE Cambrai	OOC
1015	Capt W H Farrow	64	11	Fokker DVII	NE Cambrai	D
1015	Capt D Lloyd-Evans	64	6	Fokker DVII	NE Cambrai	D
1030	Lt H J Welch	80	1	Fokker DVII	Havrincourt Wood	OOC
1045	Lt G R Hicks	74	4	Fokker DVII	S Cambrai	D
1045	Lt F E Luff	74	4	Fokker DVII	S Cambrai	D
1045	Lt A C Kiddie	74	8	Fokker DVII	S Cambrai	D

Time	Pilot/Crew	Sqdn	Vic No	E/A	Location	How
1100	Maj A Coningham MC	92	13	Fokker DVII	W Cambrai	D
1110	Capt W E Reed	92	4	Fokker DVII	SW Cambrai	D
1115	Lt E Shapard	92	2	Fokker DVII	Cambrai	D
1120	2/Lt D V Thomas &	57	1	Fokker DVII	Marcoing	OOC
	2/Lt I S Woodhouse	57	1			
1125	Lt F O Thornton &	57	3	Fokker DVII	W Marcoing	OOC
	2/Lt F C Craig	57	4			
1125	Capt A MacGregor &	57	5	Fokker DVII	SW Marcoing	DF
	Sgt J Grant	57	7			
1125	Sgt D E Edgley &	57	5	Fokker DVII	Marcoing	OOC
	Sgt J H Bowler	57	2			
1145	Lt A W Franklyn	3	7	Fokker DVII		DF
1205	Lt W Hubbard	3	11	Albatros C	Péronne	D
1215	Capt E L Zink	32	5	two-seater	N Équancourt	D
1240	Capt H A Oaks &	48	10	Fokker DVII	Courtrai-Roulers	DF
	Lt T Beck	48	1			
1240	Capt H A Oaks &	48	11	Fokker DVII	Courtrai-Roulers	OOC
	Lt T Beck	48	2			
1345	2/Lt F Suckling	65	1	Fokker DVII	Ostende	D
1345	2/Lt W Thornton	65	2	Fokker DVII	E Ostende	OOC
1345	2/Lt B Lockey	65	1	Fokker DVII	E Ostende	DF
1345	2/Lt W H Bland	65	1	Fokker DVII	E Ostende	OOC
1345	Capt Jones-Williams	65	13	Fokker DVII	E Ostende	OOC
1440	Capt J E Greene	213	11	Fokker DVII	S Varsenaere	D
1440	Lt G C Mackay	213	13	Fokker DVII	S Varsenaere	D
1500	Major R Collishaw	203	56	Fokker DVII	Inchy-en-Artois	D
1520	Capt H P Lale &	20	14	Fokker DVII	SE Cambrai	D
	2/Lt H L Edwards	20	3			
1520	2/Lt R B D Campbell &	20	1	Fokker DVII	SE Cambrai	OOC
	2/Lt G C Russell	20	1			
1520	Lt G E Randall &	20	5	Fokker DVII	SE Cambrai	OOC
	Lt G V Learmond	20	4			
1605	Capt A MacGregor &	57	6	Fokker DVII	W Avesnes-le-Sec	DF
	Sgt J Grant	57	8			
1615	'B' Flight	57		Fokker DVII	W Avesnes-le-Sec	OOC
1650	Lt G Howarth &	218	1	Pfalz DIII	Bruges	OOC
	2/Lt F Gallant	218	1			
1700	Capt S Thompson &	22	27	Fokker DVII	Douai	DF
	Sgt R M Fletcher	22	24			
1700	Capt S Thompson &	22	28	Fokker DVII	Douai	OOC
	Sgt R M Fletcher	22	25			
1700	Lt H H Beddow &	22	10	Fokker DVII	Douai	OOC
	Lt W U Tyrrell	22	1			
1700	Lt C W Thompson &	22	5	Fokker DVII	Douai	OOC
	2/Lt G McCormack	22	2			
1700	Lt F G Gibbons &	22	11	Fokker DVII	Douai	OOC
	2/Lt J McDonald	22	8			
1720	1/Lt F E Kindley	148 US	6	Fokker DVII	Saint-Quentin Lake	OOC
1720	1/Lt E W Springs	148 US	11	Fokker DVII	Canal du Nord	OOC
1730	Lt L Yerex	210	4	Fokker DVII	NE Roulers	OOC
1730	Lt I C Sanderson	210	11	Fokker DVII	SE Roulers	D
1805	Lt A H Lockley	4 AFC	3	Fokker DVII	S Brebières	OOC
1805	Lt L E Taplin	4 AFC	12	Fokker DVII	S Brebières	OOC
1810	Capt J E Doyle	60	8	Fokker DVII	Avesnes-le-Sec	DF
1810	Capt J E Doyle	60	9	Fokker DVII	Avesnes-le-Sec	OOC

Time	Pilot/Crew	Sqdn	Vic No	E/A	Location	How
1820	Lt J W Rayner	60	1	Fokker DVII	Avesnes-le-Sec	DF
1820	Lt G M Duncan	60	9	Fokker DVII	Avesnes-le-Sec	OOC
1825	Lt J W Rayner	60	2	Fokker DVII	Avesnes-le-Sec	OOC
1825	Lt G M Duncan	60	9	Fokker DVII	Avesnes-le-Sec	OOC
1830	Lt A E Reed	29	16	LVG C	SE Armentières	D
1845	Lt K B Conn &	88	10	Fokker DVII	NE Armentières	OOC
	2/Lt B Digby-Worsley	88	12			
1845	Lt V Voss &	88	3	Fokker DVII	Armentières	D
	Sgt C Hill	88	3			
1845	Capt J R Swanston	204	2	Fokker DVII	Oucken	DF
1850	Lt C Findlay &	88	10	Fokker DVII	E Pérenchies	D
	2/Lt G T Gauntlett	88	2			
1855	Lt F W Gillet	79	6	Fokker DVII	E Armentières	D
1900	Capt F I Lord	79	7	Fokker DVII	E Ploegsteert	OOC
1900	Capt H P Rushworth	79	1	Fokker DVII	NE Armentières	OOC
1900	Capt A Hepburn &	88	9	Fokker DVII	N Douai	OOC
	2/Lt H G Eldon	88	1			
1900	Capt A Hepburn &	88	10	Fokker DVII	Armentières	DF
	2/Lt H G Eldon	88	2			
1910	Lt A C Kiddie	74	9	Fokker DVII	W Lille	OOC
1910	Lt G R Hicks	74	5	Fokker DVII	W Lille	OOC

6 September 1918

Time	Pilot/Crew	Sqdn	Vic No	E/A	Location	How
0630	Lt R King	4 AFC	16	DFWC	E Wavrin	OOC
0705	1/Lt J O Creech	148 US	3	Fokker DVII	NE Bourlon	D
0830	Lt A T Iaccaci &	20	12	Fokker DVII	Cambrai-Saint-Quentin	OOC
	Sgt A Newland	20	15			
0830	Lt P T Iaccaci &	20	16	Fokker DVII	Cambrai-Péronne Road	D
	Lt A Mills	20	11			
0845	Capt H P Lale &	20	15	Fokker DVII	Saint-Quentin	DF
	2/Lt H L Edwards	20	4			
0845	Capt H P Lale &	20	16	Fokker DVII	Saint-Quentin	DF
	2/Lt H L Edwards	20	5			
0850	Lt P T Iaccaci &	20	17	Fokker DVII	Saint-Quentin	OOC
	Lt A Mills	20	12			
0850	Lt R B D Campbell &	20	2	Fokker DVII	Saint-Quentin	OOC
	2/Lt D M Calderwood	20	1			
0850	Lt A T Iaccaci &	20	13	Fokker DVII	NE Saint-Quentin	OOC
	Sgt A Newland	20	16			
0915	Lt H N Compton	23	3	Fokker DVII	Saint-Quentin	DF
0915	Lt E H Johnston &	205	4	Fokker DVII	Saint-Quentin	D
	2/Lt A Crosthwaite	205	4			
1025	Lt G N Dennis &	13	1	Fokker DVII	Bourlon Wood	DF
	Lt H G Hewett	13	1			
1030	Lt E S Coler &	11	11	Fokker DVII	W Cambrai	D
	2/Lt D P Conyngham	11	1			
1030	Capt H A Hay &	11	4	Fokker DVII	W Cambrai	D
	Lt A H Craig	11	1			
1030	Lt E S Coler &	11	12	Fokker DVII	W Cambrai	OOC
	2/Lt D P Conyngham	11	2			
1030	Capt H A Hay &	11	5	Fokker DVII	W Cambrai	OOC
	Lt A H Craig	11	2			
1100	1/Lt B Rogers	32	2	Rumpler C	E Roisel	OOC
1130	Capt J S Stubbs &	103	7	Fokker DVII	W St André-Lille	D
	2/Lt C C Dance	103	5			

Time	Pilot/Crew	Sqdn	Vic No	E/A	Location	How
1145	Lt J Whitham &	103	1	Fokker DVII	Lille	OOC
	Sgt E G Stevens	103	2			
1700	Lt G E B Lawson	32	2	Fokker DVII	Holnon	D
1700	1/Lt B Rogers	32	3	Fokker DVII	Holnon	DF
1800	Lt G W Wareing	29	4	DFWC	SE Pérenchies	D
1815	Lt F C Jenner	213	2	Fokker DVII	N Ostende	OOC
1830	Capt J B White	208	8	Fokker DVII	Arras-Cambrai Road	DF
1830	Lt J S McDonald	208	6	Fokker DVII	Arras-Cambrai Road	DF
1830	Capt W E G Mann	208	10	Fokker DVII	Canal du Nord	DF
1830	Capt W E G Mann	208	11	Fokker DVII	Canal du Nord	OOC
1835	Lt E Swale	210	12	Fokker DVII	W Ostende	D
1835	Lt C F Pineau	210	2	Fokker DVII	W Ostende	OOC
1840	Lt T S Harrison	29	13	Fokker DVII	SE Armentières	OOC
1845	Capt E J McCloughry	4 AFC	19	LVG C	N Don	OOC
1845	Lt J P Findlay &	88	4	Fokker DVII	N Douai	OOC
	2/Lt W Tinsley	88	7			
1845	Capt A Hepburn &	88	11	Fokker DVII	N Douai	OOC
	2/Lt H G Eldon	88	3			
1845	2/Lt A Fowles	201	1	Fokker DVII	Cambrai	OOC
1845	Capt R C B Brading	201	11	Fokker DVII	Cambrai	OOC
1845	2/Lt H J Ewan	201	1	Fokker DVII	Cambrai	OOC
1855	Lt V G M Sheppard	4 AFC	1	Fokker DVII	Douai	OOC
1855	Lt J W Wright	4 AFC	2	Fokker DVII	Douai	OOC
1855	Lt G Jones	4 AFC	2	Fokker DVII	Douai	OOC
1900	Lt J J Wellworth	2 AFC	4	Fokker DVII	NW Douai	OOC
1900	Lt F R Smith	2 AFC	6	Fokker DVII	NNE Douai	D
1900	Lt D A O'Leary	29	2	Fokker DVII	N Menin	D
1910	Lt A E Reed	29	17	Fokker DVII	S Lille	OOC
1915	Lt L N Caple &	22	2	Pflaz DXII	Cambrai	OOC
	2/Lt S G Barrow	22	2			

7 September 1918

Time	Pilot/Crew	Sqdn	Vic No	E/A	Location	How
0655	Lt G W Wareing	29	5	Balloon	Gheluvelt	DF
0700	2/Lt T H Barkell	4 AFC	1	two-seater	Henin-Liétard	D
0815	Capt L H Rochford	203	27	Fokker DVII	N Bourlon Wood	D
0930	Major F I Tanner	80	4	Fokker DVII	S Cartigny	D
1020	Capt G B Gates	201	10	Albatros C	Noyelles	D
1100	Capt R B Bannerman	79	7	DFWC	NE Ploegsteert	D
1120	2/Lt R Russell &	108	1	Fokker DVII	Ostende	D
	2/Lt G B Pike	108	1			
	2/Lt C R Knott &	108	1			
	2/Lt E D McClinton	108	1			
	2/Lt H L McLellan &	108	1			
	2/Lt F X Jackson	108	1			
1130	1/Lt I P Corse	84	3	Balloon	N Saint-Quentin	DF
1130	2/Lt S W Highwood	84	6	Balloon	Bellenglise	DF
1135	Capt A F W B Proctor	84	44	Balloon	Cambrai-Saint-Quentin	DF
1140	2/Lt F R Christiani	84	2	Balloon	Cambrai-Saint-Quentin	DF
1205	Lt A E Reed	29	18	Halb C	Warneton	OOC
1800	2/Lt E A R Lee &	98	1	Pfalz DXII	Demicourt	D
	2/Lt E G Banham	98	1			
1810	Capt H P Lale &	20	17	Fokker DVII	NE Saint-Quentin	D
	2/Lt H L Edwards	20	6			

Time	Pilot/Crew	Sqdn	Vic No	E/A	Location	How
1815	2/Lt T W Sleigh &	98	1	Pfalz DXII	SW Cambrai	D
	2/Lt A H Fuller	98	1			
1815	2/Lt C B Gowing &	98	1	Fokker DVII	SW Cambrai	OOC
	2/Lt J G W Holliday	98	1			
1840	2/Lt H F Taylor &	205	1	Fokker DVII	W Saint-Quentin	OOC
	2/Lt J Golding	205	1			
1845	2/Lt E J Taylor &	23	4	Fokker DVII	Ronssoy	OOC
	Lt H A White	23				
1900	Capt M E Ashton &	12	1	LVG C	Noyelles	D
	Lt T D Fitzsimon	12	1			
1910	2/Lt C G Vandyk,	54	1	two-seater	NE Marquion	D
	2/Lt Berrington,	54	1			
	2/Lt Fuller,	54	1			
	Capt G Hackwill,	54	8			
	Lt M G Burger &	54	3			
	Lt J C MacLennan	54	2			

8 September 1918

Time	Pilot/Crew	Sqdn	Vic No	E/A	Location	How
0635	Capt D H M Carberry &	59	3	Halb C		D
	Lt J B V Clements	59	2			
0645	Capt D H M Carberry &	59	4	Halb C		OOC
	Lt J B V Clements	59	3			
0650	Capt G B Gates	201	11	Albatros C	Cantaing	D
0700	Lt R K McConnell	46	7	Rumpler C	S Péronne	DF
0815	Capt T F Hazell	24	38	Fokker DVII	Le Catelet	D
0815	Capt H D Barton	24	14	Fokker DVII	Le Catelet	OOC
0820	2/Lt H L Bair	24	5	Fokker DVII	N Saint-Quentin	D

13 September 1918

Time	Pilot/Crew	Sqdn	Vic No	E/A	Location	How
1750	Lt A E Reed	29	19	Halb C	SE Deulemont	D
1850	1/Lt H C Knotts	17 US	2	Fokker DVII	–	D
2115	Capt W H Haynes	151	1	Gotha GV	Bapaume	
2145	Capt W H Haynes	151	1	EA	NE Bapaume	
2150	Lt E P MacKay	151	1	EA	Moislains	

14 September 1918

Time	Pilot/Crew	Sqdn	Vic No	E/A	Location	How
0035	Lt W Aitken	151	1	Gotha GV	Beauquesnes	DF
0115	Capt A B Yuille	151	3	Fried G	Doullens-Arras	POW
0800	Capt C W Odell,	46	3	two-seater	NE Vermand	D
	Lt N Bruce &	46	2			
	Lt P F Paton	46	3			
0815	Capt C W Odell &	46	4	Balloon	NE Vermand	DF
	Lt P F Paton	46	4			
1010	Capt C H R Lagesse	29	9	Balloon	W Quesnoy	DF
1020	2/Lt P F Bovington &	12	1	Fokker DVII	Graincourt	DF
	Lt H P Elliott	12	1			
1025	Lt A Ibbotson &	59	1	Fokker DVII	S Marcoing	DF
	2/Lt W J Carruthers	59	1			
1030	Capt W A Southey	84	14	Balloon	Gonnelieu	DF
1030	2/Lt S W Highwood	84	7	Balloon	Bantouzelle	DF
1030	2/Lt D C Rees	84	1	Balloon	Bantouzelle	DF
1325	Capt G B Gates	201	12	LVG C	E Villers-Plouich	DF

Time	Pilot/Crew	Sqdn	Vic No	E/A	Location	How
			15 September 1918			
0845	Capt R C B Brading	201	12	Pfalz DXII	W Cambrai	D
0850	Capt A W B Proctor &	84	45	Balloon	Bellicourt	DF
	Capt D Carruthers	84	3			
0955	Lt C R J Thompson	84	7	Balloon	E Saint-Quentin	DF
1040	2/Lt P E Cunnius,	148 US	1	Halb C	Épinoy	OOC
	1/Lt O A Ralston,	148 US	3			
	1/Lt E W Springs &	148 US	13			
	1/Lt H Starkey Jr	148 US	1			
1050	1/Lt F E Kindley	148 US	7	Fokker DVII	Épinoy	OOC
1100	Lt R B D Campbell &	20	3	Fokker DVII	NE Saint-Quentin	OOC
	Sgt A J Winch	20	1			
1105	Capt O M Baldwin	73	10	Fokker DVII	Cambrai	D
1105	Lt N Cooper	73	5	Fokker DVII	Cambrai	OOC
1110	Lt N S Boulton &	20	1	Fokker DVII	NE Saint-Quentin	OOC
	2/Lt G W Pearce	20	1			
1110	Capt O M Baldwin	73	11	Fokker DVII	Cambrai	D
1115	Lt A T Iaccaci &	20	14	Fokker DVII	S Lesdain	D
	Sgt A Newland	20	17			
1120	Lt A T Iaccaci &	20	15	Fokker DVII	S Morcourt	D
	Sgt A Newland	20	18			
1120	Capt O M Baldwin	73	12	two-seater	La Folie	D
1120	Lt A R Strachan &	20	2	Fokker DVII	Omissy	D
	Lt D M Calderwood	20	2			
1120	Lt A R Strachan &	20	3	Fokker DVII	Omissy	OOC
	Lt D M Calderwood	20	3			
1120	Lt W M Thomson &	20	22	Fokker DVII	Saint-Quentin	D
	2/Lt H L Edwards	20	7			
1120	Lt W M Thomson &	20	23	Fokker DVII	Saint-Quentin	OOC
	2/Lt H L Edwards	20	8			
1200	Capt E S Coler &	11	13	Fokker DVII	W Esnes	D
	2/Lt E J Corbett	11	1			
1200	Capt E S Coler &	11	14	Fokker DVII	SW Lesdain	D
	2/Lt E J Corbett	11	2			
1300	Lt O J Rose	92	7	Hannover C	W Lille	D
1320	Capt H A Whistler	80	18	Balloon	Étricourt	DF
1400	Lt B E Barnum &	204	3	Fokker DVII	Zeebrugge	D
	Lt R C Pattullo	204	1			
1400	Capt C R R Hickey	204	16	Fokker DVII	Zeebrugge	OOC
1400	Lt D S Ingalls &	213	3	Rumpler C	Ostende	DF
	Lt H C Smith	213	3			
1415	Capt D R MacLaren	46	46	Fokker DVII	N Gouzeaucourt	OOC
1520	Lt C J H Haywood &	205	6	Fokker DVII	Busigny	OOC
	Sgt S F Longstone	205	5			
1645	Capt W E Shields	41	14	Fokker DVII	Houthem	OOC
1700	Capt F O Soden	41	20	Balloon	Beaucamps	DF
1700	Capt R M Foster	209	14	Fokker DVII	Écoust-Saint-Quentin	D
1700	2/Lt F O McDonald &	205	2	two-seater	W Roisel	DF
	2/Lt J B Leach	205	4			
1705	Capt G W D Allen,	62	11	Pfalz DXII	Récourt	POW
	Capt C S T Lavers,	62	8			
	Lt D E Cameron,	62	1			
	Lt B H Moody,	62	5			
	Capt W E Staton &	62	24			
	Lt L E Mitchell	62	6			

Time	Pilot/Crew	Sqdn	Vic No	E/A	Location	How
1705	Capt W Pallister	1	1	Fokker DVII	NW Cambrai	D
1705	Lt R Schallaire &	62	3	Fokker DVII	Marquion	D
	2/Lt R Lowe	62	3			
1705	2/Lt P S Manley &	62	1	Fokker DVII	Marquion	OOC
	Sgt G F Hines	62	1			
1715	Lt C W Arning	1	1	Fokker DVII	Haynecourt	OOC
1715	Lt C G Pegg	1	3	Fokker DVII	E Raillencourt	D
1715	Capt W R May	209	11	Fokker DVII	E Épinoy	D
1720	Capt E E Cummings &	2 AFC	5	Albatros C	W Marquart	D
	Lt E E Davies	2 AFC	2			
1720	Capt R M Foster	209	15	Fokker DVII	Ecoust-Saint-Quentin	D
1745	Lt E Lussier	73	9	Fokker DVII	Aubigny-au-Bac	D
1750	Capt T P Middleton &	20	26	Hannover C	SE Saint-Quentin	D
	Lt A Mills	20	13			
1750	2/Lt H F Taylor &	205	2	Fokker DVII	Saint-Quentin	OOC
	2/Lt H S Mullen	205	1			
1805	Lt J W Warner	85	5	Fokker DVII	Bourlon Wood	D
1810	Capt W H Hubbard	73	11	Fokker DVII	Gouy-sous-Bellone	D
1815	Lt S T Liversedge	70	11	Fokker DVII	Houthulst	OOC
1815	Lt N Cooper	73	6	Fokker DVII	NE Bourlon Wood	D
1815	Capt O M Baldwin	73	13	Fokker DVII	Gouy-sous-Bellone	D
1815	Capt O M Baldwin	73	14	Fokker DVII	Gouy-sous-Bellone	OOC
1830	Capt H D Barton	24	15	Albatros C	Cambrai	OOC
1830	2/Lt M J Ward	70		Balloon	E Armentières	DF
1840	Capt G H Hackwill	54	9	Fokker DVII	Fernin	OOC
1840	1/Lt J O Creech	148 US	4	Fokker DVII	Épinoy	D
1845	1/Lt T L Moore	148 US	1	Fokker DVII	NE Hamel	D
1845	Lt G W Wareing	29	6	Fokker DVII	Roulers-Rumbeke	DF
1845	1/Lt W W Lauer	29	1	Fokker DVII	Moorslede-Roulers	D
1850	Capt S Carlin	74	10	Fokker DVII	NE Lille	DF
1850	Lt F E Luff	74	5	Fokker DVII	NE Armentières	D
1855	Capt H D Barton &	24	16	Hannover C	Hannescourt Wood	D
	2/Lt H L Bair	24	6			
2220	Capt F C Broome	151	2	Staaken	Bapaume	POW
	Lt G F Anderson &	88	3	Fokker DVII	E Seclin	OOC
	Lt T F Chiltern	88	4			
	Lt V W Kilroe &	15	1	Fokker DVII		D
	Lt G E Izzard	15	1			
16 September 1918						
0625	Lt R King	4 AFC	17	Fokker DVII	Le Quesnoy	D
0625	Capt H G Watson	4 AFC	13	Fokker DVII	Le Quesnoy	OOC
0630	2/Lt S W Highwood	84	8	Rumpler C	Selenoy	D
	& Lt C F C Wilson	84	4			
0730	Lt F R Smith	2 AFC	7	Fokker DVII	Lille	OOC
0730	Lt F R Smith	2 AFC	8	Fokker DVII	Lille	OOC
0730	Lt F Alberry	2 AFC	1	Fokker DVII	NW Lille	DF
0730	Capt R L Manuel	2 AFC	10	Fokker DVII	Habourdin	OOC
0735	Lt G E Holroyde	2 AFC	1	Fokker DVII	Habourdin	OOC
0800	Lt C H Copp	2 AFC	1	Fokker DVII	Steenvoorde	OOC
0800	Capt R L Manuel	2 AFC	11	Fokker DVII	S Droglandt	POW
0815	Lt W M Thomson &	20	24	Fokker DVII	NE Saint-Quentin	D
	2/Lt H L Edwards	20	9			

Time	Pilot/Crew	Sqdn	Vic No	E/A	Location	How
0815	Lt A R Strachan &	20	4	Fokker DVII	NW Saint-Quentin	D
	2/Lt D M Calderwood	20	4			
	Lt W M Thomson &	20	25			
	2/Lt H L Edwards	20	10			
0820	Lt W M Thomson &	20	26	Fokker DVII	Saint-Quentin	D
	2/Lt H L Edwards	20	11			
0820	2/Lt T H Barkell	4 AFC	2	Fokker DVII	Frelinghien	D
0820	Lt A J Pallister	4 AFC	I	Fokker DVII	Frelinghien	D
0820	Lt G Jones	4 AFC	3	Fokker DVII	Frelinghien	D
0825	Lt A T Iaccaci &	20	16	Fokker DVII	W Lesdain	D
	Sgt A Newland	20	19			
0825	Lt H E Johnson &	20	2	Fokker DVII	W Lesdain	OOC
	2/Lt E S Harvey	20	1			
0825	Lt N S Boulton &	20	2	Fokker DVII	W Lesdain	OOC
	Sgt R S Dodds	20	1			
0825	Lt J Nicholson &	20	2	Fokker DVII	W Lesdain	OOC
	2/Lt B W Wilson	20	1			
0825	Lt J Adam	23	3	Fokker DVII	W Saint-Quentin	D
0830	2/Lt E J Taylor &	23	3	Fokker DVII	W Itancourt	D
	Lt R L M Robb	23	1			
0830	Lt H A White &	23	5	Fokker DVII	Saint-Quentin	OOC
	Lt A P Pherson	23	3			
0830	Lt H A White	23	6	Fokker DVII	Saint-Quentin	DF
0830	Capt E S Coler &	11	14	Fokker DVII	Cambrai	DF
	2/Lt E J Corbett	11	3			
0830	Capt E S Coler &	11	15	Fokker DVII	E Cambrai	D
	2/Lt E J Corbett	11	4			
0835	1/Lt W L Dougan	29	4	Fokker DVII	S Wervicq	D
0835	Capt C H R Lagesse	29	10	Fokker DVII	S Linselles	D
0835	Lt E O Amm	29	4	Fokker DVII	Bois Warneton	D
0840	Capt E C Hoy	29	11	Fokker DVII	N Quesnoy	D
0845	Capt E C Hoy	29	12	Fokker DVII	E Becelaere	D
0845	Lt W E Macpherson &	205	1	Hannover C	N Saint-Quentin	DF
	2/Lt S F Ambler	205	1			
0845	Lt W E Macpherson &	205	2	Fokker DVII	Saint-Quentin	D
	2/Lt S F Ambler	205	2			
0900	Capt G B Gates &	201	13	LVG C	Haynecourt	DF
	Lt J M Mackay	201	1			
0917	Lt C M Wilson	29	8	Fokker Dr I	N Loos	D
0920	Lt E G Davies	29	1	Fokker Dr I	E Lille	D
0920	Lt A F Diamond	29	2	Balloon	W Pérenchies	D
0930	2/Lt K G Nairn &	205	1	Fokker DVII	W Bray	OOC
	2/Lt N R McKinley	205	1			
0940	Capt R A Del Haye	19	6	Pfalz DIII	Fort Carnot	D
0940	Lt D P Laird	19	1	Pfalz DIII	Lille	OOC
0940	Capt C V Gardner &	19	9	Fokker DVII	Lille	OOC
	Lt J D Hardman	19	6			
0940	Lt L H Ray	19	3	Pfalz DIII	Lille	OOC
0945	Capt F I Lord	79	8	Fokker DVII	Messines	OOC
1030	Capt A W Vigers	87	11	Rumpler C	N Cambrai	D
1030	2/Lt T W Sleigh &	98	2	Fokker DVII	Valenciennes	OOC
	2/Lt A H Fuller	98	2			
1030	Lt H A Kullberg	1	19	Fokker DVII	Valenciennes	DF
1035	2/Lt J H Nicholas &	98	1	Pfalz DIII	W Valenciennes	D
	2/Lt A P C Bruce	98	1			

Time	Pilot/Crew	Sqdn	Vic No	E/A	Location	How
1045	Capt O W C Johnsen &	98	5	Fokker DVII	Oisy	OOC
	2/Lt C H Thompson	98	1			
1105	Lt L H Pearson &	202	4	Pfalz DIII	Lisseweghe	OOC
	2/Lt E Darby	202	4			
1105	Capt N Keeble &	202	5	Pfalz DIII	Lisseweghe	D
	Capt E B C Betts	202	5			
1105	Lt H N Witter &	202	1	Fokker DVII	Lisseweghe	OOC
	2/Lt A E Lee	202	1			
1110	Lt C F Pineau	210	3	Fokker DVII	NW Zeebrugge	D
1115	Lt A Buchanan	210	5	Fokker DVII	N Zeebrugge	D
1125	Lt L H Pearson &	202	5	Fokker DVII	Dudzeele	DF
	2/Lt E Darby	202	5			
1125	Capt N Keeble &	202	6	Pfalz DIII	Dudzeele	DF
	Capt E B C Betts	202	6			
1135	Capt T W Nash	204	5	Balloon	S Ostende	DF
1145	Capt R B Bannerman	79	8	two-seater	N Hollebeke	D
1200	Capt R B Bannerman	79	9	two-seater	Hooge	OOC
1215	Capt C H Stokes &	57	3	Fokker DVII	Havrincourt Wood	D
	Lt R D Bovill	57	1			
1215	Lt P W J Timson &	57	1	Fokker DVII	Havrincourt Wood	DF
	2/Lt I S Woodhouse	57	1			
1230	Capt C H Stokes &	57	4	Fokker DVII	Havrincourt Wood	OOC
	Lt R D Bovill	57	2			
1230	Sgt D E Edgley &	57	6	Fokker DVII	Havrincourt Wood	OOC
	Sgt A Lovesay	57	2			
1340	Lt C V A Bucknell &	41	1	DFWC	W Roubaix	OOC
	Lt W Mitchell	41	1			
1350	Major G H Bowman	41	29	two-seater	Hooglede	DF
1400	Capt C F Falkenberg	84	12	Fokker DVII	Montigny	OOC
1410	Major G H Bowman	41	30	Fokker DVII	Houthulst	OOC
1530	Lt T W Martin &	22	6	Fokker DVII	Quesnoy Wood	D
	Sgt M Jones	22	1			
1530	Lt F G Gibbons &	22	12	Fokker DVII	Quesnoy Wood	OOC
	Sgt G Shannon	22	4			
1615	Lt J H McNeaney	79	1	Fokker DVII	NW Tourcoing	OOC
1730	Capt H J Larkin	87	11	Fokker DVII	W Abancourt	D
1735	Capt H A R Biziou	87	4	Fokker DVII	N Cambrai	D
1735	Capt H A R Biziou	87	5	Fokker DVII	N Cambrai	OOC
1735	Capt R C B Brading	201	13	Fokker DVII	SE Cambrai	D
1735	Capt R McLaughlin	201	4	Fokker DVII	SE Cambrai	OOC
1750	Lt K B Conn &	88	11	Fokker DVII	NE Havrincourt	D
	2/Lt B Digby-Worsley	88	13			
1750	Lt K B Conn &	88	12	Fokker DVII	NE Haubourdin	D
	2/Lt B Digby-Worsley	88	14			
1755	Lt H A S Molyneaux	56	4	Fokker DVII	Havrincourt Wood	D
1755	2/Lt V H Hervey	56	1	Fokker DVII	Havrincourt Wood	OOC
1800	Lt G E B Lawson	32	3	Fokker DVII	E Marquion	OOC
1810	Lt F L Hale	32	4	Fokker DVII	Brunemont	DF
1810	1/Lt B Rogers	32	4	Fokker DVII	Sancourt	OOC
1810	Lt A A Callander	32	6	Fokker DVII	Sancourt	OOC
1810	2/Lt W H Maxted	3	5	Fokker DVII	Bourlon Wood	OOC
1810	2/Lt A H Betteridge	3	1	Fokker DVII	Bourlon Wood	OOC

Time	Pilot/Crew	Sqdn	Vic No	E/A	Location	How
1815	Capt D R MacLaren,	46	47	Fokker DVII	Cambrai	DF
	Lt R Viall &	46	1			
	Lt C H Sawyer	46	2			
1815	Capt D R MacLaren	46	48	Fokker DVII	Cambrai	OOC
1840	Lt F J S Britnell	203	6	Fokker DVII	Haynecourt	DF
1845	Major C M Crowe	85	14	Fokker DVII	Souchy-Couchy	D
1845	2/Lt R A H Lloyd	85	1	Fokker DVII	Biache	DF
1850	Lt B S B Thomas &	11	2	Fokker DVII	N Cambrai	D
	Lt W T Barnes	11	5			
1855	Capt C R R Hickey,	204	15	Fokker DVII	Blankenberghe	DF
	2/Lt N Smith,	204	1			
	Lt R M Bennett,	204	4			
	Lt F G Bayley &	204	2			
	2/Lt J R Chisam	204	11			
1900	2/Lt N Smith	204	2	Fokker DVII	Blankenberghe	OOC
1900	2/Lt C L Kelly	204	1	Fokker DVII	Blankenberghe	OOC
1900	Lt R M Bennett	204	5	LVG C	Blankenberghe	D
1900	Lt P F Cormack	204	1	two-seater	Blankenberghe	D
1900	Lt B S B Thomas &	11	3	Fokker DVII	S Cambrai	D
	Lt W T Barnes	11	6			
1905	Lt W B Craig	204	3	Fokker DVII	Blankenberghe	D
1905	Lt W B Craig	204	4	Fokker DVII	Blankenberghe	OOC
1905	Lt W B Craig	204	5	Fokker DVII	Blankenberghe	OOC
1910	Capt C R R Hickey,	204	16	Fokker DVII	Blankenberghe	DF
	2/Lt N Smith,	204	3			
	Lt R M Bennett,	204	5			
	Lt F G Bayley &	204	3			
	2/Lt J R Chisam	204	2			
1910	Lt G E C Howard	204	1	LVG C	Blankenberghe	D
1910	Lt C H Moss &	62	1	Fokker DVII		D
	2/Lt R Lowe	62	4			
1910	Lt L Campbell &	62	7	Fokker DVII		OOC
	2/Lt L Egan	62	2			
1910	2/Lt P S Manley &	62	2	Fokker DVII		OOC
	Sgt G F Hines	62	2			

17 September 1918

Time	Pilot/Crew	Sqdn	Vic No	E/A	Location	How
0955	Lt A T Drinkwater	40	7	Fokker DVII	SE Cambrai	OOC
1010	Capt F I Lord	79	9	Fokker DVII	Comines	OOC
1020	Lt F Alberry	2 AFC	2	Fokker DVII	Lille	OOC
1020	Lt F Alberry	2 AFC	3	Fokker DVII	Lille	OOC
1055	Lt B S B Thomas &	11	4	Fokker DVII	Cambrai-Wasnes	D
	Lt W T Barnes	11	6			
1100	Lt L L K Straw &	25	2	Fokker DVII	E Bourlon Wood	OOC
	Lt G M Lawson	25	1			
1115	Lt R G Dobson &	25	1	Fokker DVII	Le Catelet	OOC
	2/Lt A G Grant	25	1			
1115	Capt W S Philcox	92	1	Albatros C	Le Catelet	OOC
1200	Capt D R MacLaren,	46	49	Fokker DVII	Cambrai	OOC
	2/Lt R Gilpin-Brown,	46	1			
	Lt P M Tudhope,	46	5			
	Lt C H Sawyer,	46	3			
	Capt C W Odell &	46	5			
	2/Lt L Skerrington	46	2			

Time	Pilot/Crew	Sqdn	Vic No	E/A	Location	How
1200	Capt D R MacLaren,	46	50	Fokker DVII	Cambrai	OOC
	2/Lt R Gilpin-Brown,	46	2			
	Lt P M Tudhope,	46	6			
	Lt C H Sawyer	46	4			
	Capt C W Odell &	46	6			
	2/Lt Skerrington	46	3			
1230	Capt O M Baldwin	73	15	Rumpler C	E Cambrai	D
1300	1/Lt F E Kindley &	148 US	8	Fokker DVII	Épinoy	D
	1/Lt J O Creech	148 US	5			
1305	1/Lt L T Wyly	148 US	4	Fokker DVII	NW Cambrai	OOC
1410	Capt S B Horn	85	13	two-seater	SE Graincourt	D
1825	Major K L Caldwell	74	21	Fokker DVII	N Courtrai	D
1825	Lt F J Hunt	74	3	Fokker DVII	N Courtrai	DF
1825	Lt A M Phillips &	217	3	Seaplane	Zeebrugge	D
	Lt N S Dougall	217	2			
1830	Lt C W M Thompson &	22	6	Fokker DVII	SW Douai	OOC
	Lt G McCormack	22	3			
1830	Lt C W M Thompson &	22	7	Fokker DVII	Brebières	OOC
	Lt G McCormack	22	4			
1830	Lt W S Jenkins	210	7	Fokker DVII	S Ostende	DF
1830	Lt W S Jenkins	210	8	Fokker DVII	S Ostende	DF
1840	Major K L Caldwell	74	22	Fokker DVII	NW Courtrai	OOC
1845	1/Lt W T Clements &	17 US	1	Fokker DVII	Arleux	D
	2/Lt H C Knotts	17 US	3			
2050	Lt E P Mackay	151	2	AEG G	SE Estrées-en-Chausée	D
2240	Capt D V Armstrong	151	5	Fried G	Fletre	DF
2241	Major C J Q Brand	151	10	Fried G	E Bapaume	D
2241	2/Lt P S Manley &	62	3	Fokker DVII		OOC
	Sgt G F Hines	62	3			
	Lt F Jeffreys &	88	1	Fokker DVII	Lille	DF
	Lt F W Addison	88	1			
	Lt F Jeffreys &	88	2	Fokker DVII	Lommelet	D
	Lt F W Addison	88	2			
	Lt R E Britton &	13	1	two-seater		D
	2/Lt B Hickman	13	1			

18 September 1918

Time	Pilot/Crew	Sqdn	Vic No	E/A	Location	How
1050	Lt D S Ingalls,	213	4	Balloon	La Barrière	DF
	Lt H C Smith &	213	3			
	Lt G S Hodson	213	5			
1100	2/Lt H C Burdick	17 US	1	LVG C	Rumilly	DF
1215	Capt J W Pearson	23	7	Fokker DVII	Lihaucourt	DF
1215	Capt J W Pearson	23	8	Fokker DVII	Lihaucourt	OOC
1420	Lt N D Willis	40	2	Fokker DVII	Cambrai	OOC
1445	Capt H A Whistler	80	19	Fokker DVII	E Pontruet	D
1445	Lt E O C Parsons	80	1	Fokker DVII	E Pontruet	D
1445	Lt H J Welch	80	2	Fokker DVII	E Pontruet	D
1730	Capt D Lloyd-Evans MC	64	7	Fokker DVII	E Havrincourt	D
1730	Capt D Lloyd-Evans MC	64	8	Fokker DVII	E Havrincourt	OOC

19 September 1918

Time	Pilot/Crew	Sqdn	Vic No	E/A	Location	How
0735	Capt R B Bannerman	79	10	Fokker DVII	E Houthulst Forest	D
1040	Lt G Carr-Harris	73	2	Fokker DVII	Magny-la-Fosse	D

Time	Pilot/Crew	Sqdn	Vic No	E/A	Location	How
1725	Lt F G Pym &	57	1	Fokker DVII	Havrincourt Wood	OOC
	Sgt W G E Mason	57	1			
1725	Capt W E Green &	57	9	Fokker DVII	Havrincourt Wood	OOC
	Lt A M Barron	57	2			
1810	Major R S Maxwell MC	54	8	DFW	E Havrincourt Wood	OOC

20 September 1918

Time	Pilot/Crew	Sqdn	Vic No	E/A	Location	How
0630	Capt H D Barton	24	17	LVG C	Wassigny	D
0655	Capt F I Lord	79	10	Hannover C	N Habourdin	D
0750	Lt K B Conn &	88	13	Fokker DVII	Quesnoy	OOC
	2/Lt B Digby-Worsley	88	15			
0750	Lt G R Poole &	88	5	Fokker DVII	SE Capinghem	D
	Sgt C Hill	88	5			
0755	Capt E C Johnston,	88	15	Fokker DVII	SE Quesnoy	D
	2/Lt W I N Grant,	88	5			
	Lt K B Conn,	88	14			
	2/Lt B Digby-Worsley,	88	16			
	Lt G R Poole &	88	6			
	Sgt C Hill	88	6			
0920	Capt J F Chisholm &	218	2	Fokker DVII	Bruges	OOC
	Sgt R J Williams	218	2			
0930	Lt E H Attwood &	218	1	Fokker DVII	W Bruges	OOC
	2/Lt A E Smith	218	1			
0943	Lt A M Anderson &	218	1	Fokker DVII	Stahlhille	OOC
	Sgt J Harris	218	3			
1000	Lt F G Harlock &	20	3	Fokker DVII	Mesnil	D
	2/Lt A S Draisey	20	3			
1000	Lt W J B Nel	84	6	Fokker DVII	E Mont d'Origny	D
1015	Capt N E Chandler	65	1	Fokker DVII	SW Bruges	D
1015	Lt M A Newnham	65	8	Fokker DVII	Jabberke	D
1015	Lt F G Harlock &	20	4	Fokker DVII	Mesnil	DF
	2/Lt A S Draisey	20	4			
1015	Lt N S Boulton &	20	3	Fokker DVII	NE Saint-Quentin	D
	Sgt E G Mitchell	20	1			
1015	Capt C F Falkenberg	84	13	Fokker DVII	Mont d'Origny	OOC
1020	2/Lt D F Tysoe	204	1	Fokker DVII	Beerst	D
1020	Lt M McCall &	20	2	Fokker DVII	E Longchamps	D
	2/Lt C G Boothroyd	20	4			
1020	Lt S Walters &	20	2	Fokker DVII	Saint-Quentin	OOC
	Lt T Kirkpatrick	20	1			
1025	Lt G E C Howard	204	2	Fokker DVII	NE Dixmuide	OOC
1025	Lt W B Craig	204	6	Fokker DVII	NE Dixmuide	OOC
1025	2/Lt H G Clappison	204	1	Fokker DVII	NE Dixmuide	DF
1025	Lt F R Brown	204	1	Fokker DVII	NE Dixmuide	D
1025	Lt M McCall &	20	3	Fokker DVII	N Longchamps	OOC
	2/Lt C G Boothroyd	20	5			
1025	Lt S Walters &	20	3	Fokker DVII	Saint-Quentin	D
	Lt T Kirkpatrick	20	2			
1030	Capt T P Middleton &	20	27	Fokker DVII	Rouvroy	D
	Lt A Mills	20	14			
1030	Capt T P Middleton &	20	28	Fokker DVII	Rouvroy	D
	Lt A Mills	20	15			
1030	Capt C F Falkenberg	84	14	Fokker DVII	Mont d'Origny	D
1030	Lt W B Craig	204	7	Fokker DVII	SW Ostende	OOC

Time	Pilot/Crew	Sqdn	Vic No	E/A	Location	How
1045	Lt D S Ingalls	213	5	Fokker DVII	Vlisseghem	D
1245	Lt H A White &	23	7	Fokker DVII	N Saint-Quentin	DF
	Lt C Thomas	23	1			
1455	1/Lt E W Springs	148 US	13	Fokker DVII	Canal-du-Nord-Aubigny	D
1530	Lt J W Warner	85	6	Fokker DVII	E Bourlon Wood	D
1530	Lt D C Mangan	87	3	Fokker DVII	Noyelles	D
1530	Lt L N Hollinghurst	87	7	Fokker DVII	Noyelles	D
1530	Capt H A R Biziou	87	6	Fokker DVII	Noyelles	D
1530	1/Lt H C Starkey	148 US	2	Hannover C	N Cambrai-Arras Road	OOC
1530	Lt F J S Britnell	203	7	Fokker DVII	Haynecourt	OOC
1530	Capt J D Breakey	203	6	Fokker DVII	Haynecourt	OOC
1530	2/Lt W H Coghill	203	1	Fokker DVII	Haynecourt	D
1530	2/Lt M G Cruise	203	1	Fokker DVII	Haynecourt	DF
1530	Lt H W Skinner	203	2	Fokker DVII	Haynecourt	D
1645	Capt W R May &	209	12	Fokker DVII	Sauchy-Lestrée	D
	Lt G Knight	209	1			
2135	Capt F C Broome	151	3	AEG C	Tincourt	D

21 September 1918

Time	Pilot/Crew	Sqdn	Vic No	E/A	Location	How
1015	Capt R B Bannerman	79	11	two-seater	SW Hollebeke	D
1035	Lt H M S Parsons	79	1	two-seater	E Oostaverne	D
1145	Patrol	108	–	Fokker DVII	Zarren	OOC
1150	Lt F W Gillet	79	7	Fokker DVII	Habourdin-Wavrin	D
1155	Capt F McQuistan	19	6	Fokker DVII	E Thorout	D
1745	Lt D C Rees	84	2	Fokker DVII	NNE Saint-Quentin	D
1745	2/Lt J A Jackson	84	1	Fokker DVII	NE Saint-Quentin	D
1810	Capt W E Shields	41	15	Fokker DVII	Don	D
1810	Capt W E Shields	41	16	Fokker DVII	Don	OOC
1835	Capt C H Stokes &	57	5	Fokker DVII	Fontaine-Notre Dame	OOC
	Lt R D Bovill	57	3			
1835	Capt W R May	209	13	Fokker DVII	Écoust-Saint-Quentin	D
1835	Lt G Knight	209	2	Fokker DVII	Écoust-Saint-Quentin	OOC
1840	Patrol	57	–	Fokker DVII	Bourlon Wood	DF
1840	Lt F J Hunt	74	4	Fokker DVII	Lille	D
1845	Capt C B Glynn	74	5	Fokker DVII	Lille	D
1845	Major K L Caldwell	74	23	Fokker DVII	Lille	OOC
1845	Capt B Roxburgh-Smith	74	15	Fokker DVII	Lille	OOC
2126	Major C J Q Brand	151	12	Fried G	Gouzeaucourt	POW
2135	Major C J Q Brand &	151	13	AEG G	S Gouzeaucourt	D
	Lt J H Summers	151	2			
2135	Lt A A Mitchell	151	2	Gotha G	N Péronne	D

22 September 1918

Time	Pilot/Crew	Sqdn	Vic No	E/A	Location	How
0820	2/Lt T H Barkell	4 AFC	3	Fokker DVII	E Armentières	OOC
0820	2/Lt T H Barkell	4 AFC	4	Fokker DVII	Armentières	OOC
0840	Capt H A R Biziou	87	7	Fokker DVII	Bourlon Wood	D
0840	Capt H A R Biziou	87	8	Fokker DVII	Bourlon Wood	D
0845	1/Lt G A Vaughn	17 US	8	Fokker DVII	Fontaine-Notre Dame	D
0845	1/Lt G D Wicks	17 US	2	Fokker DVII	W Rumilly	D

Time	Pilot/Crew	Sqdn	Vic No	E/A	Location	How
0845	1/Lt G A Vaughn	17 US	9	Fokker DVII	W Cambrai	DF
0910	2/Lt H C Knotts	17 US	4	Fokker DVII	SW Cambrai	D
0910	Capt A W Vigers &	87	12	Rumpler C	NE Bapaume	OOC
	Lt R M MacDonald	87	2			
0910	Lt E C Worthington	87	5	Rumpler C	NE Bapaume	OOC
1030	Capt C W Cudemore	64	9	Fokker DVII	S Cambrai	OOC
1040	Capt H D Barton	24	18	Fokker DVII	E Bourlon Wood	D
1325	2/Lt H J Evans &	12	1	Fokker DVII		D
	Lt C A Stubbings	12	1			
	Capt E C Johnston &	88	16	LVG C		OOC
	Lt W I N Grant	88	5			

23 September 1918

Time	Pilot/Crew	Sqdn	Vic No	E/A	Location	How
0835	Lt G S Bourner &	13	1	two-seater	Sains-lès-Marquion	DF
	Lt F A D Vaughn	13	1			
1425	Lt W E Grey,	213	6	Fokker DVII	E Dixmuide	OOC
	Lt M N Hancocks,	213	2			
	Lt A R Talbert &	213	2			
	Lt C P Sparkes	213	3			
1715	2/Lt G C Upson &	42	1	Fokker DVII	Fleurbaix	D
	2/Lt A N Thomson	42	1			
1725	Capt G B Gates	201	14	LVG C	Sailly	D
1745	Capt A W Vigers	87	13	Fokker DVII	NE Cambrai	OOC
1745	Lt C K Oliver	87	4	Fokker DVII	NE Cambrai	OOC
1748	Lt R M McDonald	87	3	Fokker DVII	NE Cambrai	D
1810	Lt L N Hollinghurst	87	8	Fokker DVII	Bourlon Wood	D
1810	Lt R M McDonald	87	4	Fokker DVII	Bourlon Wood	OOC
1810	Capt A W Vigers	87	4	Fokker DVII	Bourlon Wood	OOC
1815	Lt N S Boulton &	20	4	Fokker DVII	NE Saint-Quentin	D
	2/Lt H L Edwards	20	12			
1818	Lt N S Boulton &	20	5	Fokker DVII	NE Saint-Quentin	DF
	2/Lt H L Edwards	20	l3			
1820	Lt N S Boulton &	20	6	Fokker DVII	NE Saint-Quentin	D
	2/Lt H L Edwards	20	14			
1820	Lt A E Kiernander &	20	1	Fokker DVII	NE Saint-Quentin	D
	Lt C G Boothroyd	20	5			
1820	Lt E A Britton &	20	1	Fokker DVII	W Rouvroy	D
	Sgt R S Dodds	20	2			
1820	Lt E A Britton &	20	2	Fokker DVII	W Rouvroy	OOC
	Sgt R S Dodds	20	3			

24 September 1918

Time	Pilot/Crew	Sqdn	Vic No	E/A	Location	How
0625	Capt E J K McCloughry	4 AFC	20	DFW C	E Lille	D
0635	Capt E J K McCloughry	4 AFC	21	Fokker DVII	Lille	D
0645	Lt G Jones	4 AFC	4	two-seater	Lens	D
0700	Capt G J Strange	40	7	Fokker DVII	Cambrai	D
0700	Patrol	40	–	Fokker DVII	Cambrai	OOC
0700	Patrol	40	–	Fokker DVII	Cambrai	OOC
0705	Major R Collishaw	203	57	Fokker DVII	Épinoy	D
0710	2/Lt G S Smith	40	1	Fokker DVII	Cambrai	DF
0728	1/Lt F E Kindley	148 US	9	Fokker DVII	W Cambrai	D
0735	1/Lt H R Clay	148 US	8	Fokker DVII	Bourlon-Épinoy	DF

Time	Pilot/Crew	Sqdn	Vic No	E/A	Location	How
0738	1/Lt E H Zistell	148 US	3	Fokker DVII	Bourlon Wood	D
0740	1/Lt L T Wyly	148 US	4	Fokker DVII	Bourlon Wood	D
0740	1/Lt E W Springs	148 US	14	Fokker DVII	NE Bourlon	D
0740	1/Lt W B Knox	148 US	2	Fokker DVII	W Cambrai	D
0745	1/Lt E H Zistell	148 US	4	Fokker DVII	N Bourlon Wood	OOC
0810	Lt A Newman &	57	3	Fokker DVII		D
	2/Lt C Wilkinson	57	1			
0810	Lt F G Pym &	57	2	Fokker DVII		DF
	Sgt W G E Mason	57	2			
0810	2/Lt F de N Hyde &	57	1	Fokker DVII		OOC
	2/Lt L H Eyres	57	1			
0815	Capt H P Chubb	56	2	Fokker DVII	Sailly	D
0830	Lt H A S Molyneaux	56	5	Fokker DVII	Haynecourt	D
0900	Lt W Sidebottom &	203	7	Hannover C	SE Lens	D
	2/Lt W H Coghill	203	2			
0900	Sgt E Campbell &	11	1	Fokker DVII	SE Havrincourt	D
	Sgt H C Taylor	11	1			
0910	Lt W J B Nel	84	7	Fokker DVII	Estrées-Gouy	D
0915	Capt A W F B Proctor	84	46	Balloon	Gouy	DF
0915	2/Lt S W Highwood	84	9	Balloon	Gouy	DF
0915	2/Lt D C Ress	84	3	Balloon	Gouy	DF
1010	Capt A Hepburn &	88	12	Fokker DVII	Habourdin	D
	2/Lt H G Eldon	88	4			
1010	Capt C F Findley &	88	11	Fokker DVII	Habourdin	DF
	2/Lt A B Radford	88	1			
1030	Capt C W Cudemore	64	9	Fokker DVII	S Cambrai	OOC
1030	Capt R L Manuel &	2 AFC	12	Albatros C	La Bassée-Béthune	OOC
	Lt F R Smith	2 AFC	9			
1030	Lt G R Hicks	74	6	SS DIV	E Armentières	OOC
1030	Major K L Caldwell	74	24	SS DIV	E Armentières	OOC
1040	2/Lt H C Knotts	17 US	5	Fokker DVII	Loupez Mill	D
1040	2/Lt H Burdick	17 US	2	Fokker DVII	NW Havrincourt	D
1040	2/Lt H C Knotts	17 US	6	Fokker DVII	NW Havrincourt	D
1040	1/Lt W T Clements	17 US	2	Fokker DVII	NW Loupez Mill	D
1040	1/Lt J F Campbell	17 US	3	Fokker DVII	NW Havrincourt	OOC
1045	2/Lt H C Knotts	17 US	7	Fokker DVII	NW Havrincourt	DF
1045	Lt G R Hicks &	74	7	Rumpler C	Capingham	D
	Capt B Roxburgh-Smith	74	16			
1050	2Lt A J Schneider	17 US	1	Fokker DVII	Havrincourt	OOC
1350	2/Lt S W Highwood	84	10	Balloon	Cambrai	DF
1350	2/Lt S W Highwood	84	11	Balloon	Cambrai	DF
1350	2/Lt F R Christiani	84	3	Balloon	Cambrai	DF
1350	Capt C F Falkenberg	84	15	Balloon	Cambrai	DF
1440	Capt E Swale	210	13	Fokker DVII	St Pierre Capelle	D
1440	Lt W S Jenkins	210	9	Fokker DVII	Schooze-Keyem	D
1440	Lt G A Welsh	210	2	Fokker DVII	NE Nieuport	OOC
1440	Lt K R Unger	210	7	Fokker DVII	S St Pierre Capelle	OOC
1440	Lt P Boulton	210	3	Fokker DVII	S St Pierre Capelle	OOC
1440	Lt C F Pineau	210	4	Fokker DVII	N St Pierre Capelle	D
1445	Lt C F Pineau	210	5	Fokker DVII	SE Nieuport	OOC
1445	Capt C P Brown	213	9	Fokker DVII	Couckelaere	D
1445	Lt G S Hodson	213	6	Fokker DVII	SW Thorout	OOC
1450	Capt C P Brown	213	10	Fokker DVII	SW Thorout	D
1455	Lt G S Hodson	213	7	Fokker DVII	W Mitswaere	D

Time	Pilot/Crew	Sqdn	Vic No	E/A	Location	How
1600	Lt T C Traill &	20	5	Fokker DVII	W Busigny	OOC
	Lt R Gordon-Bennett	20	4			
1600	Capt G H Hooper &	20	4	Fokker DVII	E Saint-Quentin	D
	Lt H L Edwards	20	15			
1610	Lt G E Randall &	20	6	Fokker DVII	S Cléry	D
	Lt J Hackett	20	1			
1610	Lt G E Randall &	20	7	Fokker DVII	S Cléry	OOC
	Lt J Hackett	20	2			
1700	Lt L C Rowney &	22	1	Fokker DVII	Masnières-Crevecoeur	D
	Lt W U Tyrrell	22	4			
1700	Lt L C Rowney &	22	2	Fokker DVII	Masnières-Crevecoeur	OOC
	Lt W U Tyrrell	22	5			
1700	Capt S F H Thompson &	22	29	Fokker DVII	Cambrai	OOC
	Sgt R M Fletcher	22	26			
1700	Lt C W M Thompson &	22	8	Fokker DVII	Cambrai	OOC
	Lt G McCormack	22	8			
1705	Capt A A Callander	32	7	Fokker DVII	Cambrai	D
1705	Capt A A Callander	32	8	Fokker DVII	Cambrai	OOC
1705	Lt C Wilderspin	32	1	Fokker DVII	Cambrai	OOC
1705	Lt R W Farquhar	32	1	Fokker DVII	N Cambrai	OOC
1710	Lt H R Carson	32	2	Fokker DVII	N Cambrai	OOC
1710	Lt G E B Lawson	32	4	Fokker DVII	N Cambrai	OOC
1715	2/Lt R Champion &	18	2	Fokker DVII	Marquion	DF
	Sgt R H Favell	18	1			
1715	2/Lt R Champion &	18	3	Fokker DVII	Marquion	DF
	Sgt R H Favell	18	2			
1720	Capt R King	4 AFC	18	two-seater	E Ploegsteert	D
1730	Lt D S Ingalls &	213	6	Rumpler C	St Pierre Capelle	DF
	Lt G S Hodson	213	8			
1750	Capt W E Shields	41	17	Fokker DVII	W Comines	D
1800	2/Lt H C Telfer	41	1	Fokker DVII	NW Comines	OOC
1800	Capt H P Chubb	56	3	Fokker DVII	E Noyelles	OOC
1810	Capt D H M Carberry &	59	5	Halb C	Lateau Wood	D
	Lt J B V Clements					
1815	Lt L Franks	2 AFC	1	Fokker DVII	E Sequedin	D
1815	Lt F C M Mills	2 AFC	4	Fokker DVII	Habourdin	OOC
1820	Lt F R Smith	2 AFC	10	Fokker DVII	S Capinghem	D
1820	Lt F L Roberts	2 AFC	1	Fokker DVII	Habourdin	OOC
1820	Capt E L Simonson	2 AFC	1	Fokker DVII	Habourdin	OOC
1820	Capt E L Simonson	2 AFC	2	Pfalz DXII	S Habourdin	D
1820	Lt J J Wellwood	2 AFC	5	Pfalz DXII	NW Habourdin	DF
1830	Lt H J Welch	80	3	Fokker DVII	Saint-Quentin	OOC
1835	Capt A T Cole	2 AFC	9	Pfalz DIII	Habourdin-Pérenchies	D
1845	Lt W B Craig	204	8	Fokker DVII	Dixmuide	DF
1850	Lt C P Allen	204	4	Fokker DVII	Pervyse	OOC
1850	Lt P F Cormack	204	2	Fokker DVII	NE Dixmuide	OOC
1850	Capt T W Nash	204	6	Fokker DVII	Pervyse	D
1850	Capt T W Nash	204	7	Fokker DVII	Pervyse	OOC
	2/Lt P S Manley &	62	4	Fokker DVII	E Cambrai	DF
	Sgt G F Hines	62	4			
	2/Lt F S Manley &	62	5	Fokker DVII	E Cambrai	DF
	Sgt G F Hines	62	5			
	Lt L W Hudson &	62	2	Fokker DVII	E Cambrai	OOC
	2/Lt A W Palmer	62	1			
	Capt W E Staton &	62	25	Fokker DVII	E Cambrai	OOC
	2/Lt L E Mitchell	62	7			

Time	Pilot/Crew	Sqdn	Vic No	E/A	Location	How
	25 September 1918					
1740	Capt C W Cudemore,	64	10	Hannover C	Bourlon	OOC
	2/Lt T Bullough,	64	1			
	Lt A H S Youll,	64	1			
	Lt A G Donald,	64	4			
	Lt G W Graham &	64	1			
	2/Lt R B Francis	64	1			
1745	Lt W E Gray	213	5	Fokker DVII	W Thorout	OOC
1750	Capt W E G Mann	208	12	Halb C	Gouy	DF
1750	Lt Bayly	208	1	Halb C	Gouy	OOC
1755	Lt J W Warner	85	7	Fokker DVII	Urvillers	D
1810	Lt F G Gibbons &	22	13	Fokker DVII	Bourlon Wood-Cambrai	D
	2/Lt J A Oliver	22	2			
1810	Lt C W M Thompson &	22	9	Fokker DVII	Bourlon Wood-Cambrai	OOC
	Lt L R James	22	1			
1815	Capt J R Webb &	27	1	Fokker DVII	Bohain	OOC
	2/Lt W A Hall	27	1			
1815	Capt G H Hooper &	20	5	Fokker DVII	NE Saint-Quentin	D
	Lt H L Edwards	20	16			
1815	Capt G H Hooper &	20	6	Fokker DVII	NE Saint-Quentin	DF
	Lt H L Edwards	20	17			
1820	Lt T C Traill &	20	6	Fokker DVII	NE Saint-Quentin	DF
	Lt R Gordon-Bennett	20	5			
1820	Lt F G Harlock &	20	5	Fokker DVII	Magny	D
	Lt A S Draisey	20	5			
1820	Capt G H Hooper &	20	7	Fokker DVII	E Bellenglise	D
	Lt H L Edwards	20	18			
1821	Lt F G Harlock &	20	6	Fokker DVII	Lehaucourt	D
	Lt A S Draisey	20	6			
1825	2/Lt J Locksedge &	25	1	Fokker DVII	Ponchaux	OOC
	Sgt H W J Roach	25	2			
1825	2/Lt C M Allan &	25	1	Fokker DVII	Ponchaux	D
	Sgt W E Smith	25	2			
1830	Lt M McCall &	20	4	Fokker DVII	Estrées	DF
	Lt C G Boothroyd	20	6			
1830	S/Lt S L Walters	20	3	Fokker DVII	Saint-Quentin	OOC
	Lt T Kirkpatrick	20	3			
1830	Major G H Bowman	41	30	Rumpler C	NE Ypres	DF
1835	Lt C J Sims	213	4	Fokker DVII	SW Ostende	D
1835	Lt C J Sims	213	5	Fokker DVII	SW Ostende	D
2300	Lt T R Bloomfield	151	1	AEG G	Montenescourt	D
	26 September 1918					
1045	2/Lt G H Clappison	204	2	Fokker DVII	Blankenberghe	OOC
1045	2/Lt F R Brown	204	2	Fokker DVII	Blankenberghe	OOC
1045	Lt N Smith	204	4	Fokker DVII	NE Ostende	D
1050	Lt B E Barnum	204	4	Fokker DVII	Blankenberghe	OOC
1050	Capt C R R Hickey	204	20	Fokker DVII	Blankenberghe	D
1050	2/Lt S E Mathey	204	1	Fokker DVII	Blankenberghe	OOC
1120	Major C J W Darwin	87	5	LVG C	Lateau Wood	D
1125	2/Lt R C Mitten	65	1	Rumpler C	Clemkerke	OOC
1130	2/Lt W S Rycroft &	48	1	Fokker DVII	Menin	D
	2/Lt H L Ward	48	1			
1130	Capt B Roxburgh-Smith	74	17	Fokker DVII	SE Warneton	DF

Time	Pilot/Crew	Sqdn	Vic No	E/A	Location	How
1300	Lt C W H Thompson	22	10	Fokker DVII	Arras-Cambrai Road	D
	& Lt W U Tyrrell	22	4			
1300	Lt C W H Thompson	22	11	Fokker DVII	Arras-Cambrai Road	D
	& Lt W U Tyrrell	22	5			
1300	Capt J D Breakey	203	7	Fokker DVII	SW Lieu St Amand	DF
1305	Major R Collishaw	203	58	Fokker DVII	Lieu St Amand	D
1315	2/Lt W H Coghill	203	3	Fokker DVII	E Combles	D
1315	Lt F S J Britnell	203	8	Fokker DVII	E Combles	DF
1325	1/Lt F E Kindley	148 US	10	Fokker DVII	E Bourlon Wood	D
1325	1/Lt J O Creech	148 US	6	Fokker DVII	E Bourlon Wood	D
1325	1/Lt O A Ralston	148 US	4	Fokker DVII	E Bourlon Wood	D
1330	1/Lt L T Wyly	148 US	4	Fokker DVII	Épinoy	OOC
1335	Major R Collishaw	203	59	Fokker DVII	E Lieu St Amand	D
1510	Lt G R Hicks &	74	7	DFWC	SE Armentières	D
	Capt B Roxburgh-Smith	74	18			
1745	Lt G W Hales	80	1	Fokker DVII	Lehaucourt	OOC
1745	Lt R E Thompson	80	1	Fokker DVII	Lehaucourt	OOC
1815	Capt D R MacLaren	46	51	Fokker DVII	Havrincourt	D
1818	Capt A Newman &	57	4	Fokker DVII	SE Cambrai	DF
	Lt E G Pernet	57	1			
1825	Lt M C Howell	208	4	Fokker DVII	N Saint-Quentin*	OOC
1840	Capt W E G Mann	208	13	Fokker DVII	SE Saint-Quentin	OOC

27 September 1918

Time	Pilot/Crew	Sqdn	Vic No	E/A	Location	How
0715	Lt L H Ray	19	4	Fokker DrI	Haynecourt	D
0715	Lt L H Ray	19	5	Fokker DrI	Haynecourt	OOC
0720	Lt L H Ray	19	6	Fokker DrI	Haynecourt	OOC
0720	Lt L H Ray	19	7	Balloon	Haynecourt	DF
0720	Capt S F H Thompson &	22	30	Halb C	N Noyelles	D
	2/Lt C J Tolman	22	10			
0725	Capt R A Del Haye &	19	7	Pfalz DIII	Haynecourt	D
	Lt C M Moore	19	1			
0725	Lt G R Riley	3	10	Balloon		DF
0725	Lt G R Riley	3	11	Balloon		DF
0730	Lt F G Gibbons &	22	14	Fokker DVII	Sensée Canal-Cambrai	OOC
	Sgt G Shannon	22	5			
0730	Lt C W M Thompson &	22	12	Fokker DVII	Oisy-le-Verger	D
	Lt L R James	22	2			
	Lt L C Rowney &	22	3			
	Lt W U Tyrrell	22	6			
0730	Lt J R Drummond &	22	1	Fokker DVII	Oisy-le-Verger	OOC
	2/Lt C H Wilcox	22	1			
0735	Lt J A Aldridge	19	6	Fokker DVII	NW Cambrai	OOC
0755	Lt G F Anderson &	88	4	Fokker DVII	Lambersart	OOC
	2/Lt T S Chiltern	88	5			
0800	Capt H P Chubb	56	4	Fokker DVII	Cambrai	D
0800	Lt C B Stenning	56	3	Fokker DVII	Cambrai	D
0800	Lt J A Pouchot	56	1	Fokker DVII	Cambrai	D
0800	Lt W E Clarkson	56	1	Fokker DVII	Cambrai	OOC
0800	Lt I W Awde	56	1	Fokker DVII	Cambrai	OOC
0805	2/Lt W H Maxted	3	2	LVG C		DF
0810	2/Lt W H Maxted	3	3	LVG C		D
0820	Lt G R Riley &	3	12	Balloon		DF
	2/Lt W H Maxted	3	4			

Time	Pilot/Crew	Sqdn	Vic No	E/A	Location	How
0845	Lt G W Wareing	29	7	Balloon	Moorslede	D
0850	Capt A W B Proctor	84	47	Balloon	Crevecoeur	DF
0855	Lt F Woolley	79		Albatros C	Armentières	D
0915	Lt B H Mooney	1	3	Fokker DVII	Bertry	DF
0915	Lt C W Anning	1	2	Fokker DVII	Bévillers	OOC
0920	1/Lt F E Kindley	148 US	11	Halb C	Marcoing	D
0925	Capt C F King &	43	20	Fokker DVII	Cambrai	OOC
	Lt C C Banks	43	10			
0930	Lt R S Johnston	43	1	Fokker DVII	SE Cambrai	OOC
0930	2/Lt G S Smith	40	2	Fokker DVII	Oisy-le-Verger	OOC
0940	Capt G E B Lawson	32	5	Fokker DVII	Émerchicourt	DF
0940	Capt G E B Lawson	32	6	Fokker DVII	Émerchicourt	D
0940	Lt B Rogers	32	5	Fokker DVII	Émerchicourt	D
0940	Lt R E L McBean	32	3	Fokker DVII	Émerchicourt	OOC
0940	Lt M A Tancock	32	2	Fokker DVII	Émerchicourt	OOC
0940	Lt C F Cawley	32	1	Fokker DVII	Émerchicourt	OOC
0945	Lt C M Allan &	27	2	Fokker DVII	Émerchicourt	DF
	2/Lt C E Robinson	27	1			
0955	1/Lt E W Springs &	148 US	16	Halb C	Fontaine-Notre Dame	D
	1/Lt H R Clay	148 US	8			
1030	Lt F G Harlock &	20	7	Fokker DVII	NE Marcy	D
	Lt A S Draisey	20	7			
1030	Lt A T Iaccaci &	20	16	Fokker DVII	Fontaine-Notre Dame	D
	Sgt A Newland	20	20			
1030	Lt A T Iaccaci &	20	17	Fokker DVII	N Bernot	OOC
	Sgt A Newland	20	21			
1030	Lt M McCall &	20	5	Fokker DVII	W Bernot	D
	Lt C G Boothroyd	20	7			
1120	Lt L N Hollinghurst	87	9	Fokker DVII	Rumilly	OOC
1130	Capt G B Gates	201	15	Balloon		DF
1150	Capt M A Newnham	65	9	Fokker DVII	Ghistelles	D
1150	Lt G Richardson	65		Fokker DVII	Ghistelles	
1150	Lt F Edsted	65	3	Fokker DVII	Ghistelles	OOC
1150	Lt J Reid	65		Fokker DVII	Ghistelles	OOC
1240	Capt F McQuistan	19	7	Pfalz DIII	E Aubigny	OOC
1250	Capt R A Del Haye	19	8	Pfalz DIII	Aubigny	OOC
1410	Capt O M Baldwin	73	16	LVG C	N Graincourt	DF
1410	Capt E C Johnston &	88	17	Fokker DVII	Abancourt	OOC
	2/Lt H R Goss	8	3			
1720	Lt F L Hale	32	5	Fokker DVII	Cambrai	D
1720	Lt F L Hale	32	6	Fokker DVII	Cambrai	OOC
1720	Lt F L Hale	32	7	Fokker DVII	Cambrai	OOC
1735	1/Lt J F Campbell	17 US	4	Fokker DVII		OOC
1745	Lt K R Unger	210	8	Halb C	SE Nieuport	D
1800	Patrol	11	–	Fokker DVII	SE Cambrai	D
1800	Capt V S Bennett	54	2	Fokker DVII	SE Bourlon Wood	D
1800	2/Lt F de N Hyde &	18	2	Fokker DVII	Cambrai	OOC
	2/Lt L H Eyres	18	2			
1800	Lt F L Harding &	57	1	Fokker DVII	Cambrai	OOC
	2/Lt I Woodhouse	57	1			
	Lt F O Thornton &	57	4			
	2/Lt F C Craig	57	5			
1815	Capt E C Hoy	29	13	Fokker DVII	Passchendaele	D

Time	Pilot/Crew	Sqdn	Vic No	E/A	Location	How
1940	Lt C F Lane &	18	1	Fokker DVII	Wasnes-au-Bac	OOC
	2/Lt C Thompson	18	1			
1940	Lt R E Britton &	13	2	Fokker DVII		OOC
	2/Lt B Hickman	13	2			

28 September 1918

Time	Pilot/Crew	Sqdn	Vic No	E/A	Location	How
0700	Capt D H M Carberry &	59	6	Halb C	La Vacquerie valley	D
	Lt Clements	59	3			
0825	Capt A Beck	60	5	LVG C	Cambrai	D
0830	Lt W Sidebottom	203	8	Fokker DVII	Hem-Lenglet	OOC
1145	Lt O A P Heron	70	4	Fokker DVII	NE Passchendaele	D
1150	Capt W M Carlaw	70	7	LVG C	NE Gheluwe	D
1230	Capt A J B Tonks	204	13	Fokker DVII	Werckem	D
1230	Capt A J B Tonks	204	14	Fokker DVII	Werckem	OOC
1230	Capt C R R Hickey	204	22	Fokker DVII	NW Werckem	D
1235	Capt R B Bannerman	79	12	Fokker DVII	SW Comines	D
1255	Lt F W Gillett	79	9	Albatros C	Bousbecque	D
1315	Lt M G Burger	54	4	Fokker DVII	NW Raillencourt	D
1315	Capt F I Lord	79	11	Pfalz DIII	Werckem	D
1445	Capt F Cunninghame	48	2	Fokker DVII	SE Roulers	D
	& Lt R A Brunton	48	2			
1610	Lt G R Riley	3	12	Fokker DVII		OOC
1625	2/Lt S M Brown	29	3	Fokker DVII	Menin	D
1710	Lt C G Ross	29	13	Fokker DVII	S Menin	DF
1725	Lt F Boulton	210	4	Fokker DVII	E Staden	D
1730	Lt C G Ross	29	14	Fokker DVII	Menin-Gheluvelt Road	D
1745	1/Lt G A Vaughn	17 US	10	LVG C		D
1745	2/Lt H Burdick	17 US	3	LVG C		DF
1745	Lt K R Unger	210	9	Fokker DVII	NE Dixmuide	D
1750	Lt G A Welsh	210	3	Fokker DVII	SE Nieuport	OOC
1750	Lt J H McNeaney	79	2	Fokker DVII	Passchendaele	D
1750	Lt F W Gillett	79	9	Fokker DVII	SE Nieuport	D
1750	Lt G A Welsh	210	4	Fokker DVII	SE Nieuport	D
1750	Lt H D MacLaren &	218	1	Fokker DrI	Cortemarck	D
	Sgt G Barlow	218	1			
1750	Lt H D MacLaren &	218	2	Fokker DrI	Cortemarck	OOC
	Sgt G Barlow	218	2			
1750	Lt E R Brewer USMC &	218	1	Fokker DrI	Cortemarck	OOC
	Sgt Wersheimer USMC	218	1			
1755	Lt J H McNeaney	79	3	Fokker DVII	Passchendaele	OOC
1755	Lt T H Newsome &	22	4	Pfalz DXII	E Bugnicourt	D
	Lt R S E Walshe	22	1			
1810	2/Lt H Burdick	17 US	4	Fokker DVII	Cambrai	D

29 September 1918

Time	Pilot/Crew	Sqdn	Vic No	E/A	Location	How
0730	Capt J D Breakey	203	6	LVG C	Hem	D
0730	Lt L N Hollinghurst	87	10	Fokker DVII	Estourmel	OOC
0755	Lt W S Jenkins	210	10	Fokker DVII	W Lichtervelde	D

Time	Pilot/Crew	Sqdn	Vic No	E/A	Location	How
0757	Lt G W Hopkins	210	1	Fokker DVII	N Wijnendaele Wood	DF
0800	Lt G A Welsh	210	5	Fokker DVII	N Wijnendaele Wood	D
0800	Lt C W Payton	210	9	Fokker DVII	Wijnendaele Wood	D
0800	Capt E Swale	210	H	Fokker DVII	Cortemarck	D
0800	Lt A Buchanan	210	6	Fokker DVII	Wijnendaele Wood	D
0800	Lt P Boulton	210	5	Fokker DVII	Wijnendaele Wood	OOC
0805	Lt A Buchanan	210	7	Fokker DVII	Wijnendaele Wood	OOC
0810	2/Lt H H Palmer &	211	1	Fokker DVII	Roulers	D
	2/Lt W C Snowden	211	1			
0845	Lt D E Cameron	1	2	Fokker DVII	Bohain	OOC
0845	Lt D M Bisset	1	1	Fokker DVII	Bohain	OOC
0845	2/Lt T Peacock &	11	1	Fokker DVII	SE Cambrai	OOC
	2/Lt G W A Kelly	11	1			
0845	2/Lt T Peacock &	11	2	Fokker DVII	SE Cambrai	D
	2/Lt G W A Kelly	11	2			
0845	Capt J R Webb &	27	2	Fokker DVII	Busigny	D
	2/Lt W A Hall	27	2			
	2/Lt T A Dickinson &	27	1			
	2/Lt W J Dimest	27	1			
0845	Patrol	27	–	Fokker DVII	Busigny	OOC
0935	Lt J H Sprott &	218	1	Fokker DVII	Lichtervelde	OOC
	2/Lt J S Lewis	218	1			
0940	Lt F P Mulcahy USMC	218	1	Fokker DVII	Cortemarck	OOC
	Cpl T McCullough USMC	218	1			
0940	Capt C S Iron &	218	1	Fokker DrI	Thorout	OOC
	2/Lt C Ford	218	1			
0950	Lt J G Coots	84	1	Balloon	N Villers-Outréaux	DF
0955	Lt E G Davies	29	2	Balloon	SE Comines	DF
1000	Lt G W Wareing	29	8	Balloon	SE Armentières	DF
1000	Lt E O Amm	29	5	Balloon	SE Armentières	DF
1010	Lt F W Gillett	79	10	Fokker DVII	W Roulers	DF
1010	2/Lt D C Rees &	84	4	Balloon	Beaurevoir	DF
	2/Lt S W Highwood	84	12			
1010	Lt F R Christiani	84	4	Balloon	Villers-Outréaux	DF
1011	Lt E R W Miller	84	2	Balloon	N Montbrehain	DF
1015	Capt H A Whistler	80	20	Fokker DVII	N Fontain	D
1015	Capt A H Orlebar	43	9	Fokker DVII	Remaucourt	OOC
1020	Capt G H Hooper &	20	8	Fokker DVII	N Saint-Quentin	OOC
	Lt H L Edwards	20	19			
1025	Capt G H Hooper &	20	9	Fokker DVII	N Saint-Quentin	D
	Lt H L Edwards	20	20			
1025	Capt G H Hooper &	20	10	Fokker DVII	N Saint-Quentin	D
	Lt H L Edwards	20	21			
1025	Lt T C Traill &	20	7	Fokker DVII	N Saint-Quentin	D
	Capt L W Burbridge	20	6			
1030	2/Lt S L Walters &	20	4	Fokker DVII	Levergies	D
	Lt T Kirkpatrick	20	4			
1030	Lt M McCall &	20	6	Fokker DVII	Lihaucourt	D
	2/Lt C G Boothroyd	20	6			
1030	Capt C F Falkenberg	84	16	Fokker DVII	Beaurevoir	D

Time	Pilot/Crew	Sqdn	Vic No	E/A	Location	How
1030	Capt H A Whistler	80	21	Fokker DVII	Joncourt	D
1115	Capt C W Cudemore	64	11	Fokker DVII	NW Cambrai	D
1115	Capt C W Cudemore	64	12	Fokker DVII	NW Cambrai	OOC
1115	2/Lt L W Rabe	148 US	1	Fokker DVII	W Ramillies	DF
1130	Lt C T McLean	148 US	3	Fokker DVII	N Cambrai-Ramillies	D
1130	Lt R M Attwater	70	1	Fokker DVII	E Roulers	D
1130	Lt O S Clefsted	70	1	Fokker DVII	SE Roulers	OOC
1130	Lt J H Latchford &	25	2	Fokker DVII	N Cambrai	DF
	Sgt A H Mabey	25	2			
1140	Lt K B Watson	70	4	Fokker DVII	Oostnieuwkerke	D
1145	Lt E J Stephens	41	7	Fokker DVII	NE Roulers	D
1145	Lt O J Rose	92	8	Fokker DVII	E Beaurevoir	DF
1150	Lt O J Rose	92	9	Halb C	Bellicourt	D
1200	Capt C P Brown	213	11	Fokker DVII	E Roulers	OOC
1220	2/Lt C H Dickens &	211	1	Fokker DVII	Dadizeele	D
	2/Lt A M Adam	211	1			
1230	Capt J B White	208	10	Fokker DVII	N Lesdins	D
1230	Lt R C D'A Gifford	208	5	Fokker DVII	Lesdins	OOC
1230	2/Lt H J Botterill	208	1	Fokker DVII	Lesdins	OOC
1230	2/Lt H J Philip	208	1	Fokker DVII	Lesdins	OOC
1240	Capt W E Shields	41	18	Balloon	SE Comines	D
1340	2/Lt G S Smith,	40	3	Balloon	NE Cambrai	DF
	Lt Field &	40	1			
	Cpt R Chidlaw-Roberts	40	10			
1340	Lt R L M Barbour &	205	4	Fokker DVII	Montbrehain	D
	Capt M F M Wright	205	1			
1410	Lt G W Wareing	29	9	Balloon	E Comines	DF
1640	Capt D R MacLaren	46	52	Fokker DVII	Le Cateau	OOC
	& Lt C H Sawyer	46	5			
1640	Capt C W Odell	46	7	Fokker DVII	Le Cateau	OOC
1700	Capt G B Gates	201	16	Balloon	Bantouzelle	DF
1740	Capt R B Bannerman	79	13	Hannover C	Estaires	D
1740	Capt G T Richardson &	62	1	Fokker DVII		D
	2/Lt I P Aitken	62	1			
1740	Capt G T Richardson &	62	2	Fokker DVII		D
	2/Lt I P Aitken	62	2			
1740	2/Lt N J Nock &	10	1	Fokker DVII		DF
	2/Lt W E Grainger	10	1			

Appendix 2

French Air Service Victory Claims

Time	Pilot/Crew	Unit	Vic No	E/A	Location
			1 September 1918		
1840	S/Lt L Bourjade &	152	17	Balloon	St Arcy
	S/Lt E Maunoury	152	6		
	Sgt C Veil	150	2	EA	Flavy-le-Meldeux
	Lt H Stickney &	150	1	EA	Flavy-le-Meldeux
	Sgt L Bagarry	150	1		
			2 September 1918		
0900	Lt H Dencaussée	90	2	Balloon	Geline
0930	S/Lt M Ambrogi,	90	9	Balloon	Juvelize
	Adj M Bizot &	90	6		
	Adj J Pezon	90	3		
1030	Adj Dutrey &	20	1	Fokker DVII	La Neuvillette
	Sgt Latapie	20	2		
1045	Lt H Hay de Slade	159	14	EA	W Terny-Sorny
1500	Adj-Chef Thevenin &	111	1	Scout	Baslieux-les-Fismes
	Adj Thomas	111	1		
	Adj Loustalot &	111	1		
	Lt Oise	111	1		
	2/Lt de Carheil &	111	1		
	Lt Hegon	111	1		
1535	MdL Galland &	2	1	Fokker DVII	Baslieux-les-Fismes
	Lt Heuzeel	2	1		
1800	Sgt P Rozes	99	1	EA	Sorny
	Adj J Lucas	97	1	Balloon	
	Lt F Bonneton	69	7	Balloon	Beaurieux-Pontavert
	S/Lt Clavel &	20	1	Fokker DVII	N La Neuvillette
	Lt Puisieux	20	1		
	Patrol	GC14	–	DFW C	
	MdL Verges &	34	1	EA	Coucy-la-Ville
	Lt Barat	34	1		
	Adj P Bentejac &	124	2	Balloon	Manre
	Sgt E Grillot	124	2		
	Lt H Berge &	124	2	Balloon	Bois de la Taille
	Sgt M Caton	124	1		
	Adj E Pillon	98	4	Scout	Servon
	S/Lt H Pretre	91	2	two-seater	Crécy-au-Mont
	MdL de Caso &	91	1		
	Cpl Leblanc	91	1		
	Sgt P Montange	155	3	two-seater	Vauxillon
	Sgt P Montange	155	4	Balloon	Bauris
	72 Balloon Cié AA fire		POW	Fokker DVII	Prosnes
	Flak		POW	Fokker DVII	Dommartin-la-Planchette
			3 September 1918		
0830	MdL A de Freslon	152	2	Balloon	Concevreux
0930	Lt P Schneider	15	1	Balloon	N Fismes

Time	Pilot/Crew	Unit	Vic No	E/A	Location
1625	Lt G Madon	38	41	Scout	N Fismes
1730	Adj J Pezon	90	4	Balloon	Goin
	MdL A Courtieu	96	2	two-seater	
	Sgt Maillon &	96	1	two-seater	
	Sgt H Hutreau	96	1		
	Lt H Pretre	91	3	Scout	Noyon
	Adj F Guerrier,	77	4	Balloon	
	MdL J Thévenod,	77	1		
	Cpl Maria &	77	1		
	Brig Coquelin	77	1		
	Adj F Guerrier	77	5	Balloon	
	Adj-Chef Delzenne	88		Balloon	

4 September 1918

Time	Pilot/Crew	Unit	Vic No	E/A	Location
0645	S/Lt L Bourjade,	152	17	Balloon	Pont Arcy
	S/Lt E Maunoury &	152	6		
	Cpl E Manson	152	1		
1135	Adj A Berthelot,	15	8	EA	
	Sgt Fourcade &	15	1		
	Sgt Barat	15	1		
1145	Adj J Jacquot	100	1	EA	Breuil-sur-Vesles
1200	Lt R Volmeraude	38	2	two-seater	W Lavannes
1815	S/Lt A M M Coadou,	88	3	EA	Juvigny
	Adj F Delzenne &	88	4	Scout	
	Adj E Pinot	84	1		
	Capt J de Luppe	83	2	Balloon	Filain
	S/Lt M Devilder	83	2		

5 September 1918

Time	Pilot/Crew	Unit	Vic No	E/A	Location
1545	S/Lt C M Haegelen,	100	14	Balloon	Boult-sur-Suippes
	Brig Guerin &	100	2		
	Sgt P Peuch	100	1		

6 September 1918

Time	Pilot/Crew	Unit	Vic No	E/A	Location
0830	Sgt J Connelly &	163	5	Fokker DVII	Navarin
	MdL J Morvan	163	1		
1215	Sgt G Florentin	90	1	two-seater	Bayon
1930	Adj E Corso &	124	1	two-seater	W Dontrien
	Adj P Bentejac	124	3		
	Sgt Rouzand &	18	1	Scout	
	Sol Martin	18	1		
	FTL/POW			two-seater	Coucy-le-Château

7 September 1918

Time	Pilot/Crew	Unit	Vic No	E/A	Location
0730	S/Lt L Austin	92	1	Balloon	N Beaurieux
	S/Lt M Coiffard,	154	25	Balloon	
	S/Lt T Condemine &	154	2		
	Sgt C Peillard	154	1		
	S/Lt L Douillet &	124	4	Fokker DVII	W Dontrien
	Sgt M Caton	124	2		

12 September 1918

Time	Pilot/Crew	Unit	Vic No	E/A	Location
	1/Lt Nelson	131	1	Balloon	
	1/Lt Newell	131	1		

Time	Pilot/Crew	Unit	Vic No	E/A	Location
			13 September 1918		
1720	S/Lt A M de Cordou,	94	6	Fokker DVII	Viéville-en-Haye
	Lt A Laganne &	94	2		
	Lt A Carbonel	94	1		
1750	Sgt J Pustienne &	155	1	Scout	Haumont
	Cpl Charties	155	1		
1750	S/Lt P Montange	155	5	Scout	Chambley
			14 September 1918		
0910	Sgt P Bourgeois	68	1	EA	Jonville
0920	Lt C Couderc	152	P	EA	Pont Arcy
1345	S/Lt M Coiffard,	154	26	Balloon	Gernicourt
	S/Lt T Condemine &	154	3		
	Cpl M Lisle	154	1		
1350	S/Lt M Coiffard,	154	27	Balloon	Cormicy
	S/Lt T Condemine &	154	4		
	Cpl M Lisle	154	2		
1745	S/Lt M Boyau,	77	32	Balloon	Étraye
	Cpl E Corsi &	77	1		
	S/Lt C M Haegelen	100	15		
	Lt J Senart	160	3	Fokker DVII	
	MdL G Halberger &	153	4	Balloon	Goin
	MdL E Aubailly	153	1		
	Capt A Mezergues &	131	5	Scout	
	Asp Collin	131	1		
	MdL Jacquot &	131	1		
	MdL Gautier	131	1		
	1/Lt Nelson &	131	2	Scout	
	1/Lt Newel	131	2		
	MdL Pradel de Lamze &	131	1		
	Sgt Rayez	131	1		
	S/Lt Truchement &	131	1	Scout	
	Asp Hogenville	131	1		
	Sgt Depuy &	131	1		
	Cpl Magnenot	131	1		
	Capt J Jannekeyn &	132	2	Fokker DVII	
	Lt E Weissmann	132	3		
	Brig Vollet &	132	1	Fokker DVII	
	Sol Malacrida	132	1		
	Sgt Brideland &	132	1	Fokker DVII	
	Lt Pechine	132	1		
	Lt A Paillard &	132	2	Fokker DVII	
	Sgt Hincelin	132	1		
	S/Lt Resel,	46	1	Scout	
	Sol Poupougnac &	46	1		
	Sgt-Maj Lacassange	46	1		
	Sgt Duval &	23	1	Balloon	Étraye
	Sgt Bacque	23	2		
	MdL G Uteau	315	4	two-seater	
			15 September 1918		
0700	Lt M Ambrogi &	90	10	Balloon	Bourdonnay
	Adj C Mace	90	4		
0930	MdL M Sainz	94	1	Balloon	Goin
1050	Adj H Garaud	38	P	two-seater	Hermonville

Time	Pilot/Crew	Unit	Vic No	E/A	Location
1100	Lt J Lemarie &	90	3	EA	Raon l'Étape
	Lt H de Ginestet	90	1		
1130	Adj J Pezon	90	5	Balloon	Avricourt
1230	S/Lt M Boyau,	77	33	Balloon	Château-Vhehery
	Lt H Decoin,	77	3		
	S/Lt Y Barbaza &	77	3		
	Adj-Chef E Strohl	77	1		
1230	S/Lt M Coiffard,	154	28	Balloon	Brimont
	S/Lt T Condemine	154	5		
	Adj J Ehrlich	154	16		
1233	S/Lt M Coiffard,	154	29	Balloon	Cormicy
	S/Lt T Condemine &	154	6		
	Adj J Ehrlich	154	17		
1235	S/Lt M Coiffard,	154	30	Balloon	Gernicourt
	S/Lt T Condemine	154	7		
	& Adj J Ehrlich	154	18		
1300	Cpl D Chollet	92	1	two-seater	N Vieil Arcy
1520	S/Lt C M Haegelen &	100	16	Balloon	Châtelet-Chéry
	Sgt Douzant	100	1		
1630	Sgt G Courcelle	97	2	Fokker DVII	Lorry
1630	Sgt W York	97	1	Fokker DVII	Prény
1640	Sgt S Jacob	163	2	EA	N Servon
1730	S/Lt L Bourjade &	152	18	Balloon	Ailles
	S/Lt E Maunoury	152	7		
1735	S/Lt M Boyau,	154	34	Balloon	Brieulles
	Lt Decoin,	77	4		
	S/Lt Y Barbaza &	77	4		
	Adj-Chef Strohl	77	2		
1735	S/Lt L Bourjade &	152	19	Balloon	Hurtebise
	S/Lt E Maunoury	152	8		
1735	S/Lt C M Haegelen &	100	17	Balloon	Brieulles
	Sgt P Peuch	100	2		
1850	Lt M Nogues	57	11	Balloon	Boise de Buttes
1855	Lt M Nogues	57	12	Balloon	Craonne
	Lt Jallois &	19	1	Fokker DVII	Saint-Thierry
	Lt Delagoutte	19	1		
	Lt Canivet &	19	1		
	Lt Desmaroux	19	2		
	Sgt Hall &	19	1		
	S/Lt Serre	19	1		
	Lt Jallois &	19	2	Fokker DVII	Saint-Thierry
	Lt Delagoutte	19	2		
	Lt Canivet &	19	2		
	Lt Desmaroux	19	3		
	Sgt Hall &	19	2		
	S/Lt Serre	19	2		
	S/Lt G Daladier,	93	6	Balloon	Chambley
	Sgt H Meyniel &	93	1		
	Sgt E Prarond	93	1		
	S/Lt J Guertiau,	97	8	EA	Gorze
	Adj J Lucas &	97	2		
	Sgt G Courcelle	97	1		
	16 September 1918				
1030	Lt M Ambrogi,	90	11	Balloon	Cirey
	Adj J Pezon &	90	6		
	Cpl Rivière	90	1		

Time	Pilot/Crew	Unit	Vic No	E/A	Location
1117	S/Lt M Boyau,	77	35	Balloon	Harville
	Asp H Cessieux	77	1		
1200	S/Lt C M Haegelen &	100	18	Balloon	Bois de Sept-Sarges
	Sgt P Peuch	100	1		
1215	S/Lt C Nuville &	57	11	two-seater	Breuil
	Adj R Vanier	57	4		
	S/Lt R Pelissier	175	6	two-seater	
	S/Lt G Daladier &	93	9	LVG C	Juvelize
	Adj P Delage	93	1		

	17 September 1918				
1615	S/Lt C M Haegelen &	100	19	Balloon	Hannonville
	Lt C Poulin	100	1		
	S/Lt W Herisson &	75	10	two-seater	Soissons
	Sgt R Le Tilly	75	1		
	S/Lt W Herisson &	75	11	Fokker DVII	Soissons
	Sgt Baralis	75	1		
	Patrol	GC23	P	EA	
	Flak			EA	
	Adj L Marot &	37	3	EA	
	Adj G Lienhard	37	3		

	18 September 1918				
1805	Adj J Ehrlich,	154	19	Balloon	Brimont
	Adj P Petit &	154	6		
	Sgt C Peillard	154	2		
	Asp G Bonneau	48	1	Balloon	Onville
	Adj E Regnier,	89	4	Halb C	Belrupt
	S/Lt V Federoff,	89	4		
	Sgt G Lasne,	89	2		
	Cpl J Havard,	89	1		
	Sgt A Stanley &	23	1		
	2/Lt F Luke, Jr USAS	27th	13	two-seater	
	S/Lt P Gaudermen &	68	3	Halb C	Jonville
	Adj R Sinclaire	68	2		

	19 September 1918				
1545	Lt L Delrieu,	150	3	Halb C	Rezonville
	Sgt C Veil &	150	3		
	MdL P Lebigre	150	1		

	21 September 1918				
	S/Lt A Cousin	163	1	EA	Tahure
	S/Lt A M M Coadou	88	4	EA	

	22 September 1918				
1004	Adj C Mace	90	2	Balloon	Geline
1007	Adj C Mace	90	3	Balloon	Juvelize
	Cpl Taillor	124	1	Fokker	

	23 September 1918				
	Lt Denis &	Sal 40	1	EA	Mont-sans-Nom
	S/Lt Beucler	Sal 40	4		

Time	Pilot/Crew	Unit	Vic No	E/A	Location
	24 September 1918				
0745	S/Lt R d'Estainville	87	2	Balloon	Bourgogne
1215	S/Lt C Nuville &	57	12	EA	Cernay-en-Dormois
	MdL Imhoff	57	1		
	Capt H Hay de Slade	159	15	EA	N Suippes
	Capt G Lagache,	78	2	two-seater	Xammes
	Sgt G Tscheoberle &	78	1		
	Sgt Le Fustec	78	1		
	25 September 1918				
	Adj G Priollaud	159	3	Scout	Ornes
	26 September 1918				
0800	Capt A de Turenne,	12	14	Balloon	Sainte Geneviève
	S/Lt Herlemont &	12	2		
	Sgt Maurio	12	2		
0820	Sgt H Y Saxon &	12	2	Balloon	N Somme-Py
	Cpl E Haller	12	2		
1145	Lt R Fonck	103	61	Fokker DVII	St Marie-à-Py
to	Lt R Fonck	103	62	Fokker DVII	St Soupley
1210	Lt R Fonck	103	63	Halb C	Perth-les-Hurles
1245	S/Lt M Nogues &	57	13	Balloon	NE Somme-Py
	Cpl Beaume	57	1		
1410	Adj A Berthelot	15	9	DFWC	N Montfaucon
1545	1/Lt G W Eypper USAS	98	1	two-seater	NE Bouconville
1650	Sgt J Kaminsky	124	1	Balloon	Sechault
1755	Sgt L Caudry	165	1	Fokker DVII	Souain
1800	Lt P Pendaires,	67	6	Scout	S Tahure
	Adj E Parsons &	3	6		
	MdL Denneulin	3	2		
1810	Lt R Fonck	103	64	Fokker DVII	St Souplet
	Lt R Fonck	103	65	Fokker DVII	Souain
1845	Capt A de Turenne,	12	13	Scout	Ville-sur-Tourbe
	Adj E Regnier &	89	5		
	S/Lt R Schurck	91	2		
	Lt R Fonck	103	66	DFW C	E Souain
	S/Lt G Daladier,	93	10	Balloon	N Somme-Py
	Adj P Delage &	93	2		
	MdL H Meyniel	93	2		
	S/Lt J Lostalot,	97	2	Balloon	Saint Hilaire
	Adj Joubert &	97	2		
	MdL R Gaston	97	1		
	S/Lt F Guyou &	37	8	Balloon	N Cerny
	Adj G Lienhard	37	3		
	S/Lt G Daladier	93	11	EA	
	S/Lt F Guyou &	37	9	two-seater	
	Adj G Lienhard	37	4		
	Adj G Lienhard &	37	5	EA	Butte du Mesnil
	Adj L Marot	37	4		
	Adj Damanez,	46	2	EA	
	Sgt Jourde &	46	1		
	Cpl Galotte	46	1		
	S/Lt A M M Coadou	88	4	two-seater	
	S/Lt P Gaudermen,	68	4	EA	Ville-sur-Tourbe
	Adj E Prevost &	68	3		
	Cpl Chirac	68	1		

Time	Pilot/Crew	Unit	Vic No	E/A	Location
	27 September 1918				
1735	Sgt M Guillet	163	3	Pfalz	Somme-Py
	Adj J Fleury &	95	4	EA	
	Sgt L Lacouture	95	3		
	Capt G Tourangin,	89	4	two-seater	Somme-Py–Manre
	Adj E Regnier &	89	6		
	Sgt G Lasne	89	1		
	Capt de Vaubicourt,	100	2	EA	
	Lt C Poulin,	100	2		
	Sgt Coursic &	100	1		
	Sgt R Hummel	100	1		
	Sgt E Corsi &	77	2	Balloon	SE Étain
	MdL J Thévenod	77	2		
	Lt Fouan &	108	2	two-seater	
	Asp Blanc	108	1		
	Adj Robyn &	108	1		
	Adj Douville	108	1		
	Lt Coubaz &	29	1	EA	
	MdL Fremont	29	1		
	Lt Charmess &	29	1		
	Sgt Lascourrages	29	1		
	Capt P d'Argueff &	GC21	11	Fokker DVII	N Cerny
	Lt Marolle	124	1		
	Lt Thiberge	EMIV	2	EA	Grateuil
	28 September 1918				
0845	S/Lt J Romatet,	165	5	Balloon	Orfeuil
	S/Lt R Decugis &	165	3		
	Lt Besse	165	1		
0900	S/Lt M Coiffard	154	31	Balloon	SW Semide
0930	Sgt R Onillon	163	2	Balloon	Challeronge
1010	Capt P d'Argueff	GC21	12	two-seater	Manre
1030	Lt R Fonck	103	67	two-seater	N Somme-Py
1115	Sgt J Connelly	163	6	Balloon	Challeronge
1145	S/Lt F Portron,	31	4	Fokker DVII	N Bois de Bouc
	S/Lt L Chartoire &	31	3		
	MdL Jacquet	31	1		
1520	Capt P d'Argueff	GC21	13	two-seater	Sechault
1645	Lt H de Sevin	151	2	two-seater	Somme-Py
	Adj P Delage	93	3	Scout	
	Adj M L Henriot	65	6	EA	N Somme-Py
	Sgt R Damhet	65	1	EA	N Somme-Py
	29 September 1918				
0945	S/Lt R Waddington	31	12	Fokker DVII	Orfeuil
1740	Sgt G Rotureau	57	2	Fokker DVII	N Auberive
1825	Adj F Delzenne	88	5	Scout	Monthois

Time	Pilot/Crew	Unit	Vic No	E/A	Location
1845	S/Lt Cousin	163	2	two-seater	Sechault
	Adj Droziers &	69	1	Balloon	
	Sgt Fugier	69	1		
	MdL P Ducornet	93	2	Balloon	Machault
	MdL H Meyneil	93	3	Scout	
	Sgt Lucci,	240	1	Scout	
	Sol Devillers &	240	1		
	Sol O'Farrell	240	1		
	Sgt Bellat &	127	1	EA	
	Asp Steiner	127	1		

30 September 1918

Time	Pilot/Crew	Unit	Vic No	E/A	Location
1545	Sgt R Onilion,	163	3	two-seater	Cerny
	Sgt D S Paden &	163	1		
	Sgt Lefebvre	163	1		

Appendix 3

US Air Service Victory Claims

Time	Pilot/Crew	Unit	Vic No	E/A	Location
2 September 1918					
0930	2/Lt A R Brooks	22	2	Rumpler C	Armaucourt
	1/Lt C G Grey,	213	1	two-seater	Flirey
	1/Lt P Phelen &	213	1		
	1/Lt S P Gaillard, Jr	213	1		
	1/Lt G M Comey &	88	1	Hannover C	Flirey
	1/Lt R B Bagby	88	1		
	1/Lt R C Page &	88	1		
	1/Lt P F Carl, Jr	88	1		
3 September 1918					
	Capt J A Summersett &	96	1	Pfalz DIII	Aubeville
	2/Lt R I Coryell	96	1		
	1/Lt A W Gundelach	96	1		
	& 2/Lt P W Way	96	1		
	1/Lt D W Young &	96	1		
	1/Lt S M Lunt	96	1		
	1/Lt A N Alexander &	96	1		
	1/Lt J C E McLennan	96	1		
	1/Lt R C Taylor &	96	1		
	1/Lt W A Stuart	96	1		
	1/Lt E E Bates &	96	1		
	1/Lt D W Warner	96	1		
4 September 1918					
1100	1/Lt V H Strahm &	91	1	Pfalz	Rembercourt
	Capt J A Wallis	91	1		
1100	1/Lt P H Hughey &	91	–	Pfalz	Rembercourt
	Capt K Roper	91	–		
1220	Patrol	96		Pfalz	Aubeville
1330	2/Lt A R Brooks,	22	3	Fokker DVII	Barnecourt
	1/Lt F B Tyndall &	22	1		
	2/Lt C Jones	22	2		
8 September 1918					
1235	1/Lt J M Swaab	22	1	two-seater	Cirey-Saarburg
to	1/Lt J M Swaab	22	2	Fokker DVII	Cirey-Saarburg
1305	1/Lt J M Swaab	22	3	Fokker DVII	Cirey-Saarburg
10 September 1918					
1650	1/Lt W A Robertson	139	1	Pfalz	Bayonville
12 September 1918					
0655	Capt R C Bridgeman	22	2	Hannover C	Bois de Pretre
0809	2/Lt F Luke, Jr	27	1	Balloon	Marieulles
1020	1/Lt L J Rummell	93	1	Fokker DVII	Thiaucourt

Time	Pilot/Crew	Unit	Vic No	E/A	Location
1020	1/Lt C R D'Olive	93	1	Fokker DVII	Viéville-en-Haye
1210	Capt D H Arthur &	12	1	EA	Viéville-en-Haye
	1/Lt H T Fleeson	12	1		
	1/Lt D E Putnam	139	13	Pfalz	Lachaussée
	1/Lt W A Coleman &	135	1	Fokker	Limey
	1/Lt J H Nathan	135	1		
	1/Lt J J Curtin &	135	1	Fokker	Thiaucourt
	1/Lt P G Hart	135	1		
	1/Lt G D Ream &	135	1	Fokker	Thiaucourt
	1/Lt J H Nathan	135	2		

13 September 1918

Time	Pilot/Crew	Unit	Vic No	E/A	Location
1530	1/Lt V H Strahm	91	2	Fokker	Orly Ferme
	Capt J A Wallis	91	2		
1700	1/Lt C R D'Olive	93	2	Fokker DVII	Chéry
1700	1/Lt C R D'Olive	93	3	Fokker DVII	Chéry
1700	1/Lt L Carruthers &	93	1	Pfalz	Woel
	1/Lt L S Harding	93	1		
1700	1/Lt G W Furlow	103	2	Fokker DVII	Chéry
1705	1/Lt G W Furlow	103	3	Fokker DVII	Chéry
1710	1/Lt H D Kenyon	103	1	Albatros	St Julien
1710	1/Lt F O'D Hunter &	103	2	Fokker DVII	Chambley
	1/Lt G de F Lamer	103	3		
1713	1/Lt C R D'Olive	93	4	Fokker DVII	St Benoit
1830	1/Lt D E Putnam	139	14	Fokker DVII	Limey
1830	1/Lt J D Este,	13	1	Fokker DVII	Chambley
to	1/Lt J J Seerley,	13	3		
1955	1/Lt R R Converse,	13	1		
	1/Lt D W Howe &	13	1		
	1/Lt F K Hayes	13	1		
1830	1/Lt J D Este,	13	2	Fokker DVII	Chambley
to	1/Lt J J Seerley,	13	4		
1955	1/Lt R R Converse,	13	2		
	1/Lt D W Howe &	13	2		
	1/Lt F K Hayes	13	2		
1830	1/Lt J D Este,	13	3	Fokker DVII	Chambley
to	1/Lt J J Seerley,	13	5		
1955	1/Lt R R Converse,	13	3		
	1/Lt D W Howe &	13	3		
	1/Lt F K Hayes	13	3		
	1/Lt B J Gaylord &	96	1	Fokker DVII	Chambley
	2/Lt H G Rath	96	1		
	1/Lt T W Farnsworth &	96	1		
	2/Lt S E Thompson	96	1		
	2/Lt S T Hopkins &	96	1		
	1/Lt B Williams	96	1		

14 September 1918

Time	Pilot/Crew	Unit	Vic No	E/A	Location
0733	Patrol	28	–	Fokker DVII	Villers-sur-Troy
0755	1/Lt H L Fontaine &	49	1	Fokker DVII	Chambley
	1/Lt H Brewster	49	1		
0755	1/Lt H L Fontaine &	49	2	Fokker DVII	Chambley
	1/Lt H Brewster	49	2		

Time	Pilot/Crew	Unit	Vic No	E/A	Location
0805	1/Lt R Biggs &	11	2	Pfalz	Mars-la-Tour
	1/Lt H Greer	11	2		
	1/Lt E Comegys &	11	1		
	2/Lt A R Carter	11	1		
	1/Lt R Chapin &	11	1		
	2/Lt C Laird	11	1		
	1/Lt L Harter &	11	1		
	1/Lt MacC Stephenson	11	1		
	2/Lt H Schindler &	11	1		
	2/Lt H Sayre	11	1		
	2/Lt R Guthrie &	11	1		
	1/Lt V Otis	11	1		
0805	1/Lt E F Richards	13	1	Pfalz	Cernay
0805	1/Lt E F Richards	13	2	Pfalz	Cernay
0805	1/Lt R M Stiles,	13	2	Fokker DVII	Prény
	1/Lt G D Stivers &	13	1		
	1/Lt M K Guthrie	13	1		
0805	1/Lt R M Stiles,	13	3	Fokker DVII	Prény
	1/Lt G D Stivers &	I3	2		
	1/Lt M K Guthrie	13	2		
0815	1/Lt E V Rickenbacker	94	7	Fokker DVII	Waville
1000	1/Lt T F Lennon,	27	1	Balloon	Boinville
	1/Lt L H Dawson &	27	2		
	2/Lt F Luke, Jr	27	3		
1310	1/Lt C G Grey,	213	2	Fokker DVII	Spandville
	1/Lt R W Richardson &	213	1		
	1/Lt S P Gaillard Jr	213	2		
1520	2/Lt A R Brooks &	22	4	Fokker DVII	Mars-la-Tour
	1/Lt P E Hassinger	22	1		
1525	2/Lt A R Brooks &	22	5	Fokker DVII	Mars-la-Tour
	1/Lt P E Hassinger	22	2		
1635	1/Lt W W White, Jr	147	3	Balloon	E Chambley
1640	1/Lt W W White, Jr	147	4	Fokker DVII	Chambley
	2/Lt F Luke, Jr	27	2	Balloon	Buzy

15 September 1918

Time	Pilot/Crew	Unit	Vic No	E/A	Location
0810	1/Lt E V Rickenbacker	94	8	Fokker DVII	Bois de Waville
0945	1/Lt L W Powell &	91	1	Pfalz	Conflans
	1/Lt J H Strieker	91	1		
1000	2/Lt R E Wells &	24	1	Fokker	Conflans
	2/Lt A W Swineboard	24	1		
1015	Major C Spaatz	13	1	Fokker DVII	Vaux
1030	1/Lt W H Stovall	13	3	Fokker DVII	Gernay
1030	1/Lt L Brewer	13	1	Fokker DVII	Cernay
1030	1/Lt M K Guthrie &	13	3	Fokker DVII	Vaux
	1/Lt F K Hayes	13	4		
1140	1/Lt G C Kenney &	91	1	Pfalz DIII	N Gorze
	2/Lt W T Badham	91	1		
1230	1/Lt W P Erwin &	1	1	EA	Mamey
	1/Lt H W Dahringer	1	1		
	2/Lt J M Richardson &	1	1		
	1/Lt A W Duckstein	1	1		
1705	2/Lt F Luke, Jr	27	4	Balloon	S Boinville
1710	1/Lt J Wehner	27	2	Balloon	SE Bois d'Hingry

Time	Pilot/Crew	Unit	Vic No	E/A	Location
1725	2/Lt F Luke, Jr	27	5	Balloon	Bois d'Hingry
1815	1/Lt C E Wright &	93	1	Fokker DVII	Chéry
	1/Lt H D Lindsay	93	1		
1950	2/Lt F Luke, Jr	27	6	Balloon	Chaumont
	1/Lt J Wehner	27	1	Fokker DVII	Rouvres

16 September 1918

Time	Pilot/Crew	Unit	Vic No	E/A	Location
1115	1/Lt G F Fisher	49	2	Rumpler C	Benville
1245	1/Lt L C Simon	147	1	Halb C	Hadonville
1220	1/Lt C E Wright &	93	2	Fokker DVII	Chambley
	1/Lt H D Lindsay	93	2		
1940	2/Lt F Luke, Jr &	27	7	Balloon	Romagne
	1/Lt J Wehner	27	3		
1945	1/Lt J Wehner	27	4	Balloon	Mangiennes
	2/Lt F Luke, Jr	27	8	Balloon	Réville

17 September 1918

Time	Pilot/Crew	Unit	Vic No	E/A	Location
1125	1/Lt G S Robertson	147	1	Halb C	Étain
1545	1/Lt F O'D Hunter	103	3	Fokker DVII	Verneville
1545	1/Lt F O'D Hunter	103	4	Fokker DVII	Bayonville
1620	1/Lt G W Furlow	103	4	Fokker DVII	Verneville
1655	1/Lt J Frost	103	1	Fokker DVII	Bayonville

18 September 1918

Time	Pilot/Crew	Unit	Vic No	E/A	Location
1610	2/Lt J S Owens,	139	1	Pfalz DIII	Bayonville
	1/Lt R O Lindsay,	139	1		
	1/Lt G V Moy,	139	1		
	1/Lt W A Robertson,	139	2		
	1/Lt K J Schoen,	139	1		
	1/Lt R D Shelby &	139	1		
	1/Lt H A Garvie	139	1		
1610	2/Lt J S Owens,	139	2	Pfalz DIII	Bayonville
	1/Lt R O Lindsay,	139	2		
	1/Lt G V Moy,	139	2		
	1/Lt W A Robertson,	139	3		
	1/Lt K J Schoen,	139	2		
	1/Lt R D Shelby &	139	2		
	1/Lt H A Garvie	139	2		
1635	1/Lt S Sewall	95	5	Fokker DVII	Landres
1640	2/Lt F Luke, Jr &	27	9	Balloon	Labeuville
	1/Lt J Wehner	27	5		
1640	2/Lt F Luke, Jr &	27	10	Balloon	Labeuville
	1/Lt J Wehner	27	6		
1645	2/Lt F Luke, Jr	27	11	Fokker DVII	St Hilaire
1645	2/Lt F Luke, Jr	27	12	Fokker DVII	St Hilaire
1645	2/Lt F Luke, Jr	27	13	Halb C	Jonville
1650	1/Lt H A Garvey	139	3	Pfalz	
1720	1/Lt D M McClure	213	1	Fokker DVII	Mars-la-Tour
1720	1/Lt D M McClure	213	2	Fokker DVII	Mars-la-Tour
1720	1/Lt D M McClure	213	3	Fokker DVII	Mars-la-Tour
1730	2/Lt R Guthrie &	11	2	Fokker DVII	Oiley
	1/Lt V Otis	11	2		

Time	Pilot/Crew	Unit	Vic No	E/A	Location
20 September 1918					
1745	2/Lt F H Hart &	90	1	Fokker DVII	Dampvitoux
	2/Lt A T Grier	90	1		
21 September 1918					
1750	1/Lt H R Hall	95	1	Fokker DVII	Dancourt
24 September 1918					
1530	Capt R C Bridgeman,	22	3	DFW C	Woel
	2/Lt R J Little &	22	1		
	1/Lt H B Hudson	22	1		
25 September 1918					
0840	1/Lt E V Rickenbacker	94	9	Fokker DVII	Billy
0850	1/Lt E V Rickenbacker	94	10	Halb C	Spincourt
1002	1/Lt G V Moy,	139	3	Rumpler	Arnacourt
	2/Lt R O Seevers &	139	2		
	2/Lt J S Owens	139	3		
	2/Lt P W Chase &	8	1		
	1/Lt R Smith	8	1		
26 September 1918					
0552	1/Lt R M Chambers	94	1	Balloon	Nantillois
0553	1/Lt I A Roberts	27	2	Balloon	Lisson
0600	1/Lt E V Rickenbacker	94	11	Fokker DVII	Damvillers
0605	1/Lt H R Buckley &	95	2	Balloon	Nantillois
	1/Lt A H McLanahan	95	1		
0625	1/Lt I A Roberts	27	3	Balloon	Romagne
0715	1/Lt J A Sperry	22	1	Fokker DVII	Bois de Merles
0715	1/Lt H B Hudson &	22	2	Fokker DVII	Étain
	2/Lt B M Doolin	22	1		
0723	1/Lt T G Cassady	28	7	Fokker DVII	St Marie-à-Py
0730	1/Lt J D Beane	22	1	Fokker DVII	Charpentrie
0735	Capt C J Biddle,	13	6	Fokker DVII	Flabas
to	1/Lt L Brewer &	13	2		
0750	1/Lt S M Avery	13	1		
1735	Major C Spaatz	13	2	Fokker DVII	Flabas
0820	1/Lt J A Sperry	22	2	Fokker DVII	Étain
1000	2/Lt S V Peters &	24	1	Fokker DVII	Domprix
	1/Lt L A Weitishek	24	1		
1015	1/Lt B F Beverly &	96	1	Fokker DVII	Cléry-le-Grand
	1/Lt F J Newbury	96	1		
	1/Lt D M Young &	96	2		
	2/Lt R I Coryell	96	2		
	1/Lt B C Hopper &	96	1		
	2/Lt A N Kelly	96	1		
	1/Lt L S Turnbull &	96	1		
	2/Lt L C Bleecker	96	1		
	1/Lt R P Elliott &	96	1		
	1/Lt A O Ellis	96	1		
	2/Lt H J Forshay &	96	1		
	2/Lt P J O'Donnell	96	1		

Time	Pilot/Crew	Unit	Vic No	E/A	Location
1015	2/Lt H J Forshay &	96	2	Fokker DVII	Cléry-le-Grand
	2/Lt P J O'Donnell	96	2		
1050	1/Lt W W Waring &	11	1	Fokker DVII	Dun-sur-Meuse
	2/Lt S H G Norris	11	1		
1055	1/Lt P N Rhinelander &	20	1	Fokker DVII	Damvillers
	1/Lt H C Preston	20	1		
	1/Lt M C Cooper &	20	1		
	1/Lt E C Leonard	20	1		
	1/Lt R P Mathews &	20	1		
	2/Lt E A Taylor	20	1		
	1/Lt W C Potter &	20	1		
	2/Lt G W Schultz	20	1		
	2/Lt G B Wiser &	20	1		
	1/Lt G C Richardson	20	1		
	2/Lt D B Harris &	20	1		
	2/Lt E Forbes	20	1		
	1/Lt S C Howard &	20	1		
	1/Lt E A Parrott	20	1		
1140	2/Lt S J Owens,	139	4	DFW C	Bois de Consenvoye
	1/Lt S J De France,	139	1		
	1/Lt H S Garvie,	139	4		
	1/Lt L H Germer,	139	1		
	1/Lt K J Schoen &	139	3		
	1/Lt H R Sumner	139	1		
1310	1/Lt W H Stovall	13	4	Fokker DVII	Étain
1315	1/Lt J F Manning &	49	1	Rumpler C	Hagecourt
	1/Lt J Wentworth	49	1		
1350	1/Lt D H Backus &	49	1	Fokker DVII	Étain
	1/Lt H W Heiber	49	1		
1620	1/Lt M Stenseth	28	1	Fokker DVII	Grimmcourt
1630	Lt H R Buckley	95	3	Balloon	Réville
	Lt A H McLanahan	95	2		
1748	1/Lt C M Gravett	95	1	Fokker DVII	Dullancourt
1750	1/Lt J Vasconcells	27	3	Balloon	Lisson
1800	1/Lt A Nutt	94		Fokker DVII	Dullancourt
1800	1/Lt L H Dawson	27	3	Fokker DVII	Chéry
1805	1/Lt A N McLanahan	95	3	Fokker DVII	Montfaucon
1845	1/Lt H W Cook	94	2	Balloon	Grandham

27 September 1918

Time	Pilot/Crew	Unit	Vic No	E/A	Location
1600	1/Lt E R Cook &	91	1	Fokker DVII	Crépon
	1/Lt W R Lawson	91	1		
	1/Lt J W Van Heuvel &	91	1		
	1/Lt L C Hammond	91	1		
	1/Lt W F Baker &	91	1		
	1/Lt R S Jannopoulo	91	1		
1745	1/Lt E R Scroggie,	94	1	Fokker DVII	Montfaucon
	1/Lt J P Herron &	147	1		
	1/Lt W W White, Jr	147	5		
1745	1/Lt W W White, Jr	147	6	Fokker DVII	Montfaucon
1814	1/Lt H R Buckley,	95	4	Rumpler C	Brieulles
	1/Lt E P Curtis &	95	3		
	1/Lt H Poperfuss	95	1		
1825	1/Lt H R Buckley,	95	5	Rumpler C	Fléville
	1/Lt T F Butz &	95	1		
	1/Lt G O Woodard	95	1		

Time	Pilot/Crew	Unit	Vic No	E/A	Location
28 September 1918					
0500	1/Lt E V Rickenbacker	94	12	Balloon	Sivry-sur-Meuse
0600	2/Lt F Luke, Jr	27	14	Balloon	Bétheniville
0606	1/Lt H W Cook	94	3	Balloon	Cléry-le-Petit
0650	1/Lt K L Porter &	147	2	Rumpler C	Langres
	1/Lt E S Ennis	147	1		
0840	1/Lt J D Beane &	22	2	Fokker DVII	Ivoiry
	1/Lt J M Swaab	22	4		
0840	1/Lt H B Hudson	22	3	Fokker DVII	Ivoiry
0845	Capt R C Bridgeman &	22	4	Fokker DVII	Montfaucon
	2/Lt W W La Force	22	1		
0850	1/Lt F B Tyndall	22	2	Fokker DVII	Montfaucon
0900	2/Lt C Jones	22	2	Fokker DVII	Ivoiry
0900	2/Lt C Jones	22	3	Fokker DVII	Montfaucon
0915	2/Lt S J De France	139	2	Pfalz DIII	Cléry-le-Petit
0915	1/Lt R D Seevers	139	2	Pfalz DIII	Cléry-le-Petit
0915	1/Lt W A Robertson,	139	4	Pfalz DIII	Cléry-le-Petit
	1/Lt E M Haight &	139	1		
	1/Lt R O Lindsay	139	3		
1030	1/Lt J Vasconcells	27	4	Rumpler C	Forges
1240	1/Lt K L Porter,	147	2	Rumpler C	Ciérges
	1/Lt O B Myers &	147	1		
	1/Lt L C Simon	147	2		
1310	1/Lt M Stenseth	28	2	Fokker DVII	Grandpré
1310	1/Lt M Stenseth	28	3	Fokker DVII	Grandpré
1325	1/Lt W J Hoover	27	3	Halb C	Forges
1325	1/Lt A H Treadwell	213	2	Fokker DVII	Bétheniville
1330	1/Lt E G Tobin	103	6	Fokker DVII	Chatel-Chéhéry
1335	1/Lt T H Hubbard	103	1	Fokker DVII	Chatel-Chéhéry
1340	1/Lt R N Weatherbee	93	1	Fokker DVII	Granham
1550	2/Lt F Luke, Jr	27	15	Hannover C	Monthainville
29 September 1918					
0455	1/Lt W P Erwin &	1	2	Rumpler C	Fléville
	2/Lt B V Baucom	1	1		
1635	1/Lt A B Patterson, Jr	93	1	Fokker DVII	Damvillers
1635	1/Lt R H Fuller	93	1	Fokker DVII	Damvillers
1635	1/Lt L J Rummell	93	2	Fokker DVII	Damvillers
1635	1/Lt L J Rummell	93	3	Fokker DVII	Damvillers
1635	1/Lt L J Rummell,	93	4	Albatros C	Chaumont
	1/Lt A B Patterson Jr &	93	2		
	1/Lt R H Fuller	93	2		
1705	2/Lt F Luke, Jr	27	16	Balloon	Avocourt
1710	2/Lt F Luke, Jr	27	17	Balloon	Avocourt
1712	2/Lt F Luke, Jr	27	18	Balloon	Avocourt
1720	1/Lt R M Chambers &	94	2	Fokker DVII	Cunel
	1/Lt S Kaye, Jr	94	1		
1850	1/Lt G O Woodard	95	3	Balloon	Dun-sur-Meuse
1850	1/Lt L C Holden	95	1	Balloon	Cunel

Appendix 4

German Victory Claims

Time	Pilot/Crew	Unit	Vic No	E/A	Location
		1 September 1918			
1005	Vfw K Schlegel	45	19	Balloon	Oueilly
1100	Oblt R R v Greim	34b	22	Camel	St Pierre Vaast
1555	Ltn T Quandt	36	11	SE5	S Pronville
1750	Flg H Nülle	39	1	Camel	Bailleul
1830	Flak			Dolphin	Armentières
2100	Ltn W Sommer	39	3	Balloon	Tilloy
	Ltn E Bormann	B	5	BF2b	S Lecluse
	Hpt B Loerzer	JGIII	34	BF2b	
	Uffz Schaak	28w	2	DH4	Tilloy
	Vfw W Skworz	36	2	DH4	Brunemont
	Sgt F Poeschke	53	2	Spad	Brétigny
	Vfw H Gockel	33	3	Camel	Quéant
	Ltn W Blume	9	–		
		2 September 1918			
0820	Ltn T Quandt	36	12	Camel	Écoust-Saint-Quentin
0820	Uffz O Bieliet	45	1	Spad	Basieux
0955	Oblt E R v Wedel	11	10	EA	
1010	Ltn A Brandenstein	49	5	Spad	Suippes
1015	Ltn H Lange	26	5	SE5	Villers
1025	Ltn O Frühner	26	19	SE5	Baralle
1030	Ltn H Frommherz	27	17	BF2b	Hamel
1100	Ltn F Noltenius	27	5	Camel	Étaing
1100	Ltn Buddeberg	50	1	Spad 2	Braisne
1100	Gefr Jakob	17	1	Spad 2	Savigny
1110	Ltn O Frühner	26	20	SE5	Villers
1125	OStv G Dörr	45	24	Spad 2	Ormes
1130	Ltn F Noltenius	27	6	Camel	Rumaucourt
1130	OStv G Dörr	45	25	Spad 2	Reims
1130	Ltn Meixner	45	1	Spad	Reims
1150	Ltn K Brendle	45	8	Balloon	Reims
1210	Ltn Christians	21s	1	Spad	NW Reims
1220	Ltn W Sommer	39	4	RE8	Fampoux
1230	Ltn W Nebgen	7	3	AWFK8	L'Homme
1230	Vfw Maack	63		AWFK8	L'Homme
1240	Vfw C Mesch	26	7	Camel	Haucourt
1240	Oblt T H Dahlmann	JGIII	4	Camel	Haucourt
1242	Vfw C Mesch	26	8	Camel	Raucourt
1245	Ltn H Lange	26	6	Camel	NE Baralle
1245	Ltn Ehlers	26		Camel	NE Baralle
1245	Hpt B Loerzer	JGIII	35	Camel	NE Baralle
1320	Ltn H Häbich	49	2	Bréguet XIV	Châlons-Suippes
1330	Ltn M Demisch	58	5	RE8	Vis-en-Artois

Time	Pilot/Crew	Unit	Vic No	E/A	Location
1515	Gefr H Nülle	39	1	Balloon	Tilloy
1555	Ltn Krayer	45	3	Balloon	Reims
1600	Ltn U Koennemann	45	2	Spad 2	Magneux
1600	Ltn H Rolfes	45	12	Spad 2	Magneux
1605	Ltn H Rolfes	45	13	Spad 2	Magneux
1720	Ltn G Buerck	54	3	Balloon	Champenoux
1740	Ltn Christians	21s	2	Spad	E Fismes
1833	Ltn H Hentzen	9	2	Spad	W Terny-Sorny
1845	Vfw Duennhaupt	58	1	DH9	Hamel
1920	Ltn H Brünig	50	7	Spad	Fismes
1930	Flg J Wolff	17	1	Spad	Savigny
1945	Oblt E R v Wedel	11	11	RE8	Le Catelet
2000	Ltn B Hobein	20	3	BF2b	Gheluvelt
2000	Ltn R v Barnekow	20	5	BF2b	Gheluvelt
2100	Ltn W Sommer	39	5	Balloon	N Bapaume
	Ltn O Löffler	B		Camel	Palleul
	Ltn E Bormann	B	8	Camel	Sauchy-Lestrée
	Ltn F Heinz	B	2	Camel	Boiry
	Ltn E Bormann	B	6	Camel	SE Dury
	Ltn E Bormann	B	7	Camel	W Havrincourt
	Ltn O Löffler	B	4	Camel	Beugnatre
	Ltn O Löffler	B	7	Camel	S Pelves
	Hpt E v Schleich	23b	31	RE8	NW Bapaume
	Vfw A Lux	27	5	RE8	Hamel
	Vfw A Lux	27		BF2b	Vis-en-Artois
	Ltn Stoltenhoff	27	2	EA	
	Fw W Kahle	27	1	Sopwith	Beugnatre
	Vfw R Jörke	39	!3	RE8	Bailleul
	Ltn W Preuss	66	13	Bréguet XIV	Bagneux
	Flg Eyssler	66	1	Spad	N Soissons
	Ltn H Quartier	67	2	Balloon	
	Uffz Baumgarten	67	2	Balloon	
	Ltn R Otto	68	4	Bréguet XIV	Rémy Wald
	Vfw Huar	68	3	Bréguet XIV	Rémy Wald
	Ltn G Clausnitzer	72s	1	Balloon	
	Oblt G Rasberger	80b	1	Balloon	
	Ltn J Filbig	80b	2	Balloon	Laroxne
	Vfw F Classen	26	–	Camel	Bailleul
	Ltn K v Schonebeck	33	7	EA	
	Ltn F Höhn	81	11	Spad	Coucy-le-Château

3 September 1918

Time	Pilot/Crew	Unit	Vic No	E/A	Location
1015	Lt W Schramm	56	3	BF2b	Moorseele
1030	Lt W Blume	9	20	Spad	S Fismes
1031	Lt H Rolle	9	3	Spad	S Fismes
1040	Flg E Mix	54	2	Balloon	Tremblecourt
1125	Lt T Quandt	36	13	SE5	Moreuil
1515	Gefr H Nülle	39	2	Balloon	Vis-en-Artois
1517	Gefr H Nülle	39	4	Balloon	Haucourt
1625	Lt O Löffler	B	5	DH9	Épehy
1700	Lt G Wember	61	1	Balloon	

Time	Pilot/Crew	Unit	Vic No	E/A	Location
1735	Ltn O Frühner	26	21	Camel	Sin-le-Noble
1740	Hpt B Loerzer	JGIII	36	SE5	Douai
1805	Ltn A Lindenberger	B	9	BF2b	Combles
1805	Ltn T Quandt	36	14	BF2b	Éterpigny
1840	Ltn F Vollbracht	5	2	BF2b	W Havrincourt
1847	Ltn F Rumey	5	30	BF2b	S Péronne
1850	Ltn J Mai	5	24	BF2b	N Bertincourt
2000	Oblt A Auffarht	29	20	SE5	Guémappe
2000	Ltn F Weber	29	2	SE5	Pelves
2000	Uffz S Westphal	29	1	SE5	Agny
2000	Uffz P Schonfelder	29	1	SE5	Agny
2010	Ltn Hencke	31	2	Camel	Rony-le-Petit
2035	Vfw O Hennrich	46	11	SE5a	SW Moreuil
2050	Ltn Z Brockhoff	MFJ 3	3	Bréguet XIV	E Furnes
	Vfw H C Donhauser	17	5	Spad	Sissone
	Rittm H v Brederlow	JGpII	2	Spad	Sissone
	Uffz M Hutterer	23b	4	DH9	Arleux
	Uffz M Hutterer	23b	5	Dolphin	Marcoing
	Ltn H Frommherz	27	18	RE8	Beugnatre
	Ltn H Frommherz	27	19	RE8	Beugny
	Fw A Hübner	36	3	SE5	Aubenscheul
	Ltn F Thiede	38	6	BF2b	
	Uffz Mack	60	1	Spad	
	Vfw W Stör	68	4	Balloon	Rémy Wald
	Ltn F Höhn	81	12	Spad	Soissons
	Vfw D Averes	81	5	Spad	Soissons
	Vfw D Averes	81	6	Spad	Soissons
	Ltn Bleibtreu	45	1	Bréguet XIV	Condé
	Uffz F Engler	62	1	Balloon	
	Vfw W Skworz	36	3	SE5	Sancourt

4 September 1918

Time	Pilot/Crew	Unit	Vic No	E/A	Location
0910	Oblt T H Dahlmann	JGIII	5	Camel	Palleul
0910	Ltn Ehlers	26	2	Camel	Palleul
0912	Oblt T H Dahlmann	JGIII	6	Camel	Palleul
0912	Vfw E Buder	26	9	Camel	Cantin
0915	Ltn O Frühner	26	22	Camel	W Cantin
0915	Ltn O Frühner	26	23	Camel	Douai
0918	Vfw F Classen	26	6	Camel	Cantin
0920	Hpt B Loerzer	JGIII	37	Camel	Monchecourt
0925	Vfw E Buder	26	10	Camel	Gouy
0930	Ltn O Frühner	26	24	Camel	W Corbehem
0930	Oblt F Röth	16b	23	DH9	Neuf-Berquin
1010	Uffz A Müller	39	2	DH9	Chelmes
1015	Uffz H Nülle	39	5	DH9	St Aubert
1015	Uffz H Haase	21s	3	Balloon	W Sarcy
1040	Ltn Spille	58	2	DH9	Helesmes
1045	Vfw Jeep	58	3	DH9	d'Hivergies-Ferme
1100	Ltn M Demisch	58	6	BF2b	Émerchicourt
1100	Ltn R Wenzl	6	2	Camel	Raillencourt
1100	Vfw G Staudacher	1	6	Camel	Sailly-Cambrai
1100	Ltn E Bormann	2	9	SE5a	Pelves
1110	Ltn G Meyer	37	15	two-seater	W Cambrai

Time	Pilot/Crew	Unit	Vic No	E/A	Location
1115	Oblt O Schmidt	5	12	BF2b	Gouzeaucourt
1205	Ltn E Siempelkamp	64w	4	Salmson 2A2	E Thiaucourt
1230	Ltn Siefert	17	1	Spad	Soilly
1335	Uffz Bader	64w	2	Balloon	Mandres
1400	Ltn H Rolfes	45	16	Spad	N Fismes
1400	OStv G Dörr	45	26	Spad	N Fismes
1715	Ltn E Just	11	6	Balloon	Barastre
1815	Ltn W Peckmann	9	3	Spad	Soissons
1830	Ltn F Rumey	5	31	Camel	Quéant
1930	Ltn Berling	45	3	Balloon	Mont Notre Dame
	Ltn A Laumann	10	28	Camel	
	Ltn H Frommherz	27	20	EA	Récourt
	Vfw A Lux	27	6	Sopwith	Cantin
	Fw A Hübner	36	4	SE5	Mercatel
	Ltn T Quandt	36	15	SE5	Quéant
	Vfw K Schlegel	45	21	Balloon	Sarcy
	Vfw A Korff	60	4	Spad	
	Ltn W Preuss	66	14	two-seater	Crécy-au-Mont
	Uffz Baumgarten	67	3	Balloon	
	Vfw F Jacobsen	73	8	RE6/AR2	

5 September 1918

Time	Pilot/Crew	Unit	Vic No	E/A	Location
0910	Flak			Camel	N Méricourt
1005	Ltn F Rumey	5	32	SE5a	N Bouchain
1010	Ltn J Mai	5	25	SE5a	W Bugnicourt
1200	G Meyer	37	16	SE5a	E Havrincourt
1200	Ltn auf der Haar	46	–	SE5a	E Havrincourt
1210	Ltn auf der Haar	46	–	SE5a	NE Ribécourt
1210	Ltn T Himmer	37	2	SE5a	NE Ribécourt
1210	Hpt B Loerzer	JGIII	38	SE5	Inchy/Brebières
1210	Vfw HC Donhauser	17	6	Spad	Champfleury
1350	Ltn B Hobein	20	4	BF2b	Espières
1415	FTL Motor trouble			Scout	Ostricourt
1515	Vfw Krautz	46	2	Balloon	NE Bapaume
1525	Ltn R Wenzl	6	8	Balloon	Croiselles
1525	Vzflgmstr Mayer	MFJ 3	4	Camel	Stalhille
1530	Ltn F Schliewen	6	1	Balloon	Croiselles
1730	Vfw K Schlegel	45	20	Balloon	Fismes
1825	Uffz L Jeckert	56	2	Camel	Lenvelere
1827	Ltn L Beckmann	56	8	Camel	Vorsmohlen
1840	Ltn P Bäumer	B	23	BF2b	S Douai
1845	Uffz A Müller	39	3	two-seater	Douai
1900	Vfw C Mesch	26	9	Camel	Coincy
1900	Ltn H Frommherz	27	21	Camel	Marquion
1905	Ltn A Lux	27	7	Camel	Baralle
1905	Vfw F Classen	26	7	Camel	Henin-Liétard
1910	Uffz Ruppert	39	1	Balloon	S Dury
1915	Ltn E Koepsch	4	8	SE5a	S Paillencourt
2010	Ltn W Ott	16b	1	Camel	Langemarck
	Hpt E v Schleich	23b	32	Dolphin	Landres
	Ltn K Ritscherle	60	6	Spad	Leury
	Ltn W Preuss	66	15	Bréguet XIV	Villeneuve
	Flgmt K Engelfried	MFJ 5	2	DH9	W Knocke

Time	Pilot/Crew	Unit	Vic No	E/A	Location

6 September 1918

Time	Pilot/Crew	Unit	Vic No	E/A	Location
0945	Ltn W v Richthofen	11	5	Dolphin	Écoust-Saint-Quentin
0950	Oblt P Blumenbach	31	3	Dolphin	N Saint-Quentin
1053	Ltn H Maushacke	4	7	Camel	Le Catelet
1220	Ltn Buddeberg	50	2	Spad 2	S Soissons
1315	Ltn M Demisch	58	8	Balloon	Monchy
1340	Ltn M Demisch	58	7	RE8	Monchy le Preux
1455	Vfw O Hennrich	46	12	Balloon	S Le Mesnil
1635	Ltn H Rolfes	45	15	Balloon	Magneux
1645	Ltn H Rolfes	45	45	Salmson	Magneux
1645	Ltn Berling	45	2	Balloon	Magneux
1645	Ltn Krater	45	2	Balloon	Magneux
1820	Vfw H Knaak	9	1	Spad	N Soissons
1842	Ltn M Näther	62	12	Bréguet XIV	Sillery
2005	Uffz W Dost	21s	3	Spad	E Braisne
	Ltn O Löffler	B	8	BF2b	N Bourlon Wood
	Ltn P Baümer	B	23	BF2b	W Cantaing
	Ltn E Bormann	B	10	Camel	N Bourlon Wood
	Ltn A Lindenberger	B	10	Camel	Lagnicourt
	Ltn O Frühner	26	–		
	Ltn F Noltenius	27	–		
	Ltn S Garaztka	31	–	DH9	Saint-Quentin
	Vfw Amschl	31	–	DH9	Noyon
	Ltn M Haenichen	53	2	Spad 2	
	Ltn M Haenichen	53	3	Spad 2	Coucy-le-Château

7 September 1918

Time	Pilot/Crew	Unit	Vic No	E/A	Location
0810	Ltn Hofmann	79b	2	Spad	Villequier-Aumont
1125	Ltn F Rumey	5	33	DH4	Saint-Quentin
1130	Ltn F Bornträger	49	2	Spad XI	Auberive
1135	Ltn H Häbich	49	3	Spad	St Hilaire
1145	Oblt O Schmidt	5	13	Balloon	SW Bertincourt
1230	Vfw A Haussmann	13	13	Salmson 2A2	Jeandelize
1300	Ltn J Schulte-Frohlinde	11	2	SE5	
1325	Ltn O v Beaulieu-Marconnay	19	14	Salmson 2A2	NE Montsec
1400	Ltn Schulte-Schlutius	3	1	DH9	Buschweiler
1415	Vfw J Hohly	65	5	Spad 2	Essey
1415	Oblt R Nebel	Kest 1a	2	DH4	Niederbronn
1430	Uffz H Forstmann	Kest 1a	1	DH4	Frankenthal
1940	Ltn W v Richthofen	11	6	SE5a	W Le Catelet
1945	Ltn W v Richthofen	11	7	SE5a	Le Catelet
1945	Oblt E R v Wedel	11	12	SE5	Le Catelet
	Ltn G Weiner	3	5	DH9	Dassberg
	Ltn G Weiner	3	6	DH9	Burscheid
	Ltn A Laumann	10	–		
	Ltn H Stutz	71	4	Bréguet XIV	W St Ulrich
	Ltn K Seit	80b	3	DH9	

8 September 1918

Time	Pilot/Crew	Unit	Vic No	E/A	Location
	TL Motor trouble			Spad	E Étain

Time	Pilot/Crew	Unit	Vic No	E/A	Location
9 September 1918					
	Hpt E v Schleich	23b	33	Camel	Quéant
	Ltn H Frommherz	27	–	DH9	
10 September 1918					
1400	Flak			AWFK8	Hulluch
1645	Cause unknown			Camel	S Mérignies
11 September 1918					
	Flak			EA	
12 September 1918					
1135	Ltn G v Hantelmann	15	7	Bréguet XIV	W Conflans
1235	Vfw R Moosbacher	77b	3	Salmson 2A2	Thimmenheim
1310	Oblt O v Boenigk	JGII	22	Salmson 2A2	Thiaucourt
1935	Ltn G v Hantelmann	15	8	Spad	SE Limey
	Ltn F Büchner	13	21	two-seater	Viéville-en-Haye
	Ltn F Büchner	13	22	Bréguet XIV	E Thiaucourt
	Ltn Grimm	13	2	Bréguet XIV	Thiaucourt
	Ltn K Hetze	13	5	Bréguet XIV	Thiaucourt
	Ltn F Büchner	13	23	DH4	N Hattonville
	Ltn Klieforth	19	1	Spad 2	Thiaucourt
	Gefr C Schmidt	35b	1	RE8	NW Quéant
	Ltn R Stark	35b	7	AWFK8	Hermies
	OStv Trautmann	64w	1	Salmson 2A2	Flirey-Brusay
	Uffz Beschow	64w	2	Salmson 2A2	Broussey
	Uffz Bader	64w	1	Bréguet XIV	
	Oblt E Wenig	80b	4	DH4	Phyln
	MFlakzug 69			Spad	Bouxières
13 September 1918					
1005	Ltn R Stark	35b	8	DH4	Récourt
1355	Vfw G Klaudat		4	Spad	Vionville
1500	Ltn J Jacobs	7	25	RE8	N Bailleul
1720	Ltn O v Beaulieu-Marconnay	19	15	Bréguet XIV	Chéry
1720	Ltn Gewert	19	1	Bréguet XIV	Chéry
1720	Ltn Scheller	19	3	Bréguet XIV	Rembercourt
1750	Vfw H Klose	54s	2	DH4	Récourt
1750	Vfw K Delang	54s	3	DH4	St Geneviève
1805	Ltn G v Hantelmann	15	9	Spad	SW Thiaucourt
1820	Vfw G Klaudat	15	5	Spad	SE Metz
1840	Ltn H Schäfer	15	7	DH4	Pont-à-Mousson
1930	Ltn O v Beaulieu-Marconnay	19	16	Spad	Jaulny
1930	Ltn M Klieforth	19	2	Spad	Jaulny
1940	Ltn M Demisch	58	9	Balloon	Monchy
	Oblt O v Boenigk	JGII	23	Spad	Thiaucourt
	Ltn F Büchner	13	24	Spad	Allamont
	Vfw A Haussmann	13	14	Spad	Allamont

Time	Pilot/Crew	Unit	Vic No	E/A	Location
	Ltn Büchner	13	1	Spad	Allamont
	Lt H Müller	18	7	DH4	W Thiaucourt
	Ltn B Hobein	20		EA	
	Ltn B Hobein	20	–	EA	
	Ltn R v Barnekow	20	–	EA	
	Uffz Buenning	83	1	Spad	
	OStv Kapfhammer	FA(A) 298	1	two-seater	Buillonville

14 September 1918

Time	Pilot/Crew	Unit	Vic No	E/A	Location
0900	Ltn H Müller	18	8	Spad	Gorze
0900	Vfw T Weischer	15	2	DH4	Bayonville
0900	Ltn G v Hantelmann	15	10	DH4	N Gorze
0905	Ltn G v Buren	18	2	Spad	Gorze
0910	Ltn H Müller	18	9	Spad	SW Sillingen
0915	Ltn H Müller	18	10	Spad	SE Gohn
0940	Ltn M Gossner	77b	8	Balloon	Pont-à-Mousson
1000	Oblt G Rasberger	80b	2	DH9	Rolters
1005	Ltn Kandt	18	1	DH4	Pelter
1020	Ltn Buddeberg	50	3	Spad	Révillon
1020	Ltn Maletzky	50	1	Spad	Révillon
1110	Ltn F Rumey	5	34	SE5a	S Le Catelet
1120	Oblt O v Boenigk	JGII	24	Spad	Lachaussée
1120	Oblt O v Boenigk	JGII	25	Spad	N Lachaussée
1140	Ltn J Klein	15	14	Spad	St Benoit
1145	Ltn G v Hantelmann	15	11	Spad	Pont-à-Mousson
1150	Oblt H Kohze	JGp9	2	DH	Pont-à-Mousson
1155	Ltn W Blume	9	24	Spad 2	S Laffaux
1200	Ltn E Siempelkamp	64w	5	Salmson 2A2	Bonzée
1200	Ltn W Blume	9	25	Spad	Braye
1245	Ltn M Gossner	77b	7	Spad XIII	Bois de Rappes
1245	Vfw B Ultsch	77b	11	Spad XIII	Jaulny
1320	Ltn M Gossner	77b	9	Salmson 2A2	Villecrey
1440	Ltn H Müller	18	11	Spad	Pont-à-Mousson
1445	Vfw Glatz	18	1	Spad	
1532	Uffz Lohrmann	42	2	DH9	W Holnon Wood
1615	Ltn G v Hantelmann	15	12	Spad	Lachaussée
1615	Ltn J Klein	J5	15	Spad	Lachaussée
1620	Vfw K Schmuckle	I5	5	Spad	St Benoit
1620	Ltn U Koennemann	45	3	Salmson 2A2	Fismes
1630	Ltn Christiansen	67	2	Balloon	Clermont-Verdun
1630	Uffz H Marwede	67	2	Balloon	Clermont-Verdun
1634	Uffz H Marwede	67	3	Balloon	Clermont-Verdun
1635	Ltn M Näther	62	13	Balloon	Mailly
1638	Uffz H Marwede	67	4	Balloon	Clermont-Verdun
1730	Oblt G Rasberger	80b	3	Spad XIII	Champenoux
1740	Ltn F Noltenius	27	7	Balloon	Vis-en-Artois
1815	Ltn Bacher	3	2	Spad	S Thiaucourt
1920	Ltn Gewert	19	2	Salmson 2A2	Beney
	Ltn P Baümer	B	25	RE8	Cantaing
	Ltn F Kresse	7	1	RE8	SE Ypres
	Ltn H Becker	12	14	Bréguet XIV	Luttingen

Time	Pilot/Crew	Unit	Vic No	E/A	Location
	Ltn F Büchner	13	25	two-seater	Mars-la-Tour
	Ltn F Büchner	13	26	Bréguet XIV	Mars-la-Tour
	Ltn Grimm	13	3	Bréguet XIV	Conflans
	Ltn W Niethammer	13	3	Bréguet XIV	Puxe
	Ltn Büchner	13	2	Caudron	Conflans
	Ltn O v Beaulieu-Marconnay	19	17	Bréguet XIV	Jouville
	Ltn R Rineau	19	3	Bréguet XIV	Conflans
	Ltn M Klieforth	19	3	Bréguet XIV	Conflans
	OStv G Dörr	45	27	Spad XI	Blanzy
	Ltn K Ritscherle	60	7	Spad	
	Ltn G Wember	61	4	Balloon	
	Ltn E Siempelkamp	64w		Spad XIII	W Auvillers
	Ltn W Frickert	65	8	Caudron	Lateur
	Vfw J Hohly	65	6	Caudron	St Maurice
	Ltn W Preuss	66	16	two-seater	
	Vfw Hasenpusch	67	2	Bréguet XIV	Doncourt
	Vfw Wimmer	80b	2	Spad XIII	
	Uffz Goetz	1	1	Spad	

15 September 1918

Time	Pilot/Crew	Unit	Vic No	E/A	Location
0923	Uffz H Nülle	39	6	Balloon	Quéant
0924	Uffz H Nülle	39	7	Balloon	Villers
0925	Uffz H Nülle	39	8	Balloon	Villers
0926	Uffz H Nülle	39	9	Balloon	Dury
0930	Oblt R Greim	34b	23	SE5a	S Hermies
1210	Ltn H Schäfer	15	8	DH9	SW Metz
1215	Vfw T Weischer	15	3	DH9	S Metz
1215	Ltn G v Hantelmann	15	13	DH9	SE Metz
1215	Oblt H v Wedel	24s	3	EA	Nauroy-Estrées
1225	Ltn U Neckel	6	25	BF2b	Estrées
1230	Ltn H Leptien	63	6	RE8	W Armentières
1250	Vfw W Kohlbach	10	4	Camel	Cantaing
1305	Ltn Jeep	58	2	Balloon	Vitry
1305	Uffz K Pietzsch	58	2	Balloon	Wancourt
1325	Ltn M Gossner	77b	5	Balloon	Lironville
1505	Ltn H v Freden	50	8	Balloon	Juvigny
1507	Ltn H v Freden	50	9	Balloon	Juvigny
1510	Ltn zS R Poss	MFJ 4	6	Camel	Zeebrugge
1540	Vfw O Hennrich	46	13	Balloon	Bertincourt
1700	Ltn G Meyer	37	17	EA	N Marcoing
1705	Flgmt Hackbusch	MFJ 1	2	Dolphin	Coucelaere
1705	Flgmt Kutschke	MFJ 5	1	DH9	Walvhern
1710	Flgmt K Engelfried	MFJ 5	3	DH9	Walvhern
1720	Ltn Freymadl	MFJ 1	1	DH9	Middleberg
1745	Vfw R Jörke	39	14	SE5a	
1800	Gefr B Bartels	44s	1	Balloon	Saint-Simon
1900	Vfw K Treiber	5	1	Balloon	W Fins
1905	Ltn O Frühner	26	25	RE8	Palleul
1905	Ltn R Stark	35b	9	Dolphin	Cagnicourt
1906	Uffz C Schmidt	35b	2	Camel	

Time	Pilot/Crew	Unit	Vic No	E/A	Location
1908	St H Stor	35b	1	SE5a	N Marquion
1910	Ltn J Jacobs	7	26	AWFK8	Passchendaele
1920	Ltn F Reimer	26	7	SE5	Palleul
1930	Vfw C Mesch	26	10	Balloon	Boiry-Notre Dame
1940	Vfw Schneck	9	2	Spad	E Vailly
1940	Ltn W Neuenhofen	27	7	SE5a	Bourlon Wood
1945	Ltn G Meyer	37	18	SE5a	Bourlon
	Ltn F Büchner	13	27	Spad	Thiaucourt
	Ltn F Büchner	13	28	Spad	Lachaussée
	Ltn Scheller	19	4	Spad	Pagny
	Ltn R Rineau	19	4	Spad	S Pagny
	Hpt E v Schleich	23b	34	AWFK8	Marcoing
	Ltn H Seywald	23b	5	Camel	Marquette
	Uffz M Hutterer	23b	6	SE5a	St Léger
	Uffz H Kleinschrodt	23b	1	Camel	Arleux
	Flg S Braun	23b	1	Camel	Écoust
	Ltn F Classen	26	–	Camel	Reincourt
	Vfw C Mesch	26	11	SE5	Rémy
	Ltn E Thuy	28w	29	Camel	
	Ltn Meixner	45	2	Balloon	Braisne
	Uffz De Ray	58	1	Camel	
	Ltn F Höhn	60	11	Balloon	
	Ltn A Korff	60	5	Balloon	
	Ltn Leibfried	64w		Salmson 2A2	Blened
	Vfw J Hohly	65	7	Spad 2	St Rémy
	Ltn J Fichter	67	6	Balloon	Douaumont
	Ltn M Gossner	77b	6	Balloon	Lironville
	Flak			two-seater	Marimbois
	Flak			two-seater	Conflans
	FTL, became lost, POW			two-seater	Doncourt
	FTL, motor trouble, POW			Scout	Conflans

16 September 1918

Time	Pilot/Crew	Unit	Vic No	E/A	Location
0740	Fw Hoffmann	Kest3	1	Spad	SW Frescaty
0840	Ltn J Jacobs	7	27	SE5a	W Menin
0840	Ltn H Böhning	79b	16	DH9	NW Bellenglise
0845	Ltn O Frühner	26	26	BF2b	Fontaine
0845	Uffz Brungel	31	1	Scout	Gricourt
0850	Ltn H Lange	26	7	BF2b	NW Quiéry
0850	Ltn Breidenbach	44s	1	BF2b	Roupy
0900	Ltn K Plauth	20	7	DH9	Bondues
0900	Hpt B Loerzer	JGIII	39	BF2b	Dourges
0900	Ltn F Rumey	5	35	DH9A	Villers-Guislain
0915	Vzflgmstr H Goerth	MFJ 3	5	Camel	Zerkeghem
0915	Ltn Holle	31	1	DH9	NE Douchy
1120	Ltn G v Hantelmann	15	14	Spad	SW Conflans
1125	Vfw G Klaudat	15	6	Spad	St Hilaire
1150	Bz 152 FTL POW			Spad	Kemnat
1230	Ltn F Rumey	5	36	SE5a	Marquion
1235	Ltn F Rumey	5	37	Camel	Marquion
1330	Ltn G Weiner	3	7	DH4	Alt-Eckendorf

Time	Pilot/Crew	Unit	Vic No	E/A	Location
1530	Ltn G Meyer	37	19	Scout	Marquion
1540	Uffz Gengelin	37	2	Scout NW	Cambrai
1755	Ltn O v Beaulieu-Marconnay	19	19	Bréguet XIV	SW Briey
1755	Ltn R Rineau	19	5	Bréguet XIV	SW Briey
1755	Gefr Felder	19	2	Bréguet XIV	Conflans
1755	Vfw C Mesch	26	13	Camel	Reincourt
1755	Vfw F Classen	26		Camel	Récourt
1755	Ltn C Reimer	26	–	Camel	Baralle
1800	Ltn Macard	26	2	SE5	Sauchy-Couchy
1935	Ltn J Jacobs	7	28	Balloon	Poperinghe
	Ltn P Baümer	B	26	DH4	Henin-Liétard
	Ltn O Löffler	B	10	DH4	Aveluy
	Ltn O Löffler	B	11	DH4	NE Arras
	Ltn F Hoffmann	B	1	BF2b	SW Cambrai
	Vfw Lieber	7	1	SE5a	
	Uffz Piesker	7	1	SE5a	
	Ltn O v Beaulieu-Marconnay	19	18	Bréguet XIV	Fléville
	Ltn H Seywald	23b	6	DH4	W Cantin
	Uffz H Kleinschrodt	23b	2	DH4	Denain
	Hpt B Loerzer	JGIII	40	SE5	
	Ltn R Klimke	27	16	Camel	
	Ltn F Noltenius	27	8	BF2b	
	Vfw E de Ridder	27	–	SE5a	
	Ltn E Thuy	28w	30	SE5a	
	Oblt R Greim	34b	–	EA	
	OStv G Dörr	45	28	Spad	Fismes
	????	47	–	Balloon	
	Ltn J Jensen	57	4	RE8	S Sauchy-Cauchy
	Vfw A Korff	60	6	Spad	
	Ltn A Stephen	70	1	DH9A	Germersheim
	Sgt Metzger	70	1	DH9A	SE Landau
	Ltn G Frädrich	72s	3	Spad	
	Ltn H Mahn	72s	2	Spad	
	Ltn F G Anders	73	–	Voisin	Warnerville
	Ltn zS Wilhelm	MFJ 4	1	Camel	Zeebrugge
	Hpt E v Schleich	JGp8	34	AWFK8	Marquion
	Ltn zS T Osterkamp	MFJ 2	24	Camel	Coxyde
	Ltn zS T Osterkamp	MFJ 2	25	Camel	Coxyde
	Flak FTL POW			Spad	Xammes
	Ltn Ahrens &		1		
	Sgt Koppel	FA44	1	Spad	Pierrefitte
	Flakzug 422			Spad	SE St Ludwig

17 September 1918

Time	Pilot/Crew	Unit	Vic No	E/A	Location
0905	Ltn F Rumey	5	38	SE5a	Rumilly
1157	Ltn F Brandt	26	–	Camel	Hermies
1300	Ltn F Rumey	5	39	Camel	NW Cambrai
1310	Flak			DH4	Wahagnies
1510	Ltn G v Hantelmann	15	15	Spad	N Gorze
1530	Ltn F Noltenius	27	9	Balloon	

Time	Pilot/Crew	Unit	Vic No	E/A	Location
1805	Flak			Camel	Neuve Chapelle
1833	Flgmt G Hubrich	MFJ 4	4	Camel	Batt Zeppelin
1910	Ltn F Rumey	5	40	Camel	SW Cambrai
1910	Ltn J Mai	5	26	Camel	S Bus
	Ltn G Weiner	3	8	Bréguet XIV	Falkenberg
	Ltn F Büchner	13	29	Salmson 2A2	Dampvitoux
	Ltn H Frommherz	27	22	DH9	
	Ltn H Boes	34b	2	SE5a	
	Vfw A Korff	60	6	Balloon	
	Flak FTL POW			Salmson 2A2	Bruville

18 September 1918

Time	Pilot/Crew	Unit	Vic No	E/A	Location
1030	Flak			SE5	Wingles
1135	Vfw Sowa/Flak	52	–	DH9	L'Homme
1140	Ltn S Garsztka	31	2	SE5a	Lempire
1430	Ltn H Böhning	79b	17	Balloon	N Vaux
1510	Ltn F Noltenius	27	10	Balloon	
1520	Ltn C Degelow	40s	14	Balloon	Oosthoek
1540	Vfw K Trieber	5	2	Balloon	Tincourt
1645	Ltn G v Hantelmann	15	16	Spad	Vionville
1725	Ltn F Büchner	13	31	Spad	Chambley
1730	Ltn F Büchner	13	32	Spad	W Chambley
1730	Ltn U Neckel	6	26	DH4	Conflans
1730	Ltn H Becker	12	15	Bréguet XIV	W Conflans
1730	Ltn H Becker	12	16	Bréguet XIV	W Conflans
1730	Ltn H Besser	12	1	Bréguet XIV	W Conflans
1730	Flg Wilke	12	1	Bréguet XIV	SW Conflans
1730	Ltn A Greven	12	1	Bréguet XIV	SW Conflans
	Ltn F Büchner	13	30	Spad XIII	Dampvitoux
	Ltn S Garsztka	31	3	DH9	Saulcourt
	FTL, Cause unknown			Salmson 2A2	Chambley
	FTL, Cause unknown			Bréguet XIV	Conflans
	FTL, Cause unknown			Bréguet XIV	Conflans

19 September 1918

Time	Pilot/Crew	Unit	Vic No	E/A	Location
1600	Ltn J Schulte-Frohlinde	11	3	BF2b	Bellenglise
1900	Ltn J Jacobs	7	29	Camel	
	Uffz P Hüttenrauch	7	4	AWFK8	
	Ltn Maletzky	50		Balloon	Noyon

20 September 1918

Time	Pilot/Crew	Unit	Vic No	E/A	Location
0745	Ltn W Neuenhofen	27	8	Camel	Proville
0745	Ltn H Frommherz	27	23	Camel	Marcoing
0745	Ltn F Noltenius	27	11	Camel	Marcoing
0800	Ltn G Meyer	37	20	SE5a	N Hermies
1005	Ltn zS Stinsky	MFJ 2	2	Camel	SE Pervyse
1005	Vzflgmstr K Scharon	MFJ 2	1	Camel	Pervyse
1037	Oblt O Schmidt	5	14	BF2b	Fresnoy-le-Grand
1040	Uffz Leicht	5	2	BF2b	Croix Fonsommé
1050	Ltn K Odebrett	42	14	DH9	SE Montigny

Time	Pilot/Crew	Unit	Vic No	E/A	Location
1055	Ltn C Degelow	40s	15	BF2b	Annappes
1445	Ltn F Noltenius	27	12	Camel	Aubigny-au-Bac
1540	Ltn F Barndt	26	9	Camel	Écourt
1545	Ltn O Frühner	26	27	Camel	E Cagnicourt
1550	Ltn P Baümer	B	27	Camel	E Rumaucourt
	Ltn J Jacobs	7		Camel	
	Ltn F Kirchfeld	73	2	Voisin	
	OStv W Schluckebier	73	2	Voisin	
	Ltn F G Anders	73	6	Voisin	
	Ltn P Becht	MFJ 1	2	Camel	Beerst
	Ltn zS T Osterkamp	MFJ 2	26	Camel	Praet Bosch
	Ground fire			H.P.	AFP C Airfield
	Flak			Camel	N Méricourt

21 September 1918

Time	Pilot/Crew	Unit	Vic No	E/A	Location
0945	Vfw Niemeyer &		1	RE8	N Éphey
	Uffz Kappel	SchSt 29	2		
1045	Ltn C Degelow	40s	16	RE8	St Julien
1120	Flak			SE5a	E La Bassée
1210	Ltn J Jacobs	7	30	DH9	Dixmuide
1222	Ltn J Jacobs	7	–	DH9	NW Roulers
1830	Ltn Oldenberg	22s	1	DH9	Cambrai
1840	Ltn J Mai	5	27	DH9	Montecouvez-Fé
1845	Uffz Westphal	29	2	SE5	E La Bassée
1900	Vfw R Schleichardt	18	3	Spad	Facqwald
1905	Ltn H Müller	18	12	Spad	Combreshohen
1905	Ltn E Spindler	18	2	Spad	Combreshohen
	Ltn P Baümer	B	28	DH4	E Bourlon Wood
	Ltn P Baümer	B	29	DH4	E Lagnicourt
	Ltn P Baümer	B	30	DH4	E Morchies
	Ltn K Plauth	20	8	DH9	Staden
	Ltn R Klimke	27	17	Camel	
	Ltn H Frommherz	27	33	Sopwith	
	Ltn F Noltenius	27	–	EA	
	Ltn R Klimke	27	–	EA	

22 September 1918

Time	Pilot/Crew	Unit	Vic No	E/A	Location
0750	Vfw K Bohnenkamp	22s	9	Camel	N Éphey
0750	Vfw K Bohnenkamp	22s	10	Camel	N Éphey
0815	Ltn H-G v d Marwitz	30	12	Camel	S Neuve-Église
0820	Ltn F Bieling	30	1	Camel	Ploegsteert Wald
0850	Ltn W Neuenhofen	27	9	Sopwith	
0850	Vfw C Reimer	26	8	Camel	W Sauchy-Cauchy
0855	Vfw Belz	1	2	RE8	Cambrai
0858	Ltn F Brandt	26	10	Camel	Sains
0956	Ltn K Odebrett	42	15	Bréguet XIV	S Flavy-le-Martel
	Hpt B Loerzer	JGIII	41	Camel	
	Hpt B Loerzer	JGIII	42	EA	
	Ltn H Frommherz	27	24	Sopwith	
	Ltn E Thuy	28w	31	SE5a	Vitry
	Vfw H Hünninghaus	66	3	Spad	Pont Arcy
	Oblt O v Boenigk	JGII	26	Salmson 2A2	Conflans

Time	Pilot/Crew	Unit	Vic No	E/A	Location
23 September 1918					
1620	Ltn Oldenberg	22s	2	Balloon	Attilly
1620	Oblt H v Wedel	24s	4	SE5	Villers-Outréaux
1710	Ltn H Leptien	63	7	RE8	S Fleurbaix
1725	Vfw K Ungewitter	24s	4	BF2b	Levergies
1725	OStv F Altemeier	24s	–	BF2b	Levergies
1815	Ltn F Rumey	5	41	Dolphin	SW Baralle
	Ltn B Hobein	20	–	BF2b	Baralle
24 September 1918					
0730	Ltn M Demisch	58	10	SE5a	Abancourt
0820	Ltn F Rumey	5	42	SE5a	S Buissy
0830	Oblt O Schmidt	5	15	SE5a	Rumaucourt
0830	Uffz Leicht	5	3	SE5a	N Hamel
0830	Vfw R Wirth	37	4	BF2b	S Beauvois
1040	Vfw K Bohnenkamp	22s	10	DH9	Vermand
1040	Ltn K Plauth	20	9	DH9	Sainghin
1050	OStv Bansmer	44s	2	Spad 2	SW Attigny
1050	Ltn H J Gildemeister	20	3	DH9	Lorgies
1050	Ltn J v Busse	20	8	DH9	Lorgies
1100	Vfw F Poeschke	53	3	Spad XI	Besine
1120	Vfw O Hennrich	46	14	Balloon	NE Manancourt
1350	Uffz H Haase	21s	4	Balloon	S Braisne
1415	Ltn zS C Wilhelm	MFJ 4	2	Camel	Pervyse
1610	Vfw O Hennrich	46		Balloon	Fins
1612	Vfw O Hennrich	46	16	Balloon	Fins
1612	Ltn auf der Haar	46	1	Balloon	Fins
1615	Ltn J Klein	15	16	Spad	
1725	Vfw Becker	44s	3	two-seater	Metz-en-Couture
1730	Ltn J Mai	5	28	DH9	S Beauvais
1800	Ltn C Degelow	40s	17	SE5a	Zillebeke Lake
1800	Vfw Mack	63	2	SE5a	S Ypres
1815	Vfw M Kuhn	21s	9	Balloon	SE Fismes
1835	Ltn J Jacobs	7	35	Camel	Moorslede
1900	OStv G Dörr	45	29	Spad	Soissons
	Ltn P Baümer	B	31	Camel	Sailly
	Ltn P Baümer	B	32	DH9	SW Clary
	Ltn O Löffler	B	12	DH9	W Cambrai
	Oblt H v Boddien	59	4	SE5a	Anneux
	Oblt F Krafft	59	2	SE5a	Inchy
	Oblt H v Boddien	59	5	DH4	Le Pave
	Ltn Lehmann	59	1	BF2b	Boursies
	Ltn H Jebens	59	1	BF2b	Bantouzelle
	Ltn G Wember	61	2	Balloon	
	Ltn zS P Achilles	MFJ 5	2	DH9	Werckem
25 September 1918					
0805	Ltn R Fuchs	77b	1	Spad	Arnaville
0950	Ltn J Grassmann	10	6	Balloon	Pont-à-Mousson

Time	Pilot/Crew	Unit	Vic No	E/A	Location
1010	Ltn O v Beaulieu-Marconnay	19	20	Bréguet XIV	Pont-à-Mousson
1115	Gefr Meyer	3	1	DH9A	SE Sarralbe
1120	Ltn G v Hantelmann	15	17	DH4	S Metz
1430	Ltn R Schmidt	78b	1	DH4	Zabern
1430	Ltn Keisze	Kest1b	1	DH4	Zabern
1500	Vfw L Prime	78b	–	DH4	Buhl Airfield
1500	2/Flamga 911			DH9	Buhl Airfield
1750	Ltn zS P Achilles	MFJ 5	4	Camel	Hooglede
1800	Vfw K Treiber	5	3	Spad	S Saint-Quentin
1800	Ltn S Garsztka	31	4	DH9	Fresnoy
1800	Vzflgmstr A Zenses	MFJ 2	8	Camel	Wynendaele
1805	Uffz Brungel	31	2	DH9	Busigny
1805	Ltn zS P Achilles	MFJ 5	5	Camel	NW Roulers
1815	Oblt R R v Greim	34b	24	DH9	S Escaufourt
1825	Ltn F v Braun	79b	2	BF2b	Villers-Guislain
1850	Ltn F Piechulek	56	11	Camel	Kortemarck
	Ltn F Noltenius	27	13	Camel	
	Ltn F Hengst	64w	3	Salmson 2A2	
	Ltn A Stephen	70	2	DH4	Alberschweiler
	Vfw Lemke	70	2	DH4	Bergzabern
	Vfw Krist	70	1	DH4	Brumath
	Ltn F G Anders	73	5	Farman	Moronvillers
	Uffz Neilputs &		1		
	Uffz Rogge	SchSt19	1	SE5	Nurlu

26 September 1918

Time	Pilot/Crew	Unit	Vic No	E/A	Location
0710	Ltn M Näther	62	14	Spad	Bezonvaux
0810	Vfw W Seitz	8	11	Spad	Étain
0830	Ltn F Höhn	60	14	Spad 2	Somme-Py
0831	Gefr Rohr	50	1	Bréguet XIV	SE Perthies
0900	Uffz K Hoffmann	60	1	Spad	Massiges
1025	Vfw K Bohnenkamp	22s	12	Camel	NW Rossoy
1030	Flgmt K Engelfried	MFJ 5	4	Camel	Wenduyne
1030	Flgomt C Kairies	MFJ 5	6	Camel	Neumunster
1050	Uffz Ernst	49	1	Bréguet XIV	Tahure
1115	Ltn Freymadl	MFJ 1	2	DH4	Ostende
1115	Vzflgmstr Sawatzki	MFJ 1	1	Camel	Ostende
1215	Ltn W Blume	9	26	Spad 2	Tahure
1215	Ltn F Höhn	60	15	Balloon	Minaucourt
1300	OStv G Dörr	45	30	Spad 2	Fismes
1350	Vfw R Francke	8	15	Spad	
1410	Ltn F Rumey	5	43	DH4	Gouzeaucourt
1415	Ltn Hebler	68	2	Balloon	Auberive
1415	Ltn Hebler	68	3	Balloon	Réchicourt
1433	Vfw C Mesch	26	12	Dolphin	W Saint-Quentin
1535	Ltn M Näther	62	15	Balloon	Thierville
1535	Ltn Breidenbach	62	1	Balloon	Thierville
1540	Ltn H Häbich	49	4	Balloon	Minaucourt
1545	Ltn M Näther	62	16	Salmson 2A2	Abaucourt

Time	Pilot/Crew	Unit	Vic No	E/A	Location
1600	Vfw A Juehe	8	4	Spad	
1630	Oblt G Rasberger	80b	4	Spad XIII	Athienville
1645	Vfw O Hennrich	46	17	Balloon	Liéramont
1710	Oblt E Udet	4	61	DH4	SW Metz
1715	Oblt E Udet	4	62	DH4	SW Metz
1715	Vfw Seidel	3	1	DH9	SE Frescaty
1715	Ltn Bacher	3	3	DH	
1715	Vfw Glasemann	3	1	DH	
1715	Ltn R Kraut	4	1	DH9	Buch
1720	Ltn J Klein	15	17	DH4	NE Vern
1725	Ltn M Gossner	77b	8	DH9	Mannigen
1727	Vfw B Ultsch	77b	10	DH9	Kubern
1730	Vfw Schaflein	77b	1	DH9	Pullingen
1730	Vfw Agne	77b	1	DH9	Grossprunach
1740	Ltn J v Zirgesar	15	3	DH4	Pont-à-Mousson
1740	Ltn S Garsztka	31	5	SE5a	Fresnoy-le-Petit
1745	Uffz Fröhlich	46	1	Balloon	Liéramont
1755	Ltn H v Freden	50	10	Balloon	Perthes
1800	Ltn Matetsky	50	3	Spad	Perthes
1805	Ltn F Rumey	5	44	BF2b	Cambrai
1810	Ltn Matetsky	50	4	Spad	Le Mesnil
	Ltn E Bormann	B	11	Camel	N Cambrai
	Ltn v Gluszewski	4	1	DH4	N Leveningen
	Vfw K Treiber	5	4	DH4	E Le Pave
	Ltn H Becker	12	17	DH4	SE Longuyon
	Ltn H Becker	12	18	DH4	Anoux
	Ltn A Greven	12	2	DH4	Giraumont
	Vfw O Klaiber	12	1	DH4	NW Longuyon
	Ltn H Besser	12	2	DH4	Landres
	Ltn F Büchner	13	33	Spad	Consenvoye
	Ltn F Büchner	13	34	Salmson 2A2	Charpentrie
	Ltn F Büchner	13	35	Spad	Gercourt
	Ltn F Büchner	13	36	Spad	Étreillers
	Vfw A Haussmann	13	15	Spad	Bertincourt
	Ltn G v Hantelmann	15	18	Spad	Étain
	Ltn H Schäfer	15	9	Spad	SW Étain
	Hpt B Loerzer	JGIII	43	EA	
	Hpt B Loerzer	JGIII	44	EA	
	Ltn H v Freden	50	11	Salmson 2A2	Ville-sur-Tourbe
	Ltn W Frickart	65	9	Spad	S Delut
	????	69	–	Spad	Montreux
	Ltn H Mann	72s	3	EA	
	Ltn H Mann	72s	4	EA	
	Ltn G Tschentschel	72s	5	EA	
	Ltn G Frädrich	72s	4	EA	
	Ltn E Schulz	72s	1	EA	
	Vfw D Averes	81	7	Bréguet XIV	Tahure
	Vfw A Näler	81	7	Spad	Suippes
	Flak			DH4	Noyelles-le-Sec

Time	Pilot/Crew	Unit	Vic No	E/A	Location
	27 September 1918				
0755	Vfw H Juhnke	52	–	BF2b	W Armentières
0815	Oblt R R v Greim	34b	25	Camel	S Masnières
0930	Ltn R v Barnekow	1	6	SE5a	Bourlon Wood
0940	Uffz G Borm	1	3	SE5a	St Olle-Cambrai
1020	OStv F Altemeier	24s	17	BF2b	Marcy-Fontaine
1130	Ltn R Ruckle	33	2	BF2b	Busigny
1208	Ltn F Rumey	5	45	Camel	E Marquion
1210	Ltn J Mai	5	29	Camel	Sauchy-Cauchy
1250	Vfw K Treiber	5	5	SE5a	W Cambrai
1300	Ltn R v Barnekow	1	7	DH4	Sailly
1300	Uffz G Borm	1	4	Dolphin	Bourlon Wood
1403	Vfw F Classen	26	8	BF2b	S Brunemont
1550	Oblt O Schmidt	5	16	BF2b	Cattenières
1600	Vfw O Hennrich	46	18	BF2b	Neuvilly
1655	Ltn H Korner	19	4	Spad	Pagny
1655	Ltn H v Freden	50	12	Balloon	Minaucourt
1700	Vfw L Prime	78b	–	Spad VII	Herbéville
1730	Gefr Meyer	3	2	Spad	Champenoux
1735	Ltn G Bassenge	B	4	SE5a	Noyelles
1735	Vfw F Classen	26	9	SE5	S Sailly
1810	Vfe A Korff	60	8	Spad	N Tahure
1820	Ltn F Höhn	60	16	Spad	Marfaux
1820	Vfw Zimmermann	60	1	Spad	Tahure
1820	Uffz H Pfaffenreiter	60	3	Spad	
	Ltn P Baümer	B	33	SE5a	W Cambrai
	Ltn P Baümer	B	34	SE5a	W Cambrai
	Ltn H Vallendor	B	4	Camel	Marquion
	Ltn P Baümer	B	35	DH4	Oisy-le-Verger
	Ltn E Bormann	B	12	Camel	Écoust-Saint-Quentin
	Ltn E Bormann	B	13	Camel	E Épinoy
	Ltn H Vallendor	B	5	Camel	N Bourlon Wood
	Uffz K Feveres	B	1	Camel	Aubenscheul
	Ltn H Frommherz	27	25	SE5	
	Ltn H Frommherz	27	26	SE5	
	Ltn E Thuy	28w	32	SE5a	
	Ltn C Degelow	40s	18	BF2b	W Valenciennes
	Ltn F Piechulek	56	12	Camel	Torhout
	Ltn J Jensen	57	5	DH9	Féchain
	Vfw Senf	59	1	DH9	Goeulzin
	Ltn M Näther	62	17	Spad	Montville
	Vfw D Averes	81	8	Spad	Ville
	Vfw A Nägler	81	8	Bréguet XIV	N Tahure
	28 September 1918				
0800	Uffz Jeckert	56	3	AR2	Moorslede
0810	Ltn F Höhn	60	17	Balloon	Tahure
0830	Ltn F Höhn	60	18	Balloon	Béthelainville
0835	Ltn G Bassenge	B	5	SE5a	Hem-Lenglet
1024	Flak			SE5	N Carvin
1035	Ltn O v Beaulieu-Marconnay	19	21	Spad	Dannevoux

Time	Pilot/Crew	Unit	Vic No	E/A	Location
1130	Flak			Camel	S Drocourt
1145	Vfw F Poeschke	53	4	Spad 2	Somme-Py
1150	Uffz K Boness	53	1	Spad	
1230	Vzflgmstr A Zenses	MFJ 2	9	Camel	Woumen
1230	Ltn zS T Osterkamp	MFJ 2	27	Camel	Woumen
1240	Ltn E Baumgartel	56	1	SE5	Ypern
1315	Ltn Wolff	60	1	Spad	Vienne-le-Château
1430	FlgMt Nake	MFJ 1	1	DH9	Leke
1545	Ltn A Brandenstein	49	6	Spad	Cerny
1620	Vfw K Bohnenkamp	22s	15	DH9	Wassigny
1740	Ltn K Plauth	20	10	Camel	S Roulers
1740	Ltn K Plauth	20	11	Camel	S Roulers
1745	Ltn zS R Poss	MFJ 4	7	Dolphin	W Roulers
1745	FlgMstr A Buhl	MFJ 4	4	Dolphin	Roulers
1750	Ltn J J Raesch	43	4	SE5a	E Ypern
1810	Ltn zS T Osterkamp	MFJ 2	28	Bréguet XIV	Pierkenshoeck
1815	Ltn zS Bargmann	MFJ 2	1	DH9	Beerst
1815	Flgmt Pfeiffer	MFJ 3	1	Camel	Woumen
	Ltn O Löffler	B	13	SE5a	Épinoy
	Uffz K Feveres	B	2	Camel	Épinoy
	Ltn J Jacobs	7	30	SE5a	
	Ltn F Buchner	13	37	Salmson 2A2	Nantillois
	Ltn W Niethammer	13	4	Bréguet XIV	
	Uffz E Binge	16b	4	SE5a	
	Oblt R R v Greim	34b	–	Camel	S Masnières
	Ltn C Degelow	40s	19	Camel	Armentières
	Ltn F Piechulek	56		DH4	Wervicq
	Vfw Krebs	56	1	Spad	Kastelhoek
	Vfw R Ruebe	67	–	Balloon	
	Ltn G Frädrich	72s	5	AR2	Maure
	Vfw K Arnold	72s	4	AR2	Maure
	Ltn E Schulz	72s	2	Spad	Mardeuil
	Ltn H Mahn	72s	5	Spad	Mardeuil

29 September 1918

Time	Pilot/Crew	Unit	Vic No	E/A	Location
0815	Vfw Krebs	56	2	SE5	Westroosebeke
0820	Vzflgmstr Hackbusch	MFJ 1	3	Camel	SW Oostkamp
0820	Ltn Freymadl	MFJ 1	3	Camel	SW Oostkamp
0820	Flgmt Reiss	MFJ 1	1	Camel	SW Oostkamp
0830	Uffz Jeckert	56	4	RE8	Zonnebeke
0845	Vfw K Treiber	5	6	DH9	N Caudry
0850	Ltn J Mai	5	30	BF2b	N Caudry
0940	Ltn K Odebrett	42	16	SE5a	Bohain
1000	Ltn H v Freden	50	13	Spad	Somme-Py
1020	Oblt H v Wedel	24s	5	SE5	Hesdins
1020	Vfw O Hennrich	46	19	SE5a	Villers-Outréaux
1030	Ltn auf der Haar	46	2	Scout	Aubenscheul
1040	OStv F Altemeier	24s	18	Scout	Montbrehain
1050	Ltn A Lenz	22s	6	SE5a	Bellenglise
1205	Flgmt E Blaass	MFJ 3	3	Camel	Oudekapelle
1230	Ltn Kohlpoth	56	1	DH4	Beythem

Time	Pilot/Crew	Unit	Vic No	E/A	Location
1240	Ltn W Rosenstein	40s	5	BF2b	
1400	Ltn H Henkel	37	4	Balloon	Graincourt
1720	Uffz Bader	64w	3	Spad XIII	SW Chambley
1855	Ltn R Rineau	19	6	Spad	Brieulles
1900	Ltn H Rolfes	45	17	BF2b	Masnières
	Uffz Keusen	B	2	BF2b	E Irony
	Uffz K Fervers	B	2	BF2b	Cagnoucles
	Ltn P Baümer	B	36	RE8	Marcoing
	Ltn P Baümer	B	37	Camel	Bourlon Wood
	Ltn P Baümer	B	38	Camel	SE Sailly
	Ltn J Jacobs	7		EA	
	Ltn Zicke	8	2	Spad	
	Ltn K Plauth	20	12	DH9	Roulers
	Vfw H Huenninghaus	66	4	Spad	N Jouy
	Uffz O Bieleit	66	1	Bréguet XIV	N Jouy
	Ltn zS T Osterkamp	MFJ 2	29	Bréguet XIV	W Zarren

30 September 1918					
0940	Vfw W Schmelter	42	3	SE5a	Bohain
1025	Vfw F Nuesch	22s	2	Camel	Omissy
1540	Gefr Pissowotsky	54	1	Balloon	Monsard
1700	Ltn H Henkel	37	5	RE8	Crevecoeur
1800	Ltn S Garsztka	31	6	SE5a	Lehaucourt
1820	Ltn H Häbich	49	5	Spad	Maure
1820	Ltn F Ray	49	17	Spad	Somme-Py
	Ltn A Wunsch	67	–	Salmson 2A2	
	Vfw A Nägler	81	9	Spad	Ville

Appendix 5

Belgian Victory Claims

Time	Pilot/Crew	Unit	Vic No	E/A	Location	How
			3 September 1918			
	Lt W Coppens	Esc.1	29	Balloon	Tenbrielen	DF
			4 September 1918			
	Lt W Coppens	Esc.1	30	Balloon	Bovekerke	DF
			27 September 1918			
	Lt W Coppens	Esc.1	31	Balloon	Leffinghe	DF
			29 September 1918			
	Lt W Coppens	Esc.1	32	Balloon	Leffinghe	DF

Appendix 6

Known German Casualties

1 September 1918

Vfw Pilarz	FA(A)294	WIA, near Roeux	
Uffz Gottfried Ebert	"	KIA	
Ltn Hermann Aschoff	"	KIA, Hendecourt	
Ltn Friedrich Ohlf	FA208	KIA, Gendecourt	
Uffz Alfred Donnevert night of 1-2 September		KIA, Le Cateau	
Ltn Paul Berthold	BGIII	Killed, Gontrude	4 Armee
Uffz Kurt Peuckert		Killed	
Ltn Hertel		Injured	

2 September 1918

Ltn Hartung (O)	FA(A)279	WIA	Armee-A 'C'
Flg Rau (O)	FA37	WIA	"
Ltn Gottfried Clausnitzer	J72	KIA	1 Armee
Uffz Hennies	J49	WIA	3 Armee
Flg Prillwitz	J81	POW	"
Uffz Herzberg	FA250	WIA	4 Armee
Ltn Hans Quartier	J67	POW	5 Armee
Ltn Konrad Brendle	J45	POW/DOW, Reims	7 Armee
Flg Karl Pabst	J50	KIA	"
Ltn Friedrich Noltenius	J27	Safe	17 Armee
Vfw Heinrich Gockel	J33	Safe, a/c burnt	"
Uffz Josef Kraemer (P)	FA2	KIA, Nesle	19 Armee
Ltn Eugen Weber (O)	"	KIA	
Uffz Otto Reichart		KIA, Coincy	"
Ltn Adolf Thomas (O)	FA(A)210	KIA, Cambrai	"
Ltn Walter Lucas (O)	FA(A)232	WIA, DOW 22 September	"

3 September 1918

Vfw Friedrich Engler	J62	WIA	1 Armee
Gefr Wilhelm Becker	SS16	KIA. Jonkershove	4 Armee
Uffz Hugo Holtmaier	"	KIA	
Ltn Wilhelm Asimus (O)	FA(A)248	KIA, Metz-en-Couture	
Gefr Karl Noelpp (P)	"	KIA	
Uffz Karl Grunwald		KIA, Valenciennes	
Ltn Keimens Hoffstadt		KIA, Reims	
Vfw Wilhelm Skworz	J36	KIA, Abancourt	
Flg Hermann Wirth	J33	KIA, Douai	
Vfw Max Siewert		KIA, Anizy-le-Château	
Vfw Fritz Schloeter		KIA	

4 September 1918

Vfw Kurt Jentsch	J2	WIA	
Vfw Alfred Baeder	J65	WIA	Armee-A 'C'
Vfw Hans Reimers	J6	DOW, 5 September	2 Armee

Ltn Kurt Waldheim	J36	KIA, Abancourt	17 Armee
Uffz Reinhold Neumann	J36	KIA, Abancourt	"
Gefr Tegtmeyer	J57	WIA	"
Vfw Duennhaupt	J58	WIA	"
Flg Otto Wagner	J79b	POW; DVII 4504/18	18 Armee
Gefr Jakob Katzner	J43	WIA, DOW 16 September	6 Armee
Ltn Lauscher	J31	Injured	
Gefr Anton Freyler	BS27	KIA, Étreux	
Uffz Hans Lienhardt	"	KIA	
Uffz Oskar Brachmann		KIA, Charleroi	
Gefr Eugen Reud		KIA, Wambaix	

5 September 1918

Ltn Jochim v Winterfeld	J4	KIA, Avesnes-le-Sec	2 Armee
Ltn Schenk	J5	WIA	"
Gefr Jakob Katzner	J43	KIA	6 Armee
Vfw Ernst de Ritter	J27	Shot down – safe	17 Armee
Ltn Heinrich Hagar	J32b	WIA	"
Uffz Otto Rosier	J37	KIA, Flesquières	"

6 September 1918

Uffz Weiser (P)	SS20	POW	
Uffz Scharg	"	POW	
Flgr Bonifazius Baal		KIA, Bisigny	Armee-A 'C'
Ltn Karl Rommel (O)	FAA219	KIA, SW Bray	"
Flgr Otto Ruden		KIA, "	
Uffz Richard Mann		KIA	

7 September 1918

Vfw Rudolf Besel	SS30	KIA	
Ltn Rudolf Brammer (O)	FA(A) 263	KIA, Flesquières	
Flgr Otto Goldtree		KIA, Valenciennes	
Flgr Julius Jansen (P)	FA1	KIA	
Ltn Johann Neumann (O)		KIA	
Gefr Rudolf Knust (P)	FA259	KIA, St Léger	
Oblt von Neufville (O)		POW	
Vfw Hermann (P)		POW (LVG crew)	
Ltn Schneider (O)		POW	

8 September 1918

Gefr Kurt Bluemener	J6	KIA, Beaurevoir	2 Armee
Lftsch Kurt Rehn		KIA, Villers-Outréaux	"
Ltn von Scheve	FA(A) 239	WIA, near Flesquières	
Ltn Karl Rudno-Rudzinsky	FA(A) 239	WIA, near Flesquières	

13 September 1918

Ltn Eugen Kelber	J12	KIA, Mars-la-Tour	Armee-A 'C'
Ltn Kohler	FA37	WIA	"
Ltn Rudolf Rienau	J19	Baled out safely, over Chéry	
Ltn Kole	KG	POW; Friedrichshafen crew	
Ltn Schwaderer		POW	
Gefr Vowinkel		POW/WIA	

14 September 1918

Ltn Paul Wolff	J13	POW, Lachaussée	Armee-A 'C'
Ltn Eugen Siempelkamp	J64w	WIA	"
Uffz Boehm (P)	FA26	WIA, Langemarck	4 Armee
Ltn Walter Stangen (O)	"	KIA	
Fw Deinlein (P)	FAA199	Safe	
Ltn Georg Baumann (O)	"	KIA, Monhofen	19 Armee
Flgr Anton Kempa	J3	POW "	
Ltn Günther von Büren	J18	WIA	"
Gefr Willi Thom		KIA, Étreux	
Ltn Gustav Proemmel		KIA	
Flgr Wilhelm Arnold		KIA	
Uffz Erich Reinecke (P)	FA17	KIA	
Ltn Dietegen v Salis-Marschlins	"	KIA	

15 September 1918

Ltn Friedrich Gerke	FAA281	KIA, Roan l'Etape	Armee-A 'A'
Ltn Willy Beck		KIA	
Ltn Johannes Klein	J15	WIA	Armee-A 'C'
Fw Elze (P)	FAA206	WIA	"
Ltn Wilhelm Holtfort (O)	FA236	KIA, Armentières	6 Armee
Ltn Paul Vogel	J23b	POW/DOW, Amiens	17 Armee
Vfw Ernst de Ritter	J27	WIA	"
Ltn Hilmar Quittenbaum	J28w	KIA, nr Douai	"
Uffz Ottowell	J33	WIA	"
Vfw Wilhelm Lubrecht		KIA, Saint-Quentin	
Vfw Hermann Sandtvos		KIA, Cambrai	
Vfw Wilhelm Mitschein		KIA, Cambrai	
Gefr Walter Leingruber		KIA, Cambrai	
Gefr Hermann Gieseler		KIA, Cambrai	
Lftsch Otto Foshac		KIA, Cambrai	

16 September 1918

Oblt Hans Schleiter	J70	WIA	Armee-A 'A'
Two-seater	FA10	crew safe, nr Hochfeld	"
Vfw Padberg (P)	FAA279	Safe	Armee-A 'C'
Ltn Springorum (O)		Safe	
Ltn Friedrich Kresse	J7	KIA, Houplines	4 Armee
Gefr Kurt Brandt	J51	KIA, nr Quesnoy	
Flgr Siegfried Braun	J23b	KIA, Cantin	17 Armee
Ltn Friedrich Noltenius	J27	Safe, nr Mons	"
Ltn Heinrich Wessels	MFJ 1	DOW	
Vzflugmstr Sawatski	MFJ 1	WIA	
Flgmt Nake	MFJ 1	WIA	
Oblt Alfred Braungard (O)	FA40	KIA, Caudry	
Ltn Paul Marten (O)	FAA222	KIA, Laon	
Vfw Walter Sieg	J71	KIA, Habsheim	
Uffz Georg Steinemann		KIA, Rethel	

17 September 1918

Vfw Johannes	FA253	WIA	6 Armee
Fw Hans Popp	J77b	KIA, Warville-Éply	19 Armee
Ltn Max Scharf (O)	KG5	KIA, Pronville, Friedrichshafen	

Uffz Paul Noeller	"	KIA crew	
Uffz Paul Kagelmacher	"	KIA	
Ltn Josef Freck	"	KIA	
Gefr Otto Kurth (P)		KIA, Athies, AEG crew	
Ltn Gerlach		POW	
Ltn Tillmanns		POW	
Flgr Geiger (P)	BG6/BS8	POW, DFW crew	
Ltn Nolte	BG6/BS8	POW	
Ltn Hans Siemann (O)	FA227	KIA, Braisne	

18 September 1918

Ltn Erich Kaempfe	J13	WIA/DOW on 20th	Armee-A 'C'
Uffz Hoppe (P)	FA17	WIA	2 Armee
Ltn Buchwald (O)	"	WIA	
Ltn Karl Höhne (O)	FA36	KIA, Maas-Ost	5 Armee
Ltn Ernst Schulz (P)	"	KIA	
Ltn Wilhelm Thormann (P)	FAA247	KIA, Froidmont	6 Armee
Ltn Wilhelm Babetz (O)	"	KIA	
Vfw Karl Zickgraf		KIA, Nivelle, Belg	"

19 September 1918

Ltn Lorenz (P)	FA241	WIA	2 Armee
Gefr Paul Milkowski (P)	FA224	KIA, Gonnelieu	"
Ltn Robert Müller (O)	"	KIA	

20 September 1918

Uffz Eddelbuttel	FA276b	Evaded, returned 22nd	
Ltn Huss	"	Evaded	Armee-A 'A'
Ltn Helmut Gantz	J56	DOW, Armentières	4 Armee
Ltn Otto Frühner	J26	Baled out safely	17 Armee
Ltn Han Böhning	J79b	WIA, Soreil	18 Armee
Flgr Walter Fischer		KIA, Jeancourt	
Vfw Johannes Schnabel		KIA	
Ltn Karl Schneider		KIA	
Gefr Fritz Mey		KIA, Charleroi	
Ltn Walter Mohnke		KIA, Nivelles	
Fw Christian Rothweiler		KIA, Villers-Outréaux	
Flgr Wilhelm Sudmeyer		KIA, Bouriers	

21 September 1918

Uffz Gerhard Schleuter (P)	FA2	KIA, St Hilaire	
Ltn Erwin Sklarek (O)		KIA	
Flgr John (P)	F46b	KIA, Briey	
Ltn Eduard Reichenwallner		KIA	
Ltn Rudolf Klimke	J27	WIA	
Uffz August Buecker		KIA, Valenciennes	
Uffz Wilhelm Landsberg (P)		KIA, Sailly	
Gefr Bosche (O)		WIA	
Ltn Paul Baümer	J2	Baled out safely	
Gefr Wilhelm Pieper		KIA, Pass am Strumitza, Belg	

Vfw Wilhelm Güdemann (P)	BS7	KIA, Proyart	
Oblt Werner Schmidt (O)		KIA	
Flgr Konrad Wieclorek		KIA, Lanboucy-la-Ville	

22 September 1918

Ltn Karl Bauernfeind	J34b	KIA, Demicourt	2 Armee
Ltn Krayer	J45	WIA	7 Armee
Flgr Otto Muhr		KIA, Avesnes	19 Armee

23 September 1918

Fw Leopold Bach	FA(A)228	KIA, Sailly	
Vfw Paul Färber	FA(A)228	KIA	
Gefr August Brenner		KIA, St Armond	
Flgr Paul Joos		KIA, Briey	
Fw Adolf Mörch		KIA, Arras	
Flgr Josef Uklei		KIA, Valenciennes	
FlgObmt Karl Schiffmann	MFJ 2	KIA, Ichteghem	

24 September 1918

Vfw A Fittgen (P)	FA37	POW	Armee-A 'C'
Ltn G Konnigs	FA37	POW	
Vfw R Wilkens (P)	FA29	POW, Briey	"
Ltn Rudolf Kaehne (O)		KIA	
Ltn Wilhelm Meyer	J47	POW, Suippes	3 Armee
Ltn Emil Melcher	MFJ 1	WIA	4 Armee
Ltn Bruno Hobein	J20	WIA	"
Vfw Peter Stenzel	J14	KIA, Fort d'Englos	
Vfw Willi Schmidt	J27	DOW 26th	17 Armee
Ltn Martin Demisch	J58	DOW 25th	"
Offz Ernst Hanisch	FA19	KIA, Henin-Liétard	
Ltn Richard Biermann (O)	FA19	KIA, Henin-Liétard	
Gefr Max Hess		KIA, Lille	
Uffz Franz Joscht		KIA, Peuvilly	
Ltn Walter Klemann (O)	FA205	KIA, Crécy	
Ltn Emil Melcher		KIA, Ghistelles	
Uffz Paul Müller		KIA, Neuville-Cambrai	
Vfw Hermann Hoos	Sch15	POW, Somme	
Vfw Richard Wagner	Sch15	POW, Somme	

25 September 1918

Vfw Adolf Martens (P)	FA(A)207	KIA	2 Armee
Ltn Hans Stanger (O)	"	KIA	
Gefr Franz Wagner	J79b	KIA, Preselles Ferme	18 Armee
Ltn Franz Hausmann	BG4	KIA, Cambrai	
Ltn Fritz Knipp		KIA, Maas-Ost	
Ltn Reinhold Lampe	BG6	KIA, Arras	
Fw August Platte	"	KIA	
Uffz Karl Rühlicke	"	KIA	
Gefr Adolf Mörch	"	KIA	

26 September 1918

Vfw Huar	J68	WIA	5 Armee
Vfw Robert Massbacher	J77b	Safe	19 Armee

Vfw Weinmann	J50	POW	3 Armee
Ltn Ernst Udet	J4	WIA	
Vfw Meppes	J37	WIA	
Flgr Ewald Feuchtner	J69	KIA, Étain	
Flgr Michael Reiner		KIA, Montbrehain	
Flgr Georg Schmidt		KIA, Aubigny-au-Bac	
Vfw Robert Wirth	J37	WIA	
Ltn Mappes	J37	WIA	
Uffz Richard Scholl	FA(A) 233	KIA, Perthes	
Ltn Eugen Anderer	FA(A) 233	KIA, Perthes	

27 September 1918

Ltn Max Näther	J62	WIA	Armee-A 'C'
Ltn Mappes	J37	WIA	2 Armee
Vfw Robert Wirth	J37	WIA	"
Ltn Fritz Rumey	J5	KIA, Neuville	"
Ltn Fritz Heinz	J2	KIA, nr Cambrai	17 Armee
Ltn Paul Strähle	J57	WIA	"
Ltn Hans Jebens	J59	KIA, Bouchain	"
Oblt Hans v Boddien	J59	WIA	"
Ltn Holle	J31	WIA	
FlugMt Richard Arfendt		KIA, La Lovie	
Ltn Wilhelm Kreitz		KIA, La Lovie	
Gefr Heinrich Brinker		KIA, Tournai	
Flgr Gustav Dunkel		KIA, La Briquette	
Flgr Fritz Schister		KIA	
Ltn Josef Heckenberger	FA290	KIA	
Uffz Karl Kessel		KIA, Valenciennes	
Ltn Eugen Wild (O)	FA261	DOW, Rethel	

28 September 1918

Vfw Heinrich Brobowski	J53	POW	3 Armee
Uffz Karl Hofmann	J60	KIA, Argonne Forest	"
Ltn Hugo Fleisher (O)	BGIII	KIA, Ypres	
Ltn Willi Meyer (P)	"	KIA	
Flgr Josef Jansen		KIA, Marquion	
Flgr Johann Kohler		KIA, Valenciennes	
Gefr Theodor Kaufhold		KIA	
Flgr Walter Koulen		KIA, Mouchin	
Fw Otto Stollberg		KIA	
Flgr Andreas Schaetzhauer		KIA, Beauchamps	
Ltn Gustav Spaich (P)	BGIV	KIA, Câtillon	
Vfw Walter Tischmann		KIA, Harly	

29 September 1918

Ltn Gerold Tschentschel	J72	WIA	Armee-A 'C'
Fw von Kamp (P)	FA33	WIA	2 Armee
Ltn Weise (O)	"	WIA	
Gefr Kurt Grossmann (P)	FA33	KIA, Gorth	"
Ltn Richard Brauss (O)	"	KIA	

Oblt Hans Eberhardt Gandert	J51	POW	4 Armee
Ltn Fritz Hoffmann	J2	KIA, W Cambrai	17 Armee
Flgr Willi Benkert		KIA, Coudron	
Flgr August Bendrin		KIA, End-Auz	
Fw Friedrich Geiger		KIA, Bernot	
OffStv Paul Haack		KIA, Gardy	
Ltn Ernst Köther		KIA, Bonne-Evance	
Vfw Gerhard Köth		KIA, Furstenwald	
Ltn Karl Metzler	FA287	KIA, Breuil	
Gefr Gerhard Müller		KIA, Fontaine	
Uffz Fritz Stein		KIA, Harly	

30 September 1918

Ltn Gaspary (O)	FA241	WIA	2 Armee
Ltn Georg Schenker	J41	WIA	
Gefr Ernst Bruck		KIA, Hauving	
Gefr Karl Faerber		KIA, Osterode	
Gefr Friedrich Heinz		KIA	
Flgr Willi Glaser		KIA, Wahn	
OffStv Ambrosius Haas		KIA	
Vfw Wilhelm Hagendorf		KIA, Rethel	
Ltn Willi Herrmann		KIA, Putzig	
Ltn Martin Miehe		KIA	
ObMt Albert Günner		KIA	
ObflgMstr August Ponater		KIA	
Uffz Hermann Geithner	FA(A) 207	KIA, Aubencheul-au-Bac	
Ltn Johann Schwartz	FA(A) 207	KIA, Aubencheul-au-Bac	

Appendix 7

IAF Victory Claims

Date	Pilot/Crew	A/C	Sqn	E/A Type	Claim
7 Sep	Capt R J Gammon	C6274	104	Fokker DVII	DF
	2/Lt P E Appleby			Fokker DVII	D
"	Lt J W Richards		104	Fokker DVII	D
	Sgt W E Reast				
"	1/Lt D J Waterous	A7942	55	Fokker DVII	OOC
	2/Lt C L Rayment				
13 Sep	2/Lt A D Mackenzie	D3263	104	Pfalz DIII	OOC
	2/Lt C E Bellord				
"	Lt Malcolm	D5483	104	Fokker DVII	OOC
	Lt Alexander				
"	2/Lt W T Jones	C6260	99	Fokker DVII	D
	2/Lt E C Black				
14 Sep	Capt W G Stephenson	D3041	99	EA	D
	Sgt J Jones				
"	Capt E J Garland	D6023	104	Fokker DVII	D
	Lt W E Bottrell				
15 Sep	Capt B J Silly	F5701	55	Albatros DV	DF
	Lt J Parke				
"	2/Lt C Turner	A7427	55	Fokker DVII	D
	2/Lt J T L Attwood				
"	Capt R T Gammon	C6264	99	Pfalz DIII	D
	2/Lt P E Appleby				
25 Sep	2/Lt H Wood	D8392	55	Fokker DVII	D
	2/Lt J D Evans			Fokker DVII	OOC
"	Lt W G Braid	D8386	55	Pfalz DIII	D
	2/Lt G S Barber				
"	Lt J Cunliffe		55	Fokker DVII	OOC
	2/Lt G E Little				
"	Capt A C M Groom	F1008	110	Fokker DVII	OOC
	Capt G E Lange				
"	Capt A G Inglis	F1010	110	Fokker DVII	OOC
	2/Lt G W L Bodley				
"	Lt R P Brailli	F995	110	EA	OOC
	Lt R F Casey			EA	OOC
"	2/Lt A Brandrich	F980	110	EA	OOC
	Sgt T W Harman				
26 Sep	Lt D M West	D544	99	Fokker DVII	OOC
	2/Lt J W Howard				
"	110 Squadron			Fokker DVII	D
"	110 Squadron			Fokker DVII	D

Index

Belgian

German